Sustainable Preservation

Greening Existing Buildings

Sustainable Preservation

Greening Existing Buildings

Jean Carroon, FAIA | Foreword by Richard Moe

WILEY

John Wiley & Sons, Inc.

Library of Congress Cataloging-in-Publication Data available upon request.

ISBN 978-0-470-16911-7 (cloth); 978-0-470-88213-9 (ebk); 978-0-470-88214-6 (ebk); 978-0-470-88215-3 (ebk); 978-0-470-95018-0 (ebk):

Printed in the United States of America

10 9 8 7 6 5 4 3 2 1

I dedicate this book to my late father, Lamar Evan Carroon, a hydraulic engineer who began his career with the U.S. Geological Survey, Surface Water Branch, Water Resources Division in Santa Fe, New Mexico in 1946 and retired in 1980 as District Chief of the Mississippi Water Resources Division. My friend and sister, Barbara Carroon, will understand why.

CONTENTS

FOREWORD

IN JUST A FEW SHORT YEARS, the topic of sustainable development has moved from the sidelines to center stage in discussions about climate change, social equity, and economic prosperity—issues that will shape the very future of our planet. This focus on sustainability has enormous implications for historic preservation. It challenges us to think in new ways about the process by which we decide what to protect and how to protect it, about the real economic benefits of our work, and—most important—about the vital role our historic resources can play in reducing our impact on the environment.

By the same token, the practice of historic preservation has profound implications for sustainable development. As champions of wise stewardship of our legacy from the past, preservationists are particularly adept at thinking about the long-term survivability of buildings and how they can be carefully maintained, innovatively reused, and thoughtfully preserved for future generations to enjoy—tasks that represent the very essence of sustainability.

It's easy to forget that every manmade thing in our lives—the computers we rely on, the plastic bottles and aluminum cans we drink from, the buildings in which we live and work—all of them take significant resources to manufacture. Despite the high environmental price we pay for them, we too often think of these things as expendable: Last year's computer gets replaced by a newer model, the plastic bottle gets tossed into the waste basket, the building gets razed to make way for something newer and "better"—all

of it done with little regard for the impact of these actions on the world around us. For too long, our attitude toward our natural resources has been, "There's plenty more where that came from." Now, with our environment in crisis, we have to face the fact that there may not be "plenty more" of anything—except trouble.

Consider the ubiquitous plastic water bottle, which has become a symbol of our foolish, callous, and self-destructive treatment of the environment. Despite the fact that good water comes gushing out of faucets everywhere, use of plastic water bottles increased an amazing 1,000 percent between 1997 and 2006. We could recycle these containers, recovering at least some of the energy and materials that went into their manufacture—but the reality is that eight out of ten plastic bottles wind up in landfills. A new understanding is beginning to take hold: Reuse is environmentally superior to recycling. In terms of environmental impact, it's far better to buy a reusable water bottle than to buy an endless stream of plastic containers that may or (more likely) may not get recycled.

The same holds true for construction materials and demolition debris. Recent years have seen an exponential increase in the recycling of these materials—but still, a small portion of building materials gets recycled every year. The rest still winds up in landfills that are rapidly filling up. The conclusion is obvious: Instead of demolishing and replacing a building, it's better to reuse it and avoid creating all that construction/demolition debris in the first place.

Sadly, reuse isn't always easy. Just like disposable plastic containers, much of our postwar building stock was not designed to last. The Brookings Institution projects that by 2035, we will demolish and rebuild approximately 30 percent of our building stock—a staggering 82 billion square feet. This orgy of demolition and reconstruction will be enormously costly, both economically and environmentally, but the fact is that many of those existing buildings will need to be demolished because they're so poorly constructed. "They don't make them like they used to" is more than an empty phrase: It's an indictment of our thoughtlessness—and a mistake we simply can't afford to keep making.

This points up an important fact: In addition to underscoring the wisdom of reusing existing resources, historic preservation offers some valuable lessons on how we should design our new buildings and communities.

Generally speaking, older buildings employ designs and techniques that grew out of the lessons learned from centuries of tried-and-true building practice. In addition, most of them were constructed so that their individual components—such as windows, for example—can be easily repaired or replaced when necessary. Most important, unlike their more recent counterparts that celebrate the concept of planned obsolescence, older buildings were generally built to last. Because of their durability and "repairability," they have almost unlimited *renewability*.

There's also much to be learned from traditional communities that were constructed before the automobile took over our lives. Because they demonstrate a respect for traditional practices that allow manmade structures to exist in harmony with the natural environment, these places offer a vision for how our cities and towns should function in a post-auto-dependent world. No wonder smart-growth advocates and new urbanists embrace the principles these communities embody.

We've always insisted that preservation makes sense, and today that statement is truer than ever. This is not to say that preservationists can rest on their laurels. We still have plenty of work to do. Here's one very important example: While many historic buildings are remarkably energy-efficient, many others—especially older homes—are poor energy performers. We must continue to work on practical strategies for improving the performance of these buildings without compromising or destroying the distinctive character that makes them so appealing.

Happily, an increasing number of green historic rehabilitation projects show we can do just that. Jean Carroon's book *Sustainable Preservation: Greening Existing Buildings offers* case studies that show how a wide range of buildings—from historic icons such as H.H. Richardson's monumental Trinity Church in Boston to modest structures of more recent vintage in communities all over America—can "go green." As one of the country's most experienced and highly regarded preservation architects, with a particular commitment to, and passion for, sensitive stewardship of both the natural and built environments, she is uniquely qualified to explain and illuminate the sometimes-complex relationship between preservation and sustainability.

For some time, preservationists have insisted that in many cases, the greenest building is one that already exists. Now that message is beginning to be heard—and, more important, heeded. Historic preservation has always sustained America by working to protect and celebrate the evidence of its past. Now, by addressing the challenges of climate change, dwindling resources and environmental degradation, preservation can—and must—play a leadership role in the sustainable stewardship of America's future.

RICHARD MOE
President Emeritus
National Trust for Historic Preservation

ACKNOWLEDGMENTS

"If you look at the science about what is happening on earth and aren't pessimistic, you don't understand the data. But if you meet the people who are working to restore this earth and the lives of the poor, and you aren't optimistic, you haven't got a pulse."

—Paul Hawken,
commencement address to the class of 2009,
University of Portland

MY THANKS TO ALL OF THE PEOPLE across the globe who recognize that heritage and stewardship are essential for a sustainable world and are working hard to make this happen, whether by celebrating the stories of one building or crafting policy that shifts our economic structure to one of repair rather than replace. You empower me with optimism through your actions.

To the many teams that created the case studies in this book and to all of the others I could not use but learned from, thank you. To all of the practitioners I have been privileged to work with, including many great clients and great teams, I extend heartfelt thanks for my education and growth as a practitioner. Lisa Howe was and is an invaluable sounding board, friend and ally in achieving the highest levels of excellence in Goody Clancy's preservation practice and sustainability goals. To my fellow principals and the staff of Goody Clancy who felt "the book" was a never-ending story, thank you for your patience and support. In particular, I could not have started without Kathryn Bossack's initial work on case studies and images, and I could not have finished without Steve Wolf's endless patience with the illustrations and text and Jennifer Gaugler's willingness to help pursue missing pieces. Thanks to the team at Wiley for making this happen, and particularly to John Czarnecki for his persistent belief in the topic and to Amy Odum for her grace and humor.

In the public sector, the publications and leadership of the U. S. General Services Administration were and are invaluable. In the private sector, I relied on the very thorough Building Design + Construction white papers edited by Robert Cassidy and am heartened by Rob's clear understanding that how we address and maintain our existing buildings is crucial in the race to mitigate climate change. Time and again I turned to the dependable and thoughtful information provided by BuildingGreen through their original publications and more recent partnership with McGraw-Hill Construction in the form of *GreenSource* magazine. The BuildingGreen website continues to be the go-to place for case studies and product information and LEEDuser.com provides essential guidance for the U.S. Green Building Council's LEED rating systems. The beautifully written *Women in Green: Voices of Sustainable Design,* by Kira Gould and Lance Hosey, was where I garnered inspiration and comfort. Anything Kira or Lance writes is worth finding; a joint effort is a bonus.

Patrice Frey, of the National Trust for Historic Preservation, provided me with valuable data and thoughtful conversation, but she also challenges and energizes me to find the most effective ways to be a change agent. She is one of my primary reasons for optimism, and I am grateful that the National Trust provides a forum for her voice and others through its blogs. Michael Jackson FAIA, Chief Architect of the Illinois Historic Preservation Agency, is an inexhaustible fount of information and a passionate advocate for sustainable development. His constant stream of links, news bites, case studies and analytical tools is one of the great gifts springing from my involvement with APT, the Association of Preservation Technology. To the many others I know through APT—Natalie Bull, Barbara Campagna, Ralph DiNola, Carl Elefante, Jill Gotthelf, Jennifer Iredale, Andrew Powter, Susan Ross, Walter Sedovic, Ron Staley, Stephen Tilly, Wayne Trusty, and Robert Young to name only a few—who are working to advance "sustainable preservation," thank you.

Last, but never least, anything I accomplish is the result of the love, support, security, and laughter provided by my husband, Michael Payne; my children, Lydia and Carter; and my stepdaughter, Jessica.

PART I

OVERVIEW

chapter 1

BUILDINGS AND ENVIRONMENTAL STEWARDSHIP— UNDERSTANDING THE ISSUES

1.1 CLIMATE CHANGE AND BUILDINGS—THE IMPERATIVE

"BE WORRIED. BE VERY WORRIED."

—Time, *April 3, 2006*

"Human activity is putting such a strain on the natural functions of the Earth that the ability of the planet's ecosystems to sustain future generations can no longer be taken for granted."

—(2000) United Nations Millennium Ecosystem Assessment

THE NEED FOR IMMEDIATE ACTION to address climate change and the related environmental degradation is increasingly urgent, and the major role that the building industry must take in abating the crisis is unequivocal. Yet, a 2008 survey of design professionals from across the United States found that some still question the actuality of climate change,[1] even though environmental scientists have concluded with unusual unanimity that dramatic change is well under way. Two years before the survey, *Time* magazine trumpeted, "The debate over whether Earth is warming up is over. Now we're learning that climate disruptions feed off one another in accelerating spirals of destruction. Scientists fear we may be approaching the point of no return."[2]

3

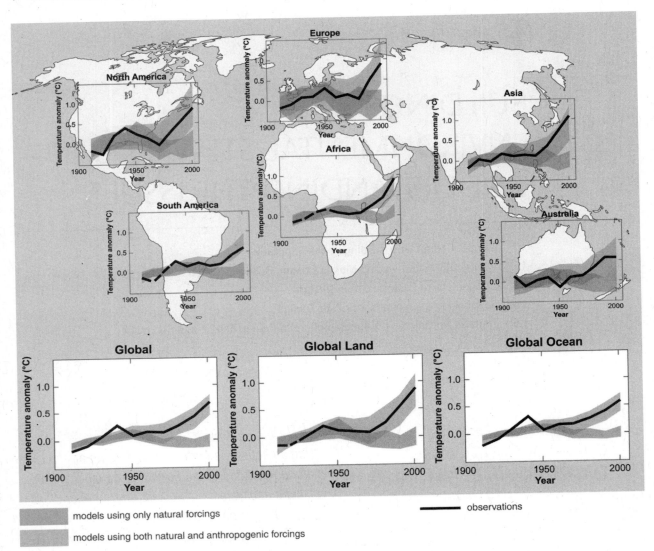

▨	models using only natural forcings
▨	models using both natural and anthropogenic forcings

—— observations

Figure 1-1 Warming of the climate system is unequivocal, as is now evident from observations of increases in global average air and ocean temperatures, widespread melting of snow and ice, and rising global average sea level. *Figure 2-5 in* Climate Change 2007: Synthesis Report *published by the Intergovernmental Panel on Climate Change of the World Meteorological Organization*

The year 2007 was noteworthy because of the new certainty and alarm expressed by international scientific groups about climate change and its rippling effects on ecosystems, biodiversity, geopolitical stability, and economic security. The *United Nations Environment Programme Year Book 2008* announced that climate change "is now recognized as a universal public issue that will dominate global attention for at least a generation."[3]

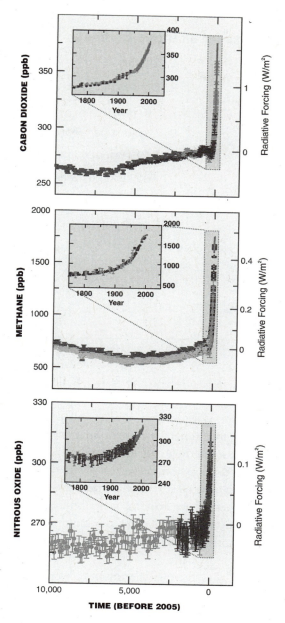

Figure 1.2 Global greenhouse gas (GHG) emissions due to human activities have grown since preindustrial times, with an increase of 70 percent between 1970 and 2004. *Figure 2-3 in* Climate Change 2007: Synthesis Report *published by the Intergovernmental Panel on Climate Change of the World Meteorological Organization.*

The reasons for climate change are complex, but the fundamental factor contributing to global warming is attributed by the Intergovernmental Panel on Climate Change [IPCC] to a dramatic increase in anthropogenic (i.e., caused by people) greenhouse gas concentrations. Atmospheric concentrations of methane (CH_4) and nitrous oxide (N_2O) have increased markedly since 1750 and far exceed preindustrial values determined from ice cores spanning many thousands of years, but the greatest concern stems from the dramatic increase in annual carbon dioxide emissions (CO_2), which grew by about 70 percent between 1970 and 2004, due primarily to the use of fossil fuels.[4] The single biggest sector responsible for creating carbon dioxide directly and indirectly in the United States is the building industry, followed by transportation, which is closely aligned with how we acquire products and move between buildings.

Building Impacts

The impact of buildings on greenhouse gas emissions and the depletion of natural resources is staggering. In terms of land use and material extraction, the building and construction industry has the greatest impact of any sector.[5] Buildings are primary contributors to environmental degradation during all phases of service—construction, operation, and deconstruction or demolition. In the United States, buildings account for the following:

- 37 percent of primary energy use[6]
- 68 percent of all electricity use[7]
- 60 percent of nonfood/fuel raw materials use[8]
- 40 percent of nonindustrial solid waste or 136 million tons of construction and demolition debris per year[9]
- 31 percent of mercury in municipal solid waste[10]
- 12 percent of potable water use[11]
- 36 billion gallons of water use per day[12]
- 20 percent loss of potable water in many urban systems due to leakage[13]

Comparison of Transportation and Operating Energy Use for an Office Building

Average U.S. commute distance (one way)	12.2 miles
U.S. average vehicle fuel economy 2006	21.0 miles per gallon
Work days	235 days per year
Annual fuel consumption	273 gallons per year
Annual fuel consumption per automobile commuter	33,900 kBtu per year
Transportation energy use per employee	27,700 kBtu per year
Average office building occupancy	230 feet^2/person
Transportation energy use for average office building	121 kBtu per square foot
Operating energy use for code-compliant office building	92.9 kBtu/ft^2/year
Percent transportation energy use exceeds operation energy use for an average office building	30.2%
Percent transportation energy use exceeds operation energy use for an office building built to ASHRAE 90.1-2004 code	137%

Source: BuildingGreen Suite, www.buildinggreen.com

- 38 percent of all carbon dioxide emissions[14]
- 49 percent of all sulfur dioxide emissions[15]
- 25 percent of all nitrous oxide emissions[16]
- 10 percent of particulate matter emissions[17]

Every year, another 1 million acres of farmland in the United States are given over to buildings, and the number of cars per household continues to climb.

Transportation is a constant reminder that buildings are not isolated events that can be individually improved, thereby solving our climate crisis and creating an environmentally sustainable world. Alex Wilson, president and founder of BuildingGreen, Inc., the Brattleboro, Vermont, publisher of *Environmental Building News (EBN)*, has suggested that the energy used by building occupants to travel to the building be incorporated into a holistic analysis of a single building's environmental impact. Typically, the aggregate energy used to get to and from a building is very high, as much as 2.4 times the building's energy use, according to Wilson.[18] No similar calculations have been done to estimate the environmental impact of the infrastructure required to transport energy, water, and waste to and from a building, but the concept of *transportation energy intensity* points out that the continuing effect of a building is not limited to its operation alone. If we are to green our buildings and our world, we must frame both problems and solutions as holistically as possible.

"Green" has become the umbrella word covering the complex issues of reducing or even eliminating adverse environmental impacts. Within the conversation of green as it relates to buildings, an evolving terminology provides a framework for analysis and judgment of issues, some of which are particularly applicable to historic buildings.

1.2 HISTORICALLY GREEN—WHAT MAKES EXISTING BUILDINGS GREEN

> "The greenest building is . . . one that is already built."
>
> —*Carl Elefante, FAIA, Quinn Evans|Architects*

Embodied Energy

Embodied energy is the description of energy used directly and indirectly in raw material acquisition, production of materials, and the assemblage of those materials into a building. Every building starts with an environmental debt that includes resource depletion, energy, and manufacturing from the impact of construction. Embodied energy is an attempt to quantify one significant part of this debt.

According to a formula produced for the Advisory Council on Historic Preservation during the energy crisis of the 1970s, a typical 50,000 ft² commercial building embodies about 80 billion Btu's of energy, the equivalent of about 640,000 gallons of gasoline. Tearing a building down not only wastes this energy but also requires more energy and more raw materials to construct a new building.

The urgent and immediate need to reduce carbon emissions makes the reuse of buildings an imperative because the embodied energy expenditure has already occurred. Even the most energy-efficient new building cannot offset its embodied energy for many years. The United Nations Energy Programme estimates that the embodied energy of a building is 20 percent if a building is operational for 100 years, which is two to four times longer than most buildings in the United States are in service. The shorter the service life, the greater the ratio of embodied energy to operating energy is. As buildings are made

Figure 1.3 A comprehensive exterior restoration of the Massachusetts State House at the beginning of the twenty-first century extends the life of a building originally constructed at the end of the eighteenth century and demonstrates a key concept of sustainability—stewardship. *Peter Vanderwarker photo, courtesy Goody Clancy*

more energy-efficient, the ratio of embodied energy to lifetime consumption also increases, placing even greater significance on the energy used in construction, recycling, and final disposal.

Embodied Carbon

Attempts to quantify embodied carbon stem from the acknowledgment of carbon dioxide emissions as a contributor to climate change. The intent in embodied-carbon calculations is to estimate the amount of carbon emitted through building construction, including the entire cycle of material extraction, fabrication,

Figure 1.4 Durable and beautiful materials, such as those shown in the lobby of 175 Berkeley Street in Boston, designed by Cram and Ferguson in 1947, have low recurring embodied energy and often reduce the need for toxic and frequent cleaning (Refer to Chapters 6, 7, and 8 for additional information about the impact of material choices, healthy interiors, and maintenance.) *Photo by Nick Wheeler © Frances Loeb Library*

transportation, and final assemblage. In 2006, researchers from the University of Bath in the United Kingdom completed a comprehensive assessment of carbon associated with building materials. Craig Jones and Geoff Hammond's draft of *Inventory of Carbon and Energy* (ICE) drew data from secondary resources, including books, conference papers, and the Web. The ICE draft selected what the researchers believed to be the best of these data to create the ICE database.

Using ICE data, *New Tricks with Old Bricks*, a 2008 study from the British Empty Home Agency compares carbon dioxide emissions in new construction with the refurbishment of existing homes. The study concludes that when embodied CO_2 is taken into account, new, energy-efficient homes recover the carbon expended in construction only after 35 to 50 years of energy-efficient operations.[19]

"Existing buildings in the United States outnumber new buildings by more than 100 to 1. If the United States is going to reduce its greenhouse gas emissions, the greening of existing buildings must be included, too."

—Charles Lockwood and Deloitte[20]

Durability

Durable, long-lived materials and composite durability of a construction system such as a masonry wall are common in many historic buildings and a logical part of sustainable design. Notes Peter Yost, a building science expert with 3D Building Solutions, LLC, "If you double the life of a building, you halve the environmental impacts [of its construction]."[21] Durable materials, especially those with low maintenance requirements such as exterior masonry, slate roofs, terrazzo floors, wood framing (properly protected from moisture), and even three-coat plaster on wood lath, can last hundreds of years, spreading the original environmental impacts over time. These materials often have a lower recurring embodied energy as well, which is the energy required to maintain, repair, and restore materials. Although less-durable materials may not involve as much energy in their manufacture, the need for frequent replacement, combined with the need to dispose of the product following removal, results in a higher total embodied energy over the life of the material.[22]

Indigenous Materials

The older a building, the more likely it is to have utilized indigenous materials, whether adobe in arid climates, redwood in the Pacific Northwest, or stone in areas of quarries throughout the country. Indigenous materials offer advantages on a number of levels, frequently including inherent durability for the climate in which they originate (such as earth construction), lower transportation requirements, and support of local economies. The appropriate use of indigenous materials is one of the many lessons that historic buildings can teach the design community.

Repairability

Repairability is at the heart of many existing buildings and building components—from wooden windows to slate roofs. When a portion of a wooden window fails, new wood can be spliced in, broken glass can be replaced, weights and pulleys can be repaired. The same can be said for slate roofs, which can be repaired with incremental replacement and consequently last 50 to 100 years. Repair rather than replacement creates an economy that values and employs local craftspeople, extends the life of products, keeps construction waste (or materials requiring recycling) to a minimum and reduces the need for new products that by definition have a negative environmental impact—regardless of how they were manufactured or the amount of recycled material they contain.

Moving from a culture of replacement to one of repair and renewal is essential for reducing our environmental impact and becoming a regenerative society, rather than one that is merely doing less harm.

Figure 1.5 The San Miguel Chapel in Santa Fe, New Mexico, is considered the oldest church structure in the United States. Its adobe walls were constructed around 1610. Vernacular architecture that responds to place is often a compelling example of sustainable design. *http://commons.wikimedia.org/wiki/index.html?curid=176797*

Passive Survivability

Passive survivability acknowledges design features in a building that allow it to function even when modern systems and energy sources fail. Vernacular and older historic buildings demonstrate passive survivability by necessity, having been constructed before dependency on off-site energy sources and mechanical systems. Rediscovery and understanding of these design strategies is an important part of building reuse, as well as a lesson for new design.

Daylighting

Many older buildings have large windows, light wells, narrow footprints, and glass transoms and doors to bring light (and air) deep into buildings. Old storefronts often still have prism glass for refracting light into the back spaces, and although it's less common, it is still possible to find examples of glass-permeated sidewalks designed to allow light into below-grade storage and work areas.

Ventilation

Natural air movement was a requirement prior to mechanical systems. Windows and doors were placed for facilitating cross-ventilation. Planning a chimney draft that brought cooler basement air up to clerestory windows or roof vents operated by wire pulls was common in church design in the nineteenth century, and the same strategy was used to allow heat to updraft through floor vents. Designs in hot climates recognized the cooling sensation of air movement by placing fans powered by people or weighted pulleys in both interior and exterior spaces.

Water

The use of cisterns is as old as recorded history, and water-storage tanks are still visible on the roofs of many nineteenth-century urban buildings. History offers significant examples of societies that understood and managed water as a communitywide resource, including the Nabateans, who created Petra and other desert cities with diverse water runoff and catchment systems.

Figure 1.6 The Clipper Mill development in Baltimore, Maryland, demonstrates long life/loose fit with creative new uses in a 150-year-old foundry complex. *Patrick Ross photo, courtesy Struever Bros. Eccles & Rouse*

Energy

Because they incorporate design for passive survivability, many older buildings use less energy than more recent buildings. Data from the Department of Energy indicate that commercial buildings constructed before 1920 use less energy per square foot than buildings from any other decade up until 2000 (see Table 1.1). A 1999 study by the General Services Administration found that utility costs in the GSA's inventory of historic buildings are about 27 percent less than in non-historic structures.[23]

**Table 1.1 Average annual energy consumption Btu/ft²
of Commercial Buildings (nonmalls)**

Before 1920	80,127
1920–1945	90,234
1946–1959	80,198
1960–1969	90,976
1970–1979	94,968
1980–1989	100,077
1990–1999	88,834
2000–2003	79,703

Source: U. S. Energy Information Agency, *Consumption of Gross Energy Intensity for Sum of Major Fuels for Non Mall Buildings* (2003). Available at: www.eia.doe.gov/emeu/cbecs2003/detailed_tables2003/2003set9/2003pdf/c3.pdf.

▼ **Figure 1.7** Ranked 97 out of 100 by Walk Score™, (www.walkscore.com) the Back Bay of Boston demonstrates the appeal, detail, and scale that historic urban cores provide. Walkable communities not only reduce automobile use but also increase both physical and mental health. Studies document lower resident weight and increased community activity. *Phil Goff photo, courtesy Goody Clancy*

Long Life/Loose Fit

Long life/loose fit is a term coined by Stewart Brand in *How Buildings Learn: What Happens After They're Built* (1994). The concept is that a building can and should last a long time but allow for changing uses over time. Many historic buildings demonstrate long life/loose fit with creative designs that successfully provide for dramatic new uses—a mill building becomes housing, an armory becomes a theater, or a barn become a visitor's center.

Transit-Oriented Design (TOD) and Walkability

Transit-oriented design recognizes the importance of providing transportation options to allow people to live and work without using personal automobiles. Families living in areas with quality public transportation are found to own approximately 50 percent fewer cars than families without public transportation options. Historic buildings frequently exist close to public transportation because they were built before automo-

biles had become a widespread transportation option. Communities with historic buildings often have characteristics that support walkability—safe sidewalks that provide easy access between buildings, physical separation from cars, generous crosswalks, and traffic-slowing street details.

1.3 TERMINOLOGY OF EVOLVING GREEN DESIGN

"When we try to pick out anything by itself, we find it hitched to everything else in the Universe."

—*John Muir*

Life-Cycle Assessment (LCA)

Life-cycle assessment (LCA) attempts to assess and quantify the environmental and cost impacts of materials and assembled systems. LCA is based on the fact that all stages in the life of a product—whether a widget or a building—generate environmental impacts on water, land, and air, that, in turn, have impacts on human health. True greenness of a product must include a holistic evaluation. The stages for a widget include raw material extraction and acquisition, manufacture, transportation, installation, use, and waste management. Economic performance is factored into the evaluation by including the initial investment and the cost of replacement, operation, maintenance and repair, and disposal. A building is more complex because it includes a composite of materials, but the same imperative to consider the holistic impacts applies. In the always-evolving approach to living more lightly on the earth, understanding the LCA of our decisions is essential because of the complexity of the issues. (For a further discussion of LCA refer to Chapter 3 and Chapter 7.)

Carbon Neutrality

Carbon neutrality is the goal of living in a way that does not create carbon dioxide—the primary gas contributing to global warming. Any effort to address this holistically—upstream, midstream, and downstream carbon impacts—considers everything from the mining of materials for fabrication, to material transportation, use, and disposal.

Most frequently, when mentioned in relationship to buildings, carbon neutrality refers only to building operation or to the CO_2 produced by the use of energy in building operations. The *2030 Challenge*—issued by Santa Fe, New Mexico-based Architecture 2030 and adopted by the American Institute of Architects—presses for designs and renovations to create buildings that operate without using fossil fuel or any greenhouse-gas-emitting energy and reduce greenhouse gas emissions by 50 percent.

This is clearly important because of our overwhelming dependence on coal to create electricity. Currently, 70 percent of the greenhouse gases created by building operations result from electricity consumption, and 50 percent of the electricity used in the United States is made with coal, which pollutes in multiple ways. The 2030 Challenge claims (www.Architecture2030.org) that extreme but uncoordinated efforts to reduce greenhouse gas are quickly reversed by the construction of new coal-fired power plants. For instance, if every college campus building in the United States reduced CO_2 emissions to zero, the "CO_2 emissions from just four medium-sized coal-fired power plants each year would negate this entire effort." The proposed far-reaching solution is to make all buildings, including those already built, reduce operational greenhouse gas emissions by 50 percent. Unlike LCA, the 2030 Challenge does not account for greenhouse gas created during construction and renovation.

New and renovated buildings begin operation with a negative balance in greenhouse gas emissions, but the greenhouse gas created by renovation is estimated to be 30 to 50 percent less than new construction for each dollar spent. All buildings also create greenhouse gas at the end of life. Even if all materials are salvaged and reused, that work still requires energy. Attempting to understand and quantify these impacts is part of the evolving focus of metric tools and guidelines used in green design (see Chapter 3) and one part of the evaluation undertaken as part of full life cycle assessment discussed on page X.

Zero Net Energy (ZNE)

Zero net energy construction attempts to design and construct buildings that operate with only energy generated on site. This approach addresses only operating energy not embodied energy or the environmental impacts of construction systems. The design requirements for a zero net energy building are very dependent on regional location and site opportunities.

Recycling and Down-cycling

Recycling and *down-cycling* are often confused. Recycling is essentially taking a product and using it to make the same product—such as paper included in the production of new paper or used ceiling tiles contributing to new ceiling tiles. Down-cycling is reusing the waste of one product in the making of another, such as adding crushed window glass to bituminous paving or new countertops. Both recycling and down-cycling postpone the transition of a manufactured material to waste, with the assumption that material recycling will keep a material in the production cycle longer than down-cycling.

Cradle to Cradle

The term and subsequent certification program, *Cradle to Cradle,* or C2C, is a concept presented by William

Figure 1.8 Fenway Park in Boston, Massachusetts, uses salvaged materials as part of a holistic strategy for greening the facilities. New bar tops were made from the salvaged materials of a bowling alley removed from one of the buildings in the complex, which is a National Historic Landmark. The Right Field Roof, State Street Pavilion, Left Field Deck all have lane bar tops. Reusing existing materials has the dual benefit of reducing landfill and avoiding the environmental impact of new products. (Refer to Chapter 7 for impacts of new materials.) © *Jordan Wirfs-Brock*

McDonough and Michael Braungart in their book of the same name in 2002, with the subtitle *Remaking the Way We Make Things.* The basic concept of C2C is the elimination of waste and the reduction of raw material use by creating products and, by extension, buildings

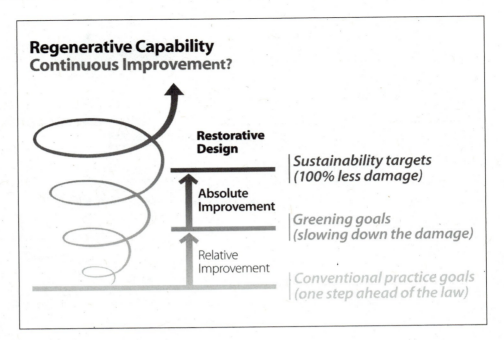

Figure 1.9 The goal of regenerative design is to produce a net positive environmental impact—to leave the world better off with respect to energy, water, and materials. Regenerative design moves beyond sustainable design, which attempts to reserve adequate resources for future generations. (Definition from *Mechanical and Electrical Equipment for Buildings,* Stein, Reynolds, Grondzik, and Kwok, John Wiley & Sons, 2006.) *Concept by Bill Reed of Regenesis, Inc., Santa Fe NM; chart by Goody Clancy*

that at the end of service life can be remade into the same product. Of course, even the remaking of a product requires resources—energy, equipment, and water.

Rapidly Renewable Resources

Many products claiming to be green use *"rapidly renewable resources"* or materials that have a shorter harvest rotation than wood, which usually means less than 10 years. (Refer to Chapter 7 for additional information about green products.)

Biomimicry Design

Biomimicry design celebrates the extraordinary systems and materials found in the natural world and attempts to apply these lessons and opportunities to human-created products and living. Biomimicry also uses design to recall and reinforce our connection to nature.

Regenerative Design

Regenerative design is sometimes characterized as being "beyond green" because of the assumption that many of the green guidelines merely create a society that is less harmful to the environment. The goal of regenerative design is to create buildings, places, and systems that actually restore or even establish environments that are truly sustainable.

Smart Growth

Smart Growth is a movement that encourages compact development that combines multiple land uses in a way that preserves open space and provides communities with options in housing and transportation that make efficient use of shared infrastructure. Regional planning and economic health are guiding principles, as well as restoration of the natural environment.

Land Use Changes, Carbon Impacts, and Neighborhood Reinvestment

By Patrice Frey, deputy director of the Sustainability Program, National Trust for Historic Preservation, with research assistance from Paul Anderson, Monica Andrews, and Carl Wolf

In recent years, land has been developed in the United States at a rate of approximately three times that of population growth [see Figure 1.10]. In fact, the average American uses five times more land than just 40 years ago. For example, while the city of Baltimore, Maryland, lost about 250,000 residents in the last quarter century, its suburbs expanded by 67 percent.[1] In yet another older Northeast city, Philadelphia, metropolitan population growth has grown by 66 percent in the past 50 years, but land development has grown by 401 percent.[2]

Land use has a tremendous impact on carbon emissions. Research has demonstrated that in the United States, people who live in more sprawling locations drive 20–40 percent more than those who live in more compact urban areas.[3] Yet as the authors of the recent *Growing Cooler* report note, "For 60 years, we have built homes ever farther

[1] Chesapeake Bay Foundation, "Growth Sprawl and the Chesapeake Bay: Facts about Growth and Land Use," www.cbf.org/site/PageServer?pagename=resources_facts_sprawl (accessed Sept. 1, 2008).

[2] Brookings Institution Center on Metropolitan Policy, "Back to Prosperity: A Competitive Agenda for Renewing Pennsylvania" (Washington DC: The Brookings Institution, 2003), http://www.brookings.edu/es/urban/pa/chapter1.pdf.

[3] Reid Ewing, Keith Bartholomew, Steve Winkelman, Jerry Waters, and Don Chen, *Growing Cooler: Evidence on Urban Development and Climate Change*, Executive Summary (Washington, DC: The Urban Land Institute, 2008), www.1kfriends.org/documents/Growing_Cooler_Executive_Summary.pdf (accessed Sept. 1, 2008), p. 4.

Figure 1.10 Every year, 1 million acres of farmland is given over to development in the United States. Housing size in the last 30 years has doubled as family size has shrunk and car ownership has increased. Sustainable design is about more than buildings. Resource consumption for construction, new infrastructure, and transportation requirements make sprawling development unsustainable even if every new house used no energy in operation. *Photo by Lynn Betts, USDA Natural Resources Conservation Service*

(continued)

from workplaces, created schools that are inaccessible except by motor vehicle, and isolated other destinations—such as shopping—from work and home."[4] The planning and transportation theory of *"smart growth"* has emerged as an alternative to such sprawling development, and promotes high concentration of growth, transit-oriented development, and walkable, mixed-use communities.

The research surveyed in *Growing Cooler* "shows that much of the [projected] rise in vehicle emissions can be curbed simply by growing in a way that will make it easier of Americans to drive less."[5] Smart growth tactics could "reduce total transportation-related emissions from current trends by 7 to 10 percent as of 2050,"[6] according to some projections. The Brookings Institution notes that carbon savings from smart growth extend well beyond those associated with decreased driving. Compact development often means reduced heating and cooling costs because homes are smaller or are in multifamily buildings. District energy systems can be used for power generation, which also creates substantial carbon savings. Municipal infrastructure requirements for roads, sewers, communication, power, and water are reduced by high-density developments. Brookings points out that the reuse of existing structures provides carbon savings, as well.[7]

Sprawl is a relatively recent phenomenon, because pre–World War II communities were built more compactly out of necessity. These neighborhoods tend to be dense, walkable, feature mixed uses, and are very often accessible to public transit. It makes sense that a significant component of a smart growth strategy would be to reinvest and redevelop in older urbanized areas to take advantage of their inherently sustainable features. Nevertheless, there are numerous obstacles to reinvestment in these older areas.

DEMOGRAPHIC SHIFTS AND THE ABANDONMENT OF SUSTAINABLE COMMUNITIES

Major demographic shifts in the last half-century have resulted in the movement of millions of Americans from older and historic communities in the Northeast and Midwestern United States to points south and southwest.[8] This southward flight has been fueled by the significant restructuring of the American economy, including the loss of manufacturing jobs that were previously concentrated in the Northeast and Midwest.

While older industrial cities (now known as rust-belt cities) hollow out, tremendous population growth has occurred in areas such as Atlanta, Phoenix, and Las Vegas, where sprawl is the dominant form of development, and where water resources in particular are scarce. The result is the movement of millions of people from more sustainably designed places to far less sustainably developed areas that face uncertain futures given rapidly escalating gas prices and water scarcity.

There is some good news, however. Reinvestment in many traditionally planned communities in some

[4] Ibid., p. 2.

[5] Ibid., p.4.

[6] Ibid., p. 9.

[7] Marilyn A. Brown, Frank Southworth and Andrea Sarzynski, *Shrinking the Carbon Footprint of Metropolitan America* (Washington, DC: The Brookings Institution, 2008), pg. 11–12 http://www.brookings.edu/~/media/Files/rc/reports/2008/05_carbon_footprint_sarzynski/carbonfootprint_report.pdf.

[8] Bruce Katz and Robert Lang, *Redefining Urban and Suburban America: Evidence from Census 2000* (Washington, DC: The Brookings Institution, 2005).

regions of the U.S.—largely on the coasts—is occurring. With gas prices increasing, Americans now have more incentive than ever to live and work in transit-accessible areas. Recent analysis suggests that while housing prices have dropped between significantly nationwide, homes in center cities or in transit accessible areas have retained, or even increased in value.[9]

Nonetheless, rustbelt cities lie fallow and remain significantly underused and potentially undervalued assets. This poses several important questions: Is it environmentally responsible to encourage growth in areas of the country that are environmentally unfit to handle it—while masses of infrastructure and buildings in sustainable designed cities rot? What are the *real* environmental consequences of such decisions? Or is disinvestment in the rustbelt just a simple—if troubling—economic and political reality with no solution?

The answers are not so clear. But with millions of square feet of abandoned building stock, the questions seem to warrant at least some consideration. This is an area in which additional research and thought is of enormous importance.

[9] Eric M. Weiss, "Gas Prices Apply Brakes to Suburban Migration," *Washington Post*, August 5, 2008, www.washingtonpost.com/wp-dyn/content/story/2008/08/04/ST2008080402649.html.

From www.preservationnation.org/issues/sustainability/additional-resources/buillding_reuse.pdf

1.4 RETHINKING ASSUMPTIONS—HOLISTIC DESIGN

"What we need is a new ethic in which every person changes lifestyle, attitude and behavior."

—*Achim Steiner*[24]

Rethinking the Linear Design Process—Integrated Design Process

The process of building design and renovations has been characterized as a linear process in which a lead designer develops concepts, then passes the design sequentially to specialized consultants who address specialty range of issues without regard to the work of others. Recognition of the interconnection and complexity of the natural systems and the need for holistic design has led to formalized presentations about integrated design, a process that gathers the entire project team together to create designs that benefit from the synergies of different areas of expertise.

Rethinking Building Costs—Can We Afford Not to Be Green?

The first costs of green building are often suggested as an impediment to environmentally responsive design. Within the construction industry, there are always comparisons between initial costs and lifetime value, but identifying the differential cost of green design has become increasingly difficult, as requirements for energy efficiency become embedded into building codes and options for green materials and building systems increase. Two reports from Davis Langdon, a consulting firm offering cost-planning and sustainable-design-management services, confirm this trend. *Examining the Cost of Green* (2004) and *Cost of Green Revisited* (2007) both concluded that there are so many cost factors in construction today that it is nearly impossible to detect any statistically significant difference between the cost of conventional and green buildings. Documentation of direct financial benefits because of environmentally sensitive design is also increasing. Benefits include energy and water savings, reduced waste, improved indoor environmental quality, greater employee comfort/productivity, reduced employee health costs, and lower operations and maintenance costs.[25]

Rethinking Space Utilization— Less Is More

Recognizing that physical space is an extremely valuable resource, universities, governments, and businesses are reexamining how they use space and how new technologies and changing social patterns have altered scheduling and shared uses. Better utilization of existing resources frees funding for other needs and significantly reduces carbon emissions by slowing the need for new facilities and making the best use of operating costs (and the resulting emissions).

The University of Michigan began the ambitious Space Utilization Initiative in 2007 to evaluate and improve the use of 29 million gross square feet of space. The initiative was developed as a key tool for reducing the university's operating costs by developing greater efficiencies and maximizing the use of facilities.

The United States General Services Administration (GSA), one of the largest landlords in the country, began an extensive review in 2002 of how workplaces are used by their tenant organizations, which ultimately led to more efficient use of office areas and a reduction in overall space needs. Here are some of the important findings of the GSA's WorkPlace 20-20 program:

- Organizations often underutilize their workspace.
- Organizations often configure the available workspace in ways that do not support the new work styles.

- The work force itself has an inaccurate idea of how it spends its time.
- Self-reporting is a poor source for reliable programming data.

Partners in the Workplace 20-20 study—including HOK, Spaulding & Slye Colliers, DEGW, Gensler, Studios Architecture, Business Place Strategies, Interior Architects, as well as Carnegie Mellon, MIT, University of California Berkeley, Georgia Tech, and the University of Michigan—confirm that underutilization of workstations is typical of both government and private sectors.[26] Hewlett-Packard, for example, has been able to reduce its total portfolio use of space by over 30 percent through the realignment of space to reflect the working habits of a mobile workforce."[27]

1.5 THERE IS NO FINISH—CREATING A CULTURE OF REUSE, REPAIR, AND RENEWAL

"A building is not something you finish. A building is something you start."

—*Stewart Brand*[28]

Much has been written about our current culture of consumption. We have created a world where it is usually easier and less expensive to replace something—whether cell phone or building—than to repair it. We are, as Carl Elefante writes in the *Forum Journal,* "drunk on the new,"[29] but new buildings cannot solve the environmental dilemma we have created. We must reshape our culture to become one of reuse, repair, and renewal that is respectful of existing resources, including buildings. It is not the makers of glitzy new green buildings who will significantly reduce carbon emissions from buildings but the facilities managers and owners responsible for the buildings that already exist.

John C. Kluczynski Federal Building

Chicago, Illinois

LESS IS MORE

In June 2006, GSA leveraged WorkPlace 20-20 tools and guidelines to renovate two floors of Chicago's timeless Mies van der Rohe-designed John C. Kluczynski Federal Building for the Great Lakes Region, Public Buildings Service. Workplace consultants conducted in-depth analyses of the organization and its work patterns through interview, focus groups, surveys, and cultural analysis. As a result, the GSA optimized the interior environment to fit the way the agency works while also maximizing environmental goals.

The analysis identified a widely held desire to increase interpersonal communications while breaking down organizational stovepipes. The resulting design created egalitarian and nimble work settings by combining:

- Stunning corner views, reserved for group spaces
- Low partitions and increased individual work surfaces
- Rapidly reconfigurable standard-sized offices and meeting rooms

- Glazed-walled private offices throughout, located away from windows
- Open, well-appointed reception and break room areas as gathering destinations

Post-occupancy surveys confirm that the new plan "strikes the right balance." Flexible configurations contributed significantly to the reduction in total space consumed and lowered churn costs to a bare minimum.

GSA also reclaimed over 16,000 square feet of inefficient file-storage space by investing in a managed 1,260-square-foot high-density system that centralized all regional document and supply management services. Not only do the occupants use space more efficiently and better control their files and supplies, but resulting savings (14,000 square feet at $32 per square foot), equate to $450,000 per year, or enough to finance the system support, file management, copy and mail operations, and plotting needs of the growing agency."

Excerpt from U.S. GSA, *Sustainability Matters* (Washington, DC: Public Buildings Service, Office of Applied Science, 2008), p. 39

The earth is not given to us by our parents, it is lent to us by our children.

—*Kenyan proverb*

Commissioning—Making Sure Buildings Work as They Should

Existing buildings represent 98 percent of the available square footage in any one year and operational inefficiencies are normal. The sixth white paper produced by *Building Design + Construction* points out that the majority of buildings, both new and existing, do not function as intended and strongly promotes *commissioning* and *recommissioning* buildings. A concept promoted by the green building movement, commissioning originated with the practice of taking newly launched ships on shakedown cruises to make sure everything was working properly.

Commissioning and recommissioning recognizes that buildings and building systems require stewardship in order to function optimally. "Building systems, particularly HVAC systems, are forever falling 'out of tune.'. . ."[30] Commissioning as applied to a building is a third-party review and inspection of building systems both before and after installation. It is probably one of the most valuable concepts to emerge from green design.

Maintenance and Repair—Caring for What We Have

Caring for what we have is at the heart of what in the United States is called historic preservation, but elsewhere in the world is referred to as heritage conservation. The technical publications and Preservation Briefs of the National Park Service include information on maintenance and repair of dozens of materials, including adobe, slate roofing, masonry, woodwork, cast stone, and terra cotta. Published in 1978, Brief #3, *Conserving Energy in Historic Buildings,* is still germane, as is the more recent Brief #47, published in 2007, *Maintaining the Exterior of Small and Medium Size Historic Buildings.* Maintenance is an inherently sustainable strategy.

Healthy Skepticism—Protecting What We Have

"Art must experiment to do its job. Most experiments fail."

—Stewart Brand[31]

At the 2005 Symposium for Sustainability organized by the Association of Preservation Technology, architect and building forensic expert John Lesak argued for the application of the precautionary principle. Professionals involved in the stewardship of historic and existing buildings, he explained, constantly address the miracle solutions of previous generations, whether lead paint or asbestos or even inadvertently created mold. The business of building forensics, which diagnoses failures of structure, material, and detailing—often focuses on recent buildings, not just historic structures. New materials and systems have not consistently stood the test of time nor have they always proved the miracle solutions advertised. Stewardship of existing buildings, especially those of great historic significance, demands that the first tenant do no harm to the existing cultural resource. Even as we move decisively to address climate change, new systems and new products must be used with caution in buildings that have already survived for decades and even centuries.

Regional Solutions—Thinking Globally

Many of the issues raised in this chapter—lifecycle analysis, building and infrastructure reuse, and transportation energy intensity—demonstrate that an individual building's impact on the environment cannot be assessed independently of the immediate region and the entire planet. The urgency of responding to climate change extends to regional planning and in urban design decisions that evaluate land use, resource depletion, transportation, and energy considerations to create true sustainable development (see Chapter 2).

People's Food Co-op
Portland, OR

Current Owner: People's Food Co-op

Building Type: Retail

Original Building Construction: 1918

Historic Designation: None

Restoration/Renovation Completion: 2003

Square Footage: 5,400 ft^2

Percentage Renovated: 45% + 55% new construction

Occupancy: 20 people (60 hrs/week) 2–20 visitors (1–2 hrs/day)

Recognitions: Businesses for an Environmentally Sustainable Tomorrow, Category/title: Energy Efficiency, 2003

Southeast Portland Uplift Community Award, 2003

"People's Food Cooperative cultivates a thriving local economy by integrating ecological responsibility, local food systems, and cooperative ownership with equitable business practices in a lively community marketplace."

—*Mission Statement*

PROJECT DESCRIPTION

The People's Food Co-op demonstrates the benefits of thinking holistically, not just in an integrated building design but in how a building and organization affects a community and neighborhood. The co-op symbolizes the ongoing process of environmental commitment by accepting the management of systems within the building to ensure human comfort and encouraging social change with inducements that invite walking, biking, and public transit use. The expansion and renovation project employed an integrated design process and biomimcry as a guide in creating a setting for gathering and learning about the environment. The small brick building was constructed in 1918 as a feed store and purchased by the PFC in 1970. The decision to renovate and double the size of the building sought to articulate a symbiotic relationship between the building and nature, with the added aspiration of employing labor-intensive construction that utilized volunteer labor and indigenous and salvaged materials.

Site Utilization and Material Synergies

- The layout of the addition takes advantage of the site to capture daylighting potential and benefit from solar heat gain. A south-facing thermal-storage bottle wall permits sunlight and heat gain in the winter, while the mass of the cob wall (straw, sand, and mud) actively cools the space in summer.
- South-facing community sunspace achieves maximum solar exposure during the winter and during the summer is protected by a roof overhang and deciduous trees.

Community Connectivity

- The L-shape of the building was intentionally chosen to create a courtyard for community gathering.
- The co-op provides incentives for biking, walking, or using public transit by displaying maps and schedules, providing discounts, offering an unusually large volume of bike parking, and providing bicycle delivery of goods.

Water

- Water is considered an asset on the site and is either harvested or infiltrated using two sections of green roof, permeable paving, bioswales, and a 1,500-gallon underground cistern beneath the courtyard.
- All plantings are drought-tolerant and watered with an efficient drip system. Paving systems are porous to promote groundwater recharge.
- The intent was to use the stored water for toilets, but this requires a permitting process that has not yet been completed.

Energy and Integrated Design

- An integrated design approach—daylighting, low-emissivity windows, insulation with an R-22 value in the walls and R-44 in the ceiling, efficient systems and monitoring—reduces energy consumption 16 percent below the Oregon Energy Code and saves roughly $1,700 per year.
- Heating and cooling use a combination of passive ventilation, direct solar gain, night flushing, ground-source heat pumps, and efficient natural gas combustion. Radiant tubing in-slab on the first floor and a conventional duct system on the second provide heat drawn from the ground-source heat pumps. The cooling sequence begins with passive ventilation drawn through a vertical shaft that extends from the first floor through the roof to facilitate night cooling. A fan can add the airflow if needed, and if night cooling proves inadequate during the day, cool water

Figure 1.11 The front wall of the People's Food Co-op in Portland, Oregon, shows the sculptural potential of the cob (a mixture of straw, dirt, and sand) used in the thermal wall. The building demonstrates the mission of promoting ecological, social, and economic sustainability. *Cheyenne Glasgow photo, courtesy People's Food Co-op*

Figure 1.12 The south-facing courtyard of the People's Food Co-op hosts community events, with permeable paving materials, rain gardens, and xeriscape planting to reduce stormwater runoff, a major source of pollution (refer to Chapter 4 for more information). *Cheyenne Glasgow photo, courtesy People's Food Co-op*

GREEN DESIGN ELEMENTS
People's Food Co-op

Sustainable Sites:
- Bicycle accommodation
- Green roof
- Permeable paving materials
- Xeriscaping
- Bioswales

Water Efficiency:
- Graywater system (planned)

Energy and Atmosphere:
- Ground-sourced geothermal heat pumps
- Solar chimney (ventilation)
- Natural ventilation

Materials and Resources:
- Over 90 percent construction waste recycled
- Recycled content materials
- Colorful recycled-glass-bottle thermal storage (placed in wall)
- Cob infill
- Forest Stewardship Council (FSC)-certified wood

Indoor Environment Quality:
- Operable windows
- Low-VOC materials and finishes

Additional Features:
- Occupant recycling program
- Vermicomposting
- Organic products

can be circulated through the in-slab radiant tubing to assist in heat removal—but this is carefully monitored to avoid condensation on the slab.

- Smart design and construction included avoiding details that allow thermal bridging from interior to exterior. For instance, the concrete slab at the entry is jointed at the door threshold to create a thermal break.

Building Envelope and Materials

- The design strategy sought the lowest possible environmental impact by first keeping all material use to a minimum, followed consecutively by seeking salvaged materials and post-consumer materials (like unused paint), biodegradable materials, and finally, new materials from local sources and near-by managed forests.

- Cob (a mixture of straw, dirt, and sand) was used as infill material in a portion of the wall. Because it is malleable, it was also used to form benches, and decorative sculpture was included in the wall. Used glass bottles were inset in the cob wall as a design feature.

- Siding on the new constructionis made from remilled cedar telephone poles from a local supplier.

Operations and Maintenance

- The designer wrote a custom and detailed operations-and-maintenance manual to promote longevity and to maintain the memory of how the building is designed to operate.

Xeriscaping: style of landsape design requiring little or no irrigation or other maintence, used in arid regions

PROJECT TEAM

People's Food Co-op

Cynthia Bankey, AIA

Dave Wadley

City of Portland Office of Sustainable Development

Hemmingson Construction, Inc.

Portland General Electric

SOLARC Architecture and Engineering, Inc.

Harris Center for Conservation Education
Hancock, NH

Current Owner: The Harris Center for Conservation Education

Building Type: Assembly/Interpretive Center

Original Building Construction: 1913

Historic Designation: None

Restoration/Renovation Completion: 2003

Square Footage: 8,580 ft²

Percentage Renovated: 73% + 27% new construction

Occupancy: 50 people (60 hrs/week)

"Building green is more than just a building process; it is the whole process. Site planning, design, construction and materials must all be considered. Recycling, energy efficiency, indoor air quality and resource conservation were blended into the renewed Harris Center because we care about our heritage, we care about our people and we care about our planet."

—*Dave Birchenough, Trustee and Building Chair*

PROJECT DESCRIPTION

The Harris Center for Conservation Education is the result of an integrated design process that began with the goal of utilizing the existing building, constructed in 1913 as a summer residence, to create an environmentally respectful modern facility for a nonprofit educational organization. The final project, by seeking low environmental impacts, is also a good example of passive survivability, or the ability to function without the support of modern mechanical systems dependent on off-site energy sources. The project employed local indigenous materials or durable new materials made from recycled or renewable products. The greatest importance was placed on energy efficiency.

Composting Toilets—In-House Waste Treatment Plant

- Waterless composting toilets that provide nutrients, instead of waste, to the earth are used throughout. Aerobic bacteria convert human waste into fertilizer and prevent nitrates from reaching the groundwater.
- The composting toilets reduced impacts on the existing septic system, and the construction cost and site disruption of a new system was avoided.

Super Insulation and Sealing of Building Envelope

- The owner chose to use the most energy-efficient windows possible, and triple-glazed fiberglass windows were installed throughout, with an estimated eight-year payback on heating costs. Two separate coatings of low-E metallic oxide and pockets of argon gas between the layers of glazing provide a 50 percent reduction in ultraviolet transmission and a 25 percent reduction in solar heat gain, as compared to typical double-glazed windows.
- Blown cellulose, from recycled newspapers, created an R22 insulation level in existing 2 feet, 4 inch exterior walls, which were strapped to achieve a 2 feet, 6 inch cavity.
- Expanding foam was used to seal the building into an airtight envelope, nearly eliminating the transfer of energy between inside and out. Blower-door testing, performed after the air barrier was completed, showed an overall leakage area for both new and renovated space of 1.05 square inches per 100 square feet of shell.

Renewable Energy and Energy Conservation

- The wood-pellet boiler was the first installed in a public building in New Hampshire, and possibly the first in New England. Wood pellets are a biomass fuel made nearby from sawdust, a recycled waste product of New England's renewable forest industry. The estimated annual energy cost is $1,200 to heat almost 10,000 square feet of space.

- The fully automated hydronic heating system uses an external silo and auger system to carry pellets to the boiler.
- Solar panels reduce dependency on commercial electric energy.
- Energy-efficient fluorescent lights and motion sensors are used throughout the building; long-lasting LED's (light-emitting diodes) are used in exit signs.

Durable, Recycled, Natural, and Renewable Products

- The Babbitt Room Addition, a post-and-beam octagon built by a local company, uses posts from Harris Center-managed and -logged stands of Eastern white pine. Reinforcing the connection of posts and rafters, the knee braces use local bent hardwood of oak, maple, and birch. The huge West Coast-grown Douglas fir rafters and compression ring were recycled from a mill building in Massachusetts, built in the early 1900s, and still show the rusting nail holes.
- All four outdoor decks were built using Trex, a manufactured plank made from recycled grocery bags and waste wood. Both second-floor decks were surrounded with railings and balustrades of recycled, century-old cypress resurrected from a river bottom in the South, which were then enhanced with cutouts of animal silhouettes by Harris Center trustees.
- Siding made of cement, sand, and wood fibers replaced less-durable wooden clapboards.
- Resilient floors, such as in the kitchen, are made from recycled SBR (styrene-butadiene rubber) automobile tires and reprocessed EPDM (ethylene-propylene diene monomer), a commercial roofing material.
- Linoleum in the bathrooms is made of all natural materials, including linseed oil, wood flour, rosin binders, and dry pigments, mixed and rolled onto a natural jute backing.
- Original wood flooring was recycled by patching existing rooms with flooring removed from other areas. All new wood flooring is FSC (Forest Stewardship Council) "green certified" yellow birch from a forest managed for sustainability.
- Office carpet tiles are made with 100 percent recycled backing and 34 percent recycled nylon face.
- Bathroom sink counters are soapstone, a natural product acquired from Vermont.

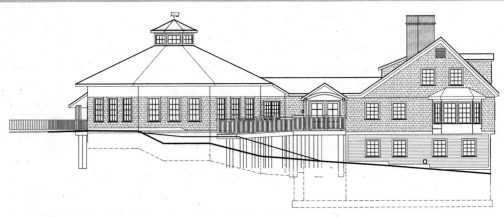

Figure 1.13 The Harris Center for Conservation Education in Hancock, New Hampshire, demonstrates an integrated design strategy to minimize impact on the environment, with a wood pellet boiler, blown cellulose insulation, and solar panels that reduce dependency on the commercial electrical grid. *© Coldham and Hartman Architects*

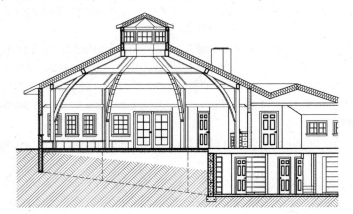

Figure 1.14 At the Harris Center for Conservation Education, local materials and timber framing created a new and dramatic daylit space that incorporates the most energy-efficient windows available at the time of construction. Expanding foam was used to seal both the old and new buildings into an airtight envelope, nearly eliminating the transfer of energy between the interior and exterior. *© Coldham and Hartman Architects*

Figure 1.15 Durability was chosen over both heritage and natural materials at the Harris Center for Conservation Education, with new siding made of cement, sand, and wood fibers replacing wooden clapboards. The same strategy was used in the decks, which are constructed of a material made from recycled grocery bags and waste wood. Decisions about "green" material selections are not always clear-cut and can engender much debate. (Refer to Chapter 7.) *© Coldham and Hartman Architects*

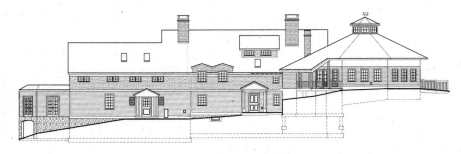

GREEN DESIGN ELEMENTS

Harris Center for Conservation Education

Sustainable Sites:
- Xeriscaping

Water Efficiency:
- Onsite well
- Low-flow plumbing fixtures
- Waterless composting toilets
- Septic system

Energy and Atmosphere:
- Photovoltaic system
- Energy (heat) recovery ventilation
- Triple-glazed windows
- Pellet boiler (automated wood chip biomass)
- Radiant baseboards
- Occupancy sensors

Materials and Resources:
- Reuse existing materials
- Recycled content materials (carpet, rubber floor)
- Forest Stewardship Council (FSC) certified wood

Indoor Environment Quality:
- Skylights/clerestory windows
- Operable windows
- Low/No-VOC materials and finishes
- Track-off matts

Indoor Environmental Quality

- The building is ventilated using an energy-recovery ventilation system that transfers most of the heat energy in stale exhaust air to incoming, fresh, outdoor air.
- To minimize harmful fumes, only water-based paints, stains, and clear finishes were used, as well as formaldehyde-free wheat-board for cabinetry.
- Vinyl products were avoided. ABS (acrylonitrile butadiene styrene) pipe was used instead of industry-standard PVC (polyvinyl chloride) pipe for plumbing.
- All outdoor, pressure-treated structural lumber was preserved using EPA-approved ACQ, an environmentally advanced formula that is arsenic and chromium free.
- Each room is an individual heating zone.
- Operable windows connect occupants with the natural world outdoors.
- The two main floors are ADA-compliant and readily accessible.
- Daylighting is used in the large meeting room in the Babbitt Room Addition.
- The Harris Center now meets all life and fire safety codes and includes a three-story emergency exit stairwell.

Maintenance and Operations

- Systems commissioning was done at project completion.

PROJECT TEAM

The Harris Center for Conservation Education
Coldham & Hartman Architects, LLC
energysmiths
Walter Cudnohufsky Associates
Ryan Hellwig
Kohler and Lewis
Downing Engineering Professional Association
Bruss Construction, Inc

Trinity Church in the City of Boston
Boston, MA

Current Owner: Trinity Church in the City of Boston

Building Type: Religious

Original Building Construction: 1877

Historic Designation: National Historic Landmark, Contributing
   Structure—National Historic District and Local Historic District

Partial Restoration/Expansion Completion: 2005

Square Footage Added: 15,000 ft^2 below the building

Percentage Renovated: 5,000 ft^2 Parish House and Sanctuary Tower

Occupancy: 3,000 to 4,000 people a week for various lengths of time

Recognition:

Recipient—Save America's Treasures Grant

Recipient—Getty Conservation Grant

National Preservation Honor Award, 2006

Tucker Design Award, 2006 (Building Stone Institute)

Preservation Achievement Award, 2006 (Boston Preservation Alliance)

Project Leadership Award, 2005 (Construction Owner's Association of
   America)

Building Massachusetts Chairman's Award, 2005 (Associated General
   Contractors)

Best New Space in Boston, Best of 2005 Boston Globe Awards

"By combining a painstaking dedication to restoring the original architectural vision of H. H. Richardson with several innovative elements of sustainable technology, you have turned Trinity Church into a symbol of all that historic preservation represents in the 21st century."

—Richard Moe, President Emeritus of the National Trust for Historic Preservation

PROJECT DESCRIPTION

Because Trinity Church in the City of Boston—designed by H. H. Richardson and richly decorated by John La Farge and others—is considered one of the most important buildings in the United States, all proposed work is reviewed by local and state historic preservation commissions. The project undertaken between 2000 and 2005 was multifaceted but sprang from the intense need for on-site space to support the many hundreds of programs hosted by the vibrant Episcopal parish, the fifth largest in the country.

Sustaining the community, protecting the building, and keeping the church fully operational throughout construction were essential elements of the work. From the first meetings, the process included a fully integrated design and construction team led by a disciplined building committee whose standard of excellence supported collaborative and creative problem solving. The project is an example of the important synergies that spring from integrated teams with overlapping goals achieved by every solution. The final work of the team included establishing an ongoing maintenance program and a long-term master plan for completion of remaining restoration work.

Figure 1.16 Completed in 2005, the partial renovation and expansion of Trinity Church in the City of Boston, a National Historic Landmark, added 15,000 square feet of space below the building and incorporated a ground-source heat pump system. Six wells set around the perimeter of the building extend 1,500 feet below the church. *Peter Vanderwarker photo, courtesy Goody Clancy*

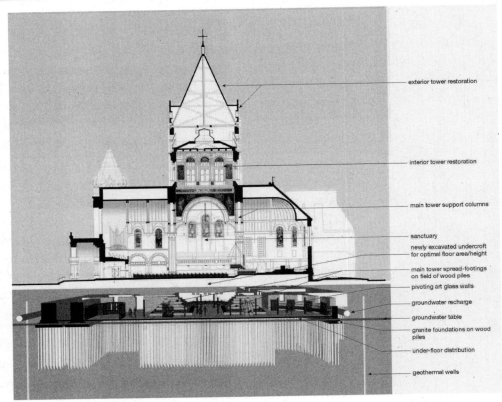

Figure 1.17 Trinity Church in the City of Boston sits on an estimated 4,000 wooden piles, which are protected by immersion in water. The new design routes all stormwater into drywells for dispersion back into the ground to maintain consistent groundwater levels and protect the integrity of the pilings.
© Goody Clancy

The labels in the figure read:
- exterior tower restoration
- interior tower restoration
- main tower support columns
- sanctuary
- newly excavated undercroft for optimal floor area/height
- main tower spread-footings on field of wood piles
- pivoting art glass walls
- groundwater recharge
- groundwater table
- granite foundations on wood piles
- under-floor distribution
- geothermal wells

Site Utilization and Rainwater Harvesting

- The building is physically constrained by a very limited site (less than 10 feet on three sides) outside of the building footprint. The only physical expansion possible required capturing space below the building without altering or impacting the wooden-friction piles that support the structure and remain intact because of the high water table. The floor level of the new spaces is approximately 7 feet above the wood pilings. All rainwater falling on the building and site is collected and stored in drywells around the perimeter of the building. When the water table, which is electronically monitored, falls to a level that might expose the wood piles to air and encourage rot, water from the wells is circulated below the building to recharge the water table.

- Strategies for claiming every available square foot of below-grade space included placing the machine room below a small area of on-site parking, locating new bath-

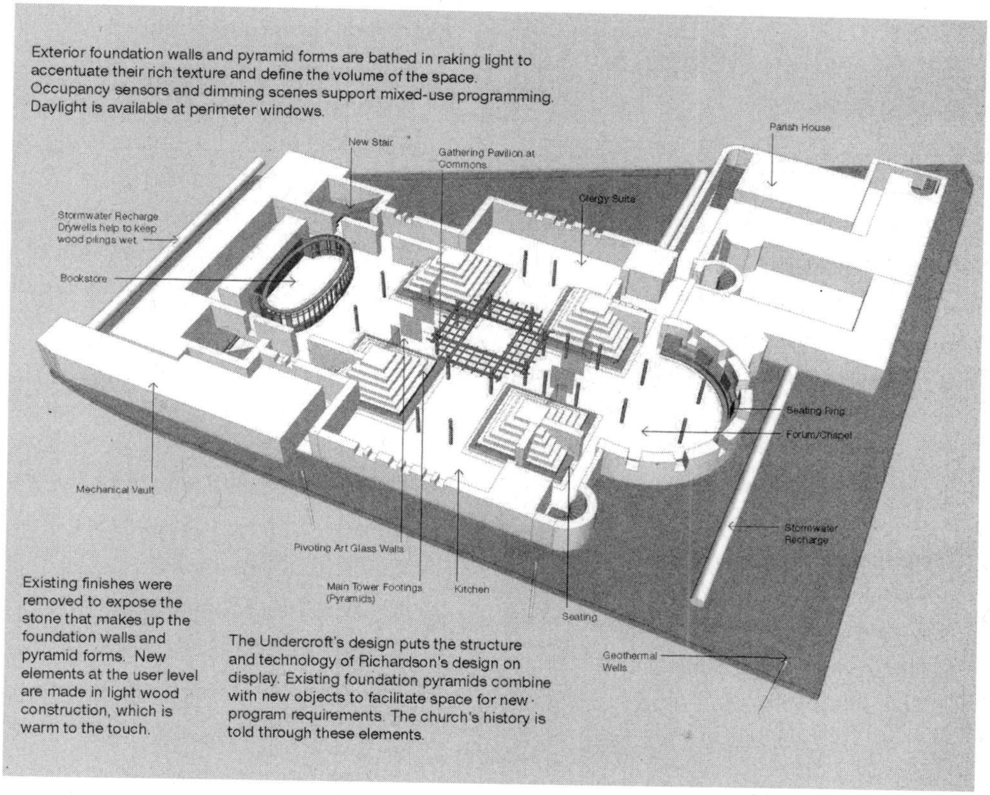

Figure 1.18 In the new below-grade spaces at Trinity Church, minimal use of new materials met multiple goals, which included reduced environmental impacts of manufacturing, aesthetic celebration of the original stone foundations, and creation of flexible open spaces. The church is a vibrant urban institution that on a daily basis hosts a diverse range of events and groups. © *Goody Clancy*

rooms below the exterior porch (an area that limited ceiling heights), placing drywell water storage beneath the broad masonry steps, and creating new storage spaces below an existing cloister garden.

Energy and Systems

- A new geothermal heat pump system reduces the energy the church must purchase by about 40 percent. The system, which utilizes six 1,500-foot vertical wells located within the 10-foot site adjacent to the building, eliminates the need for traditional cooling towers and is ideal for the air conditioning required in the new assembly spaces. No air conditioning was added to the interior of the church sanctuary. An existing connection to purchased steam was maintained for hot water and heating, but the inclusion of a variable frequency drive regulates both the heating and cooling pump systems to provide efficiency.

GREEN DESIGN ELEMENTS
Trinity Church

Sustainable Sites:
- Stormwater management
- Rain sensor irrigation system

Water Efficiency:
- Low-flow plumbing fixtures

Energy and Atmosphere:
- Ground-sourced geothermal heat pumps
- Variable frequency drives
- Four-pipe fan-cool system
- Natural ventilation
- Occupancy sensors

Materials and Resources:
- Recycled content materials
- Local/regional materials (wood)

Indoor Environment Quality:
- Operable windows
- Low-VOC materials and finishes
- CO_2 monitors

Additional Features:
- Interior excavation for undercroft

Materials and Resources

- The design of new spaces takes both structural and aesthetic advantage of the existing walls and foundations. The team sought solutions that left existing materials visually exposed and relied on pilings known to have been set in the 1870s but not used in the final structure. Salvage stone found in the excavation was used wherever possible, and new materials were selected on the basis of their recycled content and local origin.

PROJECT TEAM

Leggat McCall Properties LLC
Goody Clancy & Associates
Carol R. Johnson Associates, Inc.
LeMessurier Consultants
Walter B. Adams AIA (SBE)
Lawrence Architectural Planning
Cosentini Associates, Inc.
Nitsch Engineering, Inc.
Shawmut Design & Construction
John Canning Studio

Historic Academic Group; Mahan, Sampson & Maury Halls, U.S. Naval Academy

Annapolis, Maryland

Owner: Department of the Navy

Building Type: Institutional

Original Building Construction: 1899

Historic Designation: Buildings are contributing structures on National Historic Landmark Site.

Restoration/Renovation Completion: 2002

Square Footage: 200,000 ft²

Percentage Renovated: 100%

▼ Figure 1.19 The buildings composing the Historic Academic Group at the U.S. Naval Academy have both rich finishes and natural light that add to the beauty of the spaces. Durable finishes facilitate a green cleaning plan. *Richard Mandlekorn photo, courtesy Goody Clancy*

PROJECT DESCRIPTION

The project exemplifies 21st-century rediscovery of of passive-survivability features incorporated into an older building design. In the 1890s the need for daylight in the classrooms and offices was a critical aspect for the educational mission of the buildings. With the introduction of electrical lighting, skylights were removed and windows became secondary light sources. The energy efficiencies and user delight of reinfusing offices, classrooms, and passageways with natural daylight were a key concepts of the design.

Figure 1.20 The windows at the U.S. Naval Academy are set deep in the masonry walls, which facilitates hot-weather, high-angle solar shading. Natural ventilation was reestablished with operable windows. The thermal efficiencies of the masonry building envelope contributed to the HVAC design. Design included properly sized, high-efficiency motors, variable-frequency drives, variable air-handling distribution, and low-temperature (high delta), low-pressure air supply to reduce fan requirements. *Richard Mandlekorn photo, courtesy Goody Clancy*

Daylighting

- Reestablished skylights bring natural light to the interior of the building. Transoms and sidelights are used to share light from the perimeter. Increasing ceiling height at the perimeter windows took advantage of the entire window fenestration. The window glass has low emissivity with a shading coefficient no greater than .59. Lighting controls are provided by blinds and stepped switching. Light finish colors were used throughout for optimal surface reflectance.

Building Envelope

- Rigid insulation (2") increased both wall and roof R-values to 8. Thermal insulation blankets and board were added, using recycled material wherever possible. Convection loss through the building envelope was reduced with proper detailing, weather-stripping, and sealants. Windows were replaced with energy-efficient insulating glass units, with aluminum frames for low heat loss. Windows are set deep in the masonry walls for high-angle solar shading during the summer.

HVAC Systems

- The building's original natural ventilation was reestablished with operable windows.

- The thermal efficiencies of the masonry building envelope were a primary contributor to the HVAC design. Systems were selected for partload operating efficiency. Air-distribution zones separate perimeter from interior air-handling units. Design included properly sized high-efficiency motors, variable frequency drives, variable air handling distribution, and low-temperature (high delta), low-pressure air supply provided to reduce fan requirements.

- A direct digital control system optimizes operating efficiencies.

Figure 1.21 Historic buildings, such as these at the U.S. Naval Academy, often demonstrate strategies for greater penetration of natural light and ventilation through interior spaces. High ceilings, transoms, and transparent partitions facilitated both. General lighting levels were designed for 30 footcandles, which was lower than the established standard. Direct/indirect fixtures were used wherever possible with room occupancy sensors and stepped lighting levels. *Richard Mandlekorn photo, courtesy Goody Clancy*

Figure 1.22 The renovation at the U.S. Naval Academy reestablished skylights, which bring natural light into the interior of the building. To increase daylight penetration, two-story atria were created with glass walls that carry light into adjacent spaces. Because over 50 percent of the electricity in the United States comes from coal, reduction of lighting loads offers an important strategy for reducing greenhouse gas emissions at the same time that indoor environmental quality improves. (Refer to Chapters 5 and 6 for additional information.) *© Goody Clancy*

GREEN DESIGN ELEMENTS

Historic Academic Group; Mahan, Sampson & Maury Halls U.S. Naval Academy

Sustainable Sites:
- Sediment- and erosion-control plan
- Reduced site disturbance to preserve trees

Water Efficiency:
- Low-flow fixtures
- Self-closing water faucets

Energy and Atmosphere:
- Low-temperature and low-pressure air supply
- Economizer cycle, 100 percent outside air
- Direct digital controls
- High-efficiency motors, fans and variable-speed drives
- Additional insulation and low-E windows installed
- Energy-efficient light fixtures, 30 fc ambient level
- Direct/indirect fluorescent fixtures throughout
- Stepped lighting controls and occupancy sensors

Materials and Resources:
- Recycled content materials
- Construction waste management
- Concrete with fly ash from local source
- Wood veneers and flooring from sustainably managed source

Indoor Environment Quality:
- Lights wells, skylights, and interior windows allow daylight to flow deeper into the building.
- Stepped lighting levels (with sensors)
- 100 percent outside air available
- Low- or no-VOC-emitting products
- High level of occupant lighting and air control

Plumbing Systems
- Toilet rooms were intentionally stacked to minimize distribution runs, and distribution pipe was insulated to reduce system standby losses.
- Localized hot water heaters were used for preheat with a centralized high-temperature hot-water system.

Electrical Systems
- General lighting levels were designed for 30 foot-candles, lower than the established standard of 50 fc. Direct/Indirect fixtures were used wherever possible with room occupancy sensors and stepped lighting levels.

Indoor Air Quality
- Operable windows throughout.
- Outdoor air economizer system is capable of supplying 100 percent fresh air.
- Individual thermostatic control in each office and classroom.
- The air-filtration system includes prefilter and afterfilter.
- Separate zoning of systems is provided for each floor (use) and location (perimeter versus interior).

PROJECT TEAM
Department of the Navy
Goody Clancy & Associates
SAR Engineering
Heller & Metzger
Morton Thomas
Rolf Jensen Associates
Acentech
Hanscomb Associates
Lawrence Architecture Planning
ATC Associates
Whiting-Turner

Forbes Park

Chelsea, MA

Current Owner: Forbes Park LLC

Building Type: Multiunit Residential/Public Park/Restaurant

Original Building Construction: 1923

Restoration/Renovation Completion: Phase One September 2008

Square Footage: 400,000 ft²

Percentage Renovated: 60% + 40% addition

BUILDING DESCRIPTION

The Forbes Park loft community is a creative example of the renewal of dilapidated structures and regenerative site design. The nineteenth-century waterside industrial complex has been transformed into a mixed-use development that supports environmentally sensitive living and encourages community interaction. A series of lights called "Forbes Orbs" functions as an energy-conservation awareness system, identifying the type (and cost) of energy being supplied to the buildings at any given time. When power is "free" or coming from on-site wind generation, a blue lamp is displayed; off-peak energy is green; peak energy consumption is yellow; and grid-powered energy used during peak hours is red. This innovative lighting system is also linked to an onsite wind turbine that produces the facility's free "blue-light" energy. It is anticipated that roughly 60 percent of the energy used by the 250 lofts during the day can be supplied by the 165-foot, 600kW wind turbine. At night, the turbine recharges a fleet of hybrid electric cars at plug-in stations; the cars are available for rental use by Forbes Park residences. The same color-coded light system (minus the "free" signal) will illuminate the windmill to allow the community to share in personal energy conservation practices.

Site Regeneration

- Restored over ten acres of indigenous vegetation and natural animal habitats and established a three-quarter-mile River Walk where parking lots once were.

Figure 1.23 Radiant flooring systems were used throughout the new lofts at Forbes Park. The masonry walls act as thermal sinks for heat absorption. The units were designed to allow the large windows to facilitate natural cross-ventilation. © *Forbes Park LLC*

Figure 1.24 The developer hopes that the 600 kW wind turbine will supply roughly 60 percent of the energy used by the 250 lofts during the day. The project restored over 10 acres of indigenous vegetation and natural animal habitats and developed a ¾-mile River Walk. © *Forbes Park LLC*

GREEN DESIGN ELEMENTS
Forbes Park

Sustainable Sites:
- Shared fuel efficient cars
- Public transportation proximity
- Underground parking structure
- Water taxis
- Natural habitat restoration
- Xeriscaping
- Waste pipe removal

Water Efficiency:
- Graywater system
- Low-flow plumbing fixtures
- Dual-flush toilets

Energy and Atmosphere:
- Wind turbine
- Radiant floors
- Thermal massing
- Natural ventilation
- Energy Star appliances
- Energy conservation light system

Materials and Resources:
- Sustainable harvested materials
- Existing material reuse (brick and concrete)
- Occupant recycling program

Indoor Environment Quality:
- Atrium
- Large operable windows
- Low-VOC materials and finishes

Additional Features:
- Onsite composting
- Exterior skywalk
- Environmental education center
- Sustainable restaurant and bar onsite

Rainwater Harvesting
- Dual-flush toilets use rainwater that has been filtered through a runoff-collection system for sewage conveyance. Stormwater not used within the building is sent through an onsite canal system that creates brackish water before releasing it into the adjacent river.

Natural Ventilation and Daylight
- Central atrium provides daylight and ventilation.

Integrated Heating and Cooling Design
- Passive heating and cooling strategies are used in conjunction with energy-efficient HVAC. Masonry walls act as thermal sinks for heat absorption. Radiant flooring systems are used throughout.

Efficiency Strategies
- Certified low-energy appliances and low-water-use plumbing fixtures are used.

PROJECT TEAM

Davis Design Development Corp.
Forbes Park LLC

ENDNOTES

1. Building Design + Construction, *Green Buildings + Climate Change* (Reed Business Information, 2008).
2. Jeffrey Klugger, "By Any Measure, Earth Is at the Tipping Point." *Time* (April 3, 2006).
3. United Nations Environment Programme, *The UNEP Year Book 2008.* Available at: www.unep.org/yearbook/2008/.
4. Intergovernmental Panel on Climate Change, *Fourth Assessment Report: Climate Change 2007,* www.ipcc.ch.
5. United Nations Environment Programme, *Buildings and Climate Change: Status, Challenges and Opportunities* (UNEP, 2007). Available at www.unep.fr/shared/publications/pdf/DTIx0916xPA-BuildingsClimate.pdf.
6. U.S. Department of Energy, *Monthly Energy Review.* (Washington, DC: Energy Information Administration, U.S. Department of Energy, 2001).
7. Ibid.
8. USGS Factsheet FS-068-98, (1998) *Materials Flow and Sustainability.*
9. U.S. Environmental Protection Agency (EPA), *Characterization of Building-Related Construction and Demolition Debris in the United States* (July 1998). Available at: www.epa.gov/osw/hazard/generation/sqg/c&d-rpt.pdf; and U.S. EPA, *Municipal Solid Waste in the United States: 2000 Facts and Figures* (June 2002). Available at: www.epa.gov/waste/nonhaz/municipal/pubs/report-00.pdf.
10. U.S. Environmental Protection Agency (EPA), *Characterization of Products Containing Mercury in Municipal Solid Waste in the United States, 1970 to 2000* (April 1992). Available at: www.p2pays.org/ref/03/02026.pdf.
11. Office of the Federal Environmental Executive, The Federal Commitment to Green Building: Experiences and Expectations (n.d.). Available at: www.epa.gov/greenbuilding/pdf/2010_fed_gb_report.pdf.
12. Ibid.
13. This includes leakage from pipes in the ground, approximately one half of which are owned by the building-owner. Congressional Budget Office, *Future Investment in Drinking Water and Wastewater Infrastructure* (November 2002) Available at: www.cbo.gov/doc.cfm?index=3983&type=0.
14. U. S. Energy Information Administration, *Emissions of Greenhouse Gases in the U.S. 2005.*
15. Office of the Federal Environmental Executive, *The Federal Green Building Report,* http://ofee.gov/sb/fgb_report.pdf.
16. Ibid.
17. Ibid.
18. Wilson, Alex (2008). "What Do You Think You're Doing? Alex Wilson talks with Jeff Stein AIA," *ArchitectureBoston* (September–October).
19. Building and Social Housing Foundation and Empty Homes Agency, *New Tricks with Old Bricks* (London, U.K.). Empty Homes Agency, www.emptyhomes.com/documents/publications/reports/New%20Tricks%20With%20Old%20Bricks%20-%20final%2012-03-081.pdf. 2008.
20. Lockwood, Charles, and Deloitte (2008). *The Dollars and Sense of Green Retrofits.* Deloitte Development LLC. www.deloitte.com.
21. Wilson, Alex (2005). "Durability: A Key Component of Green Building." *Environmental Building News* 14 (11).
22. http://hem.dis.anl.gov/eehem/95/950109.html.
23. Bradley Wolf, Donald Horn, and Constance Ramirez, "Financing Historic Federal Buildings: An Analysis of Current Practice" (Washington, DC: General Services Administration, 1999.)
24. As quoted by Robert Ivy in "Shifts in the Architectural Climate," *Architectural Record,* December 2007. Available at http://archrecord.construction.com/community/editorial/archives/0712.asp.
25. Gregory H. Kats, *Green Building Costs and Financial Benefits* (Massachusetts Technology Collaborative, 2003). Available at: http://vgbn.org/whybuildgreen.php?rec=193.
26. U. S. General Services Administration, *Sustainability Matters* (Washington, DC: Public Buildings Service. Office of Applied Science, 2008), 36.
27. Ibid., p. 38.
28. Stewart Brand, *How Buildings Learn: What Happens After They're Built* (New York: Viking, 1994), p. 188.
29. Carl Elefante, "The Greenest Building Is…One That is Already Built." *Forum Journal 21* (4) (Summer 2007).
30. Building Design+Construction, *Green Buildings + Climate Change* (New York: Reed Business Information, 2008), p. 46.
31. Brand, p. 54.

chapter 2

BUILDINGS AND SUSTAINABLE DEVELOPMENT— UNDERSTANDING THE GOALS

2.1 Sustainable Development versus Sustainable Design
2.2 The Triple Bottom Line—People, Planet, and Profit
2.3 The Triple Bottom Line and Historic Preservation
2.4 Regional/Community Connectivity
2.5 Interwoven History of Sustainability and Historic Preservation

2.1 SUSTAINABLE DEVELOPMENT VERSUS SUSTAINABLE DESIGN

"Sustainability envisions the enduring prosperity of all living things."

—*American Institute of Architects Committee on the Environment*

THE TERMS *sustainable design* and *sustainable development* are often used interchangeably within the building industry. Sustainable development, however, is a much broader topic that informs the way we approach sustainable design. Sustainable development was presented in 1987 by the United Nations World Commission on Environment and Development (WCED) in the often-quoted report *Our Common Future* (aka The Brundtland Report) as: "development that meets the needs of the present without compromising the ability of future generations to meet their own needs."[1]

Our Common Future built on work begun in 1972 at the first United Nations Conference on the Human Environment in Stockholm and stressed the essential relationship between economic, social, and environmental sustainability. This interdependence has been consistently reinforced in the international conferences and charters that followed, including the 1992 United Nations Conference on Environment and

Development in Rio de Janeiro (The Earth Summit), the 1996 Habitat II Conference in Istanbul, and the Third International Conference on Urban Regeneration and Sustainability held in 2004 in Siena, Italy. All of these recognized sustainability as an overarching goal that requires the preservation of cultural heritage and stewardship of the environment, as well as social, economic, and political balance. In other words, sustainability is not limited to the environment, but encompasses human physical and emotional well-being supported by the three pillars of sustainability—social, environmental, and economic well-being.

2.2 THE TRIPLE BOTTOM LINE— PEOPLE, PLANET, AND PROFIT

"Our vision is of a life-sustaining Earth. We are committed to the achievement of a dignified, peaceful, and equitable existence. A sustainable United States will have a growing economy that provides equitable opportunities for satisfying livelihoods and a safe, healthy, high quality of life for current and future generations."

—*The President's Council on Sustainable Development, 1999*[2]

Figure 2.1 The focus of the Hudson Area Association Library during the renovation of the 1818 building was to interweave the "triple bottom line"—people, planet, profit—throughout all phases of the project. Notable achievements include the establishment of apprenticeship training programs and job opportunities for the community; incorporation of durable, salvaged and local materials; upgrading thermal efficiency of historic wood windows through restoration; and stormwater management. The master plan also includes graywater plumbing, indigenous landscaping, permeable paving, ground-source energy, and a variety of lighting technologies to reduce energy consumption and increase efficiency. © *Walter Sedovic*

Triple Bottom Line Performance Metrics of LANDCOM, a Government-owned Development Corporation in New South Wales, Australia

Social Development

- Provision of moderate-income housing
- Community facilities
- Welcome program
- Influencing design
- Effectiveness of community consultation
- Stakeholder relationship management
- Consumer education on sustainable living
- Conservation of nonindigenous heritage
- Aboriginal employment opportunities
- Employee satisfaction
- Employee retention rate
- Training

Environmental Care

- Integrated urban water-cycle management
- Reuse and recycling of construction and demolition materials
- Energy efficiency
- Sustainable or renewable energy supply
- Office use and greenhouse gas emissions
- Native vegetation management
- Riparian corridor management

Economic Development

- Profitability
- Financing capacity
- Returns to government
- Job creation and economic output

The synergies among social (people), environmental (planet), and economic (profit) stewardship are sometimes referred to as the *triple bottom line* (TBL), a term attributed to John Elkington, founder of the consulting firm SustainAbility and author of *Cannibals with Forks: The Triple Bottom Line of 21st Century Business* (1998). At its narrowest, TBL is about measuring and reporting corporate, organizational or government performance against social, environmental, and economic parameters. At its broadest, TBL concerns values, issues, and processes that must be addressed to create social, environmental, and economic sustainability.[3]

TBL evaluation tools have been adopted by businesses as well as organizations and are used by groups such as the ICLEI (International Council for Local Environmental Initiatives) to assist cities and towns in making decisions that support sustainable development. It serves as a reminder of the component, but overlapping, goals of sustainability—which are not always quantifiable and consequently may not be included in the building metric systems discussed in Chapter 3. Each category of the triple bottom line can be explored or defined at multiple levels. Each of the categories is quite broad, and the boundaries between them are often blurred.

People

The considerations under *people* involve political and social equity, the right to have equal access to education, healthcare, economic opportunities, and emotional and physical well-being to which connection to place contributes. Civic engagement is an important part of this—providing full opportunities for citizens, businesses, and communities to participate in and influence decisions that affect them.[4] *People* is about creating and sustaining communities in which all

Figure 2.2 Found artifacts reused in the railings at the Clipper Mill development in Baltimore, Maryland, reinforce the memory of place and the unique heritage of the foundry complex. All reuse of materials avoids the environmental impacts of new materials at the same time that it reduces construction waste. (Refer to Chapter 7 for additional information.) *Rick Lippenholtz photo, courtesy Struever Bros. Eccles and Rouse*

members are safe and happy and acknowledges that everyone has the right to clean air, clean water, healthy shelter, and healthy food.

Planet

Planet addresses the health of natural systems and requires that we understand and take responsibility for decisions, both immediate and long-term. Stewardship of the planet lies at at the heart of the environmental movement but cannot occur and be sustained without economic and social well-being.

Profit

Profit recognizes that economics are a critical part of achieving sustainability, both for individual businesses and for a collective standard of living that ensures comfort, health, and security for all. Profit for some cannot come at the expense of others and cannot impose on others costs resulting from pollution and environmental degradation. A healthy economy must be able to create meaningful jobs, eliminate poverty, and provide the opportunity for a high quality of life for everyone in an increasingly competitive world.[5]

"'Eco' comes from the Greek word *oikos*, meaning home. Ecology is the study of home, while economics is the management of home.... The challenge today is to put the 'eco' back into economics and every aspect of our lives."

—*David Suzuki*[6]

Figure 2.3 The swimming pool at the Clipper Mill development in Baltimore, Maryland, is enhanced by the historic character of the surrounding buildings. Adaptive reuse of buildings often addresses multiple aspects of sustainability—social, economic, and environmental. *Patrick Ross photo, courtesy Struever Bros. Eccles and Rouse*

2.3 THE TRIPLE BOTTOM LINE AND HISTORIC PRESERVATION

"Preservation is an essential tool for sustaining the environmental viability of the planet as well as the quality of life for ourselves and our children."

—*Richard Moe, President Emeritus, National Trust for Historic Preservation*

People and Historic Preservation

The act of preserving a site, a building, or a community is a gesture of respect for past decisions and a gift to future generations who may enjoy or be curious about the physical manifestation of different times and cultures. Historic preservation as a movement, not unlike the environmental protection movement, represents a reaction to decisions that seem to many to be wrong-headed, whether tearing down the house of our first president or destroying Grand Central Station in New York City or the wholesale demolition of American neighborhoods in the 1950s and 1960s in support of urban renewal, often federally funded, which reflected a belief that the only way to revitalize a community was to demolish it and start anew.

Despite the name, historic preservation (which in other parts of the world is known as heritage conservation or building conservation) is not stagnant. *With Heritage So Rich*, the document that provided the basis for the 1966 National Historic Preservation Act, makes an eloquent statement of why heritage matters. It presents the case that preservation must "go beyond saving bricks and mortar. It must go beyond saving occasional historic houses and opening museums. It must be more than a cult of antiquarians. It must do more than revere a few precious national shrines. It must attempt to give a sense of orientation to our society, using structures and objects of the past to establish values of time and place."[7]

"The importance of historic preservation is that it will help preserve each country's unique culture and history. Today, there are so many mega projects around the world that look alike regardless of the country. Each country and each city has its own character that should be valued and preserved. Because globalization is making cities look more alike, I believe we must face this challenge and reverse the trend. . . . The authentic city must be built on real architectural heritage rather than on a set formula and current fashion."

—*Weiming Lu*[8]

Historic preservation now embraces the stories of diverse marginalized communities and is providing the rallying point for multiple groups to unite in overlapping claims to neighborhoods and landmarks.[9] The civic engagement at the heart of preservation may be

Principles of Place

Standards for Creating Vibrant, Inspiring, and Sustainable Places

1.0 Build community.

2.0 Create inviting spaces.

3.0 Minimize carbon footprint and energy dependence.

4.0 Connect people and buildings to nature.

5.0 Encourage transportation alternatives.

6.0 Craft the first 30 [vertical] feet [for pedestrian pleasure].

7.0 Inspire communities with art.

8.0 Make 20-minute living real [mix uses in development].

9.0 Integrate schools and neighborhoods.

10.0 Preserve symbols that matter.

Gerding Edlen Development, Portland, Oregon, www.gerdingedlen.com

Figure 2.4 The Center for Neighborhood Technology in Chicago reclaimed and regenerated the site to create both an oasis from urban heat island effect and a place that celebrates community art. Below grade, a thermal ice-storage system supports off-peak purchase of energy. © *2008 Center for Neighborhood Technology*

as important as the buildings. As English Heritage, officially known as the Historic Buildings and Monuments Commission for England, has noted, "Historic places are a powerful focus for community action," which translates into social capital that can lead to improved health, higher educational attainment, better employment opportunities, and lower crime rates.[10]

Planet and Historic Preservation

"Buildings are unique in their longevity compared with other industrial products. The low turnover rate suggests that the environmental impact of newly built buildings is comparatively limited. Therefore...[existing] building stock must be looked upon as an unexploited asset with a great potential to improve the environment."

—*Organisation for Economic Co-Operation and Development*[11]

Studies of embodied energy, embodied carbon, and life-cycle assessment of buildings support the idea that the wisest course of action for the environment is often reuse of existing buildings, rather than replacement. In addition to avoiding the environmental impacts, energy use, and carbon created in the manufacturing and construction of new buildings, reuse significantly reduces construction waste, utilizes existing infrastructure, and sometimes creates greater density and reduced energy use per person because living units in older buildings tend to be smaller than new construction.

Because the energy required to operate a building over its life—particularly a long life—is far greater than the initial and recurring embodied energy in the materials (by a ratio of roughly 3 to 1, according to The Athena Institute), embodied energy alone might not justify saving buildings. However, a comparison between retrofitted buildings and new, high-performance buildings published in the Association for Preservation Technology *Bulletin* makes the case

that renewal of existing buildings offers the wisest energy strategy because a retrofitted building begins to benefit the environment more quickly (in 34.2 rather than 57 years) than a new building, which is burdened with its own embodied energy as well as energy costs of the demolished building (even when partially salvaged).[12]

The carbon footprint of existing buildings also supports reuse over replacement, as discussed in Chapter 1 and detailed in the 2008 report, *New Tricks from Old Bricks,* by the Empty Homes Agency and Building and Social Housing Foundation in Great Britain. This study found that refurbishment generated 70 percent less CO_2 than new construction, and that it takes anywhere from several decades to as many as 50 years for new super-insulated homes to surpass the CO_2 savings achieved by renovating existing homes to make them energy-efficient.

According to the creators of BuildCarbonNuetral.org, an online carbon calculating tool, carbon dioxide released in constructing a building represents about 17 percent of its lifetime emissions.[13] These emissions are released at the time of construction, creating an emissions peak that we can ill afford. Significant CO_2 emissions from construction will be extraordinary if, as the Brookings Institute predicts, the United States increases building stock by over 40 percent before 2030, partially by demolishing and replacing 82 billion square feet of existing buildings, or one quarter of the building stock we currently have.[14]

Life-cycle assessment (LCA) offers a more holistic metric for comparing renovation against new construction because it considers the entire life of a product or building. A recent study by Diane Ross of the University of Victoria in Canada used the most comprehensive available whole-building LCA software, Athena Environmental Impact Estimator (discussed in Chapter 3), to compare the impact of an 1867 house against a new house. The environmental impacts of the heritage building were found to be less than those of a new house, although the report is careful to note that new versus old is not always a comparison of equals.[15]

Profit and Historic Preservation

"Nearly any way the effects are measured, be they direct or indirect, historic preservation tends to yield significant benefits to the economy."

Randall Mason[16]

The Advisory Council on Historic Preservation (ACHP), an independent agency with broad federal responsibilities for promoting preservation, states unequivocally on its website that historic preservation delivers significant economic benefits to communities. The website, www.achp.gov, provides links to studies covering a broad geographic range and types of documentation, and yielding such findings as these:

- Historic preservation activities in Texas generate more than $1.4 billion of annual economic activity.
- Rehabilitation of historic properties in Georgia over a five-year period created 7,550 jobs and $201 million in earnings.
- Each dollar of Maryland's historic preservation tax credit leveraged $6.70 of economic activity in the state.

Randall Mason, associate professor of City and Regional Planning at the University of Pennsylvania's School of Design, reviewed a range of studies in 2005 for the Brookings Institution Metropolitan Policy Program—including economic impacts, development pro formas, cost-benefit analyses, property value tracking, and hypothetical market situations. He found that the literature weighted toward advocacy causes and suggested that it could benefit from more collaborative research that addresses the relative value of preservation compared to other kinds of investment. However, he concluded, "Historic preservation has important economic values and produces certain economic benefits for both private actors and the public at large. Preservation projects can be profitable; and preservation policies do make sound fiscal sense."

"The perspective on stewardship of built heritage needs to shift to a presumption in favor of reuse. As it stands, the burden to demonstrate the case for preservation rests with groups of interested citizens, often seen as an elite. Currently, the challenge is to prove that an old building is so valuable that it ought to be saved; rather the owner/developer should be required to prove that an old building cannot be adapted to new use."

—*Heritage Canada Foundation[17]*

Donovan Rypkema, author of *The Economics of Historic Preservation: A Community Leader's Guide,* frequently addresses preservation conferences about the economic benefits of historic preservation. He makes the point that new construction is equally divided between materials and labor, but dollar for dollar, rehabilitation is weighted toward labor. The higher labor intensity benefits the local economy with local jobs and increased household income. He makes a convincing case for the economic viability of a culture of renewal and repair rather than replacement.

"Across America, for every million dollars of production, the average manufacturing firm creates 23.9 jobs," Rypkema argues. "A million dollars spent in new construction generates 30.6 jobs. But that same million dollars in the rehabilitation of an historic building? 35.4 jobs.... Now, of course, the argument can be made, 'Yeah, but once you've built the building the job creation is done.' Yes, but there are two

The National Trust for Historic Preservation Sustainability Initiative

Richard Moe, President Emeritus

Through our Sustainability Initiative, the National Trust for Historic Preservation is focusing the nation's attention on the importance of reusing existing buildings and reinvesting in older and historic communities as critical elements in combating climate change. Americans already embrace as common sense the need to recycle aluminum cans, glass, and newspapers. We advocate applying that same common sense to our built environment.

We don't discount the value of new, green construction—in fact, many green technologies can and should be applied to existing buildings to improve performance. But new construction—no matter how green—still uses energy and other natural resources and generates construction waste that clogs landfills.

Through its research, the National Trust's Sustainability Initiative is demonstrating that conservation and improvement of our existing built resources are environmentally logical and economically viable elements in combating climate change.

SUSTAINABLE STEWARDSHIP OF OUR BUILDINGS AND COMMUNITIES

Guiding Principles:

- *Reuse existing buildings.* Use what you have. The continued use of our existing buildings reduces the amount of demolition and construction waste deposited in landfills, lessens unnecessary demand for energy and other natural resources, and conserves embodied energy (the amount of energy originally expended to create extant structures).

Figure 2.5 The location of The Center for Neighborhood Technology in Chicago—an urban setting well served by public transportation—reflects the Center's commitment to urban sustainability, environmental education, and amenities for employees. © 2008 Center for Neighborhood Technology

(continued)

Figure 2.6 Incorporating bike storage can be as simple as the wall racks at the Alliance Center in Denver (see Chapter 3), provided they don't create a risk for the sight-impaired. Reducing the use of cars by encouraging cycling targets greenhouse gas emissions, air quality, noise pollution, and urban heat island effects. Cars themselves are resource- and pollution-intensive in manufacturing, with both upstream and downstream impacts. *Alliance for a Sustainable Colorado*

- *Reinvest in our older and historic communities.* Older and historic communities tend to be centrally located, dense, walkable, and are often mass-transit accessible—qualities celebrated and promoted by Smart Growth advocates. Reinvestment in existing communities also preserves the energy embedded in infrastructure, such as roads, water, and sewer lines.

- *Retrofit our existing building stock.* Many historic and older buildings are remarkably energy efficient because of their site sensitivity, quality of construction, and use of passive heating and cooling, while other buildings require improvements to reduce their environmental footprint. Historic buildings can go green without compromising historic character.

OUR COMMITMENT

Focus on local, state and federal policy: The National Trust for Historic Preservation will work with several cities to develop model policies that encourage preservation as sustainable development. This work will include refining building, energy and zoning codes, as well as developing model language for comprehensive plans and climate change action plans. We will also work to expand the availability of historic tax credits at the state and federal level, encourage other financial incentives for building reuse and community revitalization and support energy policy that improves energy efficiency in older buildings. Respect for our existing built environment is an important component of the Sustainability Initiative's strategy.

National Trust for Historic Preservation, www.preservationnation.org

responses to that. First, real estate is a capital asset—like a drill press or a boxcar. It has an economic impact during construction, but a subsequent economic impact when it is in productive use. Additionally, however, since most building components have a life of between 25 and 40 years, a community could rehabilitate 2 to 3 percent of its building stock per year and have perpetual employment in the building trades."[18]

2.4 REGIONAL/COMMUNITY CONNECTIVITY

"The historical and cultural foundations of the nation should be preserved as a living part of our community life and development in order to give a sense of orientation to the American people."

—*The National Historic Preservation Act of 1966*

Because of the complexity of natural systems and of cultural heritage, every place is environmentally and historically unique. Understanding and embracing the diversity of our world represents an essential part of sustainability and is worthy of a brief description that establishes the concept of regional and community connectivity within conversations about historic preservation, environmental responsibility, and global reach.

Change is perhaps the only constant in our search for sustainability. As we seek a new world that is equitable and responsible, celebrating and reinforcing the unique characteristics and opportunities of each place become more important, because environmental sustainability is regionally specific and people have an emotional need to be connected to both nature and community. If we continue to make all places similar by erecting new buildings that look alike despite climatic differences, and if we continue to casually dispose of objects of memory, we will not achieve environmental

Figure 2.7 Home to Ecotrust, the Jean Vollum Natural Capitol Center (see Chapter 8) in Portland, Oregon, reuses a nineteenth-century warehouse building, which provides a connection to history, supports the vitality of the city center (curtailing urban sprawl) and takes advantage of public transportation. *Dan Tyrpak Photographic for Holst Architecture*

Successful initiatives share seven common characteristics that should inform and guide the development of policies and projects. Successful initiatives:

1. Serve, invest in, and respect people
2. Invest in and respect places
3. Align with or create new market forces for sustainable development
4. Leverage their ecological and social, as well as economic, assets
5. Constructively address issues of race and class
6. Build regional and multijurisdictional alliances; and
7. Are locally driven

In particular, successful initiatives understand the intrinsic value of place. They recognize that challenges extend beyond artificial jurisdictional lines and attempt to create regional solutions. They also recognize that challenges and opportunities can be best addressed by networks of people with diverse backgrounds, views, and experiences working together in inclusive planning and decision-making processes.

President's Council on Sustainable Development, Metropolitan and Rural Strategies Task Force, 3/99. http://clinton4.nara.gov/PCSD/ca.html

sustainability—in part because we will have ignored ecological variance, and in part becasue we will also have destroyed the unique heritage of place. "Meaningful places," writes Garth Rockcastle, "tend to share at least three qualities. First, they are unique to a specific location. Second, they are a reflection or embodiment of shared or constituent values. Third, they live in time; and the broader the reach they embody, the better."[19]

Human connection to nature, community, and place is a necessary element of healthy living and the ability to achieve sustainability. Connectivity to nature is now defined as biophilia and widely celebrated in sustainable design. Built responses to the natural world must vary by climatic zone and conditions unique to each area. So, too, must the memory of place, which requires that buildings and heritage areas from past generations and cultures be retained to avoid creating communities so lacking in personality that it is impossible to identify geographic location without signage.

Figure 2.8 The new porches at the Eastern Village Cohousing Condominiums in Silver Spring, Maryland (see Chapter 8), provide places for social interaction, shade the entrances to the units, and support the extensive greenery that is part of the transformation of a 1950s office building into a forward-thinking housing community. *EDG Architects*

2.5 INTERWOVEN HISTORY OF SUSTAINABILITY AND HISTORIC PRESERVATION

"The concept of preservation is built on a…balance between respect for private rights on the one hand and a concern for the larger community on the other," writes Diane Lea in "America's Preservation Ethos: A Tribute to Enduring Ideals."[20] The same can be said about the elusive goal of sustainability, which has evolved from efforts to protect the natural world (sometimes described as the "environmental movement"). Widespread concern for the environment and broad support for historic preservation emerged at the same time. Their interwoven history serves as a reminder of the relationship and interdependency between the two social movements and sets the stage for guidelines and metrics reviewed in Chapter 3.

The historic preservation movement in the United States began with the protection of natural areas and expanded into the safeguarding of individual buildings and sites. To this day, the protection of natural areas is a significant part of historic preservation in the United States, as demonstrated by the National Park Service and the Public Lands Initiative of the National Trust for Historic Preservation.

In 1872, President Ulysses S. Grant signed an act that created and safeguarded the first national park in the world on a "tract of land …near the head-waters of the Yellowstone River…as a public park or pleasuring-Ground for the benefit and enjoyment of the people."[21] Twenty years earlier, the Mount Vernon Ladies Association had formed to purchase and protect the estate of George Washington recognizing the emotional, educational, and cultural importance of the home of America's first president.

Timeline of Historic Preservation and Environmental Action/Design

1872—Yellowstone National Park created

1892—Sierra Club founded

1905—National Audubon Society

1906—The Antiquities Act

1916—National Park Service established

1931—Charleston, South Carolina, Historic District

1931—AIA Committee on Preservation of Historic Buildings, now the Historic Resources Committee

1935—Historic Sites Act

1936—Vieux Carre, New Orleans, Louisiana, protected

1936—Urban Land Institute founded

1937—Restoration Policy Statement issued by National Park Service

1938—*The Culture of Cities* (Lewis Mumford)

1949—National Trust for Historic Preservation created by congressional order

1961—*The Death and Life of Great American Cities* (Jane Jacobs)

1962—*Silent Spring* (Rachel Carson)

1963—*Design With Climate* (Victor Olgyay with Alddar Olgyay)

1966—National Historic Preservation Act

1966—Department of Transportation Act protects historic sites

1967—*Sun; Wind; Water* (Ralph Knowles)

(continued)

1968—*Form and Stability* (Ralph Knowles)

1968—*The Whole Earth Catalog* first published

1969—Friends of the Earth formed by David Brower

1969—National Environmental Policy Act affirms a commitment to historic preservation

1970—First Earth Day celebration

1970—Environmental Protection Agency formed

1970—Natural Resources Defense Council formed

1971—Executive Order for the Protection and Enhancement of the Cultural Environment

1972—*The Limits to Growth* (Club of Rome Report)

1972—UN Conference on the Human Environment, Stockholm

1973—OPEC oil embargo

1973—AIA Energy Conservation Task Force established

1973—Federal Energy Management Program chartered

1973—The Endangered Species Act

1974—Federal Energy Administration Act signed

1975—AIA Committee on Energy established (now the Committee on the Environment or COTE/Sustainability)

1976—Tax Reform Act of 1976 offers tax credits for restoration of certain kinds of historic buildings

1977—The Clean Water Act

1978—*The Secretary of the Interior's Standards for the Treatment of Historic Properties*

1978—National Park Service Preservation Brief #3, *Conserving Energy in Historic Buildings* (Baird Smith)

1978—Executive Order 12072: Federal Space Management

1979—The Australia ICOMOS Charter for the Conservation of Places of Cultural Significance (the Burra Charter)

1980—National Main Street Center established by the National Trust for Historic Preservation

1981—*New Energy from Old Buildings* (National Trust for Historic Preservation)

1988—AIA Committee on the Environment formed

1992—UN Conference on Environment and Development, Rio de Janeiro

1993—U.S. Green Building Council formed

1993–1999—President's Council on Sustainable Development

1994—Greening of Grand Canyon National Park

1996—Executive Order 13006: Locating Federal Facilities on Historic Properties in Our Nation's Central Cities, 1996

1997—The Kyoto Protocol to limit greenhouse gas emissions

1999—Executive Order 13123 "Greening the Government through Efficient Energy Management"

2001—*Greening Federal Facilities: An Energy, Environmental and Economic Resource Guide for Federal Facility Managers and Designers,* second edition

2002—UN World Summit on Sustainable Development, Johannesbug

2003—Executive Order 13287 "Preserve America" emphasizes federal policy for the protection and enhancement of historic properties

2007—Intergovernmental Panel on Climate Change Fourth Assessment Report

2009—Preservation Green Lab opens in Seattle, Washington

Learning from the Past

NATURAL VENTILATION IN THE OLD EXECUTIVE OFFICE BUILDING (OEOB)

The OEOB was opened in 1888 with an intricate natural ventilation and passive cooling system. Air channels were built throughout the granite walls, allowing fresh air to enter through slots under the windows and be drawn across the room into the corridors. At each corner of the building, stained glass domes top open stairwells. Hot air would rise into the domes and exhaust through vents into glazed sky-lit spaces, creating negative pressure that pulled air through the rest of the building.

Excerpt from *Greening of the White House, Six Year Report,* November 1999

Protection of resources in the United States and the world has moved back and forth between the public and private sectors for over 150 years, with private groups often leading the way. In 1891, the first private regional land trust in the world, The Trustees of Reservations, was formed in Massachusetts, followed by the founding of the National Trust in the United Kingdom in 1895 to "act as a [private] guardian for the nation in the acquisition and protection of threatened coastline, countryside and buildings."[22]

Policies and standards created by the United States in the late nineteenth and early twentieth centuries—and emulated around the world—maintained the dual goals of protecting natural and cultural heritages. The year 1906 saw passage of the Act for the Preservation of American Antiquities, the National Park Service was created in 1916, and in 1935 the Historic Sites Act declared "that it is a national policy to preserve for public use historic sites, buildings, and objects of national significance for the inspiration and benefit of the people of the United States."[23] The Historic Sites Act expanded the scope of federal preservation by enabling the NPS to buy and own private buildings, maintaining and operating them for the public benefit.

The era after World War II saw sweeping changes in the world and in values, but in the early 1960s, two remarkable women refocused attention in the United States on environmental stewardship and cultural sustainability. With two books, Jane Jacobs and Rachel Carson challenged the arrogance of American culture. In *The Death and Life of Great American Cities* (1961) Jane Jacobs questioned the wholesale demolition of urban neighborhoods to make way for new construction intended to improve on what it replaced. In *Silent Spring* Rachel Carson decried the widespread use of chemical toxins as pesticides.

Other seminal books rapidly followed in reaction to the destruction required to build the interstate highway system, the spread of urban renewal, and a continuing disregard for the impacts of industry and "modern" buildings. *Design with Climate,* by Victor Olgyay with Aladar Olgyay, was released in 1963, and Ralph Knowles wrote *Sun; Wind; Water* for publication in 1967, followed by *Form and Stability* in 1968. In 1966, the Rains Committee published *With Heritage So Rich.*

Safeguarding resources and heritage was again affirmed as a central concept of the National Historic Preservation Act of 1966 and the National Environmental Policy Act of 1969. Both laws reflect the link between environmental preservation and heritage protection. The National Historic Preservation Act identifies historic properties as "irreplaceable" and catalogs the rewards of preservation, including "cultural, educational, aesthetic, inspirational, economic, and energy benefits…"[24] The National Environmental Policy Act establishes six goals, among them to "preserve important historic, cultural, and natural aspects of our national heritage…."[25] Both laws, word for word, state the purpose of ensuring "social, economic, and other requirements of present and future generations,"[26] directly acknowledging the holistic and interrelated complexities of both preservation and environmental sustainability. The National Environmental Policy Act went further, stressing an interdisciplinary approach and "the integrated use of the natural and social sciences and the environmental design arts in planning and decision-making...."

An interdisciplinary approach and the integrated use of the natural and social sciences often take a back seat to more visible and immediate aspects of environmental protection. In the 1970s, the single most visible environmental issue was energy. The 1973 OPEC oil embargo supported the case that natural resources were limited and called into question the wisdom of relying on technologies dependent on extensive and pollutant-producing consumption of fossil fuels. The federal government responded by establishing the Federal Energy Office and chartering the Federal Energy Management Program in 1973.

The Energy Policy Act of 2005—which expedites energy development on public lands and targets vast regions of the American West for the mining of oil, gas, and coal—has caused "the emergence of an unprecedetnted alliance between environmentalists, historic preservationists, and archeologists, all working toward a common goal of preservation of cultural resources"[27] Noting that the extraction of hydrocarbon fuels dominates public lands policy these days, to the detriment of ancient archeological sites, Jerry Spangler quotes President Theodore Roosevelt as saying "no man is justified in doing evil on the ground of expedience." Roosevelt's legacy included the Antiquities Act of 1906, which reflected his firm belief that public lands and the resources found on them—including the archeological ones—were treasures owned by all Americans.

Figure 2.9 The recent renovation of the Candler Library at Emory University in Atlanta, Georgia (see Chapter 8) restored the space to its appearance shown in this historic photograph. The room had been floored over and its character lost. Sustainable design addresses intangibles such as a sense of place and the emotional satisfaction of aesthetically pleasing places rich in heritage. *Courtesy Emory University Archives*

The Department of Energy and the Solar Energy Research Institute were created in 1977.

During this time, the preservation community played upon the emotional momentum of what became known as the "energy crisis" to emphasize the point that the demolition and replacement of existing buildings uses more energy than their renovation. Banners draped across structures proclaimed the amount of oil saved by preservation. Such efforts led to the passage of the Public Buildings Cooperative Use Act, which encouraged the rehabilitation of historic federal properties. In 1981, the National Trust for Historic Preservation published *New Energy from Old Buildings,* which, although now out of print, remains a definitive text for understanding the economics of preservation and material resource conservation.

The American Institute of Architects (AIA) responded to the energy crisis of the 1970s by establishing the Energy Conservation Task Force, which evolved in 1989 into the Committee on the Environment (COTE). COTE began an ambitious project to assess building products based on life-cycle analysis. The resulting *AIA Environmental Resource Guide,* published in 1992, accelerated the emergence of an evolving construction market that supports ecologically sensitive building materials in the same way that the preservation industry has revived the use of historic reproductions.

▼Figure 2.10 The Solar Umbrella House in Venice, California, renovated and added onto an existing house in a design built on multiple strategies for reducing environmental impacts during construction and operation. The design approach to an existing building depends on the character of the surrounding neighborhood and the historical importance of the building. *Marvin Rand photo, courtesy Pugh+Scarpa Architects*

▶Figure 2.11 Buildings are often beloved for the stately character to which they contribute as part of a historic environment. The extensive renovation of the Lion House at the Bronx Zoo (see Chapter 5), embodies a masterful weaving of new technology, including a fuel cell, with the beauty of the original building. *© David Sundberg/Esto*

The federal government has become a leader in renovations that implement sustainable design. The "Greening of the White House" began in the early 1990s, followed by properties such as the Pentagon, the Presidio, and the U.S. Department of Energy head-quarters, as well as Grand Canyon, Yellowstone, and Denali national parks. These projects successfully and significantly reduced energy and water consumption, as well as landscaping and solid-waste costs, while lowering atmospheric emissions.[28]

Greening of the White House—Measures Taken between 1993 and 1999

"We're going to identify what it takes to make the White House a model for efficiency and waste reduction, and then we're going to get the job done. I want to make the White House a model for other federal agencies, for state and local governments, for business, and for families in their homes. Before I ask you to do the best you can in your house, I ought to make sure I'm doing the best I can in my house."

—President Bill Clinton, April 21, 1993

The initiative launched by President Clinton on Earth Day 1993 identified opportunities to reduce waste, lower energy use, and make appropriate use of renewable resources, while improving indoor air quality and building comfort. The final report in 1999 estimated that the operational savings achieved reached approximately $300,000 annually, with the elimination of 845 metric tons of carbon emissions a year.

LIGHTING

- Completed in 1800, the White House sits on an east-west axis, allowing for maximum use of the sun for lighting and heating. Originally, candles and lard-oil lamps were used at night.

Gas lighting was added in 1848 and electrical lighting in 1891, but sunlight still provides light for most of the day.

- In 1993, 95 percent of the building's incandescent table lamp bulbs were replaced with compact fluorescents, saving 1,600 kilowatts-hours per year.

HEATING, VENTILATION AND AIR CONDITIONING (HVAC)

- Installation of a new HVAC system in the Executive Residence was completed in 1999. The chillers were replaced with high-efficiency units without chlorofluorocarbon coolant (CFC). Estimated savings were 400,000 kilowatt-hours of electricity, 24,000 gallons of water, and $32,000 per year.
- All pipes were insulated.
- Steam traps were replaced to prevent steam loss.

WASTE

- Shredded paper documents were sent to an off-site composting facility, where they were mixed with yard trimmings to make a compost product called LEAFGRO. LEAFGRO, in turn, was used as compost on White House grounds.

- Internal policies were put in place to educate staff to reduce paper consumption, limit the use of disposables, conserve office supplies, and eliminate unnecessary items.

- Furniture was refurbished rather than disposed of to avoid cutting new wood and manufacturing of other materials required for new furniture.

TRANSPORTATION

- Flexible-fuel ethanol vehicles were tried.

- A pilot program, sponsored jointly by the Potomac Electric Power Company and the Department of Energy, tested Ford's electric 1998 Ranger pickup truck.

- A transit-subsidy program was implemented to encourage employees to use public transportation.

- A shuttle service was provided for official travel to Capitol Hill.

LANDSCAPING

- New plantings used only species that are native to Washington.

- Preference was given to organic practices whenever possible. Pesticide use was reduced 80 percent by eliminating blanket sprays and improving pest management.

- In 1994, sprinkler heads were adjusted and/or replaced and watering was switched to the early morning, saving 15,000 gallons in one year.

- Trimmings and yard waste from 18 acres of grounds were composted off-site and returned for use as soil amendments.

Source: *Greening of the White House, Six Year Report,* November 1999

The 1990s also saw the launch of the EPA's Energy Star labeling program and a green pilot project in eight Navy buildings, including a 150-year-old gunnery-assembly plant and the Naval Facilities Engineering Command headquarters. In 1997, the Navy initiated the development of the *Whole Building Design Guide,* an online resource that incorporates sustainable design requirements into mainstream building specifications and guidelines. (Refer to Chapter 3 for tools and metric systems.)

In the late 1990s, a series of executive orders focused on "greening" the government and laid the foundation for many of the federal environmental policies in place today. Executive Order (EO) 13123, "Greening the Government through Efficient Ener-

gy Management," signed in June 1999, was the first to mention sustainable design. That order charged an interagency team, led by the General Services Administration and the Department of Defense, to define precisely what sustainable design and development principles would mean to the federal government.[29] Subsequent publications and projects have documented the significant savings in operational costs, the reduction of energy use, and holistic strategies that improve occupant comfort and productivity by creating healthier places to work.

Sustainable design, as both a requirement and a voluntary strategy, continues to spread, as does the impact of historic preservation. *Building Design + Construction* magazine describes sustainable design

Figure 2.12 The Forbes Park development in Chelsea, Massachusetts (see Chapter 1), reuses an existing building, restores natural habitat, offers water views and access to a water taxi in addition to utilizing an on-site wind turbine, incorporating all aspects of sustainability—social, economic, and environmental. © *Forbes Park LLC*

as "the most vibrant and powerful force to impact the building design and construction field in more than a decade."[30] Frank Matero, writing in the preface of *Managing Change: Sustainable Approaches to the Conservation of the Built Environment,* states that many people now consider the field of historic preservation "among the most significant and influential sociocultural movements that affect the built environment," helping to position heritage center stage in the discourse on place, cultural identity, and ownership of the past.[31] However dire the data are about impending climate change, it is an exciting and hopeful time in which actions can make a significant difference and the ability to merge common goals can offer a positive legacy for future generations.

The case studies demonstrate diverse and inventive regenerative design solutions that capitalize on existing resources and renew communities, as well as buildings.

CCI Center

Pittsburgh, PA

Current Owner: Conservation Consultants Inc.

Building Type: Commercial Office

Original Building Construction: 1910

Restoration/Renovation Completion: 1998

Retro-commissioned: 2002

Square Footage: 11,500 ft^2

Percentage Renovated: 100%

Occupancy: 40 people (40 hrs/week)

Recognition: LEED EB Pilot—Gold; AIA/COTE Top Ten Green Projects, 1999; City of Pittsburgh, Category/title: Preservation Award; Governor's Award for Environmental Excellence

Northeast Green Building Awards, Category/title: Commercial and Institutional Buildings (3rd place), 2001

"The CCI Center is a multifaceted endeavor that combines architectural history, community economic revitalization, environmental stewardship and architecture as pedagogy. Collectively, the structure speaks to the mission of CCI as one of Pittsburgh's leading nonprofit organizations specializing in energy conservation, environmental education, sustainable design and neighborhood development. By reusing an existing building, the project honors the building's place in the history of the community and the physical fabric of the neighborhood. In addition, the embodied energy and resources contained in the existing building are retained, lessening the drain on natural resources that typically take place in new construction."

—*CCI Development Committee Grant Application*

PROJECT DESCRIPTION

The CCI Center renovation combined two turn-of-the-century buildings to create office spaces and work areas that demonstrate the principles of the tenants, which include not only Conservation Consultants, Inc., which promotes responsible energy use but also The Green Building Alliance, Healthy Home Resources, and branches of the Pennsylvania Resources Council and Earthforce. The CCI actively monitors the building to ensure that mechanical systems are performing as designed and pursues a green housekeeping policy for cleaning, integrated pest management, and environmentally conscious procurement to avoid chemical toxicity.

Figure 2.13 Two buildings are combined to create the office spaces and work areas of multiple tenants that are committed to sustainability. Photovoltaic awnings shade the front porch and the access to the roof deck above. Added skylights and large windows reduce lighting-energy loads. © 2008 Conservation Consultants, Inc.

GREEN DESIGN ELEMENTS

CCI Center

Sustainable Sites:

- Public transportation proximity
- Permeable pavement
- Rooftop garden
- Xeriscaping

Water Efficiency:

- Graywater system
- Low-flow plumbing fixtures

Energy and Atmosphere:

- Photovoltaic panel system
- Natural stack ventilation
- Renewable energy certificates (100% wind)
- Ceiling fans
- High-internal-thermal-mass building

Materials and Resources:

- Reclamation of existing materials
- Recycled content materials
- Locally harvested/manufactured materials

Indoor Environment Quality:

- Skylights/clerestory windows
- Operable windows
- Low-VOC materials and finishes
- IAQ construction management plan

Additional Features:

- Solar panels as shading device
- Green cleaning policy
- Occupant recycling program
- Environmental education programs

Energy

The building utilizes passive survivability strategies to reduce energy requirements and provide a high-quality interior environment. Skylights and clerestory windows keep lighting-energy loads to a minimum, and ceiling fans, coupled with operable windows, allow occupants to work comfortably without using the mechanical system. The building employs natural stack ventilation along with a waste-heat recovery system that maintains a cleaner indoor environment for occupants.

The south side of the building is shaded with overhangs, trees, and shrubs to reduce summer cooling loads. A 2.5kW photovoltaic system provides renewable energy to the building and also functions as a shading device over a south-facing balcony, displaying both active and passive solar systems. Hot water needed in the building is preheated with a solar domestic hot water heater and pumped to low-flow plumbing fixtures.

Separate mechanical systems serve spaces with different heating and cooling needs. Thermostats are seven-day programmable and are located in a central area out of the direct sun.

DESIGN TEAM

Tai + Lee Architects
Conservation Consultants, Inc.
Green Building Alliance
Pennsylvania Resources Council
Clearview Project Services Company
Bert Davis & Associates
Tudi Mechanical Systems, Inc.
Sustainaissance International, Inc.

Center for Neighborhood Technology

Chicago, IL

Current Owner: Center for Neighborhood Technology

Building Type: Commercial Office/Institutional

Original Building Construction: 1924

Restoration/Renovation Completion: 2004

Square Footage: 13,800 ft^2

Percentage Renovated: 100%

Occupancy: 65 people (40 hrs/week)

Recognition: LEED NC v2.0—Platinum; Mayor Daley's GreenWorks Award for Outstanding Non-Residential Building, 2004; Sustainable Buildings Industry Council Exemplary Sustainable Building Award, 2004

"Since 1978, the Center for Neighborhood Technology (CNT) has worked to show urban communities locally and all across the country how to develop more sustainably. By combining thoughtful data analysis with creativity and innovation, well before the term sustainable development was even widely used, CNT has been demonstrating its unique brand of sustainable development: development that is good for the economy and the environment; makes better use of existing resources and community assets; and improves the health of natural systems and the wealth of people—today and in the future…. Our … building demonstrates how we work—from innovation to implementation—within a framework that values places."

—Center for Neighborhood Technology, www.cnt.org, accessed January 2009

PROJECT DESCRIPTION

The Center for Neighborhood Technology moved into a former textile factory in 1987 and began its second renovation in 2000 to accommodate greater space needs. The new office space offers an exemplary model of sustainable adaptive reuse that takes advantage of environmentally responsible products and technologies not available in the 1980s.

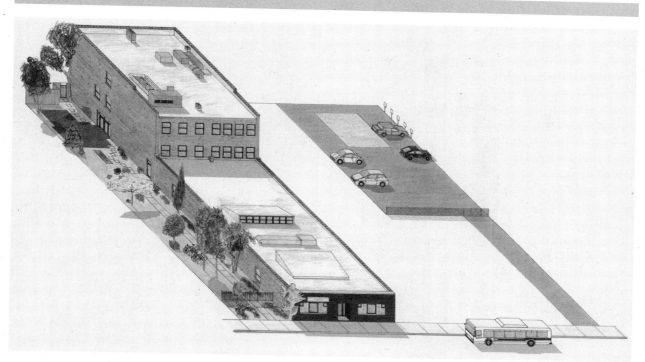

▲ Figure 2.14 Clerestories and skylights were added to increase daylight penetration and facilitate natural ventilation. The light-colored roof reduces absorption of the sun's heat and keeps interior air temperature lower. A roof-mounted photovoltaic system partially meets the building's energy needs. © 2008 Center for Neighborhood Technology

▶ Figure 2.15 Energy use is reduced by the careful monitoring of interior and exterior conditions for temperature, sunlight, carbon dioxide levels, humidity, and time of day. Large skylights and operable windows, adjustable lights, and nontoxic materials all contribute to indoor environmental quality. © 2008 Center for Neighborhood Technology

Figure 2.16 The sliver park adjacent to the building serves as an oasis for the neighborhood, but it also provides shading that reduces the heat load of the building. Stormwater percolates into the ground through pervious pavements in both the garden and the parking area. © 2008 Center for Neighborhood Technology

The original decision to relocate to Chicago's northeastern side was to enhance public transportation options for employees and visitors. The Center's website notes that people can easily come and go, do errands, or eat lunch by walking or using public transportation. The commitment to urban sustainability and environmental education has attracted hundreds of visitors, and tours are held almost daily to enlighten the community on ecological design.

Site and Water
A light-colored roof was installed to reduce the absorption of the sun's heat and reduce interior air temperature during warm months. An adjacent lot is planted as a sliver park using native, drought-tolerant vegetation to provide a cool oasis for the neighborhood and trees that shade the building to further lower air-conditioning requirements. Rainwater percolates through the garden and pervious parking lot to replenish aquifers. Low-flow fixtures inside the building have reduced potable water consumption by 30 percent.

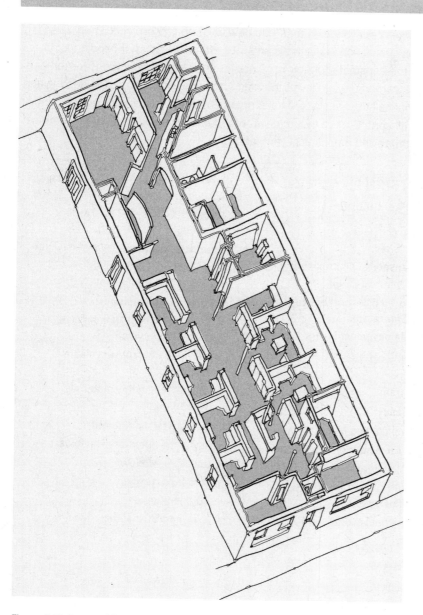

Figure 2.17 Low partitions take advantage of shared light and ventilation. Toxic functions, like printers and copiers, are ganged in a room with direct exhaust. © 2008 Center for Neighborhood Technology

Energy

The building uses 50 percent less energy per square foot than a new building constructed to standard codes through a combination of holistic strategies, including a below-grade thermal ice-storage system that efficiently cools the building using off-peak energy. This system utilizes a storage tank filled with 4-inch-diameter spheres made from a high-performance polyethylene. Filled with water, the spheres are either cooled to form ice or thawed by a glycol-based solution. During off-peak hours, typically at night, the glycol solution is pumped from a chiller that has lowered the liquid's temperature enough to turn the water in the spheres to ice and circulated through the spheres. Since the chiller runs at times when systemwide demand for energy is low, the Center avoids high electrical rates and does not add to systemwide demand spikes, which often lead utilities to build additional generating capacity solely to address those peaks. When the building is occupied during the day, the chiller can be shut off and the "ice balls" alone provide air conditioning and process cooling.

A roof-mounted photovoltaic system supplies the building with over 5 percent of its energy needs; 50 percent of the remainder is offset by purchase of renewable energy certificates that fund new wind-energy projects. Energy use is reduced by new insulation in the walls and roof, efficient equipment and, most important of all, the constant monitoring of interior and exterior conditions for temperature, sunlight, carbon dioxide levels, humidity, and time of day to adjust heating and cooling automatically. Large skylights and operable windows, adjustable lights, and indoor plants all contribute to indoor environmental quality and reduce dependence on artificial lighting and mechanical ventilation.

GREEN DESIGN ELEMENTS
Center for Neighborhood Technology

Sustainable Sites:
- Public transportation proximity
- Bicycle accommodation
- Light-colored highly reflective roof (Energy Star rated)
- Permeable pavement layers
- Xeriscaping
- Bioswales
- Shading trees

Water Efficiency:
- Low-flow plumbing fixtures

Energy and Atmosphere:
- Renewable Energy Green-e certificates
- Photovoltaic system
- Ice Ball Thermal energy storage system
- Natural ventilation
- Additional insulation
- High-efficiency T-8 fluorescent lighting
- Automatic occupancy and daylight sensors
- Energy Star appliances

Materials and Resources:
- 75 percent construction waste reused or recycled
- Recycled content/recyclable materials
- Rapidly renewable materials (wheatboard)

Indoor Environment Quality:
- Skylights/clerestory windows
- Operable windows
- Indoor garden
- CO_2 monitors
- Low-/no-VOC materials and finishes

PROJECT TEAM

Center for Neighborhood Technology
Farr Associates
EME Consulting Engineers
Phoenix Builders
J. T. Katrakis & Associates

Philadelphia Forensic Science Center
Philadelphia, PA

Current Owner: City of Philadelphia

Building Type: Laboratory

Original Building Construction: 1929

Restoration/Renovation Completion: 2003

Square Footage: 58,700 ft^2

Percent Renovated: 100%

Occupancy: 72 people (50 hrs/week) 110 visitors (2 hrs/week)

Recognition: AIA/COTE Top Ten Green Projects, 2006

"Philadelphia has a huge supply of empty older buildings. Sadly, most of them are knocked down—but this project really set an example for how those buildings can be reused."

—*Spencer Finch, director of Sustainable Development, Pennsylvania Environmental Council*[32]

PROJECT DESCRIPTION

Located in a physically deteriorating neighborhood of North Philadelphia targeted for revitalization, the adaptive reuse of the abandoned 1920s art deco building (Mary Channing Wister School) as a Forensic Science Center created a sustainable development model for future projects undertaken by the Philadelphia Capital Program. The project demonstrates restorative qualities—reintroducing a cultural asset, reinvigorating a troubled neighborhood, replenishing natural assets and hydrology—and economic logic. Construction cost was approximately 33 percent less than comparable projects, and the cumulative payback on all sustainability features was 2.2 years.

Site and Water

The 2.16-acre site was completely covered in asphalt, making storm runoff a significant problem, with storm surges forcing as many as 48 sewage outfalls into the nearby Delaware River. The site design reduced the hardscape and created linear vegetated swales

Figure 2.18 The picture suggests the grim character of the building before reclamation of the two-acre site removed asphalt and created vegetated swales and stone-reinforced water pathways that dramatically improved water catchment and reduced the heat island effect. © 2009 Croxton Collaborative Architects, PC

and stone-reinforced water pathways parallel to the parking rows to capture storm water, allowing evaporation, ground infiltration, and filtering the water before it enters storm drains. Water catchment has improved by roughly 33 percent.

Energy

The energy savings on the project are impressive, especially for a laboratory building that is particularly energy-intensive. The project was fully simulated using the latest versions of PowerDOE and Superlite 2.0 modeling program and was projected to achieve the following improvements over a comparable building designed in minimal compliance with ASHRAE 90.1—1989:

- 72 percent reduction in total annual source energy
- 69 percent reduction in 25-year carbon dioxide emissions
- 67 percent reduction in total annual utility bill
- 65 percent SO_2 + NOx 25-year emission reductions (acid rain + ozone-smog precursors)
- 61 percent reduction in annual peak electrical demand

Innovative mapping was done of areas requiring 100 percent outside air, and air-pressure vestibules were extended to create a "building within a building" (this achieved over 50 percent of the energy savings) to minimize HVAC loads. Angled ceilings facilitate deep daylighting, and high-performance glass reduces visible transmittance. After project completion, a 15kW photovoltaic array was added on the roof. High-efficiency fluorescent bulbs are used throughout the building and task and ambient lighting are separated. Occupancy sensors control both lighting and air systems.

Figure 2.19 Interior spaces before renovation show the desirable high ceilings and large windows common to many historic buildings. *© 2009 Croxton Collaborative Architects, PC*

Figure 2.20 An AIA COTE Top Ten winner in 2006; the Philadelphia Forensic Science Center revitalized both a building and a community. The design takes advantage of the large windows to reduce lighting loads as part of a strategy that allows a cumulative payback on all sustainability features in 2.2 years. *© 2009 Croxton Collaborative Architects, PC*

Green Materials

All glues and adhesives are low- to no-VOC (volatile organic compounds). The project uses no PVC piping; all piping is stainless steel, glass, cast iron, or copper. No CFCs or HCFCs are used in any of the equipment in the building, including the water fountains, refrigerators, and mechanical system equipment. Rapidly renewable products (linoleum, agriboard) or recycled products (cellulose, carpeting, tile, steel, gypsum board) were used wherever possible.

GREEN DESIGN ELEMENTS

Philadelphia Forensic Science Center

Sustainable Sites:
- Reduce paved areas
- Xeriscaping
- Bioswales

Water Efficiency:
- Waterless urinals

- Low-flow plumbing fixtures

Energy and Atmosphere:
- Photovoltaic panel system
- Heat recovery ventilation

Materials and Resources:
- Rapidly renewable materials
- Recycled materials

Indoor Environment Quality:
- Low-VOC materials and finishes

PROJECT TEAM

Croxton Collaborative Architects, PC

Cecil Baker & Associates

Ortega Consulting

Vinokur-Pace Engineering Services, Inc.

Andropogon Associates, Ltd.

Health Education + Research Associates, Inc.

Brewers Hill, Natty Boh Building

Baltimore, MD

Current Owner: Obrecht Commercial Development and Struever Bros., Eccles and Rouse

Building Type: Commercial Office/Storage/Daycare

Original Building Construction: 1892, 1890, 1950

Historic Designation: Individual listing National Register for Historic Places

Restoration/Renovation Completion: 2007

Square Footage: 186,500 ft^2

Percentage Renovated: 100 percent

Occupancy: 250 people (40 hrs/week)

"We are committed to urban redevelopment because, after all, that is the most logical route to green and sustainable living. Long commutes and an inability to use public transportation have a negative impact on our environment. So, we work to create a *green way of life* through a focus on renewing historic buildings and neighborhoods, and creating 24-hour, live/work communities."

—*Struever Bros. Eccles and Rouse Marketing Brochure www.sber.com*

PROJECT DESCRIPTION

The restoration of the Brewers Hill complex was the first project to combine the newly created Maryland Green Building tax credits with federal and state historic tax credits. An industrial site that had been abandoned for many years, the complex was particularly challenging to renovate because of large areas of windowless walls, but the team creatively manipulated the program to locate storage and systems in the areas lacking natural daylight. The building and its signature neon sign of Natty Boh—symbol of National Bohemian beer—are well known, representing a once-thriving beer industry that was closely linked with Baltimore's dominant German population. It was National Brewery that first introduced the six-pack in the 1940s.

Site and Water

One of the building's unique qualities is a rainwater-harvesting system that collects roof runoff and drains into salvaged brewery tanks. Located beneath the parking lot, the tanks provide ample storage. The water is filtered for spot irrigation needs and toilet flushing throughout the building. This recycling process greatly reduces both the amount of water used within the building and pressure on the city stormwater-management facilities. A large green roof also absorbs significant amounts of water before it reaches the storm system, allowing natural evaporation and reducing the site's overall heat island effect. (Refer to Chapter 4 for discussion of green roofs and heat island effect.) Highly reflective surfaces and a rainwater pool fill areas of the roof not covered by vegetation and dramatically reduce the amount of energy needed to cool the building.

Energy

During the day, most of the occupied areas of the building are flooded with natural light with the help of light shelves that bounce light further into the building from the large original window openings. Workstations have low partitions, and wherever possible, dividing walls are made with translucent materials. Sensors monitor and balance the amount of artificial light needed to supplement the daylight. The building envelope is thoroughly insulated and high-performance windows were installed.

Material Use Reduction

The design team intentionally pursued an "industrial chic" theme within the building, which allowed them to leave existing structural members exposed and reduced the need for new finish materials.

◀Figure 2.21 The visible signage of the former brewery continues to act as a landmark and beacon for the adaptive reuse. © 2006 Patrick Ross Photography

▼Figure 2.22 Multiple integrated strategies lie at the heart of all interior design. At Brewers Hill, these include light shelves to increase daylighting, light sensors, recycled materials, high-efficiency HVAC, low, translucent partitions, nontoxic materials, high-performance windows, an insulated building envelope, planted green roof and graywater irrigation and toilet flushing with rain and stormwater stored in salvaged brewing tanks. © George Holback, CBH+A

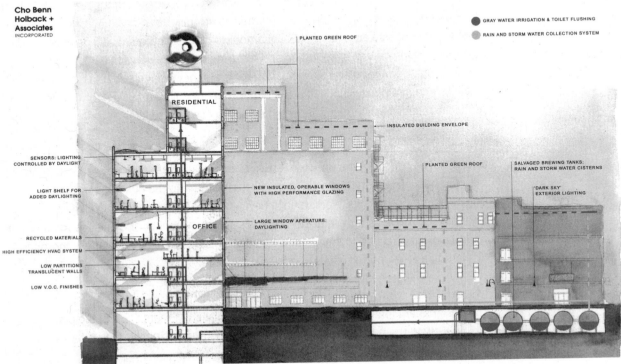

GREEN DESIGN ELEMENTS

Brewers Hill, Natty Boh Building

Sustainable Sites:
- Public transportation proximity
- Green roof

Water Efficiency:
- Graywater system (brewing tanks now provide storage for rainwater)

Energy and Atmosphere:
- High-efficiency HVAC and lighting
- Increased insulation in envelope
- New high-performance windows

- Occupancy and daylight sensors
- Building commissioning

Materials and Resources:
- 75 percent construction waste recycled
- Most materials harvested less than 500 miles from site
- Recycled content materials used

Indoor Environment Quality:
- Light shelves
- Low-VOC finishes

Additional Features:
- Green tenant standards

PROJECT TEAM

Obrecht Commercial Development

Struever Bros., Eccles and Rouse

Cho Benn Holback + Associates Inc.

Burdette Kohler and Murphy Engineers

Skarda Engineers

STV Engineers

Betty Bird & Associates

Denver Dry Building

Denver, CO

Current Owner: Denver Urban Renewal Authority and Affordable Housing Development Corporation

Building Type: Multiunit Residential/Retail/ Commercial Office

Original Building Construction: 1888

Historic Designation: Listed on the National Register of Historic Places, 1978

Project Completion: Phases completed between 1993 and 1997

Square Footage: 330,000 ft^2

Percentage Renovated: 100%

Recognition: AIA/COTE Top Ten Green Projects, 1999; American Institute of Architects, Colorado Design Award, 1997; Ahwahnee Community Livability Award, 1997; ULI Awards for Excellence Finalist, 1995 and 1996; National Trust for Historic Preservation, National Preservation Honor Award, 1995; Council of Urban Economic Development's Public/Private Partnership Award, 1994; Downtown Denver Partnership Rehabilitation of the Year Award, 1994; Colorado Historical Society Award for Rehabilitation, 1994; *Denver Business Journal,* Deal Maker of 1993 for Economic Development

"At the heart of every city is a downtown, a hub that determines the city's success or failure. Much of the momentum for our economic turnaround in Denver originated in our strategy for downtown. ... We created a downtown housing office to market our inventory of vacant buildings to housing developers and to provide developers and investors with accurate information on properties and market conditions. We also made sweeping changes in downtown zoning to encourage housing and transit-oriented development and to protect historic buildings."

—Wellington E. Webb, mayor of Denver 1991–2003, Brookings Review *article,* Brookings Institute, Summer 2000

PROJECT DESCRIPTION

Renovation of the 1888 Denver Dry building through a public–private partnership was the vanguard project that inspired similar revitalization efforts in Denver's historic downtown area (the city established the Downtown Denver Historic District in 2000), which in total have brought more than 2,000 residents back to the city in an area that is now fully supported by public transportation and bike paths. The project encompasses two city blocks and six floors of mixed-use space, including retail, offices, and housing, which were completed in phases over four years.

Creative Financing

Financing was complex and came from different sources, including federal historic and affordable-housing tax credits and a state bond issue. Over 20 lenders provided funding for Denver Dry. As a result of their aggressive fundraising efforts, the developers obtained loans for $40.7 million of the development—85 percent of total funding. Private sources provided $25.2 million, over half of the amount lent, and public agencies provided an additional $15.5 million in loans. Other sources of funding include tax credit equity of $4.7 million, cash equity of $2.3 million, and grants of $60,000 and equity.[33]

Exterior Envelope

The renovation maintained and restored the building's exterior integrity. Wooden-frame windows were dismantled and rebuilt with dual-layer insulated glass after more than 30 layers of toxic lead paint were removed from the wood. The original façade of the build-

Figure 2.23 The Denver Dry Building was one of the first projects in the revitalization of downtown Denver that began in the 1990s, fueled by sweeping changes in downtown zoning to encourage housing and transit-oriented development and to protect historic buildings. The Downtown Denver Historic District was established in 2000. © *Urban Design Group*

ing was restored, removing all exterior paint and revealing the original sandstone, limestone, and brick detailing.

Energy

The building benefits from its significant masonry mass, which boasts very slow thermal momentum that creates a flywheel effect, keeping the internal temperature stable. The thermal momentum of materials is different than insulative value and describes the ability of a material to remain at a given temperature over time.

Energy-efficient evaporative coolers for the residential units take advantage of Denver's relatively low humidity. The commercial areas are cooled by rehabilitated and new central chillers, controlled by a digital BMS system. The building also featured early applications of variable-speed motors and other energy-saving devices recommended by the Rocky Mountain Institute's Green Building Program.

Figure 2.24 The Denver Dry Building encompasses two city blocks and is fully supported by public transportation and bike paths. © *Urban Design Group*

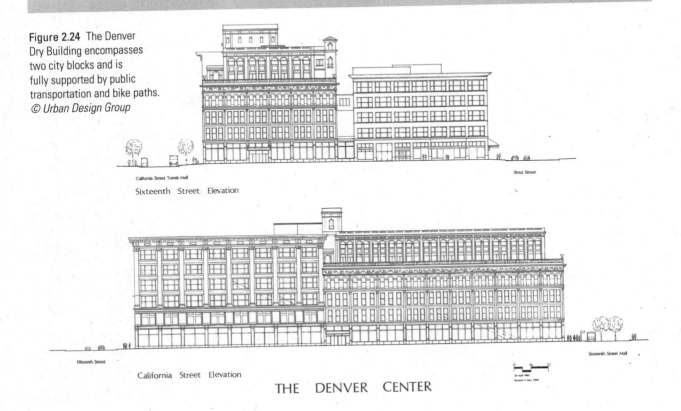

California Street Transit Mall

Stout Street

Sixteenth Street Elevation

Fifteenth Street

Sixteenth Street Mall

California Street Elevation

THE DENVER CENTER

GREEN DESIGN ELEMENTS

Denver Dry Building

Sustainable Sites:
- Public transportation proximity
- Highly reflective roof

Energy and Atmosphere:
- Low-emission insulated glass
- Evaporative cooling (residential)
- Flat-plate heat exchanger
- Variable-speed motor
- Waste heat from city central heating system (steam)
- Natural ventilation
- Direct digital control system

Materials and Resources:
- Original façade restored
- Recycled carpet tiles
- Demolition materials recycled

Indoor Environment Quality:
- Abundant daylight
- Operable windows
- Removal of toxic chemicals (lead paint)
- Low-VOC finishes

Additional Features:
- Green tenant policy

Figure 2.25 Six floors of mixed-use space include retail, offices, and housing, which were built out over four years. Over 20 lenders provided funding for 85 percent of the total project cost. © *Urban Design Group*

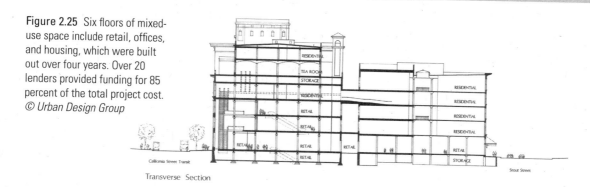

Transverse Section

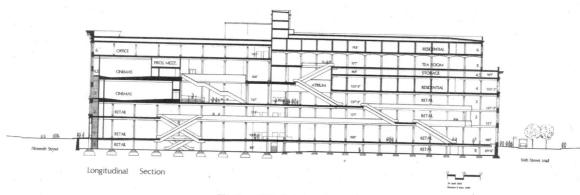

Longitudinal Section

THE DENVER CENTER

PROJECT TEAM

Denver Urban Renewal Authority
Affordable Housing Development Corporation
Urban Design Group
Perry Rose LLC
Jonathan Rose Companies LLC
B-Corp (condos)

ENDNOTES

1. United Nations World Commission on Environment and Development, *Our Common Future,* p. 43.

2. President's Council on Sustainable Development, *Towards a Sustainable America (Final Report).* (Washington, DC: U.S. Government Printing Office, 1999).

3. ICLEI, presentation by Kate McKeand, Executive Manager, ICLEI-A/NZ Sustainability Services, 2 May 2007. "Triple Bottom Line Tools for Embedding Sustainability in to Council Operations." Available at: www.iclei.org/anz/iss.

4. President's Council on Sustainable Development, *Sustainable America—A New Consensus* (Washington, DC: U.S. Government Printing Office, 1996), Chapter 1.

5. Ibid.

6. David Suzuki, *The Sacred Balance: Rediscovering Our Place in Nature.* Vancouver, BC: Greystone Books, 2007.

7. Richard Moe, "Introduction: Celebrating a Year of Preservation Anniversaries," *Forum Journal* (Fall 2006).

8. "An Interview with Weiming Lu," *CRM Journal* (Summer 2008), pp. <<PAGE NUMBER(S) FOR NOTE 8?>>

9. Angel David Nieves (2008"), "Revaluing Places: Hidden Histories from the Margins," *Places: Forum of Design for the Public Realm* 20 (1) (2008). www.places-journal.org.

10. English Heritage, *The Heritage Dividend Methodology: Measuring the Impact of Historic Projects* (2005).

11. Organization for Economic Co-Operation and Development, "Urban Policy Development Workshop: Towards Sustainable Use of Building Stock," January 15–16, 2004.

12. Mike Jackson, "Embodied Energy and Historic Preservation: A Needed Reassessment," *APT* 38 (4) (2005): 45–52.

13. Sean Cryan and Mark Simmons, "BuildCarbonNeutral.org; Measuring a Construction Project's Carbon Footprint," *Eco-structure* (November–December 2007), www.eco-structure.com.

14 Arthur C. Nelson, *Toward a New Metropolis: The Opportunity to Rebuild America,* The Brookings Institution Metropolitan Policy Program (2004).

15. Diane Ross, "Life Cycle Assessment in Heritage Buildings," Work Term Report, Victoria, British Columbia, 2007.

16. Randall Mason, *Economics and Historic Preservation: A Guide and Review of the Literature* (Washington, DC: The Brookings Institution, September 2005).

17. Heritage Canada Foundation, *Exploring the Connection between Built and Natural Heritage* (2006). www.heritage-canada.org.

18. Donovan D. Rypkema, "Downtown Revitalization, Sustainability, and Historic Preservation, National Main Streets Conference Closing Plenary Session, Seattle, Washington, March 28, 2007,

19. Garth Rockcastle, *Places, A Forum of Environmental Design* (Spring, 2008).

20. Robert E. Stipe (2003). *A Richer Heritage: Historic Preservation in the Twenty-First Century* (Chapel Hill and London: The University of North Carolina Press, 2003), p. 1.

21. "An Act to Set Apart a Certain Tract of Land Lying Near the Headwaters of the Yellowstone River as a Public Park." 17 Stat. 32 (March 1, 1872).

22. See www.nationaltrust.org.uk/main/w-trust/w-thecharity/w-thecharity_our-past.htm.

23. Historic Sites Act of 1935, 16 U.S. C. (Aug. 21, 1935, ch. 593, sec. 1,49 Stat. 666.).

24. Title 1, Section 1(b)(4) of the National Preservation Act of 1966, as amended.

25. The National Environmental Policy Act of 1969, as amended, Title 1, Sec. 101 (b)(4).

26. The National Environmental Policy Act of 1969, as amended. Title 1, Sec.101(a), The National Preservation Act of 1966, as amended. Section 2 (1).

27. Jerry D. Spangler, "Cultural Resources and Energy Development: What Would Saint Theodore Do?" *Forum Journal* (Summer 2008).

28. "Greening Federal Facilities," Department of Energy, Federal Energy Management Program, May 2001. Available at: www.nrel.gov/docs/fy01osti/29267.pdf.

29. U.S. General Services Administration, *Sustainability Matters* (Washington, DC: Public Buildings Service, Office of Applied Science, 2008), p. 11.

30. Building Design and Construction, *White Paper on Sustainability* (Oak Brook, IL: Reed Business Information, November 2003), www.bdcmag.com.

31. Frank Matero, *Managing Change: Sustainable Approaches to the Conservation of the Built Environment* (Los Angeles: The Getty Conservation Institute, 2001), Preface.

32. As quoted by Krista Walton in "Philadelphia Police Forensic Science Center," *Preservation* (Jan./Feb. 2008).

33. Source for financing information: Horizon Solution Site, www.solutions-site.org/artman/publish/article_113.shtml, accessed January 2009.

chapter 3

TOOLS, GUIDELINES, AND PROCESS—BALANCING THE GOALS

3.1 BALANCING OBJECTIVE AND SUBJECTIVE GOALS— INTEGRATED DESIGN

Law No. 229—If a builder build a house for someone, and does not construct it properly, and the house which he built fall in and kill its owner, then that builder shall be put to death.

—*Hammurabi's Code of Laws, ca. 1760 B.C.*

BUILDING CODES, whether Hammurabi's Code of Laws or the International Building Code, are intended to create buildings and communities that provide an acceptable level of health, safety, and general welfare regardless of ownership.

The cost of meeting the building code or the appropriateness of a public enforcement of mandates applied to private property is not usually questioned. We accept that we need rules that physically protect us (often against ourselves) in terms of fire and life safety, structural requirements, and building system design and installation. We also accept, but not without frustration, that rules—whether building codes, zoning restrictions, or design and preservation guidelines—can be subject to interpretation.

"All these [buildings] must be built with due reference to durability, convenience, and beauty. Durability will be assured when foundations are carried down to the solid ground and materials wisely and liberally selected; convenience, when the arrangement of the apartments is faultless and presents no hindrance to use, and when each class of building is assigned to its suitable and appropriate exposure; and beauty, when the appearance of the work is pleasing and in good taste, and when its members are in due proportion according to correct principles of symmetry."

—*Vitruvius Pollio, ca. 25 B.C.[1]*

Changes in building codes often arise in response to major tragedies such as the citywide fires in Chicago (1871) and Boston (1872). These events also spawn new technologies as solutions—for instance, the development of automatic sprinkler systems, first patented in 1874 and now routinely required as a proven means of saving lives.

Codes and technologies resulting from a major catastrophe are similar to what is currently happening in the building industry as the larger society grapples with issues ranging from sick building syndrome to a sick environment. New requirements for communities and buildings are developing at the same time that new technologies and products are appearing in the marketplace.

"An integrated approach is needed to address GHG emissions from the U.S. building sector—one that coordinates across technical and policy solutions, integrates engineering approaches with the architectural design, considers design decisions within the realities of building operation, integrates green building with smart growth concepts, and takes into account the numerous decision makers within the fragmented building industry."

Pew Center for Global Climate Change[2]

Requirements imposed on building design are both objective and subjective, both prescriptive and performance-based, and they become all the more complex when balancing modern expectations with the stewardship of heritage sites and buildings. The tension among multiple goals is often portrayed as conflict, but it is a natural part of the design process and managing change. The practice of historic preservation is just that—the thoughtful management of change through design.

The most successful design often springs from convening numerous sources of expertise for a fully integrated approach that balances many points of view, requirements, and goals. This is not unusual in the world of historic preservation, where teams can include historians, finance experts, conservators, architects, engineers, and craftspeople, and where the interface with public agencies such as the National Park Service and historical commissions and community interest groups is part of the design process.

More widespread and formalized team integration is now being triggered by the complex requirements for sustainable design and changing delivery technologies such as *building information modeling* (BIM), which offers the potential for creating three-dimensional drawings that provide coordinated product and material information that expedites construction. The American Institute of Architects (AIA) champions *integrated project delivery*, or IPD, as a new contract mechanism that can create a collaborative team to counter the prevailing waste and inefficiency of the traditional linear design and construction process. Described as transformative, IPD is intended to create a process of mutual respect and trust rather than blame. It builds on the assumption that new expectations for building performance, project costs, and user satisfaction can be met with innovation and decisions resulting from the early involvement and consensus

Figure 3.1 Repurposed to meet the needs of the Western Pennsylvania Conservancy, the Barn at Fallingwater (see Chapter 7) focused on preserving features that convey the historical, cultural, and architectural heritage of the Barn. The project utilized the LEED metric system of the U.S. Green Building Council and was recognized as an AIA Committee of the Environment Top Ten Project in 2005. *Nic Lehoux photo courtesy Bohlin Cywinski Jackson*

of all key participants. IPD is idealistic, but so is design. Many design professionals would agree that, regardless of size, successful projects have always sprung from strong collaborative teams that remain involved with the project through completion and implementation. Formalizing an integrated process represents a contractual acknowledgment of shared responsibility that benefits all parties with a better final product and addresses the multiple goals and requirements inherent in every design project.

IPD OVERVIEW

Integrated project delivery [IPD] uses business structures, practices, and processes to collaboratively use the talents and insights of all participants in the design, construction, and fabrication process. Beginning when the project is first conceptualized, the integrated process continues throughout the full life cycle of the facilities.

Integrated project delivery encourages early contribution of knowledge and experience and requires proactive involvement of key participants. Responsibility is placed on the most able person, with decisions being made on a "best for project" basis.

—*AIA California Council*[3]

3.2 GREEN TOOLS AND METRICS— URBAN AND CAMPUS

More and more states and cities are developing Climate Change Action Plans that outline how they intend to fight global warming—usually through efforts such as expanding recycling programs and encouraging the use of mass-transit. Many of these plans make little or no provisions for green retrofits. Even fewer establish retention and reuse of existing buildings as a priority. This is a serious misstep, and we need to correct it.

—Richard Moe
President Emeritus, National Trust for Historic Preservation[4]

The community in which a building exists dictates much that can and must happen during a renovation and/or addition. Buildings are shaped by local codes, zoning, transportation options, energy, and historic preservation policy, to name just a few factors. Many organizations and tools exist to help cities and neighborhoods implement both sustainable development and sustainable design. Given the importance of using existing resources, including buildings, it is discouraging that most climate action plans and green measurement systems seem to focus on new construction and new development, with the notable exceptions of The Natural Step and ICLEI—Local Governments for Sustainability.

The Natural Step

Founded in Sweden in 1989, the Natural Step has developed a process that can help communities and businesses better understand and integrate environmental, social, and economic considerations as they work to create a sustainable society. With affiliated nonprofit groups in 11 countries, the organization promotes "The Natural Step (TNS) Framework," which it de-scribes as a "comprehensive model for planning in complex systems." The TNS Framework provides a basis for strategic decision making, and according to the organization, it creates a clear definition of sustainability while reducing financial risk and supporting design and innovation.[5]

Swedish towns described as ecocommunities have used the TNS Framework to approach sustainability holistically, rather than on a project-by-project basis. In the United States, cities utilizing the TNS Framework include Pittsburgh, Pennsylvania, Santa Monica, California, and Madison, Wisconsin.

Sarah James and Torbjorn Lahti, in their book *The Natural Step for Communities: How Cities and Towns Can Change to Sustainable Practices*,[7] describe the four guiding objectives of The Natural Step and how these might be implemented in a community.

BENEFITS OF THE NATURAL STEP FRAMEWORK

Some of the benefits Madison [Wisconsin] might expect from using the TNS Framework to implement its sustainable city goals include:

- Alignment of municipal departments and staff toward a common vision of sustainability
- Clarity in assessing and organizing actions and programs for sustainable municipal operations
- Enhanced policies and programs incorporating a sustainability perspective (e.g., procurement policies, environmental management systems)
- Enhanced reputation as a proactive contributor to a more sustainable community

Toward a Sustainable Community; A Toolkit for Local Government[6]

Figure 3.2 The 1911 Balfour-Guthrie Building in Portland, Oregon, was listed on the National Register of Historic Places in 2003 in order to take advantage of Oregon Historic Tax Credits in its renovation. State business energy tax credits and a small business loan were also part of funding, and the City of Portland offered financial incentives for achieving a U.S. Green Building Council LEED rating. Portland has had a carbon dioxide reduction strategy since 1993. It signed the U.S. Mayors Climate Protection Agreement in 2005. © *Thomas Hacker Architects*

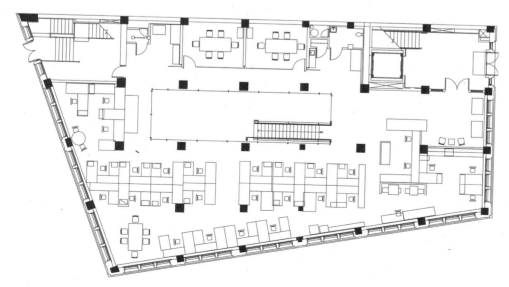

Figure 3.3 Home to Thomas Hacker Architects, the open floor plan of the Balfour-Guthrie Building in Portland, Oregon, was maintained during renovations. Low-e interior storm windows were added, and the new open stairwell allows daylight to penetrate to the basement. Thanks to a downtown location, 75 percent of the building's employees get to work without using cars. © *Thomas Hacker Architects*

The Natural Step Guiding Objective No. 1

Eliminate our community's contribution to fossil fuel dependence and to wasteful use of scarce metals and minerals.

Types of Community Practices

Transit and pedestrian-oriented development; development heated and powered by renewable energy; alternatively fueled municipal fleets; incentives for organic agriculture that minimizes phosphates and petrochemical fertilizers and herbicides.

The Natural Step Guiding Objective No. 2

Eliminate our community's contribution to dependence on persistent chemical and wasteful use of synthetic substances.

Types of Community Practices

Healthy building design and construction that reduces or eliminates use of toxic building materials; landscape design and park maintenance that uses alternatives to chemical pesticides and herbicides; municipal purchasing guidelines that encourage low- or nonchemical product use.

The Natural Step Guiding Objective No. 3

Eliminate our community's contribution to encroachment on nature (i.e., land, water, wildlife, forest, and ecosystems).

Types of Community Practices

Redevelopment of existing sites and buildings before building new ones; open space, forest, and habitat preservation; reduced water use and recycling of wash water.

The Natural Step Guiding Objective No. 4

Meet human needs fairly and efficiently.

Types of Community Practices

Affordable housing for a diversity of residents; locally based business and food production; use of waste as a resource; ecoindustrial development; participatory community planning, and decision making.[8]

ICLEI—Local Governments for Sustainability

The ICLEI was founded in 1990 as the International Council for Local Environmental Initiatives when more than 200 local governments from 43 countries convened at United National headquarters for the inaugural World Congress of Local Governments for a Sustainable Future. Now known as ICLEI—Local Governments for Sustainability, the international association counts as members more than 1,000 cities, towns, counties, and their associations that have made a commitment to sustainable development.

The ICLEI U.S. website, www.idleiusa.org, states that ICLEI specializes in developing and distributing tools that "that will empower local governments to achieve their climate and sustainability goals."[9] The range of tools listed is broad and, among other things, includes skills trainings, calculators for comparing the impact of residential developments of varying densities, and multiple types of assistance for improving greenhouse gas emissions.

Playbook for Green Buildings + Neighborhoods

Launched by a consortium of more than 20 local governments, nonprofit organizations, government agencies, and utilities, Playbook (www.greenplaybook.org)

Dubuque, Iowa, Vision Statement

Dubuque is a viable, livable, and equitable community. We embrace economic prosperity, social/cultural vibrancy, and environmental integrity to create a sustainable legacy for generations to come.

DUBUQUE'S 11 SUSTAINABLE PRINCIPLES

Economic Prosperity

Regional Economy: Sustainable Dubuque is a community that values a diversified regional economy with opportunities for new and green markets, jobs, products, and services.

Smart Energy Use: Sustainable Dubuque is a community that values energy conservation and expanded use of renewable energy as a means to save money and protect the environment.

Resource Management: Sustainable Dubuque is a community that values the benefits of reducing, reusing, and recycling resources.

Community Design: Sustainable Dubuque is a community that values the built environment of the past, present, and future, which contributes to its identity, heritage, and sense of place.

Social/Cultural Vibrancy

Green Buildings: Sustainable Dubuque is a community that values a productive and healthy built environment.

Healthy Local Food: Sustainable Dubuque is a community that values the benefits of wholesome food from local producers, distributors, farms, gardens, and hunters.

Community Knowledge: Sustainable Dubuque is a community that values education, empowerment, and engagement to achieve economic prosperity, environmental integrity, and social/cultural vibrancy.

Reasonable Mobility: Sustainable Dubuque is a community that values safe, reasonable, and equitable choices to access live, work, and play opportunities.

Environmental Integrity

Healthy Air: Sustainable Dubuque is a community that values fresh air, reduced greenhouse gas emissions, and minimized health risks.

Clean Water: Sustainable Dubuque is a community that values water as a source of life and seeks to preserve and manage it in all forms.

Native Plants and Animals: Sustainable Dubuque is a community that values biodiversity through the preservation, restoration, and connection of nature and people.

www.sustainabledubuque.org, Strategic partners with the National Trust for Historic Preservation, ICLEI, Carbon Disclosure Project and the AIA Communities by Design

is an online resource that helps promote the goals set out in the U.S. Conference of Mayors Climate Protection Agreement. Playbook offers strategies, tips, tools, and leading actions. It also demonstrates how green development promotes economic development, leads to healthier communities, strengthens energy independence, and supports climate protection.

EPA's Green Communities

The U.S. Environmental Protection Agency provides a toolkit for Green Communities, built around a five-step planning process. In each step, the toolkit provides strategic guidance and links to resources, case studies, model codes, and tools.

Step One—Community assessment, or Where are we now?

Step Two—Trends analysis, or Where are we going?

Step Three—Vision statement, or Where do we want to be?

Step Four—Sustainable action plans, or How do we get there?

Step Five—Implementation, or Let's go!

LEED—Neighborhood Development (ND)

The U.S. Green Building Council (USGBC) has created a family of green rating systems using the acronym LEED®, for Leadership in Energy and Environmental Design. Originally focused only on buildings, the USGBC released a pilot program for neighborhood design in 2007 that was developed in collaboration with the Congress for the New Urbanism and the Natural Resources Defense Council. The intent is to integrate green building principles with larger concerns such as smart growth, but like the other LEED systems, LEED-ND seems targeted toward new construction and not the effective reuse of existing buildings or the sustainable development of existing communities.

"With the current LEED metrics giving little credit for the inherent 'greenness' of historic structures and no penalties for the environmental impact of discarding the old structures, one might expect some county commissioners to prefer to sell or demolish rather than refurbish existing structures."

—James T. Kienle[10]

STARS

STARS (Sustainability Tracking, Assessment and Rating System) is currently being developed as a voluntary, self-reporting framework for recognizing and gauging progress toward sustainability in all sectors of higher education, from education and research to operations and administration. Developed by the Association for the Advancement of Sustainability in Higher Education with public feedback openly solicited, the intent of STARS is to provide a framework for schools to measure progress in sustainability goals and to learn from the efforts of their peer institutions.

3.3 GREEN TOOLS AND METRICS— BUILDING AND SITE

"A complete assessment system should address the whole life-cycle sustainability issue, including design, construction, operation and maintenance."

—Building Grading Systems: A Review of the State-of-the-Art[11]

Rating systems for green projects can function as tools that assist in thoughtful creative design and in changing systems and operations. They can encourage intellectual discussion among the project team members about goals and help educate those not familiar with basic concepts about resource conservation, environmental impacts, and health issues. Rating systems sometimes provide an organizing framework, discipline, and a common language for reviewing a design, but because rating systems cannot intuit the creative opportunities available in every project, an integrated process remains essential. Nor do rating regimes always acknowledge or reward bioclimatic design and passive design strategies that improve buildings without relying on systems.

Figure 3.4 Relocation of a colony of brown bats to a new bat house was necessary to allow renovation of The Barn at Falling Water (see Chapter 7) for use as a visitor center for the Western Pennsylvania Conservancy. Metric systems designed to provide incentives and guidelines for environmentally appropriate design cannot always recognize the unique challenges of every project. *Nic Lehoux photo courtesy Bohlin Cywinski Jackson*

LEED may be the fastest-growing and most recognized of rating systems in the United States, but it is by no means the only system available, nor is it the oldest. Other systems encountered in North America are BREEAM, Green Globes, SBTool, and the Living Building Challenge. Energy Star, created by the U.S. Department of Energy, recognizes both products and buildings for energy efficiency.

Writing about the status of green rating systems in 2008, University of Sydney professors M.Y.L. Chew and Sutapa Das classified systems by generation: first-generation systems are pass-fail systems, such as Energy Star; second-generation systems are simply additive, like LEED; and third-generation systems are weighed-additive systems that include BREEAM, SBTool, and Green Globes. They describe the third generation as extending the scope beyond "what the building does" to address more fully such factors as embedded energy, life-cycle evaluation, and operation and maintenance.[12]

LEED®

The most commonly used system to promote "green" design in the United States is the LEED® Green Building Rating Systems. Established in 1998 by the U.S. Green Building Council, LEED (Leadership in Energy and Environmental Design) is a family of rating systems in which the owner accumulates points by implementing building standards that are deemed environmentally beneficial. Depending on type of project, the system used might be NC (New Construction and Major Renovations), EB (Existing Buildings: Operations and Maintenance), CI (Commercial Interiors), Core and Shell, Schools, Retail, Healthcare, or Homes. For further descriptions of LEED-EB and LEED-Homes, refer to Chapters 7 and 8, respectively.

"In 2004, in response to concerns about the
first costs of green buildings, GSA [General
Services Administration] examined the costs
of LEED certification for its most recent
construction projects and found that LEED
ratings could indeed be achieved within a
standard GSA budget. In fact, the potential costs
for either certified or silver LEED certification
were below the 5 percent estimate variance
normally associated with early conceptual cost
estimates. As a result of a 2006 evaluation by
GSA of sustainable building rating systems, the
Administration concluded that LEED remains the
most credible rating system available to meet
GSA's needs. The GSA is required to re-evaluate
the rating systems every five years."

—U.S. General Services Administration,
Sustainability Matters[13]

The LEED rating systems for buildings comprise
five categories: Sustainable Sites, Water Efficiency,
Energy and Atmosphere, Materials and Resources,
and Indoor Environmental Quality. A sixth category
offers additional credits that reward design innovation. The total number of points acquired through
these categories leads to an overall rating by which
a building is designated as certified, silver-, gold-, or
platinum-rated. More important, the components
within each category establish common standards for
environmentally responsible design.

Each LEED category concentrates on different factors necessary to achieve environmentally responsible
design.

- **Sustainable Sites** offers points for urban redevelopment and access to alternative transportation, as
  well as for on-site infiltration of stormwater.
- **Water Efficiency** supports water-efficient landscaping.

- **Energy and Atmosphere** rewards minimized depletion of the ozone layer, use of green power, and
  continued performance of systems.
- **Materials and Resources** recognizes both building and material reuse.
- **Indoor Environmental Quality** monitors for carbon dioxide and encourages daylight and views.

USGBC membership is available not to individuals but to organizations or agencies, ranging from
engineers and scientists to the American Society of
Interior Designers. Government members include
not only the Department of Energy but also some
of the largest landlords of historic buildings in the
country, including the U.S. General Services Administration, the U.S. Navy, Army and Air Force, the Forest Service, and the National Park Service. With the
support of such significant and well-known building
owners, the LEED Green Building Rating System has
rapidly become a common acronym within the building industry and is specifically cited or required in
climate action plans, both public and private.

The LEED systems continue to evolve through
committee action and member comments. Current
proposed changes address life-cycle analysis and regional considerations. Despite its continuing evolu-
tion, the LEED program's mission remains the same:
to promote buildings and communities that are "environmentally responsible, profitable and healthy
places to live and work."[14] Although the LEED point
standards and their effectiveness are vigorously debat-
ed, both within the organization and by vocal outside
critics, there is no question that the USGBC has succeeded in substantially raising awareness of environmentally focused design through the LEED systems.

BREEAM

BREEAM is the UK Building Research Establishment
(BRE) Environmental Assessment Method, created in

1990. Buildings outside the United Kingdom can be assessed using BREEAM International, which is tailored to suit local circumstances. A BREEAM International assessment relies on the BRE's setting up a list of criteria specifically for the project, or for series of projects with similar characteristics. It is carried out by an accredited assessor, who then submits a report to the BRE for Quality Assurance, resulting in a rating such as Pass, Good, Very Good, Excellent, or Outstanding and a BREEAM certificate. BREEAM has certified more than 110,000 buildings, most of them residential projects. In 2005 the historic Van de Kamp Bakery Building in Los Angeles became the first building in the United States to achieve a BREEAM rating.

Green Globes™

Green Globes™ is a Web-based tool that was developed and first released in Canada in 2002. It was released in the United States in 2005 and competes directly with the LEED systems. Licensed for use in the United States by the Green Building Initiative and in Canada by Building Owners Management Association (BOMA), Green Globes consists of a series of online questionnaires, customized by project phase and role. Unlike LEED, Green Globes does not hold projects accountable for nonapplicable strategies, so available points vary by project. Because of its ease of use and relatively low cost compared to LEED, Green Globes is considered by some a more viable tool, particularly during design. Green Globes incorporates life-cycle assessment, which is still being developed in LEED.

The software developer for the online tool, Green Globes is ECD, Energy and Environment Canada. ECD was acquired by Jones Lang LaSalle, a giant global real estate services firm, in 2008 but will continue to provide technical support for Green Globes. Green

Figure 3.5 Renovations by the firm of Tanner, Leddy Maytum at the Presidio in San Francisco, a National Historic Landmark, used the Green Building Challenge (SBTool) assessment method and met the requirements for a 20 percent historic tax credit by following *The Secretary of the Interior's Standards for Rehabilitation.* The building houses the Thoreau Center for Sustainable Design. *Richard Barnes photo, courtesy Leddy Maytum Stacy Architects.*

Globes, in turn, may achieve more visibility if Jones Lang LaSalle applies it in its building management.

SBTool

SBTool, formerly known as GBTool, is the software implementation of the Green Building Challenge (GBC) assessment method that has been under development since 1996 by a group of more than a dozen teams. Natural Resources Canada launched the GBC but handed over responsibility to the International Initiative for a Sustainable Built Environment (iiSBE) in 2002. SBTool is a generic framework for rating the sustainable performance of buildings and projects. The system addresses a wide range of sustainable building issues, not just green building concerns, but its scope can be modified to be as narrow or as broad as desired. SBTool takes into account region- and site-specific context factors, which it links to carbon weights. The system can provide approximations of annualized embodied energy for structural and building envelope components.

A third-party team establishes the qualitative and quantitative measures used to evaluate sustainable design achievements and expected building performance. The numerous updates that have occurred since inception reflect experiences gained through use. Because of its flexibility, applying SBTool tends to require greater technical expertise than other rating systems, a fact that has limited its exposure in the U.S. market.

The Living Building Challenge

The Living Building Challenge first appeared in 2006, launched by the Cascadia Region Green Building Council, a chapter of both the U.S. Green Building Council and the Canada Green Building Council. The challenge is described as a building "informed by its eco-region's characteristics, and that generates all of its own energy with renewable resources, captures and treats all of its water, and uses resources efficiently and for maximum beauty." [15]

Energy Star

The Environmental Protection Agency introduced Energy Star in 1992 as a labeling program intended to promote energy-efficient products that would, in turn, reduce greenhouse gas emissions. By 1996, the EPA had joined with the Department of Energy (DOE) to set guidelines for energy-efficient appliances, home electronics, HVAC equipment, and other residential and commercial products. The Energy Star label identifies these products as environmentally sound. Recently, the guidelines set by the EPA and the DOE have grown to include new homes and buildings. Just as important as the labeling system that it uses to identify energy-efficient products is the technical information Energy Star offers to consumers and builders on how to cut energy use and costs. In partnership with the EPA, Energy Star provides an energy management strategy to measure and set new goals for energy performance. Energy Star also offers loans, rebates, and special financing to homebuyers.

Buildings and plants that rate in the top 25 percent of facilities in the nation for energy performance may qualify for the Energy Star. Many types of commercial and industrial buildings can be rated based on a comparison of energy use with other, similar types of buildings. Currently, Energy Star–rated buildings include offices, bank branches, financial centers, retailers, courthouses, hospitals, hotels, K–12 schools, medical offices, supermarkets, dormitories, and warehouses. Architecture firms can also display the "Designed to Earn the Energy Star" graphic to distinguish their projects as among the nation's best in energy performance.

Athena® EcoCalculator for Buildings and the Athena® Impact Estimator for Buildings

The Athena Sustainable Materials Institute and its collaborator in software development, Morrison Hirshfield, have released two tools for design and renovation that utilize life-cycle assessment, the Athena Impact Estimator for buildings and the Athena EcoCalculator for assemblies. The Impact Estimator allows users to evaluate whole buildings and assemblies based on internationally recognized LCA methodology and assists in design decisions by providing comparative information about building systems selections by region and, in the case of new construction, the shape and placement of a building. The EcoCalculator provides instant LCA results for more than 400 common building assembles and was developed in association with the University of Minnesota and commissioned by the Green Building Initiative™ for use with the Green Globes™ rating system. The tools are accessed through the Athena Web site, www.athenasmi.org.

3.4 HISTORIC PROPERTY DESIGNATION AND TREATMENT GUIDELINES

"Basically, it is a saving of people and lives and cities—not just buildings—that is important to all of us. We have before us an unparalleled opportunity, if we are determined, to contribute significantly to upgrading the quality of human existence. If we can achieve this, to some extent at least, the architecture and the history will fall into place."

Robert E. Stipe[16]

Historic Property Designation

Recognizing the cultural importance of a building and/or site and determining guidelines for stewardship are usually separate actions. In the United States, the National Historic Preservation Act of 1966 authorized the National Register of Historic Places, the official inventory of the "irreplaceable heritage" of the country, dedicated to the enrichment of future generations. Maintained by the National Park Service, the National Register lists over 80,000 properties representing more than 1.4 million individual resources. It includes districts, sites, buildings, structures, and objects that possess integrity of location, design, setting, materials, workmanship, feeling, and association. Additional identification and registration of historic properties and neighborhoods occurs on the state and local levels, swelling to many millions the list of designated properties and those eligible for designation. Designation indicates some level of documentation and review has occurred. It reflects an important distinction, because the adjective *historic* is often attached to a building description, with the implication that it is a designated historic property. All old buildings do not meet the criteria applied to achieve historic designation on a local, state, or national level.

A designated historic property is often recognized in multiple ways. For instance, The Gibson House in Boston is historically designated in five ways:

1. within the City of Boston's Back Bay Architectural District created in 1966;
2. as part of the Back Bay National Register District created in 1973, which has slightly different boundaries than the local district;
3. as a City of Boston Registered Landmark (1992);

4. on the *Commonwealth of Massachusetts Register of Historic Places;* and

5. as an individual listing on the National Register of Historic Places as a National Historic Landmark (2001), which means it is one of only a few thousand properties of outstanding national significance.

Figure 3.6 The new entrance canopy at the Thoreau Center for Sustainable Design (see Chapter 3) incorporates photovoltaic cells as a demonstration of alternative energy options. This did not prevent the building—part of a National Historic Landmark—from qualifying for the highest possible historic tax credit, which requires the project to follow *The Secretary of the Interior's Standards for Rehabilitation. Richard Barnes photo, courtesy Leddy Maytum Stacy Architects.*

A building and site can also be judged *eligible* for designation on a local, state, or federal level; in terms of review, this has the same impact as actual designation.

What designation as a historic property means and what jurisdictional review can occur as a consequence is widely misunderstood. In the essential textbook, *Historic Preservation: An Introduction to Its History, Principles, and Practice,* architect and planner Norman Tyler identifies what listing on the National Register does and does not mean.

Having properties listed on the national register does:

- Encourage the preservation of historic properties by documenting their significance and by lending support to local preservation activities.
- Protect the property by providing for review of federally funded, licensed, or sponsored projects that may affect the property, such as urban renewal projects, highways, or new buildings.
- Make owners of historic properties eligible to apply for federal grants-in-aid for preservation activities.
- Encourage the rehabilitation of income-producing historic properties that meet preservation standards through tax incentives; discourage the demolition of income-producing properties through federal income tax disincentives.

Listing of the National Register does not:

- Restrict the rights of private property owners in their use, development, or sale of privately owned historic property.
- Lead automatically to local historic district or landmark designation.
- Stop federal, state, local, or private projects.
- Provide for review of state, local, or privately funded projects that may affect historic properties (al-

though some states have tied such designation to environmental reviews).

■ Guarantee the grant funds will be available for all significant historic properties.

■ Provide tax benefits to all owners of residential historic properties, unless those properties are rented and treated as income producing by the Internal Revenue Service.[17]

Historic designation, whether national, state, or local, does not automatically mean that alterations to the property will require review, nor are properties in different communities reviewed with matching criteria. The basis for any review depends on the authority of a designated local group, such as a historical commission and/or a planning board. The extent of local review and jurisdiction varies from community to community. Federal review, through the auspices of the state, is often triggered by some type of federal funding or tax credit.

The states, through the auspices of the State Historic Preservation Office (SHPO, referred to as "ShipO") are the principal agents for identifying, enhancing, and protecting historic resources.[18] It is the SHPOs that are charged with recognizing historic places through surveys, distributing grants, and protecting properties affected by federal funding, including federal tax credits.

Treatment Guidelines for Historic Properties

In 1976 the National Park Service issued *The Secretary of the Interior's Standards for Rehabilitation and Guidelines for Rehabilitating Historic Buildings*, primarily to address the billions of dollars of renovations and adaptive reuse triggered by federal tax incentives for rehabilitation of income-producing historic properties. Revised several times, the standards were codified in 1995 under the title, *The Secretary of the Interior's Standards for the Treatment of Historic Properties with Guidelines for Preserving, Rehabilitating, Restoring and Reconstructing Historic Buildings*. According to the National Park Service, *The Standards and Guidelines* are intended to promote responsible preservation practices, but they are neither technical nor prescriptive. In and of themselves they cannot be used to make essential decisions about which features of the historic building should be saved and which can be changed. The standards provide "philosophical consistency" once one of the four treatments is selected for application on a building.[19]

"For more than 30 years, the federal Historic Tax Credit (HTC) Program has helped revitalize communities by encouraging the flow of private funds to facilitate the rehabilitation of historic buildings. Under the program, owners of historic properties partially finance the costs of rehabilitation and restoration of certified historic properties by selling the credits to third parties, which may include national banks.

"Since the Tax Reform Act was enacted in 1976, the HTC program has leveraged more than $45 billion in private funds to create nearly 382,000 rehabilitated housing units, of which 24 percent are low- and moderate-income (LMI) housing units.

"For more than 30 years, the federal HTC program has been used to attract new private capital to the historic cores of cities and Main Streets across the nation. These funds have enhanced property values, created jobs, generated local, state, and federal tax revenues, and revitalized communities."

—*Historic Tax Credits: Bringing New Life to Older Communities*[20]

The treatments, in hierarchical order, are:

1. *Preservation,* which places a high premium on the retention of all historic fabric through conservation, maintenance and repair. It reflects a building's continuum over time, through successive occupancies, and the respectful changes and alterations that are made.

2. *Rehabilitation,* which emphasizes the retention and repair of historic materials but provides more latitude than preservation because it is assumed that the property is more deteriorated prior to work.

3. *Restoration,* which focuses on the retention of materials from the most significant time in a property's history, while permitting the removal of materials from other periods.

4. *Reconstruction,* which establishes limited opportunities to re-create a nonsurviving site, landscape, building, structure, or object in all new materials.[21]

Application of *The Standards and Guidelines* is not an exact science but a philosophical position. Arguments about their application and interpretation can occur between professionals who use them on every project, and local guidelines may actually take a stronger position about alterations and additions than the standards do. Even if two different projects both receive historic tax credits and both are reviewed by the National Park Service, it cannot be assumed that the parameters are exactly the same, since the specific history and condition of each building, the proposed uses, and the performance demands of codes and other compliance may be very different. A warehouse in an industrial neighborhood will meet different criteria than a townhouse in a nineteenth-century residential district, and a National Historic Landmark will not be regarded in the same way as a contributing building in a local historic district. A continuum of approaches is possible and necessary in the stewardship of historic buildings, which opens the door to a wide range of solutions.

3.5 BALANCING SYSTEMS AND GUIDELINES—WHOLE BUILDING DESIGN

Sustainable design is not just about how to make a new building and pass it on to future generations. Sustainable design is about the ability to use resources wisely and to create places of enduring value to society—places that can be utilized by many generations.

—Mike Jackson[22]

"Clearly, the sub-disciplines of heritage conservation and green-building design fell under the umbrella of sustainable design and had much to offer each other," writes John Lesak in discussing the addition of a sustainability track for the 2004 APT (Association for Preservation Technology) conference and a two-day symposium the following year.[23] Both events and the formation of the APT Technical Committee on Sustainable Preservation sprang from an expanding group of members who recognized the urgency of environmental issues, but who also had concerns that

▼Figure 3.7 Installation of the ground-source heat pump system at the Sisters, Servants of the Immaculate Heart of Mary Motherhouse in Monroe, Michigan (see Chapter 4), a closed-loop system, required 232 holes drilled 450 feet deep, totaling 19.77 miles and using 47 miles of piping. The installation is part of a strategy that will ultimately make the historic complex independent of nonrenewable energy sources. *Denyse Burkhart photo courtesy Sisters, Servants of the Immaculate Heart of Mary*

▶Figure 3.8 The construction process can be extremely disruptive of the site and has a carbon footprint rarely captured by green building metric systems, which focus on the completed building and not the process that produces it. Holistic strategies take into account minimal disruption to the site, protection of watersheds, and reduction of worker transportation needs. *Denyse Burkhart photo courtesy Sisters, Servants of the Immaculate Heart of Mary*

Figure 3.9 Reuse of existing resources, whether buildings or building elements, may be the greenest action of all (refer to Chapter 7). Over 100 period light fixtures were retrofitted and reused at the Sisters, Servants of the Immaculate Heart of Mary Motherhouse in Monroe, Michigan (see Chapter 4). 600 wood doors were salvaged and 450 reused in the 376,000-square-foot renovation. *Denyse Burkhart photo courtesy Sisters, Servants of the Immaculate Heart of Mary*

the emerging standardized measuring tools were inadequately addressing heritage properties. In particular, the common measuring tools for "green" buildings were seen as overlooking the impact of projects on cultural value; failing to consider the performance, longer service lives, and embodied energy of historic materials and assemblies; and placing a disproportionate emphasis on current or future technologies while neglecting how past experience helps to determine sustainable performance.[24]

Many of the articles and papers that discuss the conflicts or tensions between green building design and heritage conservation really address conflicts between building stewardship and the application of green building rating systems or current preferences for the most sustainable course of action. For instance, Donovan Rypkema—president of PlaceEconomics, a Washington, D.C.–based consulting firm specializing in the economic revitalization of city centers—suggests that the acronym LEED really stands for "Lunatic Environmentalists Enthusiastically Demolishing" because of projects that have demolished a building as part of new LEED-certified construction and won LEED ranking by diverting a minimum of 75 percent of the demolition debris from landfill. (There are no penalties in the LEED system for the demolition of existing or historic buildings.) "Green buildings in and of themselves are not sustainable development," says Rypkema, "They are just one aspect of overall sustainability, but they are being touted as the whole thing."[25] In Rypkema's judgment, the removal of a building deemed of cultural value is an unsustainable action, regardless of how the materials are reclaimed.

Historical commissions are frequently criticized for not accepting relatively new "green" materials, replacement windows, and visible statements of sustainable intent such as photovoltaic panels, but

Whole Building Design Guide

WBDG is a Web-based portal that provides government and industry practitioners with access to up-to-date guidance toward holistic sustainability.

Maintained by the National Institute of Building Sciences, it is the primary Web portal for architects and engineers in government and industry looking for current information on a wide range of buildings-related guidance, criteria, and resources.

"Design Objectives," the website's first section, focuses on eight critical aspects of designing, delivering, and operating almost any building:

- Accessibility
- Aesthetics
- Cost effectiveness
- Functionality
- Historic
- Productivity
- Safety and security
- Sustainability

More than 1 million documents are downloaded each month from the site and over 10 million visits were expected in 2007. Access to the site is free to all.[26]

the commissions are charged with the protection of cultural resources and the character of individual buildings and neighborhoods. Too often, requests for dramatic interventions are made when simple but important measures, such as attic and basement insulation, haven't been instituted. Instead of adding storm windows, caulking, or making repairs, owners ask permission to install new windows—often with no guarantees about their quality or the effectiveness of the installation. Professionals dealing with historic buildings are all well aware that many modern "miracle" components, including windows, have a much shorter life cycle than original materials and, rightly or wrongly, in addition

to voicing aesthetic concerns, resist the installation of materials that further a culture of replacement rather than repair.

Clearly, moving toward sustainability is critical, and identifying how to do this is an ongoing conversation. Every building project has multiple constraints and requirements, encompassing social, environmental, and fiscal responsibility. The only way to address and balance these is through an integrated team process (see Integrated Project Delivery in section 3.1) and a whole-building design process that recognizes competing performance goals.

Within the current framework of manufacturing and operation, even new green buildings merely do less harm, regardless of how much energy they take from or return to the grid and regardless of the amount of recycled material they employ. Existing buildings (and sites) must also do less harm, but they provide valuable resources, as well, serving not just to reduce carbon impacts but as cultural touchstones that anchor our hearts and minds and those of generations to come. That emotional intangible creates conflict and leads to dismissal of "hysterical" commissions from proponents of green.

Not all existing buildings are precious, and not all elements of precious buildings are precious, but if our current throw-away culture has created this mess, finding our way to sustainability is not always about the solution of the moment, but, rather, thoughtful evaluation of the options and implications for decisions. We must act responsibly, yet with humility, as we move forward in modifying our society to become truly sustainable. As Barbra Batshalom, executive director of the Green Roundtable (www.greenroundtable.org) wisely notes, "Healthy, efficient (green) design is still too often referred to in a context of 'either/or.' Either affordable, or green. Either historic preservation, or green—as if green is always an alternative that you must compromise to achieve….the process of design—the degree to which it is collaborative—influences the extent to which a project is green much more than technology or products do." Green design, she goes on to say, is interwoven with economic and social issues as well as with design excellence.[27]

"Preservation and sustainability share the vision of a viable, meaningful future for our children and the generations that will follow them. We stand on common ground—but we can't stand still.

"We have a choice: We can do nothing for a while longer—until we are forced to take action by soaring energy costs, the disappearance of the irreplaceable resources, and the realities of climate change. Or we can forge a strong partnership *now* to develop a smart sustainable development ethic and the policies that will support it.

"Historic preservation has always sustained America by working to protect and celebrate the evidence of its past. Now, by addressing the challenge of climate change, preservation can—and must—play a leadership role in the sustainable stewardship of America's future."

Richard Moe, President Emeritus,
National Trust for Historic Preservation[28]

Metric tools for green design and guidelines for historic preservation have the same goal—creating a sustainable world for future generations. Both should address the immediate urgency of climate change as well as the long-term legacy we deliver to the future. The case studies include a cross section of preservation projects, building types, and geographic locations to demonstrate the compatibility and feasibility of incorporating environmentally responsible design with historic preservation practices, including federal tax credit utilization.

Whitaker Street Building

Savannah, GA

Current Owner: Melaver, Inc.

Building Type: Retail/Restaurant/Commercial Office

Original Building Construction: 1890

Historic Designation: National Register of Historic Places, Savannah National Landmark Historic District

Restoration/Renovation Completion: 2003

Square Footage: 14,000 ft^2

Percentage Renovated: 100%

Recognition: LEED NC (2.0)—Silver (33/69 points), Historic Savannah Foundation Merit Award, Georgia Trust for Historic Preservation Excellence in Rehabilitation Award

"The original design of the building already supplied durability. From many viewpoints, we rehabilitated the building in a manner consistent with the original building design. And by using LEED guidelines, we created a high-performance, environmentally friendly, healthy place to work that will be historically certified in the process."

—*Randy Peacock, Melaver, Inc.*[29]

PROJECT DESCRIPTION

The restoration of the 1890s building in Savannah's National Landmark Historic District demonstrated the compatibility between the LEED system and historic rehabilitation, which required review on a national and local level for certification under the federal Historic Preservation Tax Credit Program and the Georgia Historic Rehabilitation Property Tax Freeze Program. The realized goal of the owners was a renovation that was historically accurate to serve as a demonstration project for environmentally sensitive design and construction.

Figure 3.10 Restoration of the 1890s Whitaker Street Building in Savannah's National Landmark Historic District was an intentional demonstration of the compatibility between *The Secretary of the Interior's Standards for Rehabilitation* and the LEED certification system. *Phil Bekker for Melaver, Inc.*

Figure 3.11 The before picture of the building shows the loss of the historic storefronts, which were recreated during the renovation to qualify the project for the Federal Historic Preservation Tax Incentives program. *Courtesy of Dawson Wissmach Architects*

Energy and Envelope

Attaining energy savings 18.35 percent above the baseline performance of ASHRAE 90.1 was a considerable achievement on this project. The existing building had uninsulated, multi-wythe masonry walls, an uninsulated roof and large areas of uninsulated windows. To improve envelope performance, the roof was insulated above the deck in order to retain exposed timber and decking on the second floor. The existing masonry walls were furred out to create a 4-inch interstitial space for insulation and moisture barriers.

To preserve and recreate the historic appearance of the building, existing double-hung, single-pane windows were retained, uninsulated stained-glass transoms were recreated, and large-pane storefront windows were installed with clear and nonreflective glass. An energy-efficient storefront glass was found that features 72 percent less ultraviolet light transmittance than standard clear glass. While transmitting about 48 percent less solar energy, the glass allows in about 88 percent as much visible light as standard glass.

Figure 3.12 The recreated details of the storefront arcade add to the rich character of the renovated building and symbolize the visual delight that historic districts provide for pedestrians. *Courtesy of Dawson Wissmach Architects*

GREEN DESIGN ELEMENTS
Whitaker Street Building

Sustainable Sites:
- Carpool program
- Bicycle accommodation
- Urban site/walkable
- Public transit proximity

Water Efficiency:
- Dual-flush toilets
- 15-second faucet discharge
- Low-flow showers

Energy and Atmosphere:
- Perimeter insulation
- Low-e storefront glass
- High-efficiency HVAC systems
- Cooling system with a non-Freon coolant
- High-efficiency lighting

Materials and Resources:
- Reuse of the building and existing materials
- Reclaimed materials from other buildings
- Wheatboard cabinets—formaldehyde-free

Indoor Environment Quality:
- Low-VOC products

Material Reuse

By virtue of its masonry-bearing structure, timber framing, and heart pine flooring, this project made reuse of the main building components a desirable way to meet both preservation and environmental goals, while reducing construction costs. One of the most notable highlights of the project was the reuse of salvaged building components. Several 3-inch-by-14-inch antique heart pine beams had rotted, but a significant portion of their overall length and section remained usable. The beams were de-nailed, planed, and reused as stair treads. A clear, low-VOC finish on the treads highlights the density and beauty of this old-growth lumber. Other miscellaneous pieces of heart pine were de-nailed, planed, and milled for reuse as handrails.

Education

The building incorporates signage pointing out key features of environmentally efficient design, and the project team has made presentations on the building to hundreds of key leaders in the local building industry—including appraisers, developers, brokers, architects, engineers, and others—to demonstrate that environmental efficiency offers a prudent way to design and renovate buildings.

PROJECT TEAM

Melaver, Inc.
Dawson Wissmach
MFI Construction, LLC
Elements
John T. Blewett, P.E.
Fred Blackburn, P.E.
Air Services Refrigeration
Holistic Test and Balance

Alliance Center for Sustainable Colorado
Denver, CO

Current Owner: Alliance for Sustainable Colorado

Building Type: Commercial Office

Original Building Construction: 1908

Restoration/Renovation Completion: 2005

Square Footage: 38,609 ft^2

Percentage Renovated: 100%

Occupancy: 130 people (40 hrs/week)

Recognition: LEED CI v2.0—Silver; LEED EB v2.0—Gold; Mayor's Design Award, It's Easy Being Green 2007; Governor's Energy Office Colorado Energy Champion; USGBC National Award for Education in Green Building (Greenbuild 2006); Bike Denver Bicycle-Friendly Workplace

"The mission of Alliance for Sustainable Colorado is to catalyze the shift to a truly sustainable world by fostering collaboration among nonprofits, businesses, governments, and academia. We are working to advance economic, environmental, and social sustainability in Colorado by building cross-sector alliances and networks. A tool for social advocacy, the Alliance Center also demonstrates how sound building design and technologies create healthy workplaces and reduce environmental impacts."

—www.sustainablecolorado.org[30]

PROJECT DESCRIPTION

The Alliance Center utilized the USGBC LEED systems to measure interior and operational improvements and achieved two certifications, LEED-CI (Commercial Interiors), which address the tenant improvements the organization implemented and LEED-EB (Existing Buildings: Operations and Maintenance), which measures operations, systems improvements and maintenance. The building was also awarded an Energy Star rating by the Environmental Protection Agency.

Figure 3.13 The Alliance for Sustainable Colorado is sowing the seeds for a statewide sustainability movement in Colorado by using a high-performing historic building as a hub for activity. The building is a showcase for sound building renovations, which reduce environmental impacts, create healthy workplaces, and promote collaboration. The windows had been replaced in previous renovations. *Alliance for a Sustainable Colorado*

Located in a 1908 warehouse structure in the heart of downtown Denver, the Alliance Center for Sustainable Colorado improved a building that had already been modified for offices and had had significant alterations, including the replacement of the windows. Many of the changes made do not require a gut rehabilitation, which is an important demonstration for all property owners.

Energy

A segmented energy system programmed by specific time of day and location (zone) in the building increases energy efficiency and contributes to 18 percent reductions in the energy bill, even though occupancy has doubled. All electrical energy needed for the building is purchased through Green-e certificates that help

Figure 3.14 Shared spaces mean reduction in resource use. Shared services for tenants include conference rooms, telecom services, copiers, and catering kitchens. Conference rooms are also available for use by organizations outside the building as well as for tenants. Furniture in lobbies and common areas had previous lives at a convention center, or as a rubber tire or reclaimed pallet. Plastic walls molded into honeycombs provide a sound barrier without sacrificing light penetration. The wheatboard in the walls is a nontoxic fiberboard made from wheat chaff, an agricultural waste. *Alliance for a Sustainable Colorado*

fund the advancement of wind power technologies. A Mylar film that reflects over 60 percent of the sun's heat was installed on the interior of the window glass, and cotton-based fiber insulation made from recycled blue jeans has been added to the walls.

Water

Water consumption was reduced by 84 percent when all fixtures were replaced or retrofitted with low-flow systems, dual-flush toilets and waterless urinals. The new fixtures reduced the water bill by $4,500 per year and paid for themselves in five years.

Education

Throughout the building, touch screens and educational signs explain the green strategies utilized in the building, and a direct digital control system allows occupants and visitors to monitor energy systems in real time. The lobby displays documents that explain the history of the building and how the neighborhood has changed with time.

GREEN DESIGN ELEMENTS

Alliance Center for Sustainable Colorado

Sustainable Sites:
- Public transportation proximity
- Bicycle accommodation
- Xeriscaping

Water Efficiency:
- Low-flow plumbing fixtures
- Waterless urinals
- Dual-flush toilets
- Aerating faucets/showerheads

Energy and Atmosphere:
- Direct digital controlled building systems
- Green-e wind power certificates
- Energy-efficient doors/windows
- Bronze Mylar film (windows)
- T-8 efficient fluorescent lighting
- Automatic daylight and occupancy sensors

Materials and Resources:
- Recycled content and recyclable materials
- Refurbished furniture
- Recycled cotton-based fiber insulation
- Sustainable/rapidly renewable materials

Indoor Environment Quality:
- Translucent interior glazing
- Low-VOC materials and finishes

Additional Features:
- Single-stream recycling program
- Green cleaning policy
- Walk-off mats
- Environmental education

Figure 3.15 The educational exhibits at the Alliance Center are designed and fabricated from green materials by local green companies. Educational signage throughout the building points to sustainable features and describes the history of the building and surrounding area. Guided and self-guided tours are provided. *Alliance for a Sustainable Colorado*

PROJECT TEAM

Alliance for Sustainable Colorado
St Charles Town Company
ShearsAdkins Architects
Sprung Construction
Ambient Energy
E Cube
ESCO

Thoreau Center for Sustainability
San Francisco, CA

Current Owner: National Park Service and Thoreau Center Partners

Building Type: Commercial Office

Original Building Construction: 1899

Historic Designation: National Historic Landmark Site, 1962

Restoration/Renovation Completion: 1996 and 1998

Square Footage: 75,000 ft^2 (phase 1); 37,000 ft^2 (phase 2)

Percentage Renovated: 100 percent

Occupancy: 300 people (45 hrs/week)

Recognition: National Trust for Historic Preservation Honor Award; California Preservation Foundation Honor Award; AIA California Design Award 1998; Green Building Challenge 2000

"The pleasant office environments, the inviting and well-placed staircases that discourage the use of the elevator, the feel of natural/organic materials in the selection of finishes, the natural gardens and experimental medicinal herb production utilizing captured rainwater, the open café in the wide historic corridors, and the ease with which accessibility requirements were integrated has been beneficial to all—the tenants, the individual historic building, the Presidio, and the larger environment. It is a model that can and should be considered when historic buildings are being rehabilitated."

—*Sharon C. Park, FAIA, Senior Historical Architect for Heritage Preservation Services of the National Park Service*[31]

PROJECT DESCRIPTION

The Thoreau Center for Sustainability utilized the Green Building Challenge metric system (refer to SBtool on page 94). Renovation of the Letterman Hospital Buildings demonstrates multiple sustainable design features that take advantage of the attributes of the historic buildings, which served the Army during World War II, and integrates new technologies and new materials.

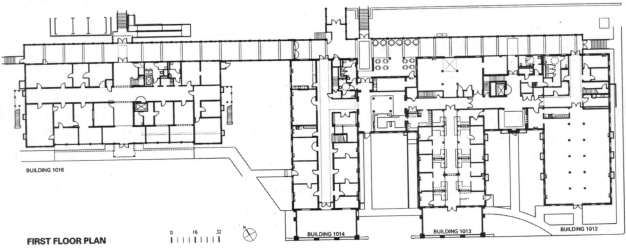

BUILDING 1016

FIRST FLOOR PLAN

0   16   32

BUILDING 1014   BUILDING 1013   BUILDING 1012

◀ Figure 3.16 The Presidio of San Francisco was designated a National Historic Landmark in 1962, and these buildings, part of the Letterman Hospital complex built for the U.S. Army between 1899 and 1933, now house the Thoreau Center for Sustainable Design. An early model for the synergies of environmentally sensitive design and rehabilitation of historic buildings, the Center houses more than 60 nonprofits in 12 buildings. *Richard Barnes photo, courtesy Leddy Maytum Stacy Architects*

As a demonstration to the community, photovoltaic panels used in the skylights above the entry canopy can be seen beneath the glass. Even though the PV panels provide a minimal amount of electricity, visibility to occupants and visitors was a noteworthy advantage to their installation.

The interiors display materials chosen after thorough research demonstrated them to be environmentally safe in both their production/manufacturing and their use within the building. Recycled-content materials are used throughout, including cotton insulation and bathroom tiles made from car and airplane windshield glass.

◀ Figure 3.17 Naturally ventilated office spaces take advantage of narrow office wings, operable windows, and attic roof vents. The open office plan allows air to circulate naturally and facilitates daylighting, which benefits from the use of glass office partitions and light-colored walls. *Courtesy Leddy Maytum Stacy Architects*

Figure 3.18 A basic tenet of sustainable design is creation of a healthy workplace with good ventilation, natural lighting, appealing work spaces, and circulation patterns that encourage pedestrian movement. It should also facilitate elimination of chemicals, air particulates, formaldehyde fumes, solvents and volatile organic compounds. The Thoreau Center strives to use materials that are biodegradable and recyclable and have been manufactured in a way that has not damaged the environment or created social inequity. *Richard Barnes photo, courtesy Leddy Maytum Stacy Architects*

GREEN DESIGN ELEMENTS
Thoreau Center for Sustainability

Sustainable Sites:
- Electric-car charging stations
- Xeriscaping

Water Efficiency:
- Graywater system
- Low-flow plumbing fixtures

Energy and Atmosphere:
- Photovoltaic system
- Cotton insulation in walls
- Hydronic heating control system
- Occupancy and photoelectric sensors
- Natural cross-ventilation

Materials and Resources:
- Majority of construction waste recycled
- Recycled-content materials
- Cotton insulation in walls
- Recovery and reuse of existing materials
- Sustainably harvested wood

Indoor Environment Quality:
- Interior glazing (shared light)
- Operable windows
- Low-VOC materials and finishes

Passive Survivability Features

The design team used passive building systems as much as possible since the building is located in a climate with relatively clement weather. Operable windows allow employees to draw fresh air into the building and reduce dependence on mechanical HVAC systems. Skylights provide natural lighting, and occupancy sensors provide efficiency when a room is empty. Open by design, the floor plan allows natural daylight and ventilation to pass throughout the building.

Site

Portions of the grass lawn were replaced with native ground cover, which requires very little upkeep and eliminates most landscaping maintenance. Rehabilitation of existing vegetation and the addition of drought-resistant plants minimize outdoor use of potable water. Remaining irrigation needs are met by a rainwater-catchment system, which, as a result, keeps stormwater runoff to a minimum.

PROJECT TEAM

National Park Service
Thoreau Center Partners
Leddy Maytum Stacy Architects
GL&A
Steven Tipping and Associates
Flack and Kurtz Consulting Engineers
Plant Construction
Simon and Associates
Architectural Lighting Design
Charles M. Salter Associates
Cheryl Barton

Gerding Theater at the Armory
Portland, OR

Current Owner: Portland Historic Rehabilitation Fund

Building Type: Assembly

Original Building Construction: 1891

Historic Designation: National Register of Historic Places, 2004

Restoration/Renovation Completion: 2006

Square Footage: 55,000 ft^2

Percentage Renovated: 36% + 64% (excavation)

Occupancy: 30 people (40 hrs/week) 650 visitors (2 hrs/week)

Recognition: LEED NC v2.1—Platinum 2006; AIA/IIDA Interior Design Award 2007; AIA/COTE Top Ten Green Projects, Honorable Mention 2007; Urban Land Institute Awards for Excellence (The Americas) 2007

"In assessing the goals of the project, the team quickly recognized the role of sustainability as an essential driver of both the theater design and a statement about Portland Center Stage's relationship to its community. An historic building, built to LEED Platinum standards, could offer a space that was more humane, intimate and uniquely 'Portland.' In Portland, green building has come to be an expression of civic responsibility, a commitment to civic ecology and reflection of the city's identity."

—*Project Statement, Gerding Edlen Development Company*

PROJECT DESCRIPTION

Utilizing The Natural Step principles throughout design and construction, the team for the Gerding Theater at the Armory achieved multiple firsts in the successful design. The theater represents one of the earliest and largest projects to combine New Markets Tax Credits with a historic preservation tax-incentive program, and it was the first building on the National Register of Historic Places and the first theater in the U.S. to achieve a LEED Platinum rating from the U.S. Green Building Council.

◀ Figure 3.19 The Gerding Theater at the Armory is one of the earliest and largest projects to combine New Market Tax Credits with the Historic Preservation Tax Incentive program. It was the first building on the National Register of Historic Places and the first theater in the nation to achieve a LEED Platinum rating from the U.S. Green Building Council. *Marcus Lima photo, courtesy GBD Architects, Inc.*

▼ Figure 3.20 Built to the edge of the property and sharing the block with a 15-story residential tower, the Armory is a completely urban site. An opaque façade and minimal solar envelope offered almost no opportunity for a bioclimatic response to solar energy flows. The design focuses on flows of water and air and on creating high-quality indoor and outdoor environments. *© GBDArchitects*

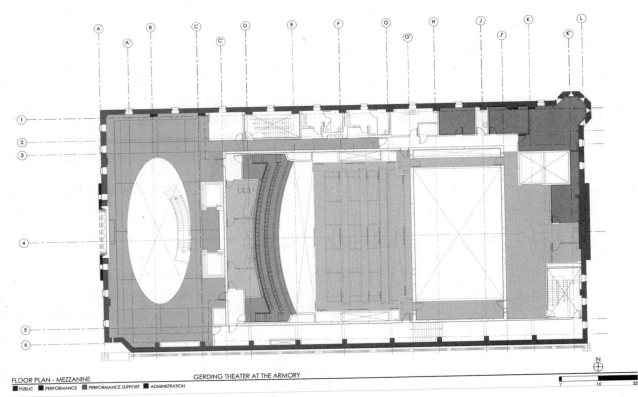

FLOOR PLAN - MEZZANINE   GERDING THEATER AT THE ARMORY

■ PUBLIC ■ PERFORMANCE ■ PERFORMANCE SUPPORT ■ ADMINISTRATION

Excavating 30 feet into the ground allowed the design of the new spaces to accommodate a program larger than the original structure could have housed without removing its existing roof and beautiful Douglas fir trusses. In order to avoid damaging the structure, all major excavation was performed within the shell of the building (roof and all). Despite its urban environment, steps were taken to minimize heat islands and stormwater runoff by using pervious pavers. A "sliver park" alongside the building includes benches designed to encourage visitors to enjoy a small urban landscape planted with native vegetation. A graywater system captures rain water to use in toilets and urinals; that feature, combined with low-flow plumbing fixtures, helps the building achieve an 88 percent reduction in its use of potable water. The building emphasizes pedestrian rather than automobile transportation and provides storage and showers for bikers.

▼ Figure 3.21 The challenge of the project involved balancing the programmatic needs of a modern theater, aesthetic goals of high-quality design, historic-preservation requirements, and high levels of energy, water, and material resource efficiency, while preserving the existing roof and shell. The process was likened to building a "ship inside a bottle." The "Sliver Park" along the long edge of the building adds outdoor seating and a swath of native vegetation in a neighborhood with few parks and open spaces. © GBDArchitects

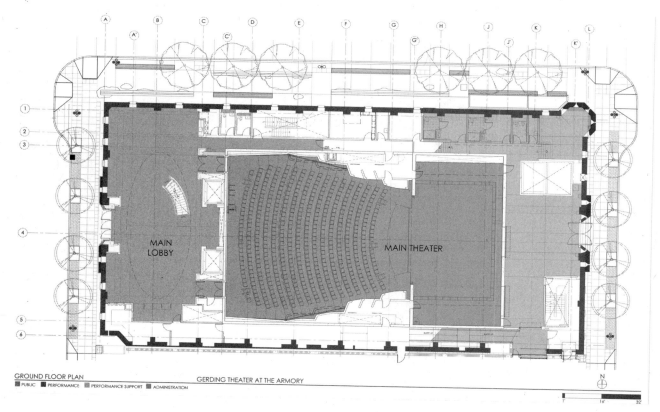

GROUND FLOOR PLAN
GERDING THEATER AT THE ARMORY

PUBLIC   PERFORMANCE   PERFORMANCE SUPPORT   ADMINISTRATION

Stormwater Management

The nearby Willamette River's water quality is affected by overflows during large storms from Portland's combined sewer overflow (CSO) system. The rainwater-harvesting system, 10,000-gallon storage tank, and exterior swales combine reuse, detention, transpiration, and mechanical filtration to cut the stormwater entering the sewer system by by 26 percent over a conventional system.

Energy

The building utilizes radiant heat and low-velocity, low-energy systems where possible to reduce energy use. Excavating provided greater insulation and earth-coupling benefits. The existing building mass, along with new concrete floors and walls, functions as a thermal flywheel to absorb heat gains and dampen temperature swings. Operable skylights were strategically positioned on the roof to provide adequate daylight to regularly occupied work spaces and the entrance lobby. Connection to a district chilled-water plant eliminated the need to install chillers onsite.

Materials

Ninety-five percent of construction waste was diverted from landfills through an aggressive waste-management plan. 45 percent of materials were manufactured within 500 miles of the site, and 25 percent of the project materials came from recycled

Figure 3.22 The Armory has had a long, rich history in the cultural life of the city. The theater introduced an essential cultural institution to the revitalized Brewery Blocks neighborhood, adding to the neighborhood's diversity of uses and intensity of activity. The theater's lobby evolved into a stage for the expression of public life—with its doors open all day, as much attention was paid to the design of the lobby as a place for "public theater" as was given to the two stages. *Josh Partee photo, courtesy GBD Architects, Inc.*

sources. Nearly 60 percent of the wood used in millwork, finish carpentry, doors, and form-work meets Forest Stewardship Council (FSC) certification standards. All paneling is locally harvested FSC Douglas fir, and all composite wood is urea-formaldehyde-free. All carpets contain high amounts of recycled content and meet CRI Green Label requirements.

GREEN DESIGN ELEMENTS
Gerding Theater at the Armory

Sustainable Sites:
- Public transportation proximity
- FlexCar shared vehicle
- Bicycle accommodation
- Interior excavation of site
- Permeable paving materials
- Xeriscaping
- Bioswales

Water Efficiency:
- Rainwater-harvesting system
- Ultra-low-flow plumbing fixtures
- Dual-flush toilets

Energy and Atmosphere:
- District chilled-water plant (offsite)
- Chilled beams
- Radiant heating (lobby-floor slab)
- Thermal mass
- Displacement ventilation
- Occupancy and photoelectric sensors
- Building commissioning

Materials and Resources:
- 95 percent construction waste recycled
- Recycled-content materials
- Flyash concrete substitute
- Forest Stewardship Council- (FCS-) certified wood
- Locally manufactured materials

Indoor Environment Quality:
- Skylights
- Operable windows
- CO_2 monitors
- Low-VOC materials and finishes

Additional Features:
- Occupant recycling program
- Green cleaning policy

PROJECT TEAM

Gerding Edlen Development
GBD ARCHITECTS Incorporated
Portland Historic Rehabilitation Fund
Hoffman Construction Company
Glumac International
Green Building Services, Inc.
KPFFConsulting Engineers
Murase & Associates

Howard M. Metzenbaum U.S. Courthouse
Cleveland, OH

Current Owner: US General Services Administration

Building Type: Public Order and Safety

Original Building Construction: 1910

Restoration/Renovation Completion: 2005

Historic Designation: National Register of Historic Places, 1974

Square Footage: 235,600 ft^2

Percentage Renovated: 100%

Occupancy: 110 people (40 hrs/week) 50 visitors (1–3 hrs/day)

Recognition: LEED NC v2.0—Certified; Builders Exchange Award for Craftsmanship 2005; AIA Cleveland Honor Award 2005; Ohio Historic Preservation Office Preservation Merit Award 2005; AIA Ohio Design Merit Award 2006; Contract Interior's Award for Restoration 2007; AIA Ohio Design Honor Award (Interior Design) 2007; Center for the Built Environment 2008 Livable Buildings Award; Energy Star® designation.

"The GSA's objective is to modernize the building and make it fully functional and equipped to serve well into its second century. At the same time, we want to preserve its remarkable art and architecture for future generations to enjoy."

—*Pam Wilczynski, project manager, U.S. General Services Administration, Region*

PROJECT DESCRIPTION

The Howard M. Metzenbaum U.S. Courthouse is an exceptional example of a highly decorative historic building that has been beautifully restored and successfully modified, following *The Secretary of Interior's Standards,* to meet multiple functional requirements while significantly decreasing the environmental impact of day-to-day operations. The project has been recognized with both LEED and Energy Star certification and more than a dozen awards for design, historic preservation, engineering, and environmental stewardship.

Figure 3.23 The General Services Administration renovated and expanded the Howard M. Metzenbaum U.S. Courthouse, a National Historic Landmark, to preserve the original 1910 structure and bring it up to modern standards. This remarkable achievement has resulted in more than a dozen awards for design, historic preservation, engineering, and environmental stewardship. © *Kevin G. Reeves, courtesy of Westlake Reed Leskosky, Architect and Mechanical/ Electrical Engineer*

The GSA's modernization of the Metzenbaum was a reinvestment in one of downtown Cleveland's most significant structures, a landmark with a unique sense of place for the city. It was the first building erected in Cleveland's Group Plan at the turn of the century, and it embodies the spirit of the nationally influential City Beautiful movement. Adjacent to Cleveland's Public Square, the Metzenbaum today anchors an economic revival of the city's central core.

Occupancy Satisfaction

An independent survey of building occupants by the University of California, Berkeley's, Center for the Built Environment demonstrates an exceptional level of enthusiasm for the project as a work environment. Overall, occupant satisfaction with the building scored in the 86th percentile of surveyed buildings. No attribute of indoor environmental quality—acoustic quality, air quality, cleanliness and maintenance, thermal comfort, and lighting—ranked below the 73rd percentile of all surveyed buildings.

▶Figure 3.24 The project reinstalled restored murals and rebuilt an original chandelier to accommodate low-energy lamps. Other reused materials include hardware, grills, wood doors, glazed brick, and marble from the basement to patch floors and wainscots. © *Kevin G. Reeves, courtesy of Westlake Reed Leskosky, Architect and Mechanical/Electrical Engineer*

▼ Figure 3.25 The original five-level courtyard was converted into functional space, repurposing it to house a security screening area and new circulation balconies. To prevent heating and cooling loss through the walls and windows surrounding the courtyard, a glass skylight caps the space, dramatically reducing the building's energy use. © *Kevin G. Reeves, courtesy of Westlake Reed Leskosky, Architect and Mechanical/Electrical Engineer*

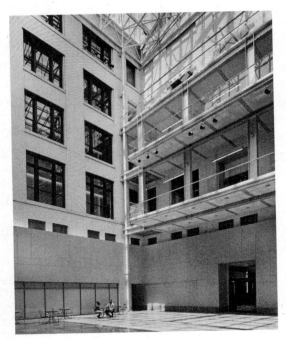

Building Performance

The courthouse scored well in a study of a dozen GSA Buildings. "Assessing Green Building Performance, A Post Occupancy Evaluation of 12 GSA Buildings," found the Metzenbaum Courthouse's operating costs to be 23 percent below the industry baseline. Building CO_2 equivalent emissions were 34 percent below baseline and energy-use intensity (EUI) was 22 percent below the CBECS (Commercial Buildings Energy Consumption Survey) regional average.

Energy and Building Security

The building's original light well was enclosed to provide an area for security screening and public circulation separate from secure court circulation. Temperature control in the atrium was addressed by a study of the adjacent building shadows, high-performance glazing in the skylight, and demand-control ventilation. Regularly occupied

GREEN DESIGN ELEMENTS

Howard M. Metzenbaum U.S. Courthouse

Sustainable Sites:

- Public transportation proximity
- Transit-subsidy program
- Bicycle accommodation
- Parking relocated underground

Water Efficiency:

- Low-flow plumbing
- Elimination of unneeded fixtures
- Automatic sensor faucets

Energy and Atmosphere:

- Demand-controlled ventilation
- Natural ventilation
- Waste-heat recovery

Materials and Resources:

- Over 50 percent construction waste recycled
- Recycled-content materials
- Existing-materials restoration/reuse
- Locally manufactured materials

Indoor Environment Quality:

- Skylights/atrium
- Operable windows
- CO_2 monitoring
- Low-VOC materials and finishes
- Humidity control
- IAQ construction management
- Tenant space preoccupancy air flush-out

Additional Features:

- Occupant recycling program
- Green cleaning policy

perimeter areas above the ground floor have access to lighting controls and numerous large, operable windows typical for a building of this era.

Water

Water consumption within the building was reduced to 60 percent of pre-renovation levels. All existing bathrooms were demolished and refitted with newer, low-flow models that require significantly less of water. Over 70 fixtures were eliminated entirely to adjust the fixture count to new occupancy levels.

PROJECT TEAM

U.S. General Services Administration
Westlake Reed Leskosky
Dick Corporation
Barber & Hoffman, Inc.
Project & Construction Services
Rolf Jensen Associates
Schiff & Associates
Hinman Associates
McKay Lodge Fine Arts Conservation Laboratory, Inc.
EverGreene Studios, Inc.
John Canning Studio
Supersky

ENDNOTES

1. Vitruvius Pollio, *The Ten Books of Architecture*, Book 1, Chapter III, Morris Hicky Morgan, ed. (Cambridge, MA: Harvard University Press, 1914). Accessed online February 24, 2009, www.perseus.tufts.edu.

2. Marilyn A. Brown, Frank Southworth, Therese K. Stovall, Oak Ridge National Laboratory, "Towards a Climate-Friendly Built Environment," (Arlington, VA: Pew Center on Global Climate Change, 2005), p. ii; www.pewclimate.org.

3. *Integrated Project Delivery: A Working Definition.* Version 2, updated June 13, 2007. (Sacramento, CA: AIA California Council, 2007), p. 4. Available at www.ipd-ca.net/images/Integrated%20Project%20Delivery%20Definition.pdf. (Accessed May 2010.)

4. Richard Moe, "Historic Preservation and the Climate-Change Challenge." Presented at the Growing Sustainable Communities Conference, Dubuque, Iowa, February 19, 2009.

5. www.naturalstep.org/our-approach#quick-overview. Accessed February 25, 2009.

6. Sherrie Gruder, Anna Haines, Jerry Hembd, Lisa MacKinnon, Jane Silberstein, "Toward a Sustainable Community; A Toolkit for Local Government," (Madison, WI: Solid and Hazardous Waste Education Center, 2007). Available electronically at www.shwec.uwm.edu.

7. Sarah James andand Torborn Lahti, *The Natural Step for Communities: How Cities and Towns Can Change to Sustainable Practices* (Gabriola Island, BC: New Society Publishers, 2004).

8. Ibid.

9. www.icleiusa.org/action-center/tools. Accessed February 25, 2009.

10. James T. Kienle, (2008) "That Old Building May Be the Greenest on the Block," AIA Web post. *Think About It: The Architects Voice,* February 8, 2008, www.aia.org/architect/this week08/0208p_pres.cfm.

11. M.Y.L. Chew and Sutapa Das, "Building Grading Systems: A Review of the State-of-the-Art," *Architectural Science Review* 51(1) (2008): p. 6.

12. Ibid, p. 3

13. U.S. General Services Administration, *Sustainability Matters* (Washington, DC: Public Buildings Service, Office of Applied Science, 2008), p. 14.

14. Leadership in Energy and Environmental Design Reference Guide Version 2.0 (Washington, DC: U.S. Green Building Council, 2001).

15. Cascadia Region Green Building Council Brochure. Available for download at http://ilbi.org/stuff/lbc-web-brochure.pdf/view (accessed May 2010).

16. Robert E. Stipe, "Why Preserve?" *Preservation News* (July 1972).

17. Norman Tyler, *Historic Preservation: An Introduction to Its History, Principles, and Practice* (New York: W. W. Norton, 2000), p. 47.

18. James A. Glass, "The National Historic Preservation Act: A 40th Anniversary Appraisal," *Forum Journal* (Fall 2006), p. 13.

19. National Park Services, *Introduction to Standards and Guidelines,* www.nps.gov/history/hps/tps/standguide/overview/choose_treat.htm. Accessed March 2, 2009.

20. U.S. Department of the Treasury, Community Affairs Department, *Historic Tax Credits: Bringing New Life to Older Communities* (Washington, DC: Community Development Insights, Comptroller of the Currency, Administrator of National Banks, 2008), pp. 1, 15.

21. Descriptions of treatments are taken directly from the National Park Service Web site, *Introduction to Standards and Guidelines, Choosing an Appropriate Treatment for the Historic Building,* www.nps.gov/history/hps/tps/standguide/overview/choose_treat.htm. Accessed March 2, 2009.

22. Mike Jackson, "Building A Culture That Sustains Design," APT Bulletin, *The Journal of Preservation Technology,* XXXVI (4), p. 3.

23. John D. Lesak, "APT and Sustainability: The Halifax Symposium," *APT Bulletin,* XXXVI (4), 2005, p. 3.

24. Ibid., p. 24.

25. Constantine A. Valhouli, "Natural Allies: Preservation and Sustainable Development," *Urban Land* (June 2008), p. 146.

26. U.S. General Services Administration. *Sustainability Matters.* (Washington, DC: Public Buildings Service, Office of Applied Science, 2008), p. 12.

27. Barbra Batshalom, Letter to the editor, *ArchitectureBoston* 10 (3), (2007).

28. Richard Moe, "Promoting Historic Preservation as Part of the Climate Solution." Presented at the Growing Sustainable Communities Conference, Dubuque, Iowa, February 19, 2009.

29. As quoted in Christina Koch, "Timeless Savannah; A Southern City Believes in Maintaining its Historic Reputation," *Eco-structure* (July/August 2004).

30. Alliance for Sustainable Colorado Web site, www.sustainablecolorado.org. Accessed February 26, 2009.

31. Sharon C. Park "Sustainable Design and Historic Preservation," *CRM,* no. 2 (1998).

PART II

TARGETED RESOURCE CONSERVATION

chapter 4

WATER AND SITE

4.1 WATER—THE MOST PRECIOUS COMMODITY

"Water is one of our most critical resources—even more important than oil. Water sustains agriculture and, thus, our food chain. Vast quantities of water are used to make the silicon chips that help power our computers and cell phones. Electric power plants depend heavily on water, and account for a staggering 39 percent of freshwater withdrawals in the United States. It could be said our economy runs on water."

—Mindy Luber and Peter Gleick[2]

"If we could see a watershed fully . . . we'd treat water with as much reverence as our own blood, because that's actually what it is—the lifeblood of the planet and of all the creatures that live here, including ourselves."

—Donella H. Meadows[1]

THE SUBJECT OF WATER will dominate global conversations about sustainability in the twenty-first century. How we use water contributes to climate change, and climate change is changing access to water. Only a small fraction (less than one-fifth of 1 percent) of the earth's water is freshwater available

127

to humans and other organisms. Already overappro-priated in much of the world, demand for this finite resource will grow more pressing. By 2025, the United Nations estimates that roughly 5 billion people, or two-thirds of the entire world population, will live in water-stressed countries.

More than one billion people currently lack access to safe drinking water. Nearly 2.5 billion (one-third of the world's population) lack access to proper sanitation facilities. In developing countries, 90 percent of wastewater goes straight into rivers and streams without treatment. Water-related diseases are the leading cause of death in the developing world, killing more than 14,000 people each day and causing more than 80 percent of all illness.[3]

Recognizing the crucial role that water plays in all aspects of sustainability and the necessity of an integrated approach to reconciling competing demands, the United Nations launched the "Water for Life" decade in 2005, following the establishment in 2003 of an interdisciplinary action group called UN-Water. In an informational brochure, UN-Water states the essential importance of water as well as the complexity of the issues:

> "We must manage freshwater sustainably so that everyone has enough water to drink and stay clean and healthy: food producers have enough water to satisfy the demands of growing populations; industries have enough water to meet their needs; and countries have opportunities to secure a reliable supply of energy. In addition, as our world changes, we need to adapt to changes in the availability of freshwater and prepare ourselves for changes in weather patterns and an increase in both the number and severity of water-related disasters. All of these issues must be addressed in ways that safeguard the health of our environment and protect ecosystems."[4]

International concern about water is not limited to developing countries. Water resources cross political boundaries, and the approach that each country takes to water alters the overall availability of water in the world. No country, including the United States, is immune to the impacts of changing water availability, nor are these impacts isolated to arid desert areas.

"The water industry in the United States ranges from the production of pipes and meters to desalination plants, wastewater treatment systems, water utilities, and water-related consulting. In 2003, the U.S. water industry had revenues of just under $100 billion, with a projected annual growth of around 10 percent."
—*Peter Gleick*, The World's Water 2008–2009[5]

Droughts in the southeastern United States have created feuds and litigation between states. In 2007, South Carolina sued North Carolina over a plan by two cities to withdraw 10 million gallons a day from the Catawba River. That same year, in the midst of an unprecedented regional drought, Alabama and Florida sued Georgia over a plan for withdrawing water from Lake Lanier, the main source of drinking water for the Atlanta metro region. Lake Lanier feeds the Chattahoochee River, which supplies water to towns in Alabama and Florida. Florida also sued the U.S. Army Corps of Engineers in 2008 over plans to reduce water flows from reservoirs in Georgia into the Apalachicola River, which runs through Florida from the Georgia-Alabama border. The river discharge is essential to the oyster industry in Apalachicola Bay, valued at $134 million.[6]

"I am convinced that, under present conditions and with the way water is being managed, we will run out of water long before we run out of fuel."
—*Nestlé Chairman Peter Brabeck-Letmathe*[7]

Water demonstrates the interconnection of all resource use and the need to think holistically as humans seek a sustainable existence. Water is in constant across the entire planet in a cycle that involves liquid, vapor, and crystals (ice or snow). Decisions about the built environment alter this cycle through the collection, processing, and redistribution of water for use within and around buildings, the addition of chemicals, biological material, and heat during use, additives from transportation, landscaping and materials, collection and rerouting of stormwater, and the use of water in the production of electricity. This cycle also affects the health of our planet: water vapor can absorb airborne pollutants and redistribute them across the Earth in precipitation.

Humans employ water to transport heat and waste, from fecal matter to soapsuds. Water is mined from subsurface aquifers and dispensed for agriculture, industry, and domestic purposes. The way we address water requires complex and expensive infrastructure and has resulted in the pollution and disruption of every watershed and ocean in the world. Even more than the use of nonrenewable fuels for energy, our attitude toward water proclaims our arrogance and ignorance about the natural world. Unlike oil, there is no substitute for water.

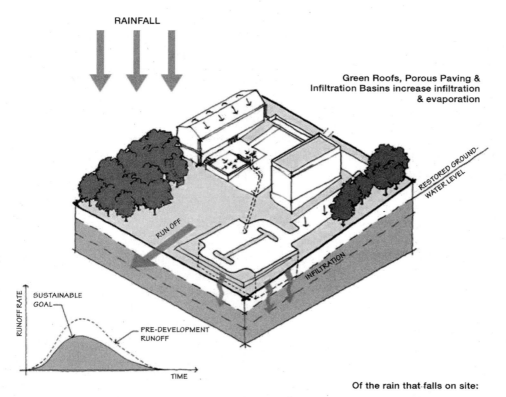

RAINFALL

Green Roofs, Porous Paving & Infiltration Basins increase infiltration & evaporation

RESTORED GROUNDWATER LEVEL

RUN OFF

INFILTRATION

RUNOFF RATE

SUSTAINABLE GOAL

PRE-DEVELOPMENT RUNOFF

TIME

SUSTAINABLE GOAL

Of the rain that falls on site:

1/3 runs off on the surface &
2/3 infiltrates to the groundwater table

Figure 4.1 Urban development dramatically expands hardscaping, increasing stormwater runoff and reducing natural infiltration and evaporation. Green roofs, porous paving, and infiltration basins can mitigate or reverse this expansion and maintain the natural systems while reducing infrastructure costs. *Courtesy Nitsch Engineering*

Embodied Water

We live in a world where water is collected and moved as a commodity—either directly as water or as food or product—many thousands of miles. Every object purchased contains *embodied water* in the same way it contains embodied energy and embodied carbon. A new car, on average, requires 39,090 gallons of water to make—as much as the average American consumes in a year.[8] A 2004 study in Australia estimated that a typical Australian house represents about 15 years worth of operational water—15 years of water for cooking, cleaning, washing, drinking, toilet flushing, and gardening, all embedded within a single home.[9] Imagine the water required to create a new high-rise building.

The Drive for Competitive Advantage Leads to Water Benefits

"Eco-efficiency, a microeconomic objective, focuses on reducing the amount of water, energy, chemicals, and raw materials used per unit of output. Eco-efficiency is motivated not only by environmental concerns but also by prospects of financial savings through reduced energy and water bills, less money spent on raw materials and fewer regulatory hurdles.

Swiss-based ST Microelectronics cut electricity use 28 percent and water use 45 percent in 2003 and reported saving $133 million. DuPont committed to keeping energy use flat no matter how much production increased, which has reportedly saved it more than $2 billion over the past decade. Advanced Micro Devices tracks kilowatt-hours per manufacturing index and reports a 60 percent reduction from 1999 to 2005.

Although motivated by the need to innovate and increase profitability, competitiveness, and market shares, these measures have all had the added benefit of decreasing water use and limiting pollution."

Source: Worldwatch Institute 2008.[10]

4.2 WATERSHEDS, STORMWATER, AND SITE DESIGN

"A watershed is an area of land that drains into a common water source. Because watersheds connect and encompass terrestrial, freshwater, and coastal ecosystems, they perform a wide variety of valuable services, including the supply and purification of fresh water, the provision of habitat that safeguards fisheries and biological diversity, the sequestering of carbon that helps mitigate climatic change, and the support of recreation and tourism. In the parlance of ecological economics, watersheds are natural assets that deliver a stream of goods and services to society."

—*"Watershed Protection: Capturing the Benefits of Nature's Water Supply Services"*[11]

Water forces us to think in terms of ecosystems not arbitrary site or regional boundaries. Utilizing natural filtration of water by protecting the watersheds that supply drinking water allows large urban areas such as Boston, Seattle, and New York City to avoid the costs of expensive water-filtration plants. New York City is avoiding $6 billion in capital costs and $300 million in annual operating costs by spending $15 billion for multifaceted agreements with private land owners in the watershed that supplies its drinking water.[12]

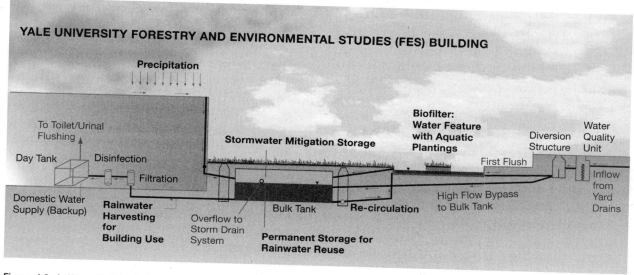

Figure 4.2 At Kroon Hall, the building that houses Yale University's Forestry and Environmental Studies program, a rainwater-harvesting system channels water from the roof and grounds to a garden in the south courtyard, where aquatic plants filter out sediment and contaminants. This graywater, held in underground storage tanks, is pumped back into the building for flushing toilets and is used for irrigation. The system avoids the use of an estimated 500,000 gallons annually of potable water from the New Haven system and lowers overall burden on city sewers by reducing the amount of storm runoff from the site. *Courtesy Nitsch Engineering*

"Providing public water and sewer (a government enterprise) is the second highest category of local government spending next to public education. More than $82 billion was spent in 2005 on water and sewer services and infrastructure, and from 1992 to 2005 total expenditures exceeded $841 billion."

—*Richard F. Anderson*[13]

Cities are also rethinking approaches to stormwater and the associated costs. Developed land creates an impervious barrier from buildings and paving, forcing a constructed collection system. Costs are not only for infrastructure and water purification, but the resulting ecosystem degradation and health issues. The leading cause of water pollution in the United States is not industry, but surface water runoff—not just from agricultural land, where surface water collects pesticides, but from lawns, roads, and parking lots, including the flooding of overloaded stormwater systems that combine with sewage. In addition to waste and chemicals, many millions of gallons of petroleum find their way into rivers, lakes, bays, and the ocean from individual vehicles, runoff, and careless disposal.[14]

Green Infrastructure

Greening of cities treats precipitation as an asset instead of a liability. Experience in many cities has shown that green infrastructure can be cost-competitive with conventional stormwater systems. Environmental benefits include improved water and air quality, reduction of radiant hot surfaces, and a more appealing urban setting.[15] Strategies vary according to climatic zone, but are all structured around the utilization of natural systems to manage and utilize stormwater.

The City of Chicago has established itself as a leader in this movement, both in policies and in education. As part of a city greening initiative, Chicago has built 90 miles of landscaped medians, refurbished more than 100 miles of streetscapes, planted a half-million new trees, and created more than 200 acres of parks and open spaces.[16] The Chicago Center for Neighborhood Technology (see Chapter 2) offers an online booklet, *Water: From Trouble to Treasure* (available at http://greenvalues.cnt.org) that provides guidance for creating natural environments that capture and utilize rainwater on even the smallest of sites by replacing impervious paving with more permeable materials and creating multiple catchment areas around street trees and parking areas.

Permeable Paving

Chicago has a program to green its public alleys, which in aggregate represent approximately 3,500 acres of paved surface, the equivalent of five mid-size regional airports. Replacing the impervious pavement with pavers or pervious paving set on stone beds provides a natural way for water to filter into the ground, recharging the water table instead of becoming polluted runoff. The pervious pavements and pavers also tend to reflect heat instead of absorbing it, which keeps the city cooler on hot days and reduces the demand for air conditioning, which in turn reduces the heat exhausted by air-conditioning systems.

Studies at the University of New Hampshire Stormwater Center (http://unh.edu/erg/cstev) demonstrate that pervious paving systems—everything from porous concrete mixtures to bricks made from recycled rubber—have the added benefit of facilitating snowmelt, which lowers the amount of salts and chemicals required in winter and reduces removal costs. Conversely, research has also found that the sealcoat used as a maintenance technique on traditional parking lots and driveways dramatically increases the polyaromatic hydrocarbons—more commonly known as PAHs and found in diesel and crude oil—that otherwise enter waterways from stormwater runoff. PAHs are considered carcinogenic.[17]

Low-Impact Site Design

Provides for:

Conservation of natural hydrology, trees, vegetation

Minimized impervious surfaces

Dispersal of stormwater runoff

Conservation of stream and wetland buffers

Ecological landscaping

Water distribution

LID techniques to reduce stormwater runoff and to treat non-point source pollution such as:

- Site-planning techniques (e.g., narrower roads, conserved natural areas, preserved natural areas, preserved natural depressions/topography)
- Dry wells for rooftop runoff
- Grassed (vegetated) swales
- Filter buffer strips
- Bioretention areas
- Sand/organic filters
- Permeable pavers
- Green roofs
- Rain barrels and cisterns
- Stormwater planters

Massachusetts Smart Growth Toolkit, www.mass.gov/envir/[18]

Figure 4.3 The Clipper Mill development in Baltimore, Maryland, reactivated a long-underused 17.5-acre site with five deteriorating buildings in a mixed-use community. The project addressed the environmental remediation of a brownfield site and integrated new strategies in water management. A 1,600-square-foot green roof forms the floor of an open-air atrium, lowering temperatures in the building and reducing and purifying stormwater runoff. An office parking lot employs a porous paving system, and water-saving fixtures are used throughout the complex. *Rick Lippenholtz photo, courtesy Struever Bros. Eccles & Rouse*

Biofiltration and Bioretention

There are many names for areas that gather stormwater and allow it to soak slowly into the ground while being filtered by native plants. Most of the pollutant removal occurs when the plants physically block the flow, slowing it and allowing the contaminants to settle out. Sometimes called rainwater gardens, the areas can be effective even when quite small. They are designed to sit slightly below grade and be filled with native plants that can thrive under typical local rainfall. The sunken area of the garden captures precipitation and allows it to filter into the ground. The plants help filter pollutants from the water. Locating any site water away from buildings avoids below-grade moisture problems, but properly located rain gardens can help slow rushing stormwater while providing a natural habitat that encourages biodiversity.

"People who would never come to a meeting about stormwater will flock to a rain garden presentation. We lure them in with the prospect of beautiful rain gardens, and they leave feeling empowered to protect their local waterways; and that was the last thing on their minds when they came to us."

—Patricia Pennell, Western Michigan Environmental Action Council[19]

Constructed wetlands are artificial versions of natural wetlands that use reeds and wetland vegetation to filter stormwater. Filter strips are areas of land slightly sloped and planted with native vegetation that collects stormwater pollutants as the water moves across the strip. Swales are wide ditches with sloped banks and a bottom planted with filtering turf. As the case studies show, one site often combines a series of filtration and retention areas.

Infiltration

Infiltration systems temporarily store water either above or below grade and allow it to percolate slowly into the ground. This not only reduces peak flows but converts 98 percent of blue water (surface water) into green water (ground water). It also cools stormwater and removes most of the nitrogen and copper. Infiltration is sometimes preferred because the water is cooled as it flows through the ground, reducing detrimental thermal effects on aquatic systems.

Above-ground retention ponds or trenches are recessed areas filled with rocks and gravel that create holding areas for the water. Dry wells or French drains are deeper retention basins that capture water directly from roofs.

Green Roofs

A highly publicized green roof on the historic Chicago City Hall and passionate advocacy by nonprofit organizations such as Green Roofs for Healthy Cities (www.greenroofs.org) have helped promote gardens on flat roofs as another strategy for managing urban stormwater and for keeping cities cooler in summer. The surface temperature of planted roofs has been measured as 50 percent lower than adjacent unplanted roofs. Lower surface temperatures allow architects and building owners to scale back heating and ventilating (HVAC) systems in response to lower air temperature at intake valves. HVAC savings attributed to reduced temperatures fostered by Chicago City Hall's green roof have reached 10 percent of total use. Green roofs also add aesthetic appeal, extend the life of a roof (depending on installation methods) and provide bird and butterfly habitat.[20]

The ability to add green roof or wall systems to existing buildings depend on existing structural and material characteristics. Since the failure of roof systems dominate building insurance claims, some engineers remain skeptical about adding moisture-retaining ma-

Figure 4.4 The green roof at the Eastern Village Cohousing development in Silver Springs, Maryland (see Chapter 8), takes advantage of the flat roof and robust structure of the four-story, concrete-frame building constructed for offices in the 1950s. The roof provides rainwater runoff control, thermal protection for the building, and reduced heat island effect for the site. The development devotes a portion of the roof to community gardens and recreation. *EDG Architects, LLC*

terials above a roof, but evolving systems, including removable trays, offer other options for protecting existing roof fabric. Sometimes, as is the case with the Chicago City Hall, one roof supports multiple systems, allowing deeper soil and more expansive plantings at areas of greatest structural capacity.

The merits of green roofs for building insulation, energy-use reduction, natural habitat, improved air quality, stormwater collection, and cooling of urban areas have become so accepted that in 2008, New York City created a significant tax credit, estimated to compensate 25 percent of total cost, for building owners who treat at least 50 percent of a flat roof area as a green roof. The measure was championed by a group dedicated to protecting the waters around Manhattan. "Each 10,000 square foot green roof can capture between 6,000 and 12,000 gallons of water in each storm event," according to Dr. Paul S. Mankiewicz, executive director of the Gaia Institute and board member of the New York City Soil and Water Conservation District. "This is rainfall that will never enter the combined sewer. At the same time, the evaporation of this rainfall will produce the equivalent of between a thousand and two thousand tons of air conditioning, enough heat removal to noticeably cool 10 acres of the city. This is a management practice that increases biodiversity and can literally add enjoyable landscape to all the boroughs of New York."[21]

Heat Island Mitigation

The higher summer temperatures in urban areas that result from dense dark absorptive materials like roofs and paving that radiate collected heat are well documented. Most green rating systems encourage the use of light-reflecting (high-albedo) materials on roofs and paving to decrease heat island effect even when plantings and/or shading aren't possible. High-rise buildings, narrow streets, and vehicle emissions also contribute to increased urban temperatures, which have very real costs in energy and health. The Lawrence Berkeley National Laboratory has estimated that

Figure 4.5 The green roof at 17 Gordon Avenue in South Providence, Rhode Island, is part of the strategy that helped the building, a business incubator owned and operated by the South Providence Development Corporation, secure a U.S. Green Building Council LEED Silver certification. Green roofs can be quite small and installed in pallets that are easy to place atop an existing roof. Structural capabilities should always be checked, but many of the systems are lightweight. *Photo: richardmccaffrey.com*

the "increase in air temperature is responsible for 5 to 10 percent of urban peak electric demand for air conditioning use, and as much as 20 percent of population-weighted smog concentrations in urban areas."[22] During the 1995 Chicago heat wave, over 600 people died in a five-day period.[23]

Xeriscaping

Xeriscaping represents a change in attitude about plantings in both gardens and yards to utilize plant schemes that are drought-tolerant and native to an area. Ideally, this includes the removal of turf, which is water- and chemical-intensive. This can represent a conflict in historic settings, where gardens and lawns may be part of the heritage, but water-reduction strategies are still possible. More drought-tolerant turf can be installed and above-ground watering systems replaced with drip systems. Switching from flood irrigation to drip can improve water-use efficiency by as much as 40 percent,[24] offsetting the cost of new systems. Moisture sensors instead of automatic timers can turn watering systems on only when needed as well as at night to keep evaporation to a minimum.

Edible Landscapes

Thinking more holistically about our environmental impact has contributed to a resurgence of locally produced food in urban areas, on rooftops and in areas that once might have been considered too small for a garden. It takes very little space for herbs, a squash plant, or tomatoes, and a decorative tree or bush can also bear fruit.

Phytoremediation

Phytoremediation involves the use of plants to contain, degrade, or remove toxic chemicals and pollutants from soil or water. A technique still in the early stages of development, it may someday prove effective in treating large areas of urban land contaminated with

Figure 4.6 Prior to renovation, more than 90 percent of the site of the Eastern Village Cohousing development in Silver Springs, Maryland (see Chapter 8), was impervious. Conversion of the central parking court to a garden and the provision of a green roof decreased the hardscape by 54 percent. The existing storm drainage system was repaired, with the green roof acting as a filtration and detention device. The green wall shades the face of the building, reducing cooling loads in summer at the same time that it creates a place for community. *EDG Architects, LLC*

lead and other pollutants. Scientists are investigating phytoremediation's potential with such plants as sunflower, ragweed, cabbage and geranium, as well as less familiar species. Many disposal and metal recovery-methods are still being explored, including sun-drying, composting, and leaching.[25]

Advantages and Disadvantages of Phytoremediation

ADVANTAGES

- Treatment is environmentally friendly, cost-effective, and aesthetically pleasing.
- Metals absorbed by the plants may be extracted from harvested plant biomass and then recycled.
- Phytoremediation appears effective for a large variety of contaminants.
- Phytoremediation may reduce the entry of contaminants into the environment by preventing their leakage into the groundwater systems.

DISADVANTAGES

- It relies on natural cycle of plants and therefore takes time.
- Phytoremediation works best when the contamination is within reach of plant roots, typically 3 to 6 feet underground for herbaceous plants and 10 to 15 feet for trees.
- Some plants absorb high levels of poisonous metals, making them a potential risk to the food chain if animals feed on them.[26]

4.3 WATER AND ENERGY SYSTEMS

"Prolonged U.S. Southwest drought is affecting the cooling water for over 24 of the nation's 104 nuclear energy reactors."

—"The Energy Challenge"[27]

We cannot separate water from energy. We consume massive amounts of energy for our water infrastructure and massive amounts of water to generate energy.

The two greatest users of freshwater are agriculture and power plants. Thermal power plants—those that consume coal, oil, natural gas, or uranium—generate more than 90 percent of U.S. electricity, and they are water hogs.[28] According to the U.S. Geological Survey, thermoelectric-power accounts for 39 percent of total freshwater withdrawals in the United States and 52 percent of all fresh surface-water withdrawals.[29]

Power plants draw 39 billion gallons of clean drinking water from aquifers daily, equivalent to the daily drinking water requirements of 62 billion people, about 10 times the Earth's population.[30] In making the case for wind energy, Paul Gipe, author of *Wind Energy Comes of Age,* states that while wind uses only occasional water for cleaning the blades, conventional power plants consume the following amounts of water (through evaporative loss, not including water that is captured and treated for further use):[31]

- Nuclear plants consume the most water: 0.62 gallons per kWh (nuclear plants contribute 19 percent of all electricity generated)
- Coal-fired plants consume 0.49 gallons per kWh (49 percent of all electricity generated)
- Oil-fired plants consume 0.42 gallons per kWh (2 percent of all electricity generated)
- Combined-cycle natural gas power plants consume 0.25 gallons per kWh (22 percent of all electricity generated)[32]

Hydropower and first-generation biofuel are even more intensive in the consumption of water, using 30 and 100 times more water than coal respectively.[33] Hydroelectricity accounts for an estimated 3.8 billion gallons of water loss per day.[34] Although considered a renewable source of energy, hydroelectricity is the subject of an ongoing debate about the amount of methane released by reservoirs and the water moving through the turbines. The source of 7 percent[35] of total

U.S. electricity production, it may not be as environmentally sound as once thought.

Transmission inefficiency multiplies the volume of water needed to create electricity. Only about 10 percent of electricity produced actually reaches end users, so each single kWh of energy used in a home—the electricity required to keep one 100-watt lightbulb burning overnight (ten hours)—requires anywhere from 25 to 180 gallons of water to produce, the equivalent of anywhere from a sink full of water to three full bathtubs.

"Like energy, water is used for a variety of purposes. And like energy, the efficiency of water use can be greatly improved by changes in technologies and processes. Unlike oil, however, fresh water is the *only* substance capable of meeting certain needs. Thus, while other energy sources can substitute for oil, water has no substitutes for many uses."
—*Meena Palaniappan and Peter H. Gleick*[36]

4.4 WATER AND MECHANICAL SYSTEMS

Mechanical systems and leakage account for as much as half the potable water consumption in commercial and institutional buildings. Audits of commercial buildings in Australia indicate that cooling-tower consumption represents 31 percent of water usage, and leakage from taps, urinals, piping, valves and pumps accounts for a substantial 26 percent.[37] The U.S. Federal Energy Management Program also flags leaks as a significant issue but estimates the loss for a 1940s military facility at 10 percent.[38] The National Renewable Energy Laboratory (NREL) in Golden, Colorado, attributes 44 percent of its current water usage to cooling towers, 19 percent to evaporative cooling, and 7 percent to single-pass cooling.[39]

Of the 14 best management practices (BMP) for water efficiency outlined by the U.S. Federal Energy Management Program, three address mechanical systems directly and several others address mechanical systems under broader topics. The practices, which provide guidance for replacement, retrofits, and operations and maintenance, are:

BMP # 1—Water Management Planning

BMP # 2—Information and Education Programs

BMP # 3—Distribution System Audits, Leak Detection and Repair

BMP # 4—Water-Efficient Landscaping

BMP # 5—Water-Efficient Irrigation

BMP # 6—Toilets and Urinals

BMP # 7—Faucets and Showerheads

BMP # 8—Boiler/Steam Systems

BMP # 9—Single-Pass Cooling Equipment

BMP #10—Cooling Tower Management

BMP #11—Commercial Kitchen Equipment

BMP #12—Laboratory/Medical Equipment

BMP #13—Other Water Use

BMP #14—Alternate Water Sources

These practices are available online. The Federal Energy Management Program is part of the U.S. Department of Energy, Energy Efficiency, and Renewable Energy site (www1.eere.energy.gov/femp).

The American Society of Heating, Refrigerating and Air-Conditioning Engineers (ASHRAE) maintains www.engineeringforsustainability.org, a stand-alone website about sustainable design. The site serves as a virtual home for ASHRAE's *Green Guide* and *Green Tips,* sidebars on techniques, processes, measures, or

Figure 4.7 The landscape plan at S. R. Crown Hall (see Chapter 10), designed by Mies van der Rohe and completed in 1956, was integral to the cooling strategy for the building, with trees planted on the western side so that long shadows stretched across the structure in the afternoon and significantly reduced solar gain. Operable vents at the perimeter of the building combined with an open floor plan allow fresh air to flow through the space during the day and bring cool air in at night. *Photography by Todd Eberle*

systems with links to additional sources. Of 29 Green Tips, five directly concern water conservation:

Green Tip #27—Rainwater Harvesting

Green Tip #25—Point-of-Use Domestic Hot Water Heaters

Green Tip #24—Graywater Systems

Green Tip #23—Water-Conserving Fixtures

ASHRAE Green Tip #14 describes the use of chemical-free water treatment with pulse-powered technology. Developed by the food industry for pasteurization, this method eliminates chemical use in water treatment. Most chemically controlled cooling towers operate at two to four cycles of concentration. Chemical-free methods often allow six to eight cycles of concentration, with an annual reduction in water usage costs and associated environmental impacts, thanks to reduced water volumes and chemicals. As with all design, of course, no one solution fits every circumstance. The complexity of water treatment in cooling towers must be managed by a treatment expert to address health and equipment issues affected by water conditions.

Figure 4.8 Rain gardens, porous paving, and stormwater retention at the Portland Food Co-op (see Chapter 1) capture stormwater and allow it to filter into the ground instead of flowing into storm sewers. The leading cause of water pollution in the United States is runoff that carries petroleum products and other urban contaminants directly into the waterways rather than allowing its filtration by natural methods. *Cheyenne Glasgow photo, courtesy People's Food Co-op*

4.5 WATER AND SEWAGE SYSTEMS

"For the last 100 years, we've basically done everything wrong. The toilet is simply a receptacle on one end of a huge chain of stupidity created in a misguided effort to protect the public from disease and embarrassment. By using water to convey waste over long distances to industrial treatment facilities, we've committed two great environmental sins. One, we've polluted our water supply: Huge amounts of energy and toxic chemicals are required to make it clean again. Two, we've become the only species on Earth that disrupts nature's nutrient cycle because we destroy those found in our waste. An entire industry has arisen just to replace them."

—Jason R. McLennon,
Cascadia Region Green Building Council[40]

The management of human waste represents a major expense in land and infrastructure. Using highly treated drinking water to remove human waste, increases the cost substantially. Water scarcity and rising urban density are changing the approach to amenity uses of water—toilets, sinks, laundry, dishwashers, and showers. Appliances and fixtures that use less water are becoming more effective and more common. In many areas, they are now required by law. Not using water at all for human waste removal and/or managing waste within a building or site is also being explored. Some cities are developing systems that treat human waste as a resource. A combination of approaches often represents the most appropriate solution, depending on location. Combined approaches will probably require dual piping for a hierarchy of water flows, from clean to gray to black (refer to section 4.6) as the new norm.

Low-flow Fixtures

Installing low-flow fixtures has become commonplace and is often required by building codes. Replacing an old toilet with either a low-flush or dual-flush system can reduce water usage by as much as 75 percent. This is a cost-effective strategy, since toilets account for the largest part of the amenity category. Aerating faucets and showerheads are also effective. Appliances continue to incorporate new technologies to become more environmentally friendly; Reuters reported in 2008 the development of a clothes-washing machine intended to use less than 2 percent of the water and energy required by a conventional machine.[41]

The 2004 Clean Watershed Needs Survey of the EPA estimates $202.5 billion is the nationwide capital investment needed to control wastewater pollution. This includes $134.4 billion for wastewater treatment and collection, $54.8 billion for combined sewer overflow corrections, and $9.0 billion for stormwater management.

—www.epa.gov[42]

Composting Toilets

Two tracks dominate the conversations about human waste: one concerns the water used to move waste—reducing its volume and finding substitutes for highly treated potable water—and the other addresses human waste's possibilities as an organic resource. Although hardly a new idea, the latter idea has been sidetracked by a single-minded focus on sanitation and health. Introducing eight companies that sell various composting toilets, the website www.buildinggreen.com describes the advantages of the process as "dramatic reductions in water use, reduced groundwater pollution or sewage-treatment impacts, and a recycling of nutrients." Case studies in Chapter 1 (Harris Center for Conservation

Education) and Chapter 5 (S.T. Dana Building at the University of Michigan) both have composting toilets. The Vermont Law School in South Royalton, Vermont, has composting toilets in both new and historic buildings, including Debevoise Hall, an 1893 wood-framed Victorian building renovated and expanded in 2005.

"This 'flush and forget' attitude creates a new problem which we have to revisit."

—Jack Sim, founder of the World Toilet Organization[43]

Treatment Plants on the Site

Innovative environmental designer Dr. John Todd, pioneered the idea that sewage can be treated on site or in a greenhouse by replicating and accelerating the natural purification processes of streams, ponds, and marshes. Todd's Eco-Machine™ can be a tank-based system in a greenhouse or a combination with exterior constructed wetlands. Usually created as an attachment to a new building, such as Oberlin College's Lewis Center, an onsite natural treatment center could be attached or sited next to an historic building if the conditions allowed. Unlike low-water-use fixtures, which can and should always be installed, more complex approaches to water management and sewage are part of a whole-system decision process that identifies most appropriate opportunities for each project.

Treatment Plants in the Building

It is possible to install a sewage treatment plant inside a building that can produce nonpotable water for things like toilet flushing and a cooling tower. An example of an in-house system is found at The Solaire, a 28-story apartment building in New York City, completed in 2003. Renovations at a similar scale, which almost always include complete system replacement, could utilize the same system.

Sludge as a Resource

Since 1989, Austin, Texas, has used treated sewage sludge as part of a composted nutrient, Dillo Dirt™, that is sold back to the community for lawns and gardens. The compost includes all yard trimmings, which reduces landfill loads and provides a safe organic material that improves plant life and reduces the need for watering. Austin's biosolids management plant, Hornsby Bend, integrates the treatment of urban waste with the conservation, protection, and restoration of the ecology. The area is renowned as a birdwatching site. Treated biosolids not used in Dillo Dirt™ are applied to publicly owned farm land that produces hay, pecans and row crops. Water from the treatment ponds is used for irrigation.

4.6 CLOSING THE CIRCLE—REUSE, MANAGEMENT, EDUCATION, DELIGHT

"Good design and management should concentrate on developing an appreciation and understanding of where water comes from and where what you put down the drain goes..."

—Sandy Halliday[44]

Reusing water allows it to be employed in multiple ways before being returned to the natural system. Assuring multiple uses represents a creative way to conserve a scarce resource. Reuse takes three primary forms—keeping water within an existing system, such as water captured from condensate and used for cooling tower makeup water; salvaging less pure wa-

Figure 4.9 17 Gordon Avenue in South Providence, Rhode Island, converted a small parking area into a more sustainable environment by adding permeable paving, xeriscape landscaping, and natural areas to collect stormwater. Sliver parks help reduce stormwater runoff but also reduce heat island effect, which benefits pedestrians. Lower air temperatures mean reduced cooling loads and less operation of heat-producing air conditioners. *Photo: richardmccaffrey.com*

ter for another application, such as sink water that as graywater can be used to flush toilets; and capturing water from roofs and elsewhere on site before it can enter a stormwater system or the ground.

Rainwater Capture—Legal Issues

Using and "capturing" the rainwater or precipitation that falls on a building site is a part of many green buildings, including routing roof runoff into storage cisterns for later use either in graywater systems or garden irrigation. Trinity Church in Boston, Massachusetts (see Chapter 1), stores stormwater in drywells to supplement groundwater that protects the integrity of wood friction piles under the building. The legality of rainwater capture depends on location. Some communities require that roof downspouts be tied to stormwater collection systems, and in many parts of the western United States it is illegal to sequester the

water that falls on a property because century-old water laws allow ownership of the water downstream.

> "It is the proper destiny of every considerable stream in the west to become an irrigating ditch."
> —Mary Austin, The Land of Little Rain, 1903[45]

Graywater Reuse

Graywater includes filtered, untreated wastewater from washing machines, showers, bathtubs, and lavatory faucets. Collected in separated drain lines, it can be reused for irrigation or flushing of toilets. Regulations on the reuse of water, how it is treated, and what it can be used for vary from community to community, but residential-size graywater systems are widely available and include a simple system that collects sink water for flushing an adjacent toilet.

Blackwater is water from sewage systems that can be captured within a building or on a site and treated for reuse for nonpotable applications. Because of the health risks, blackwater is also closely controlled, and the ability to capture and treat blackwater depends on local regulations.

"Water issues are, by nature, interdisciplinary and multifaceted."

—*Yale Center for Environmental Law & Policy*[46]

Air-Conditioning Condensate Recovery

Condensate generated by air-conditioning equipment, which once might have been disposed of as wastewater, is now more commonly recovered and piped directly into cooling towers as make-up water, or it can be stored for use in irrigation and toilet flushing.

Cooling Tower Blowdown Reuse

Water is regularly removed from cooling towers in a process called blowdown in order to reduce concentrated contaminants, minerals, and sometimes bacteria. The water, after treatment, can be used for irrigation, but only if the mineral concentration is not too high.

Municipal Graywater Systems

The WateReuse Association, originally formed in California in 1990, became a national organization in 2000. It maintains a national database that documents 1,600 reclaimed-water systems operating in 25 states. Nonpotable recycled water uses a separate pipeline system and is kept completely separate from the drinking water pipeline. Nationally, the U.S. Environmental Protection Agency's *Guidelines for Water Reuse*, published in 2004, addresses recommended practices for reclaimed water use.[47]

Municipal Water Recycling

In the United States, Orange County, California (2008 Stockholm Water Award recipient), focused on reuse in its groundwater replenishment system, which diverts and purifies highly treated sewer water that was previously discharged into the ocean. It returns the cleaned water to the groundwater basin. The system will provide enough additional water to meet the needs of 500,000 more people without diminishing groundwater resources for current users (2.3 million).

Source: Adapted from Benoit and Comeau 2005 and www.siwi.org/sa/node.asp?node=77.[48]

Water Management

In the bigger picture, water management ties a building and facility directly to the health of the watershed and the entire planet. The Commonwealth of Australia, a country intimately familiar with water shortages, offers a commonsense hierarchy of decisions that builds on the three Rs of reduce, reuse, and recycle.

1. *Rectify* leaks.
2. *Review*—Is the process/activity really necessary? Is it necessary to use water, or is there a cost-effective alternative?
3. *Reduce*—Could water be used more efficiently? Is there an alternative process/activity that could be used?
4. *Reuse*—Could the water be treated/filtered and reused within the process/activity?
5. *Recycle*—Can the water be recycled for use elsewhere (e.g., process/gray water/groundwater recharge)?[49]

Systems Approaches and Performance Contracting

Between 1998 and 2005, Eastern Illinois University reduced annual water consumption 49 percent from 157 million gallons to 81 million gallons, while resident student population stayed steady at around 4,500. A holistic and systematic approach included upgrading equipment, changing operations, and educating users. The university took these actions to cut water use:

1998—Installed a central campus chilled-water loop

1999—Installed west campus chilled-water loop and lower-flow (2.5 gpm) showerheads in residence halls

2001—Under a performance contract, replaced five steam-driven chillers with electric units and installed a south campus chilled-water loop

2002—Under a performance contract, replaced 1,117 toilets, 1,469 faucet aerators and 118 washing machines with low-consumption units, blended in new electric chillers

2003—Replaced the Physical Science Building cooling tower, ran more electric chillers for load, started water-chemistry initiative

2004—Replaced Carman Building cooling tower, replaced O'Brien Stadium turf with artificial surface, continued water-chemistry program

During this period the university's water rates rose by 42 percent, but its actual costs declined 49 percent. Eastern Illinois saved 385 million gallons of drinking water, worth $2,825,000 in 2005 rates.[50]

Education and Delight

"To stick your hands into the river is to the feel the cords that bind the earth together in one piece."
—*Barry Holston Lopez,*
River Notes: The Dance of Herons[51]

Water is central to all that humans do. Water will never be a single-issue problem nor lend itself to a uniform solution. This resource offers untold opportunities to introduce us and continually reintroduce us to the natural world. Once you understand the journey that the drops take to get there, it's hard to remain casual about the water pouring from a spigot.

"Because the demands on water are many and diverse, water management needs to be guided by broader social and economic development objectives that clarify expected outcomes."[52]

The Welcome and Admission Center at Roger H. Perry Hall (Champlain College)

Burlington, VT

Current Owner: Champlain College

Building Type: Student Services/Admissions

Original Building Construction: 1860

Historic Designation: South Willard Street (National) Historic District

Restoration/Renovation Completion: 2010

Square Footage: 29,900 ft^2

Percentage Renovated: 40% + 60% new construction

"If we can teach our students the dangers of certitude, if we can instill perpetual curiosity in them, if we can make our students intellectually pugnacious, and if we can give them marketable skills, then we will have fulfilled the promise of a Champlain education."

—*President David Finney, Champlain College*

PROJECT DESCRIPTION

Champlain College is a small, innovative urban college set on a steep site in a National Historic District of Burlington, Vermont. The college has demonstrated a high level of commitment to community amenities and the stewardship of the historic properties. The college voluntarily provided a 50-year open space easement to the city to allow public access to its lawn, and meeting areas within Champlain building are available for community functions. Perry Hall consists of a nineteenth-century house with an addition on a multiacre lot with views of Lake Champlain. The house is relatively intact, with rich historic finishes that have been fully restored.

Programmatic needs for offices, assembly, and student services are met in two wings of new construction that flank the original house and are set behind it to maintain the residential character of the streetscape. This arrangment maintains the original views from the house and sets the wings on an east–west axis for maximum solar gain and daylighting on the southern exposure.

Figure 4.10 The 1860 house, seen before renovation, is part of the South Willard Street National Historic District. The substantial addition sits as far behind the original building as possible in order to maintain the residential character of the street. Champlain College elected to completely restore both the interior and exterior of the house rather than execute the gut renovation common in many "green" projects. The original rooms are used for reception and shared offices. © Goody Clancy

The office wings are clear-span to provide long life and loose fit. The design intends to provide an exterior "area of delight" for each part of the building, with a south-facing balcony protected by a green screen, an outdoor terrace, and two outdoor porches that overlook the lake.

Originally designed following the guidelines of the Athena Eco-Calculator™, the project was registered for LEED in 2009 and is expected to achieve a Platinum certification.

Site and Water

Preproject planning afforded the opportunity to explore new technologies in addressing, capturing, and controlling release and redirection of stormwater. The site is designed to mitigate and treat stormwater runoff from other parts of campus, as well as to handle runoff generated on-site. Subsurface detention beneath the lawn releases stormwater slowly after a storm to reduce peak flows. The water passes through a subsurface gravel wetland with wetland plants at grade on the downhill end of the site, a process that removes pollutants, before reaching the city's storm sewer system. Water is treated below ground to avoid ponding, and positive drainage away from building entrances reduces the potential for ice.

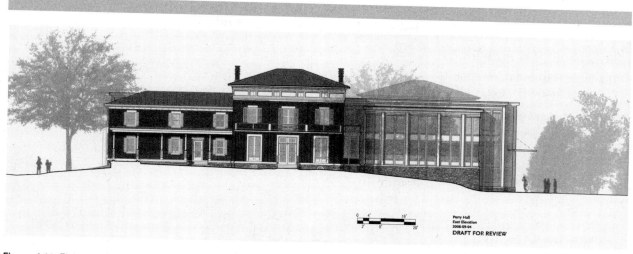

Figure 4.11 The new elevation to the right of the original building sits behind the existing building, maintaining itshistoric facades. The design intentionally located new construction to protect views from the house to Lake Champlain. © *Goody Clancy*

Figure 4.12 The new spaces can accommodate meetings and presentations that overlook the lawn, which the college has made available to the community as common space. Every part of the building intentionally has an exterior "area of delight" that is easily accessible and provides views to Lake Champlain. © *Goody Clancy*

Walks, promenades, gates, and public areas are woven into the site to provide pedestrian-friendly flow and ambiance. The attention paid to the site during the project both physically repaired and enhanced the historic structure, while giving the site into a more public and engaging community role.

GREEN DESIGN ELEMENTS

The Welcome and Admission Center at Roger H. Perry Hall

Sustainable Sites and Water:
- Permeable pavement
- Green roof
- Constructed wetland
- Xeriscaping
- Bicycle parking
- Public transportation access
- Parking shuttle service
- Low-flow fixtures
- Green screen on south elevation

Energy and Atmosphere:
- Ground-sourced heat pumps
- Natural ventilation
- Automatic light sensors
- Thermal setback
- East-west orientation of additions
- Natural daylighting

Materials and Resources:
- Local materials (brick, stone, slate, wood)
- Recycled content
- Durable low-maintenance materials

Indoor Environment Quality:
- Daylighting and views
- Operable windows
- Low-VOC materials and finishes
- Demand-control ventilation
- CO_2 sensors
- Areas of delight (porches/terraces/lake views)
- Biophilic design—connection to nature

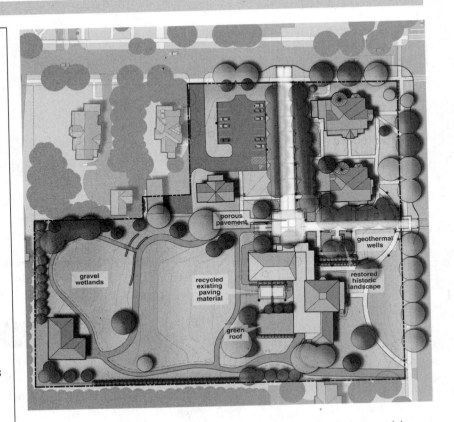

Figure 4.13 The site plan shows the large area of public lawn behind the house and the gravel wetlands at the lowest end of the site to allow natural filtration of stormwater. Other site features include recycled paving materials, porous pavements, restored historic landscape, and geothermal wells. The additions have green roofs and greenscreens shading the southern exposure. © *ORW Landscape Architects & Planners*

PROJECT TEAM, THE WELCOME AND ADMISSION CENTER AT ROGER H. PERRY HALL

Champlain College

Goody Clancy

Engelberth Construction

ORW Landscape Architects

Engineering Ventures

L.N. Consulting, Inc.

Llewellyn-Howley, Inc.

GeoDesign, Inc.

CX Associates

Liz Pritchett Associates

Collaborative Lighting

Rolf Jensen & Associates, Inc.

Chicago Center for Green Technology
Chicago, IL

Current Owner: Chicago Department of Environment

Building Type: Assembly/Commercial Office

Original Building Construction: 1952

Restoration/Renovation Completion: 2002

Square Footage: 40,000 ft^2

Percentage Renovated: 100%

Occupancy: 35 people (50 hrs/week) 100 visitors (2 hrs/week)

Recognition: LEED NC v1.0—Platinum

AIA/COTE Top Ten Green Projects 2003, Chicago Building Congress Merit Award for Rehab Construction 2003, ASHRAE Award for Engineering Accomplishment 2006

"The City of Chicago understands that it must engage its residents and provide them the necessary tools, information and resources to reduce our impact on all natural resources."

—*Suzanne Malec-McKenna, Commissioner of the Chicago Department of Environment.*

PROJECT DESCRIPTION

Located in one of the country's most ecologically aware cities, the renovation for the Chicago Center for Green Technology facilitates a plan to cut electrical power usage in Chicago by 20 percent in the next year through alternative energy sources. Other entities sharing the facility include GreenCorps Chicago, a city-run job-training program with a horticultural focus) and Spire Solar Chicago (a solar panel manufacturing/marketing company).

Figure 4.15 A wetland adjacent to the building and bioswales (the ditches located in the front of the parking areas) slow the flow of rainwater so that many contaminants can settle out of the water before it sinks into the ground or reaches sewers. Vegetation in the wetland and bioswales also helps filter debris out of the water. The wetland can hold large volumes of rainwater at a time and slowly release it to the ground during drier periods. *Okrent Associates, Inc.*

Figure 4.16 Cisterns connected to the building downspouts catch rainwater and reduce the amount of water flowing into the sewers. The four cisterns have a 12,000-gallon water-storage capacity and hold the captured water for irrigation. Native plants were selected to minimize maintenance and water needs. *© Farr Associates Architecture | Planning | Preservation, Chicago, Illinois*

Figure 4.14 Light-colored paving, along with extensive tree coverage, helps decrease the heat island effect in parking and walking areas. A green roof on part of the building supports the same goal through evapotranspiration; the rest of the roof is painted white to decrease heat absorbance. *© Farr Associates Architecture | Planning | Preservation, Chicago, Illinois*

Site and Water

A four-part water-conservation system reduces the amount of water flowing into sewers, which helps avoid water pollution and eases pressure on the sewer system itself. One-third of the building is covered by a green roof. Four 12,000-gallon cisterns capture rainwater from the roof and store it for irrigating the landscape.

Rainwater on the roof that is not collected by the green roof or in the cisterns flows directly into the landscape via conventional downspouts. Rainwater falling on the ground at CCGT flows from parking lots and sidewalks into bioswales, which feed into a wetland. On a rainy day, an average of 3 inches of rain falls on the site within a 24-hour period. Stormwater runoff is reduced by 50 percent, diverting 85,000 gallons of water.

GREEN DESIGN ELEMENTS

Chicago Center for Green Technology

Sustainable Sites:
- Public transportation proximity
- Bicycle accommodation
- Electric-car charging station
- Constructed wetland
- Green roof
- Xeriscaping
- Bioswales

Water Efficiency:
- Graywater system
- Low-flow plumbing fixtures

Energy and Atmosphere:
- Photovoltaic system
- Ground-source geothermal heat pump
- Displacement ventilation
- Low-energy fluorescent lighting

Materials and Resources:
- Recycled materials
- Locally manufactured materials

Indoor Environment Quality:
- Hazardous material decontamination (asbestos)
- Low-VOC materials and finishes

Additional Features:
- Canola-oil-run elevator
- Occupant recycling program

Energy

The addition of solar panels, both on the roof and as shading devices on the south-facing windows of the new construction, is estimated to replace 20 percent of annual electrical power usage. With the addition of the energy saved by using a ground-source heating and cooling system, the building requires 40 percent less energy than a building of equivalent size (a saving of just under $30,000 each year).

Materials

Interior green elements include an elevator that runs on vegetable oil as opposed to petrochemical-based oil that is harmful to the environment, fluorescent light sensors, recycled, and locally sourced materials. 100 percent of the existing structural shell was reused, reducing the need for new materials as well as the amount of waste; the project achieved a total reduction of about 83 percent in construction debris.

DESIGN TEAM

Farr Associates Architecture and Urban Design

IBC Engineering Services

OWP&P Architects

Prisco, Serena, Sturm Architects

Sieben Energy Associates

Site Design Group

Spectrum Engineering, Inc.

Spire Solar Chicago

Terra Engineering

Tylk Gustafson Reckers Wilson and Andrews, LLC

Blackstone Station Office Renovation
Cambridge, MA

Current Owner: Harvard University Operations Services

Building Type: Academic/Offices

Original Construction: 1887–1929

Renovation Completion: 2006

Square Footage: 42,000 ft^2

Percentage Renovated: 100%

Occupancy: 142 people (40 hrs/week)

Recognition: LEED NC v2.0/2.1—Platinum, Honor Award for Sustainable Design 2007, Build New England Merit Award 2007, Go Green Award 2007

"This project is not only a great historic (and now LEED Platinum) building, but it shows how an effective planning process and leadership commitment can achieve phenomenal results."

—Harvard Green Campus Newsletter, *Spring 2007, Volume 10*

PROJECT DESCRIPTION

Originally built as part of a coal-fired electricity plant in the 1890s and converted in 2006 into the first consolidated headquarters for Harvard's University Operations Services (UOS), the Blackstone office renovation epitomizes the doctrines of green design in a LEED Platinum-certified facility. Harvard and its Green Campus Initiative regard the sustainable design and construction practices established in this project as "the model for use in future Harvard projects."

Indoor Environmental Quality

The primary challenge was to transform three of the historic masonry structures on the site into a single, state-of-the-art sustainable building that would provide a collaborative workspace while ensuring occupant health and comfort. The design solution maximizes the principles of sustainable design in a modern facility. A vertical light-slot connects two previously detached buildings, delivering daylight to newly discovered interior

Figure 4.17 The landscape solution is integral to a design that combined three separate nineteenth-century warehouses into one modern, energy-efficient and sustainably built complex. Earth excavated during construction was used to create a landscaped courtyard, and an asphalt parking lot was removed to allow the addition of trees, grass, and native plants. No site irrigation is required. A sloping walkway, created from earth otherwise destined for landfill, connects the sidewalk to the main entrance. © 2007 Richard Mandelkorn

space and announcing a contemporary intervention within the original framework. Similarly, a large skylight canopy allows light to penetrate an interior three-story communicative stairway. Use of translucent and transparent materials diffuses natural light throughout interior spaces. The open floor plan encourages interaction among occupants and affords an outdoor view to over 90 percent of the workstations. The original timber frame and decking are incorporated into the interior design. The building also features operable windows to allow occupants to use natural ventilation to maintain a comfortable working environment.

Energy

A valance unit system heats and cools spaces through convection, and the university purchases energy certificates for 100 percent of the site's demand as well. Ground-source heat pumps provide for both heating and cooling. The building is designed to be 42 percent more efficient than a code-compliant building. Other eco-friendly design elements include energy-efficient equipment such as a hydraulic-fluid-free elevator, use of low-VOC materials, occupancy and lighting sensors.

Water and Site

Xeriscaping eliminated the use of potable water outdoors by introducing drought-tolerant plants; earth excavated from the site was relocated to sculpt a courtyard. The addition of bioswales and permeable pavement mixed with green spaces reduces heat islands and stormwater runoff up to 37 percent. Dual-flush toilets, waterless urinals, and other low-flow plumbing fixtures reduce indoor water consumption by 43 percent.

Sustainable Construction

Nearly 100 percent of construction waste was recycled, virtually eliminating any contribution to local landfills.

Figure 4.18 Renovation of the Blackstone Power Plant transformed a neglected industrial site into an environmentally responsible space. An alternative interpretation of the traditional campus quad employs recycled excavated material to structure a rainwater-remediation system that reinforces interactions between ecological performance and campus life. © 2005 Landworks Studio

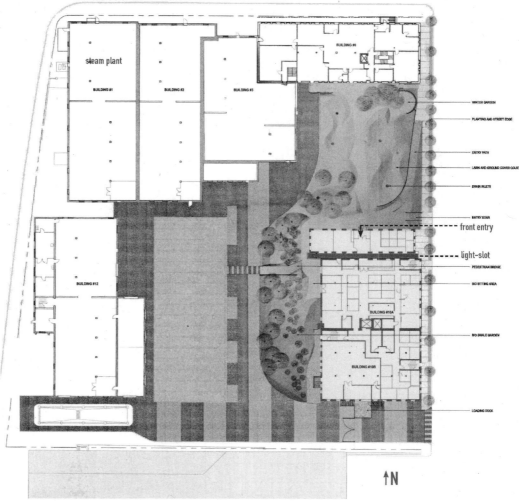

Site plan and landscaping

GREEN DESIGN ELEMENTS

Blackstone Station Office Renovation

Sustainable Sites:
- Public transportation proximity
- Bicycle accommodation
- Permeable paving materials
- Xeriscaping
- Bioswales

Water Efficiency:
- Dual-flush toilets
- Waterless urinals
- Low-flow plumbing fixtures

Energy and Atmosphere:
- Renewable energy certificates
- Ground-source heat pumps
- Enthalpic heat recovery
- Demand control ventilation
- Occupancy and photoelectric sensors
- Machine-room-free elevator

Materials and Resources:
- 99.4 percent construction waste diverted/recycled
- Recycled materials used
- Rapidly renewable materials used

Indoor Environment Quality:
- Skylights/abundant daylighting
- Operable windows
- Transparent/translucent glazing (interior and exterior)
- Low-VOC materials and finishes

Figure 4.19 A new "light-slot" connects two formerly detached buildings, provides daylight, and announces a modern intervention within this historic complex. The translucent skylight, stairwell, and partitions, as well as operable windows, allow daylight into the whole building. Bioswales treat stormwater runoff, and the newly landscaped, no-irrigation exterior courtyard creates an attractive entrance, as well as a connection to the rest of the complex. © 2006 Leland Cott

PROJECT TEAM

Bruner/Cott Architects and Planners, Inc.
Harvard Real Estate Services
Harvard University Operations Services
Ove Arup & Associates
Haley & Aldrich
Landworks, Inc.
Green International Affiliates
Consigli Construction Co., Inc.
Shawmut Design & Construction
Harvard Green Campus Initiative

Immaculate Heart of Mary Motherhouse
Monroe, MI

Current Owner: Servants of the Immaculate Heart of Mary

Building Type: Special Needs Housing

Original Building Construction: 1932

Restoration/Renovation Completion: 2003

Square Footage: 380,000 ft²

Percentage Renovated: 100%

Occupancy: 440 people (80 hrs/week) 300 visitors (2 hrs/week)

Recognition: LEED NC v2.1—Certified

Awards: EPA Energy Star Award 2007; AIA/COTE Top Ten Green Projects 2006; Interfaith Forum's Faith and Form Honor Award 2005; Honor Award for Preservation from the Michigan Historic Preservation Network 2003; EPA Clean Air Excellence Award 2003

"Our IHM community considers sustainability a moral mandate for the 21st century. It is a mandate that requires transformation. Our vision for this project was rooted in our deepening awareness that all of life is intricately connected, and choices made by individuals, corporations and nations can have profound global influence."

—*IHM, www.ihmsisters.org*

PROJECT DESCRIPTION

The Monroe campus of the Sisters, Servants of the Immaculate Heart of Mary, is 280 acres, including the 376,000-square-foot Motherhouse built in 1932 and 35 acres of native woodlands. A primary goal of the renovation was creation of a space that was sensitive to the surrounding environment and that would minimize the Sisters' dependence on resources and grid-supplied energy. The building incorporates multiple strategies to maximize energy efficiency, including ground-source heat pumps, daylighting, and energy-efficient lighting designed to consume 20 percent less energy than a conventional building.

Water and Site

Restoration activities included the reintroduction of indigenous plant life and replacement of high-maintenance lawn with native meadows, eliminating mowing and watering. These strategies reduce both irrigation and maintenance needs and, in turn, the polluting equipment and fertilizers required to maintain lawns. A constructed wetlands virtually eliminates stormwater runoff and recharges the groundwater basin. The wetland not only slows the water's course back to the ground, but also naturally filters out harmful chemicals that contaminate the city's sewer system. The wetland also purifies building graywater for reuse.

Figure 4.20 The 376,000-square-foot Motherhouse renovation project demonstrated the holistic philosophy of the Sisters, Servants of the Immaculate Heart of Mary. Water conservation was a key goal in the work. Low-flow water-conserving fixtures and fittings achieved a 35 percent reduction in freshwater consumption. In addition, graywater collected from sinks and showers moves through a separate piping system to constructed wetlands for treatment. Once the wastewater has been treated and marked with blue dye, it is returned to the building as recycled graywater for use in toilet flushing and make-up water in the mechanical plant. This system reduces water use an additional 55 percent. © Halkin Photography

Figure 4.21 The entire campus encompasses 280 acres, including 35 acres of native woodlands and a 4-acre island. The entire site was carefully preserved and restored. Topsoil removed during the earthwork was reused in the landscaping; existing trees and landscape features were either preserved or enhanced. The meadows and constructed wetlands now process and treat rainwater. Vegetated swales in parking lots provide a natural drainage system, and a management plan intentionally reduces the requirements for mechanical cutting of grass. Denyse Burkhart photo courtesy Sisters, Servants of the Immaculate Heart of Mary

GREEN DESIGN ELEMENTS
Immaculate Heart of Mary Motherhouse

Sustainable Sites:
- Public transportation proximity
- Constructed wetlands
- Xeriscaping
- Bioswales

Water Efficiency:
- Graywater system
- Low-flow plumbing fixtures

Energy and Atmosphere:
- Ground-source heat pumps
- Enthalpic heat recovery ventilation
- Natural ventilation
- Occupant and photoelectric sensors

Materials and Resources:
- Over 75 percent of construction waste recycled
- Reclaimed/recycled materials
- Roughly 70 percent of new materials harvested locally
- Rapidly renewable materials

Indoor Environment Quality:
- Enlarged existing windows
- Operable windows

Additional Features:
- Occupant recycling program
- Environmental education display
- Green Team implementing new measures

The Sisters significantly reduced hardscape by removing 300-plus parking spaces, implementing a car-/van-pooling system, and lobbying for a bus route that stops by the Motherhouse. Vegetated swales at remaining paved areas help mitigate stormwater runoff.

Planning for the Future
Planning both for the present and for a future with more elderly occupants, two interior courtyard spaces were revitalized and the existing cloistered walkways around them were restored as promenades to provide a connection to the outdoors—a necessary element, since many of sisters are in fragile health, which prevents them from going outside.

Materials—Reduce, Reuse, Recycle
The project reused entry doors, closets, and cabinets, and all of the building's wood windows were restored with energy-efficient insulated glass. Wood trim, wood wainscoting, and parquet floors were also restored. Salvaged marble pieces were used for countertops on cabinetry and windowsills, and more than 100 existing period light fixtures were retrofitted. Original cork floors were retained. The Ann Arbor, Michigan, Reuse Center also removed used building materials like sinks, toilets, wiring, and ductwork.

PROJECT TEAM
Sisters, Servants of the Immaculate Heart of Mary
SMP Architects (formerly Susan Maxman & Partners, Architects)
H.F. Lenz Company
Viridian Landscape Studio (formerly Rolf Sauer & Partners, Ltd.)
Gredell & Associates
Clanton & Associates, Inc.
Mannik & Smith Group, Inc.
The Christman Company

Lazarus Building

Columbus, OH

Current Owner: Columbus Downtown Development Corporation

Building Type: Commercial Office/Retail

Original Building Construction: 1908

Restoration/Renovation Completion: 2007

Square Footage: 750,000 ft^2

Percentage Renovated: 90% + 10% new

Occupancy: 2,000, 9 hours per day

Recognition: LEED CS (Pilot)—Gold (37/65 points); AIA Ohio Merit Award 2007; National Association of Industrial and Office Properties Green Development Award 2007

"We not only renovated a historic Columbus landmark, we created space for 1,800 jobs downtown in the most significant 'Green' building in the Midwest."
—Mayor Michael B. Coleman

BUILDING DESCRIPTION

Built in the early 1900s as the premier department store in downtown Columbus, the local landmark has been transformed for a diverse and vibrant mix of uses, including office, retail, artists studios, exhibition space, and restaurants. As a major component of the mayor's vision for a green Central Ohio, the renovation used numerous design and construction techniques to reduce the building's impact on the environment.

Water and Site

The building has a decorative green roof to reduce heat island effect, slow stormwater runoff, and reduce summer cooling loads. The landmark L-ball tower, an integral part of the rainwater harvesting system, stores graywater for flushing toilets and irrigating the roof garden. Low-flow plumbing fixtures and waterless urinals are used throughout the building. Sliver parks adjacent to the street reduce heat islands and slow stormwater runoff.

Figure 4.22 Renovation of this historically significant Midwestern landmark transformed a former department store and corporate headquarters into a mixed-use space with offices, retail, artists' studios, and exhibition space. In addition to interior renovations, the façade was restored, windows that had been infilled were replaced, and decorative grillwork ornaments the storefront windows, emphasizing the building's art deco style. *Photography © Brad Feinkhopf 2007*

Figure 4.23 The Lazarus Building received a LEED Gold certification for existing buildings. The Ohio Environmental Protection Agency and the Ohio Jobs and Family Services Agency, housed in the building, remained operational throughout the renovation. The building anchors the north end of a proposed urban redevelopment effort and has space for 1,800 jobs downtown. *Photography © Brad Feinkhopf 2007*

Figure 4.24 A new seven-story sky-lit lightwell was added at the heart of the building. The new art deco lobbies include hotel-style concierge reception desks. The project received a Green Development Award in 2007 from the National Association of Industrial and Office Properties. *Photography © Brad Feinkhopf 2007*

Materials and Resources

- Terrazzo flooring utilizing recycled glass
- Toilet partitions made from soft drink bottles
- Flooring made from tires
- Metal used in the renovation also contained recycled content

- Solid surface plastic with recycled content
- Bamboo flooring
- Cork baseboards
- Gypsum board with recycled paper facing
- Millwork with wheatboard panel cores
- Low-VOC paint, carpet, adhesives, and sealants to improve air quality

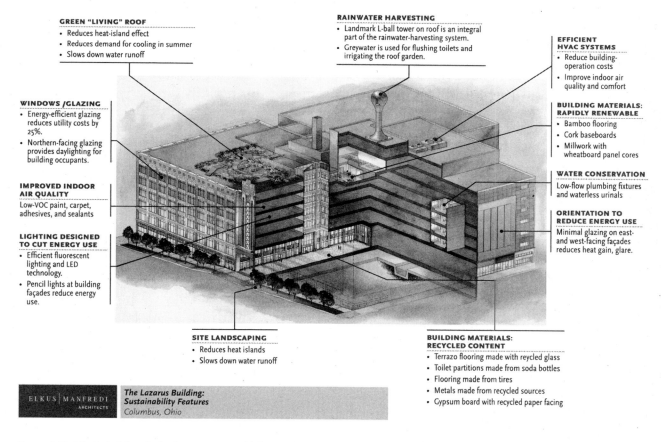

GREEN "LIVING" ROOF
- Reduces heat-island effect
- Reduces demand for cooling in summer
- Slows down water runoff

RAINWATER HARVESTING
- Landmark L-ball tower on roof is an integral part of the rainwater-harvesting system.
- Greywater is used for flushing toilets and irrigating the roof garden.

EFFICIENT HVAC SYSTEMS
- Reduce building-operation costs
- Improve indoor air quality and comfort

WINDOWS /GLAZING
- Energy-efficient glazing reduces utility costs by 25%.
- Northern-facing glazing provides daylighting for building occupants.

BUILDING MATERIALS: RAPIDLY RENEWABLE
- Bamboo flooring
- Cork baseboards
- Millwork with wheatboard panel cores

IMPROVED INDOOR AIR QUALITY
Low-VOC paint, carpet, adhesives, and sealants

WATER CONSERVATION
Low-flow plumbing fixtures and waterless urinals

ORIENTATION TO REDUCE ENERGY USE
Minimal glazing on east- and west-facing façades reduces heat gain, glare.

LIGHTING DESIGNED TO CUT ENERGY USE
- Efficient fluorescent lighting and LED technology.
- Pencil lights at building façades reduce energy use.

SITE LANDSCAPING
- Reduces heat islands
- Slows down water runoff

BUILDING MATERIALS: RECYCLED CONTENT
- Terrazo flooring made with recycled glass
- Toilet partitions made from soda bottles
- Flooring made from tires
- Metals made from recycled sources
- Gypsum board with recycled paper facing

ELKUS | MANFREDI ARCHITECTS

The Lazarus Building: Sustainability Features Columbus, Ohio

Figure 4.25 Whole-building design incorporates multiple greening strategies, including reuse of the landmark water tower on the roof as part of the rainwater-harvesting system that uses graywater for flushing toilets and irrigating the roof garden. A green roof and site landscaping reduces cooling loads and stormwater runoff. *Elkus Manfredi Architects*

GREEN DESIGN ELEMENTS
Lazarus Building

Sustainable Sites:
- Green roof
- Brownfield site

Water Efficiency:
- Rainwater capture for toilets and irrigation
- Low-flow fixtures and waterless urinals
- Water use reduced by over 80 percent

Energy and Atmosphere:
- Energy-efficient windows
- High-efficiency HVAC system

Materials and Resources:
- Nontoxic paint, carpet, adhesives, and sealants
- Terrazzo flooring with recycled glass
- Toilet partitions made from pop bottles
- Flooring made from tires
- Solid surface plastic with recycled content
- Rapidly renewable materials—bamboo flooring
- Cork baseboards
- 50 percent of construction waste (11 tons) diverted

Indoor Environment Quality:
- Lobby filled with natural light from a multistory atrium
- Daylighting

PROJECT TEAM

Columbus Downtown Development Corporation
Georgetown Company
Elkus Manfredi Architects
Schooley Caldwell Associates
Turner Construction Company
Kabil Associates
LAM Partners
Steven Winter Associates
Heapy Engineering
EMH&T
HVAC
Dalmation Fire Protection
The Schachinger Group
Roofscapes, Inc.
Desman Associates
Moody/Nolan, Inc.

ENDNOTES

1. The Donella Meadows Archive, Sustainability Institute, Hartland, VT, www.sustainer.org/dhm_archive/index.php?display_article=vn644watered. Accessed April 28, 2009.

2. Mindy Luber and Peter Gleik, "Foreword," in Jason Morrison, Mari Morikawa, Michael Murphy, and Peter Schulte, *Water Scarcity & Climate Change: Growing Risks for Businesses and Investors* (Boston: CERES, 2009), p. i. www.ceres.org.

3. www.un.org/summit/water.html. Accessed April 28, 2009.

4. "A Guide to UN-Water," www.unwater.org. Accessed April 2009.

5. Peter Gleick, *The World's Water 2008–2009: The Biennial Report on Freshwater Resources* (Washington, DC: Island Press, 2008).

6. John Manual, "Drought in the Southeast: Lessons for Water Management," *Environmental Health Perspectives* 116, no. 4(April 2008). www.ehponline.org/members/2008/116-4/spheres.html. Accessed April 28, 2009.

7. "A Water Warning: Peter Brabeck-Letmathe, *The Economist* (November 19, 2008), chairman of Nestlé, argues that water shortage is an even more urgent problem than climate change."

8. U.S. EPA, "Water Facts," EPA 816-F-04-036 (June 2004), www.epa.gov. Accessed April 2009.

9. G. Treloar, M. McCormack, L. Palmowski, and R. Fay, "Embodied Water of Construction," *Environment Design Guide* (May 2004), pp. 1–8. The Royal Australian Institute of Architects.

10. World Water Assessment Programme, *The United Nations World Water Development Report 3: Water in a Changing World* (Paris: UNESCO, and London: Earthscan, 2009), p. 279.

11. Sandra L. Postel and Barton H. Thompson Jr., "Watershed Protection: Capturing the Benefits of Nature's Water Supply Services," *Natural Resources Forum* 29 (2005): 98–108.

12. Ibid.

13. Richard F. Anderson "National City Water Survey 2007; The Status of Asset Management Programs in Public Water and Sewer Infrastructure in America's Major Cities," The United States Conference of Mayors Mayors Water Council (2007), http://usmayors.org/pressreleases/documents/watersurvey_report_0907.pdf. Accessed April 2009.

14. Kevin Coyle, *Environmental Literacy in America; What Ten Years of NEETF/Roper Research and Related Studies Say About Environmental Literacy in the U.S.* (Washington, DC: The National Environmental Education and Training Foundation, 2005), www.neetf.org.

15. Christopher Kloss and Crystal Calarusse, *Rooftops to Rivers: Green Strategies for Controlling Stormwater and Combined Sewer Overflows* (Washington, DC: Natural Resource Defense Council, June 2006), www.nrdc.org.

16. Susan Saulny, "In Miles of Alleys, Chicago Finds Its Next Environmental Frontier," *New York Times* (November 26, 2007),

17. "UNH: Pavement Sealcoat A Source of Toxins in Stormwater Runoff," (April 8, 2009), www.unh.edu/news/cj_nr/2009/apr/rz8sealcoat.cfm. Accessed April 29, 2009.

18. Massachusetts Smart Growth Toolkit, www.mass.gov/envir/. Accessed May 2007.

19. Dave Dempsey, "The Greening of Stormwater: Michigan communities: Saving Money, Beautifying Neighborhoods and Protecting Lakes and Streams," Clean Water Fund (2006), www.cleanwater.org and American Rivers, www.americanrivers.org.

20. Bruce Dvorak and Marcus de la Fleur, "Seeing Green Up Top," *Fabric Architecture* (January/February 2008).

21. E-Wire press release, http://www.ewire.com/display.cfm/Wire_ID/4844, June 24, 2008.

22. Cited from Hashem Akbari, "Energy Saving Potentials and Air Quality Benefits of Urban Heat Island Mitigation," prepared for the Office of Building Technologies of The Department of Energy and the California Energy Commission in 2001.

23. Benjamin Engelhard, Seth Geiser, and Will Payne, "Chicago's Green Alley Program; The Green Alley Handbook—Chicago, Illinois, USA," ARCH 503/LARC 504 (Autumn 2008). Accessed April 2009.

24. Natural Resources Defense Council, *Water Efficiency Saves Energy: Reducing Global Warming Through Water Use Strategies* (Washington, DC: March 2009). www.nrdc.org.

25. www.biobasics.gc.ca/english/View.asp?x=742. Accessed March 29, 2009.

26. www.biobasics.gc.ca/english/View.asp?x=742. Accessed March 29, 2009.

27. Mike Hightower and Suzanne A. Pierce (2008), "The Energy Challenge," *Nature* 452/20 (March 2008), pp. 285–286, Nature Publishing Group.

28. EIA www.eia.doe.gov/cneaf/electricity/epa/epa_sum.html. Accessed April 2009.

29. Susan S. Hutson, Nancy L. Barber, Joan F. Kenny, Kristin S. Linsey, Deborah S. Lumia, and Molly A. Maupin (2004). "Estimated Use of Water in the United States in 2000," U.S. Geological Survey, http://pubs.usgs.gov/circ/2004/circ1268. Accessed April 2009.

30. Ed Brown (2005), *Renewable Energy Brings Water to the World, Renewable Energy World* (August 23, 2005). www.renewableenergyworld.com/rea/news/article/2005/08/renewable-energy-brings-water-to-the-world-35664. Accessed April 2009.

31. Paul Gipe, *Wind Energy Comes of Age* (New York: John Wiley & Sons, 1995).

32. Percentage of electricity from EIA. www.eia.doe.gov/cneaf/electricity/epa/epa_sum.html. Accessed April 2009.

33. Pacific Institute, *Water Scarcity and Climate Change: Growing Risks for Businesses and Investors,* (Boston, MA: Ceres, February 2009), www.ceres.org.

34. U.S. Department of Energy, *Energy Demands on Water Resources* (2006), p. 20.

35. Hydroelectric Power Water Use, http://ga.water.usgs.gov/edu/wuhy.html. Accessed April 2009.

36. Peter H. Gleick (Author), Meena Palaniappan, Mari Morikawa, Jason Morrison, Heather Cooley (Constributors), *The World's Water 2008-2009: The Biennial Report on Freshwater Resources* (Washington, D.C. , Island Press, 2009), p.8.

37. The Department of the Environment and Heritage, "Water Efficiency Guide: Office and Public Buildings," Commonwealth of Australia (2006). http://www.environment.gov.au/settlements/publications/government/pubs/water-efficiency-guide.pdf. Accessed April 2009.

38. www1.eere.energy.gov/femp/water/water_bmp3.html. Accessed April 2009.

39. www.nrel.gov/sustainable_nrel/water.html. Accessed April 2009.

40. Quoted in Michael Grozik, "Throne Off Course," *Dwell* (July/August 2008).

41. "UK to Give Waterless Washing Machine a Spin," London (Reuters) June 9, 2008. www.reuters.com/article/environmentNews/idUSL0967346220080609. Accessed April 2009.

42. Environmental Protection Agency (EPA), "Clean Watersheds Needs Survey 2004 Report to Congress.," (2004). www.epa.gov/owm/mtb/cwns/2004rtc/toc.htm. Accessed April 2009.

43. Don Duncan, "Is It Time to Kill off the Flush Toilet?," *Time* (November 6, 2008).

44. Sandy Halliday, *Sustainable Construction* (Oxford, UK, and Burlington, MA: Butterworth-Heinemann, Elsevier Linacre House, 2008), p. 311.

45. Mary Austin, *The Land of Little Rain* (Boston: Houghton-Mifflin, 1903; reprinted by Penguin Books, 1997).

46. Yale Center for Environmental Law and Policy and the Center for International Earth Science Information Network, Columbia University, 2008 Environmental Performance Index, p. 48, June 16, 2008, Yale Center for Environmental Law & Policy, http://epi.yale.edu.

47. Alex Wilson, "Toward Wiser Water Strategies," *GreenSource* (July 2008).

48. Water Assessment Programme, *The United Nations World Water Development Report 3: Water in a Changing World* (Paris: UNESCO, and London: Earthscan, 2009), p. 276,

49. The Department of the Environment and Heritage, "Water Efficiency Guide: Office and Public Buildings," Commonwealth of Australia. www.environment.gov.au/settlements/publications/government/pubs/water-efficiency-guide.pdf. Accessed April 2009.

50. Gary Reed (2006), "Water Conservation Opportunities in Illinois Higher Education, June 28, 2006, Sustainable University Symposium, greed@eiu.edu provided by Mike Jackson, FAIA, Chief Architect of the Preservation Services Division of the Illinois Historic Preservation Agency.

51. Barry Holston Lopez, *River Notes: The Dance of Herons* (Kansas City, KS: Andrews and McMeel, 1979), p. 100.

52. Water Assessment Programme, p. 294.

chapter 5

ENERGY—NOT THE ONLY ISSUE, BUT…

5.1 ENERGY OVERVIEW

"Current energy trends are patently unsustainable—socially, environmentally, economically."

—Dr. Fatih Birol, Chief Economist,
International Energy Agency, November 2008[1]

THE USE OF ENERGY to meet human needs is so integral to any discussion of sustainability that, when buildings are the focus, energy often, mistakenly, becomes the only topic addressed. The urgency of decreasing energy use in buildings cannot be overstated. At the same time, as every chapter in this book stresses, the issues around the greening of buildings and of our society are interconnected—and all directly and indirectly address energy. A greener society will require less energy for transportation, for unnecessary product production, for resolving water issues, and for treating the health problems resulting from poor indoor air quality, toxic materials, and pollution. Moving toward environmental sustainability and slowing carbon emissions demands aggressive actions on many fronts while we rigorously and constantly evaluate each decision to ensure that we do not solve one problem while creating bigger concerns upstream, downstream, and into the future.

No Universal Solution

Dramatically reducing the direct energy required to occupy all existing buildings and altering the impact of energy sources used to power buildings and the activities within them is essential to slowing climate change that results from greenhouse gas emissions. This statement cannot be stressed enough. Reusing buildings avoids the far-reaching environmental impacts of making something new, especially something as big as a building, but that represents only part of a solution. Especially in the United States, humans use unnecessary and excessive amounts of energy to heat, cool, and light space, to meet plug loads, and to power the activities within the estimated 300 billion square feet of existing buildings.

> "It is clear that there are no universal solutions for improving the energy efficiency of buildings. General guidelines must be adjusted to the different climate, economic and social conditions in different countries."
> —*United Nations Environment Programme*[2]

No one-size-fits-all solutions will reliably reduce energy use in existing buildings, especially those with heritage value and a range of defining characteristics that might include highly decorative interior and exterior elements. The solutions for a landmark masonry church in the northeast U.S. will be completely different than those developed for a wood-framed warehouse in a historic district in a subtropical or desert climate.

No other part of sustainable design so completely requires buy-in from all parties—owners, engineers, architects, facility managers, and occupants—and demands partnerships beyond the building site—with power companies, funding programs, and reviewing authorities—as does energy use in a building. The best

Figure 5.1 Lowering a fuel cell into a new below-grade space at The Lion House at the Bronx Zoo illustrates the success of an integrated project team and a partnership with the New York Power Authority. Employing multiple strategies—including ground-sourced heat pumps balanced with the fuel cell, the zoo's cogeneration plant, and condensate waste heat—the project reduced energy use in the building 57 percent below the ASHRAE 90.1 standard. *FXFOWLE Architects*

creative brainstorming and problem solving necessitates holistic thinking that solves multiple problems and supports a commitment to ongoing stewardship, system maintenance, commissioning and user responsibility. An integrated project team and the involvement of the maintenance staff and building occupants are essential to establishing and maintaining a successful energy-use-reduction strategy.

Energy and Carbon Dioxide

Combustion of fossil fuels such as petroleum, natural gas, and coal in power plants, vehicles, industrial facilities, and buildings is the primary source of anthropogenic greenhouse gas emissions. In the United States, which contributes one-fifth of the greenhouse gas in Earth's atmosphere, emissions from fossil fuels represent 86 percent of the total and 97 percent of the CO_2.[3] Transportation, which depends on petroleum, and electricity generation, which relies primarily on coal combustion, account for 33 percent and 41 percent, respectively, of total U.S. carbon emissions. By volume, only 27 percent of U.S. energy comes from coal, but coal produces more CO_2 per unit of energy than petroleum or natural gas.[4]

"Coal is the single greatest threat to civilization and all life on our planet."

—James Hansen, NASA's top climate scientist[5]

Atmospheric concentrations of CO_2 are already higher than they have been at any time in the past 20 million years. Business as usual and increasing population mean that by 2050, the CO_2 in the atmosphere will reach a level twice what it has been in the preceding million years and probably higher than in 100 million years. Atmospheric CO_2 has great staying power (its lifetime is estimated at about 3,000 years), meaning our energy choices today are creating a legacy that will stretch as far into the future as the history of modern civilization. Melting permafrost and ice also release methane and CO_2, which will further affect the atmosphere. Two hundred and thirty million years ago, CO_2 levels spiked and, according to the fossil record, about 90 percent of the species on Earth went extinct.[6] Can even the greatest skeptics about climate change consider our current experiment with energy and greenhouse gases worth that risk?

Energy, Buildings, and Greenhouse Gas Emissions

Two different facts appear almost inseparable when discussing buildings and energy. The first reflects the dominance of the building sector in total energy use and the second describes the resulting greenhouse gas emissions. In the United States, buildings are responsible for 41 percent of all energy consumed,[7] and they produce 37 percent of all U.S. greenhouse gas emissions.[8] Rarely mentioned in the discussion of greenhous gas emissions from buildings in the U.S. is the fact that the majority of them (75 percent) come from the purchase of electricity, which is often generated by coal in inefficient plants that release byproducts such as mercury and carbon dioxide. The most effective ways to reduce greenhouse gas emissions from buildings are to reduce electricity usage and switch to electricity, whether from microgeneration or the grid, that originates in more efficient and/or largely carbon-free generation.

"Depending on how the electricity is ultimately used, as much as 97 percent of the energy in the coal used to produce electricity can be lost as waste heat."

Brookings Institution[9]

Zero-Carbon Sources of Energy

Energy sources that do not overtly throw off greenhouse gas are increasing, but worldwide only 8 percent of all energy produced is described as "renewable," including hydroelectricity (about one-third of the renewable total). Nuclear electric power, often labeled zero carbon, contributes another six percent of the world's energy.[10] Renewable energy can take many forms, ranging from giant regional wind and solar farms to micro-generation units for single buildings (refer to section 5.3). Increasing awareness of the unsustainability of our current energy production has spurred research into additional sources of renewable energy such as waves and tides, geothermal, photosynthesis, concentrated solar power, solar chimneys, and biofuels.

It cannot be assumed that *renewable,* or *zero carbon,* energy has no environmental impacts. Nuclear power requires a massive infrastructure, consumes large amounts of water, and presents considerable disposal problems. The construction and maintenance required to install wind farms can alter ecosystems through the clearing of vegetation, soil disruption, and the potential for erosion and noise.[11] Biofuel farms may involve clearing via fires, changing land use, and converting forests, peatlands, savannas, and grasslands into agricultural land[12]—which in turn consumes large amounts of water, is vulnerable to erosion, and sheds chemical- and pesticide-laden runoff. Rare earths required in batteries that store "green" power have already begun to leave a new legacy of environmental degradation from strip mining.[13]

> "Some (energy) options may prove unsustainable due to serious health and environmental damages. Some may inadvertently enhance global warming."
> —*Healthy Solutions for the Low Carbon Economy*[14]

In energy production, there is no environmentally free lunch, but some lunches are far more appetizing than others. Improving efficiency and taking full advantage of natural systems to avoid the need for energy at all is the most preferable option in buildings. Examples include reducing heat island effect (see Chapter 4) to avoid cooling loads and using passive solar, natural ventilation, and daylighting.

Energy Use Statistics

The United States was self-sufficient in energy until the 1950s, when energy consumption began to outpace domestic production and the country began to import energy to fill the gap. In 2008, net imported energy in the United States accounted for 26 percent of all energy consumed. The 1950s also marked the beginning of a steady rise in energy use per person in the country. By 2008, average per capita consumption for a U.S. resident reached 52 percent above the 1949 rate.[15] This is more than twice the consumption of a European and 14 times more than someone living in China or India.[16]

In an immensely complex topic, one basic truth about energy exists—historically, energy use per person has always increased even as the sources of energy have changed. Given that the world population is projected to grow from 6 billion to 10 billion in the next 40 years, there is little doubt that humans will continue to use more and more energy. The good news is that energy is not a desired commodity in and of itself. Increased energy consumption is based on wanting more of what energy does, not more energy. Achieving more with less and shifting to sources of energy that do not produce greenhouse gas are both important goals.

Within buildings, reducing energy use requires a holistic approach that addresses the environmental impacts and opportunities of a site, a building enclosure, efficient systems and equipment, occupant plug loads, and operational diligence. Operational energy-use reduction and management in buildings is never a single task to be completed and checked off. The goals require a continuous pattern of awareness and improvement.

5.2 LESS IS MORE—AVOIDED IMPACTS

> "All building sector stakeholders need to adopt a sense of urgency and a new mindset in which building energy is a top priority."
>
> —*World Business Council for Sustainable Development, April 2009*[17]

Efficiency—The Great Opportunity

Achieving more with less is the basis of energy efficiency and can potentially not only halt the growth of demand for energy but actually shrink it. According to McKinsey Global Energy and Materials practice, a management consulting firm, investing in energy efficiency in the United States could reduce non-transportation energy consumption by 23 percent in the next ten years, saving $1.2 trillion—against the $520 billion investment total—and potentially avoiding 1.1 gigatons of greenhouse gases annually.[18] The report, issued in 2009, notes that unlocking the full potential of energy efficiency in buildings demands a whole-building approach, a challenging goal in an industry where specialization by component is the norm.

> "The most inefficient buildings can be considered the conservationist's equivalent of a gold mine; when retrofitted with efficient lighting and other basic measures they often consume one-fourth of the energy they previously used. The net cost savings and net increase in available energy is the greatest for the worst offenders."
>
> —*Victor Olgyay, Rocky Mountain Institute*[19]

Whole-Building (Site) Thinking—Greater Efficiency and Savings

"Increasing energy end-use efficiency," writes Amory Lovins, "is generally the largest, least expensive, most benign, most quickly deployable, least visible, least understood, and most neglected way to provide energy services."[20] He stresses whole system design in which combined strategies, such as reduced heat island effect, reduced interior heat from more efficient lighting, and increased shading through window treatments, can lower demand for air cooling, facilitating the installation of smaller equipment and reducing operating costs. Replacing the cooling equipment without changing the situations that create a need for cooling simply yields new, more efficient equipment without the synergy of reduced demand.

Lovins demonstrates that "optimizing whole systems for multiple benefits, rather than single benefits, can often…make very large energy savings cost less than small or no savings."[21] His organization, the Rocky Mountain Institute, is currently implementing this strategy as a consultant in the retrofit of the Empire State Building in New York City, where multiple linked strategies are projected to cost-effectively reduce energy use 38 percent.[22] A website about the project, www.ebsustainability.com, offers extensive information on process, tools, evaluation, and implementation—all applicable to any project, regardless of size.

> "It is important to strive for whole-building solutions that address each building's unique situation in an intelligent, cost-effective, and historically sensitive manner."
>
> —*A Guide for Historic District Commissions, Clean Air-Cool Planet* [23]

Every project requires identification of linked opportunities, evaluation and weighting of the potential actions, a sequencing of steps for financing and for construction, and an understanding of the post-construction operations and maintenance that will sustain the intent. Multiple reports indicate that the financial gains from energy-use reduction in buildings are real but not being pursued. A SmartMarket Report released by McGraw Hill Construction in 2009 found that only 32 percent of owners and 38 percent of tenants are capturing the achievable benefits of energy savings.[24]

Functional Density—Seeking the Right Metrics

Many paths can lead to increased efficiency. Using less space to meet a need reduces the use of energy and material resources. Hence, as noted in Chapter 9, a small older home may use less energy (and far fewer natural resources) per occupant than a large new "energy-efficient" house. Measuring energy use by area, such as energy required per square foot, distorts the goal of reducing overall energy use by failing to measure and compare the total amount of energy used (in a building, by an individual, or to provide a service). Operational energy used in a building should be measured in the efficiency of the function provided and not the energy, however efficient, required for what might be unnecessary space and redundant appliances or equipment.

"Basing comparisons on BTUs [British Thermal Unit] per square feet rather than BTUs per person clouds the analyses."

—*Michelle Addington*[25]

A 2007 study on energy usage by the Britain's Ministry of Justice found that energy-efficient court buildings built in the previous decade use 68 percent more energy than pre-1900 buildings "to provide the identical function of justice" with the equivalent

Figure 5.2 A 10 kW photovoltaic solar array on the roof at 17 Gordon Avenue in South Providence, Rhode Island, is part of the strategy that helped secure LEED Silver certification. Flat roofs on historic buildings are often invisible from the street and can accept photovoltaic systems without creating tension with a local historic commission that may be charged with maintaining the historic appearance of a neighborhood. *Photo: richardmccaffrey.com*

user satisfaction. Why? The new buildings represent a 42 percent increase in floor area per court over the older structures. The report recommends reconsidering the policy of replacing multiple smaller buildings with one large one, since the additional floor area of the modern buildings "cannot be justified in terms of construction cost and energy costs in use."[26] It also recommends that redundant and underutilized space (e.g., attics, basements and outbuildings) be refurbished and brought into use. [27]

Old Is Bad, New Is Good—Misperceptions

It is widely assumed that the older a building is, the more energy will be required to use it comfortably. The data about commercial buildings say otherwise. In Canada, commercial buildings built before 1920 have a lower energy use per square meter than any period until 2000–2004. The worst performance groups were built in 1960–1969 and 1980–1989.[28] The U.S. Energy Information Administration confirms a similar pattern the United States (see page 11).

It is possible that the oldest buildings use the least energy because they have not been modernized—although this runs contrary to the belief that old buildings are energy hogs unless "leaky" windows are replaced. Studies by government agencies comparing modern applications and expectations of comfort within large and diverse real estate portfolios, verify that the oldest buildings use the least energy per unit of physical area and, in some cases, by function.

A 1999 report by the U.S. General Services Administration found that the historic buildings in its portfolio (although it did not separate them by age) used 7 percent less energy than nonhistoric buildings; 98 percent of them matched or used less energy than the industry standard, while only 86 percent of nonhistoric met industry standards.[29] The 2007 Ministry of Justice study on energy usage in 256 court buildings in the United Kingdom found that the oldest buildings (pre-1900) have the lowest energy use per square meter, and only the buildings of the 1990s and 2000s matched their performance in energy efficiency per building area. As noted in previously, however, the modern buildings use significantly more energy per courtroom (68 percent) to "provide the identical function of justice" because the new courts the new are so much larger than the old.[30]

Passive Solutions—Relearning Physics

Buildings and communities that predate widespread reliance on mechanical systems offer lessons in working with nature to achieve comfort and functionality for occupants. "Passive" strategies such as evaporative cooling, thermal mass, attics that serve as solar-powered passive ventilators, cross-ventilation that captures and moves heat in high-ceilinged spaces, night cooling and sun shading cannot necessarily meet new requirements of fire safety or mitigate the added internal heat impact of office equipment. Nevertheless, recognizing buildings as systems in the natural world provides opportunities to satisfy occupant needs without full dependence on manufactured energy.

"Heritage buildings that predate the development of four-season climate management systems typically had some inherent capability to moderate external influences on interior conditions," writes Michael Henry, an engineer and architect specializing in preservation of historic buildings and environmental management. "In these older structures, the building itself was the system for ventilation and human comfort. The hygrothermal performance of these buildings relied on building materials, thermal mass, moisture buffering, landscape, siting, overall form, horizontal and vertical communication among interior spaces, and exterior wall openings."[31]

Henry took part in an Expert's Roundtable on Sustainable Climate Management Strategies organized by The Getty Conservation Institute (GCI) in 2007. Those present at the Roundtable agreed that requirements for interior environments had become more rigid, but demonstrated through case studies and computer modeling that heritage buildings provide opportunities to moderate environmental conditions as a viable alternative to complete reliance on mechanical systems.

"Many cultural institutions are housed in historic buildings, which were often ingeniously built to passively control the indoor environment. However, the knowledge of how to use and operate these buildings has nearly been lost."
—*Getty Conservation Institute*[32]

Getty Conservation Institute studies of this issue focus on alternatives to air conditioning and methods for controlling relative humidity through ventilation and heating or dehumidification, while allowing for larger variations in temperature. The studies, located in tropical and subtropical regions have demonstrated an "impressive capability to improve climates with systems that, relative to air-conditioning, are inexpensive and simple to install, operate, and maintain."[33]

The climate control system installed by the GCI at Hollybourne Cottage, an 1890s mansion on Jekyll Island, Georgia, consists of sets of supply and exhaust ventilators, as well as convection heaters or dehumidifiers, all of which are integrated with the environmental-monitoring system by control programs. Operational costs are as much as 73 percent lower than a conventional system, and installation costs never rose above $2.50 per square foot.[34]

GEOTHERMAL WELL

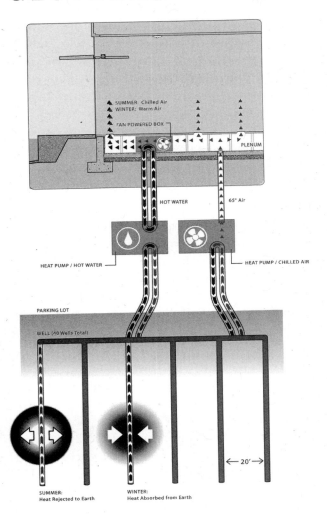

Figure 5.3 Geothermal wells are the term often used to describe ground-source heat pumps, or GSHP. Geothermal more accurately describes systems that use hot water or rocks in the earth. A GSHP rejects and collects the heat from the typical ground temperature of around 55 to 60 degrees Fahrenheit. The systems, which can be laid either vertically or horizontally, can be very effective but must be sized and spaced to avoid actually changing the temperature of the ground. © *Valerio Dewalt Train Associates, Inc.*

Adaptive Thermal Comfort

Climate control systems are designed to maintain specific measurable environmental factors—air temperature, surface temperature, air motion, and humidity—at levels that assure thermal comfort, or at least cause no complaints, for 80 percent of building occupants. The American Society of Heating, Refrigerating and Air-Conditioning Engineers (ASHRAE) has defined comfort zone boundaries in the United States and Canada since 1966, when it first released ASHRAE *Standard 55, Thermal Environmental Conditions for Human Occupancy. Standard 55* defines thermal comfort so narrowly, however, that it essentially mandates dependence on mechanical systems to achieve or at least attempt a perfect and consistent indoor environment.

In 2004 ASHRAE modified *Standard 55* to allow "adaptive thermal comfort" in buildings that use a passive or nonmechanical approach to tempering indoor environments. Adaptive thermal comfort allows for a wider and more natural range of conditions, but it is not currently applicable to buildings that have any mechanical system. Advocates for reduced operational energy in buildings argue that adaptive comfort is essential because of the many variables in how people experience comfort.

Research has shown that reporting of discomfort varies by gender (women report more discomfort than men) and can shift based on an impression of the space itself. The more people like the space they occupy, the less physical discomfort they report.[35] Adaptive comfort acknowledges perceptual comfort, which is influenced by nonmeasurable factors and even the need for environments that reflect seasonal change and a change in clothing. Color, texture, sound, movement, and light can all influence perceptual comfort.[36]

5.3 REDUCING AND SHIFTING ELECTRICAL LOADS

"Based on energy usage, opportunities to reduce greenhouse gas emissions appear to be the most significant for [electric] space heating, air conditioning, lighting, and water heating."

—*Pew Center on Global Climate Change*[37]

Reducing electricity usage in buildings and shifting the purchase of electricity to off-peak demand periods are cost-effective opportunities.[38] Reducing energy bills, however, does not directly link to reducing carbon emissions. As John Straube, a building

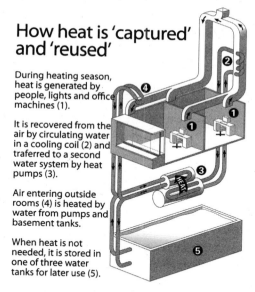

How heat is 'captured' and 'reused'

During heating season, heat is generated by people, lights and office machines (1).

It is recovered from the air by circulating water in a cooling coil (2) and traferred to a second water system by heat pumps (3).

Air entering outside rooms (4) is heated by water from pumps and basement tanks.

When heat is not needed, it is stored in one of three water tanks for later use (5).

Figure 5.4 Recognizing heat as a resource is becoming more common. The heating system installed at the Massachusetts State Transportation Building in Boston in the 1980s relies completely on the heat generated by people, lights, and office machines to temper the air. Total energy use for the 900,000-square-foot office building is 30 percent below current code requirements and saves the Commonwealth an estimated $1 million per year in utility charges.
© *Goody Clancy*

scientist from the University of Waterloo, points out, "Energy consumption should be measured in terms of environmental damage, such as carbon emissions, resource depletion, or habitat destruction.... All energy is not equal when it comes to environmental impact.... Measuring energy in the form of dollars presumes that environmental damage is related to dollars. It is not, and this format should be avoided."[39] Of the energy used in buildings, electricity is often the most environmentally detrimental, regardless of cost.

Seventy-six percent of the emissions created by building operations and plug loads in the United States in 2007 came from the use of electricity.[40] About half the electricity in the U.S. is generated from coal, but this half contributes 80 percent of the CO_2 emitted by the electrical industry, the sector that is the largest producer of greenhouse gas in the country. (Refer to page 169.) Most electricity, 70 percent,[41] is used in buildings and, according to Architecture2030 (www.architecture2030.org), an even higher percentage of the electricity generated by coal goes to buildings.

The primary use for electricity in commercial buildings is lighting (38 percent), followed by cooling, ventilation, and refrigeration (all three total another 36 percent).[42]

Electricity usage in buildings continues to climb, even as other areas of energy use have flattened or declined. Growing use is attributable to strong demand for commercial lighting and cooling; increased demand for computers and electronics in homes and offices; and substitution of new electricity-intensive technologies, such as electric arc furnaces for steelmaking.[43]

Lighting and Daylighting

Every energy-use reduction plan, regardless of building type, begins with a recommendation to replace existing lighting with more efficient systems. This may be as simple as changing light bulbs and adding motion and daylight sensors, or as complex as increasing natural daylighting through added building elements such as internal light shelves, skylights, or solar tubes.

The Royal Institute of Chartered Surveyors in the United Kingdom estimates that energy-efficient lighting can reduce both energy use and internal heat gain by approximately 60 percent and suggests that the use of pale colors on walls and ceilings can reduce energy used for lighting by another 5 to 10 percent.[44] Changing building codes are also redefining how much light is needed in what locations for safety and task completion.

Daylighting must be part of an integrated energy-management strategy that considers the amount and type of glass in a building. Increased natural light can significantly reduce the amount of artificial lighting used, but it may also contribute to increased cooling loads if the windows allow too much solar gain or increased heating loads if they allow too much heat to escape through the glass and frame.

Light Shelves

Methods for increasing light penetration into building spaces historically included glass prisms placed over storefront doors and glass blocks embedded in sidewalks to daylight below-grade storage areas. New products such as interior light louvers and light shelves are often described as "throwing light" deeper into a building. Typically, an interior light shelf does not have this effect, but it will create a more uniform light distribution in the 15-foot perimeter zone, reducing glare and providing a more comfortable environment.[45]

Lighting for Retrofit—Two Promising Technologies

By Robert J. Osten, Jr. IALD, RA
Principal, Lam Partners Inc. Architectural
Lighting Design

DALI

What's DALI (Digital Addressable Lighting Interface)? It's a lighting control system. Why are controls important? In addition to having a big impact on energy consumption, maintenance, and the flexibility of a lighting system, they also can involve a lot of wiring, which can be especially difficult or expensive in retrofit installations. DALI is not a product, and it's not controlled by any manufacturer. It's a control system structure, and an open-source standard for communication between actual system hardware components, so products from various manufacturers can be mixed-and-matched in a single installation. Take a simple dimmer controlling several luminaires as an example. In a conventional system, the dimmer resides in an electrical wallbox or in larger systems in a dimmer rack in an electric closet, and each of the luminaires to be dimmed is hard-wired back to the dimmer using line-voltage wire. When the dimmer is adjusted, all of the luminaires are dimmed equally. In a DALI system, the dimmers reside in each luminaire, and a digital network cable connects each luminaire to the DALI controller. Since each luminaire has its own unique digital address, they can all be controlled together, as in the conventional system, but they can also all be controlled individually or in any grouping. And that grouping can be changed simply by reprogramming, with no change in the wiring.

Perhaps it's no accident that the DALI system originated in Europe, where it's been in use for years, and where a high proportion of buildings are older structures that have been restored or adapted for new uses, because it has a lot of advantages for retrofit installations:

- Greatly simplified wiring—the luminaires can be powered from any circuit, and no "home-runs" are required. All luminaires can share the same data wire circuit, in any pattern that's convenient.

- No dimming or relay racks are required—just small routers or hubs.

- Data hubs can be wireless—simplifying wiring even more.

- Simply by providing a data port connection, plug-in luminaires can be controlled by the dimming system, with no change to the power wiring.

- Daylight sensors and occupancy sensors can share the same data wiring as the DALI luminaires—offering great, programmable system flexibility at low relative cost.

- With DALI track lighting (power and data from the same track), DALI and conventional heads can be intermixed—so dimming or multiscene control can be bought only for the heads that need it.

- This means some of the cost of a DALI track or plug-in system can be spread over time—more DALI luminaires can be bought later and installed without any rewiring.

- Two-way data—the DALI luminaires also talk *back* to the controller, allowing central monitoring of on-off or dimmed status and lamp burnouts, facilitating maintenance, building control, and load-shedding.

(continued)

LEDS (LIGHT-EMITTING DIODES)

LED luminaires are emerging from their Wild-West period and are beginning to become a dependable and cost-effective light source. They offer particular advantages for lighting in historic or other existing buildings:

- LED wiring can be low-voltage—without the need for conduit and junction boxes, it can be much more compact and easier to route and conceal in existing structures.

- LED luminaires themselves can be physically very small—making it easier to fit them in to existing construction or keeping them unobtrusive if exposed to view.

- LEDs are intrinsically directional—without the need for large reflectors they can be effective at accenting architectural features and artwork, and in grazing washes of light, highlighting textures such as stonework.

- Retrofit LED lamps are widely available—so life and efficiency can be improved simply by screwing a new lamp into an existing luminaire. This is true of compact fluorescent lamps also, of course, but they lack focused, directional beams. LED retrofit lamps can effectively replace the punch of halogen lamps in tall spaces and in accenting artwork and building features.

- The very long life of LEDs makes them good for locations where maintenance access is difficult—for example, tall vaults, lobbies, and façade lighting.

HVAC Distribution Systems

Composed of air handlers, electric motors, ductwork, diffusers, energy and humidity exchangers, control boxes, and associated control systems, the heating, ventilating, and air conditioning (HVAC) distribution system is a major consumer of energy in commercial buildings. Full renovations usually entail complete replacement of these systems and offer opportunities to implement new technologies that use less energy and may find new ways to capitalize on the attributes of the existing building. Examples presented in the ASHRAE Green Tips include Variable Air Volume Systems, Variable Flow/Variable Speed Pumping Systems, Ventilation Demand Control Using CO_2, and different strategies for heat recovery, including combined heating and power systems.[46]

Mixed-Mode Ventilation Systems

Mixed-mode ventilation systems combine both passive and mechanical solutions for ventilation and cooling. Natural ventilation can come from operable windows, louvers, or dampers that are mechanically or manually operated. Simple controls can ensure that air conditioning systems are deactivated when windows or other elements are open for natural ventilation.

Mixed-mode systems can provide many of the benefits of a natural ventilation system and can reduce fan and cooling plan energy consumption 15 to 80 percent, depending on climate, cooling loads, and building type.[47] The Center for the Built Environment's helpful online resource describes different systems in detail (www.cbe.berkeley.edu/mixedmode/aboutmm.html).

Figure 5.5 A radiant-cooling system, in which cold water runs through copper pipes at the ceiling, was added to the S. T. Dana Building at the University of Michigan School of Natural Resources and Environment. The cold water acts as a heat sink for warm air in the room, replacing the air in a traditional forced-air system. This translates into substantial energy savings, as water is about three times more efficient than air as a heat-transfer medium. © *Quinn Evans / Architects 2005*

Precooling and Thermal Mass

Night precooling involves circulating cool air within a building during nighttime hours, which are off-peak periods for electrical grids. The cooled structure acts as a heat sink during daytime hours, reducing the mechanical cooling required. The naturally occurring thermal storage capacity of high-mass buildings smoothes swings in the load curve.[48] An unoccupied building can be cooled more effectively because comfort constraints are reduced.

Thermal Energy Storage for Cooling

Active thermal storage systems utilize a building's cooling equipment to produce ice or chilled water during off-peak energy hours for delivery of cooling at a later time. Chillers are the single largest energy users in commercial buildings, consuming about 20 percent of the total electrical energy generated in North America.[49] Thermal storage allows a chiller plant to run at peak efficiency during its operating period because the demand for cooling is decoupled from the production of cooling.[50] Many historic buildings have basement or site areas large enough to allow for thermal storage. (Refer to Figure 5.6.)

Photovoltaic

The technologies for producing photovoltaic panels are changing rapidly. A 2009 Massachusetts Institute of Technology analysis of energy used in their manufacture notes that "the inherent inefficiency of current solar panel manufacturing methods could drastically reduce the technology's lifecycle energy balance—

that is, the ratio of the energy the panel would produce over its useful lifetime to the energy required to manufacture it."[51] Even with that caveat in mind, photovoltaics used in individual projects still decrease dependency on larger energy plants and are environmentally less harmful.

"It will always be more cost-effective to use low-energy bulbs, good control, draught-proofing or more insulation than to install PVs or a wind turbine to an existing inefficient building."

—*Sandy Halliday, Sustainable Construction*[52]

A study published in *Environmental Science and Technology* in 2008 concluded that 89 percent of air emissions associated with electricity generation could be prevented if electricity from photovoltaics displaced electricity from conventional fossil-fuel-based electricity. The study found that all photovoltaic technologies generate far less life-cycle air emissions than conventional grid electricity, but among the current photovoltaic technologies, it identified thin-film cadmium telluride PV as generating the least amount of harmful air emissions because that process requires the least amount of energy during the module production.[53]

An expanding group of communities and organizations internationally and regionally have addressed the installation of photovoltaics in heritage neighborhoods and on heritage buildings. Examples include *Renewable Heritage: A Guide to Microgeneration in Traditional and Historic Homes | A Changeworks Initiative*, based on work in the World Heritage Site of Edinburgh's Old Town, which appeared in 2009; *Small Scale Solar Electric (Photovoltaics) Energy and Traditional Buildings* was published by English Heritage in 2008; and the City of Boulder (Colorado) Office of Environmental Affairs released *Making Your Historic Building Energy Efficient* in 2007.

Figure 5.6 Off-peak energy purchase is useful as a budget strategy and as a means of better using available energy infrastructure systems. At the Center for Neighborhood Technology in Chicago (www.cnt.org), water-filled plastic balls float in a glycol bath in the storage tank for the building's new cooling system (buried next to the building during renovation. The balls are frozen at night, using off-peak, lower-cost energy. During the higher-cost hours, food-grade, glycol-based fluid transfers the chill from the ice balls to the building cooling system (see Chapter 2). © 2008 Center for Neighborhood Technology

Figure 5.7 The ice storage balls used at the Center for Neighborhood Technology (see **Figure 5.6**) contain water. When they freeze, the food-grade glycol around them in the building's cooling system becomes cold and runs through the pipes to cool the building. To make the best use of energy, conditions inside and outside the building are constantly monitored for temperature, sunlight, carbon dioxide levels, humidity, and time of day. Heating and cooling are adjusted automatically. © 2008 Center for Neighborhood Technology

Building Automation Systems

Building automation systems (BAS) offer a coordinated management of multiple systems in a building. A BAS can control each piece of equipment separately, but it can also integrate the separate systems into a single network that can react to and evaluate the interaction between the components for efficiency.

Solar Shading

Solar shading provides a means of reducing solar heat gain during the summer months, while allowing a degree of low-angle winter sun to provide some passive solar heating. This can be accomplished through site trees, awnings, and blinds (both external and internal). For a renovation in Los Angeles, XTen Architects added dramatic fixed textile panels to the exterior of a three-story commercial office building. The building owner recoverd the cost of the three-week installation in fewer than four years due to a 42 percent drop in energy consumption following installation.[54]

Energy Star—Staged Approach to Building Upgrades

Stage 1 *Retrocommissioning* (refer to Chapter 8)—tune-up systems

Stage 2 *Lighting*—upgrade lighting and maximize daylighting

Stage 3 *Supplemental load reductions*—from occupants and equipment

Stage 4 *Air distribution systems*—adjust and improve building fan systems

Stage 5 *Heating and cooling systems*—upgrade and properly size

Energy management is a path of continuous improvement. After completion of the fifth stage, the process begins again with recommissioning and a *green team* (refer to Chapter 8) to determine where further savings can be found.

www.energystar.gov[55]

Sample Action Plans for Energy Management

Lighting

- Match operating hours to activities.
- Minimize lighting of unoccupied spaces.
- Add occupancy sensors.

Air Systems

- Match running time to activities.
- VAV boxes with different occupancy.
- Lower hot-air temperatures.
- Fan static pressure setpoint.
  - Lower the fixed manual setpoint.
  - Dynamic reset using VAV damper positions.
  - Schedule time of day.
- Verify ventilation quantities.

Hot Water Systems

- Match running time to activities.
- Lower hot-water temperatures.
- Lower pump pressure in piping.
- Reset pump pressure using valve positions.
- Verify proper flow.
- Experiment with staging multiple boilers.

Chilled Water Systems

- Match running time to activities.
- Raise chilled-water temperatures.
- Lower pump pressure in piping.
- Reset pump pressure using valve positions.
- Verify proper flow-throttle balance valves or trim pump impeller.
- Condenser water reset.
- Optimize tower fan speed control—start low speed and ramp up.
- Optimize chiller staging—avoid operating unnecessary chillers.

Additional action items may be found in Chapter 35, *ASHRAE 2007 Handbook*, Richard J. Pearson, P.E. FASHRAE, Pearson Engineering, Madison, Wisconsin.

5.4 THE BUILDING ENCLOSURE

"Too often the scope of concerns and complexity of issues regarding sustainability are oversimplified. ... No amount of energy efficiency, nor any other single-issue campaign, will deliver sustainable development, although it will help. Oversimplification encourages one-dimensional solutions, short cuts, shallow questions and potentially bad laws."

—*Sandy Halliday*[56]

The character of the exterior enclosure of a building is a significant contributor to the amount of energy used to heat, ventilate and cool interior space as well as lighting. In the supposed conflict between historic buildings and environmental sustainability, treatment of the exterior walls and windows is usually the area of greatest contention. Changes in the building enclosure, even when executed on the interior, are often the most visible, require the most removal of existing materials such as windows and wall plaster, have potential to cause long-term damage, and are less reversible than new mechanical systems might be.

The Precautionary Principle

The debate centers on how the building enclosure can be "improved." For some, this is simplicity itself—insulation, new air-tight details, and new windows with the lowest U-value possible regardless of climatic zone or internal load types. For others, such an approach raises alarms about aesthetic and social values because it entails replacement and alteration of original materials. It also causes concern about whether new materials are nontoxic, upstream and downstream environmental and health impacts, potential long-term damage to buildings because of moisture entrapment, possible poor indoor-air quality and creating a cycle of mandatory replacement, since many new products cannot be easily repaired.

"Studies conducted by the Canadian government during the 1990s confirmed that the energy conservation benefits of installing weatherstripping and sealing gaps between walls, window frames and sash to reduce infiltration offered greater operational savings in relation to dollars invested than any other window upgrade alternative, including installation of thermal replacement windows."

—*U. S. General Services Administration Technical Guidelines*[57]

The "precautionary principle" supports both sides of the argument. The Rio Conference of 1992—the United Nations environmental conference that laid the groundwork for the Kyoto Protocol—declared in Principle #15 that, "the precautionary approach shall be widely applied....Where there are threats of serious or irreversible damage, lack of full scientific certainty shall not be used as a reason for postponing cost-effective measures to prevent environmental degradation." The crisis of operational energy use consequently drives the push for "deep energy retrofits," because maximum reduction of a building's energy-use intensity is deemed by many to be the paramount issue, regardless of the amount or type of materials used to achieve an improved building enclosure.

Advocates for protecting existing physical resources—buildings and building components—often insist that conclusive and holistic environmental information precede dramatic, potentially irreversible interventions. In this case, interpretations such as "the precautionary principle applies where scientific evidence is insufficient, inconclusive or uncertain and ...there are reasonable grounds for concern...."[58] serve as the basis for a conservative rather than aggressive approach to changing a building enclosure, especially on buildings of national or international heritage value, where "do no harm" should be the guiding principle.

The conflict over whether and how to change a building enclosure springs from different perspectives on the same issue, a belief that humans are living in unsustainable ways. Despite the often-vociferous debate, solutions need not be polar opposites. Protecting what already exists does not, by any means, preclude "improving" a building envelope, but, rather, suggests a less-is-more approach that focuses on solutions that create the biggest impact with the least amount of risk—for instance, draft-proofing and installing attic insulation, repairing windows and adding reversible storm window systems. New tools and new uses for old tools are improving the ability to evaluate opportunities and balance decisions.

"Installation of roof insulation can reduce heat loss through the roof by 60 percent."

—*Royal Institution of Chartered Surveyors*[59]

Design and Evaluation Tools

Computerized Energy Analysis

Computer modeling of a building's energy-use intensity is now commonly used to determine the size of mechanical equipment needed; to allow comparison between design decisions, including window alterations; and to estimate annual energy consumption. Windows and walls are just one part of an *integrated energy analysis* of the building as a whole system. Altering windows to improve the thermal barrier may adversely affect lighting loads or limit productive heat gain. Energy modeling offers a useful tool for optimizing energy performance, but it is just a tool for decisions and not a definitive prediction of how a building will actually perform. Building performance still requires continuous operational monitoring, improvements, and the participation of occupants (refer to Chapter 8).

Computerized Hygrothermal Modeling

Hygrothermal modeling tools characterize the change in heat, air and moisture regimes within building wall assemblies. A commonly used software is WUFI, which was jointly developed by the Fraunhofer Institute for Building Physics (IBP) in Holzkirchen, Germany, and Oak Ridge National Laboratory in Oak Ridge, Tennessee, both internationally established in the area of building-energy performance and durability assessments. The program can help select repair and retrofit strategies with respect to the hygrothermal response of a wall assembly in a particular climate. A WUFI analysis is not foolproof. The program cannot address all types of historic wall types, nor does it account for air movement and two-dimensional effects on moisture movement through a wall system, both of which can elevate moisture levels.

Thermal Transfer Modeling

A common software used to model heat-transfer effects in building components is THERM, developed at the Lawrence Berkeley National Laboratory. Heat-transfer analysis helps identify potential thermal bridges in the geometry of building elements, including windows, walls, foundations, and roofs.

Infrared Thermography

Used for many decades as a nondestructive tool in the stewardship of heritage buildings, infrared thermography (IRT) presents emitted radiation as a two-dimensional image representation of the distribution of temperatures on an emitting surface. It permits researchers to evaluate the locations, shape, material characteristics, and state of decay of building elements and systems. IRT can also identify structural members, defects and moisture diffusion in buildings.[60] This information allows evaluation of building enclosures to determine areas of thermal inefficiency and check the effectiveness of alterations such as added insulation or changes in the windows.

The design team used high-resolution thermography as a tool in retrofitting the 1960s-constructed 18-story Richard Bolling Federal Building in Kansas City, Missouri. The phased renovation, completed in 2010, included improvements in the metal, glass, and granite curtain wall. Thermal imaging helped the team evaluate mocked-up insulation options and unexpectedly highlighted high-exterior windowframe temperatures that led to improvements in the thermal break design. During construction, thermographic imaging helped to verify even and thorough distribution of spray-applied polyurethane-foam insulation of 0.5 lb/cubic foot.[61]

Air Infiltration Tests

The airtightness of a building directly affects the ability of the exterior enclosure to reduce heating and cooling loads with mechanical equipment. Testing air infiltration can be done in two ways.

Tests of residences or limited areas often employ a blower door. A powerful fan mounted in the frame of an exterior door pulls air out of the space. The resulting differential between air pressure in the interior and higher pressure outside draws air in through any

"Draught proofing is a common practice to prevent wind from blowing in through traditional windows. The test window was draught proofed, and…the airtightness of the window was improved considerably, reducing the air leakage by 86 percent. The window is tighter than the recommended 4,000 mm² trickle vent for domestic new build."

—*Paul Baker,* Improving the Thermal Performance of Traditional Windows[62]

unsealed cracks and openings. A smoke pencil can be used to detect exact points of leakage.

A PFT (perflourocarbon tracer) gas test, developed by the Brookhaven National Laboratory, measures changes in a building's air-infiltration rate over time. After the release of a small amount of colorless, odorless, and harmless perfluorocarbon gas, the technique measures its concentration—the tighter the building, the higher the concentration. The PFT technique can use different gases to measure transfer from one zone of a building to another, and it can also be used to quantify pollutant source strengths.[63]

Existing Walls and Insulation

In a 2009 article about the importance of durability in *GreenSource* magazine, Peter Yost wrote, "Before the focus on energy conservation that began, for the most part, in the 1970s, a wet building dried quickly because so much heat was blasting through its walls. Now we stuff our walls full of insulation, interrupting that heat flow. That creates the risk that moisture will be trapped in the wall, leading to mold growth, rot and corrosion. As a result, we get air-quality problems and even structural failures…to be green and durable and energy efficient, we need a new mantra: Manage energy and moisture with equal intensity."[64]

Adding insulation inside or on the interior face of building walls that have never had insulation creates the potential for moisture entrapment. This does not mean that insulation can never be added, nor does it mean that without wall insulation energy efficiency cannot be achieved. What to do depends on the building, the climate and, sometimes, the budget.

The National Trust for Historic Preservation's website (www.preservationnation.org/issues/weatherization/ insulation), although directed primarily toward homeowners, provides links and resources about insulation, including region-specific guides. As always, the more precious the building, the more cautious the approach to change or the introduction of hard-to-reverse materials (such as spray-foam insulation) should be.

Ongoing research into how buildings perform when insulated properly continues to provide new information about how heritage materials perform when not insulated. Historic Scotland, in addition to providing thorough guides for improving energy efficiency, has carried out thermal tests on different building components across a range of building types and ages. The *in situ* testing found that many traditionally built masonry walls have better U-values than previously assumed.[65]

A report funded by the Canadian government and published in 2007 by the Canadian Housing and Mortgage Corporation documents the preliminary performance of nine masonry buildings that received different forms of interior insulation and one that received no insulation. The report suggests that increasing thermal resistance along the inside face of the existing masonry wall in most cases produced conditions that could increase the rate of condensation in the wall assembly, with an increased possibility of masonry deterioration.[66]

"Adding insulation to the walls of such [load-bearing brick and stone] masonry buildings in cold, and particularly cold and wet, climates may cause performance and durability problems."

—Straube and Schumacher, "Interior Insulation Retrofits of Load-Bearing Masonry Walls in Cold Climates"[67]

A study documented in the *Journal of Building Enclosure Design* in the summer of 2009 found that closed-cell spray-foam insulation added to the interior of a 1950s masonry building created a low freeze-thaw risk for the brick in the wall, but it increased the risk of embedded steel corrosion. This suggests that a survey—and possible replacement—of metal components might be desirable prior to insulating a masonry wall in a cold climate.[68]

Common materials used to insulate masonry from the interior are fiberglass insulation with independent air flow and/or vapor control layers, open-cell spray-foam insulation, and closed-cell spray-foam insulation.[69] In general, open-cell foam (polyicynene) allows water vapor to move through the material more easily than closed-cell foam (polyisocyanurate and polyurethane). However, open-cell foams usually have a lower R-value for a given thickness, so closed-cell foams may be needed where space is limited. English Heritage considers closed-cell foam an incompatible material for masonry walls. Because the foam is impervious and can trap moisture, it may damage the wall, and it will also neutralize the masonry's ability to buffer moisture levels in the internal air, reducing comfort for people using the building.[70]

English Heritage cautions that the challenge when adding insulation to a building is to achieve coverage that avoids thermal bridges, as where floors meet external walls. Areas left with reduced or no insulation coverage will be colder as a result. They will attract more condensation because other surfaces are warmer, putting them at risk for deterioration.[71]

Windows—No Single Solution

The impact of windows on energy use within a building cannot be dismissed or blithely assumed to be the same in every building and every location; assumptions, even those made by the most experienced project teams, can prove incorrect. At the Massachusetts Institute of Technology, a 2009 study of the windows and facades of the buildings known as the Main Group identified heat loss as the primary source of energy consumption, although the expectation had been that cooling loads would dominate. An initial assumption that a double window, which would prevent solar loads from entering the building, offered the best the solution proved incorrect, because solar gains through a window in winter can offset heating loads.[72] (See Section 5.2 for discussion of holistic solutions.)

Windows performance comprises five factors—U-factor, solar heat gain coefficient (SHGC), visible transmittance (VT), air leakage (AL), and condensation resistance (CR). The website www.efficientwindows.org describes each of these as well as optimum window (and glass) by geographic area. Such information is helpful in understanding the goals for windows, but the website—jointly developed by the University of Minnesota Center for Sustainable Building Research, the Alliance to Save Energy, and the Lawrence Berkeley National Laboratory to promote knowledge of new high-performance windows—cannot address the window as part of the whole building system and does not yet include life cycle assessment data. Ways of improving existing windows are given and the durability of new products discussed.

"Window salespeople are particularly aggressive and promise huge savings in energy. They are lying toads."

—Lloyd Alter[73]

Decisions about replacing or retaining windows are often based on preconceived opinions rather than rational evaluation. Heritage advocates protest that most newer windows lack the repairability characteristics of older windows (particularly wood), which can extend service life for centuries. An ever-growing body of articles and guidelines document and demonstrate how existing windows can be repaired to reduce air infiltration and can come close to matching the performance of new windows with combinations of added shading, storm windows, films, shutters, and insulated curtains.[74] This extends service life (refer to Chapter 7) and is accomplished with less financial cost and fewer new products.

"[A] solid one-piece aluminum window (with a life-span of only 15 years) is NOT a sustainable solution, no matter how energy efficient it is… repairable products last much longer, and keep money in the local economy by valuing labor and creating jobs for craftspeople and skilled workers. There are many, varied benefits of a 'repair instead of replace' culture."

—Energy Efficiency, Renewable Energy and Historic Preservation: A Guide for Historic District Commissions[75]

Not every existing window, however, is well made and worthy of repair. Retention of an original window must be considered in the context of the whole building, existing conditions, toxic materials, the aesthetic importance of the window to the building and the benefits—environmental, financial, and comfort—of change. The U.S. General Services Administration uses a weighted decision matrix to evaluate different scenarios for windows on a building. Depending on the situation, compared strategies might include many possible actions, from repair of an existing window to its replacement with a new material, in order to determine the best strategy overall.

Weighting factors include:

1. Historic materials, design, and appearance
   - Retention of historic material
   - Matching historic appearance
   - Risk of damage to adjacent areas/ constructability
2. Occupant impact
   - Providing operability
   - Thermal performance and proximity comfort
   - Meeting security requirements
3. Operation, maintenance, and repair
   - Expected lifespan/long-term performance
   - Maintenance requirements/convenience
4. Short- and long-term costs (both financial and environmental)
   - Initial financial cost (includes abatement of toxic materials if applicable)
   - Life cycle (financial) cost analysis (LCCA)
   - Environmental impact estimates/life cycle analysis (LCA)[76]

Windows—Life-Cycle Analysis

An Australian study completed in 2007 suggests the complexity of evaluating window choices (or any building component) with a life-cycle analysis (upstream and downstream environmental impact).[77] (The report authors acknowledge the need for additional work to establish appropriate data for various components of the analysis, including landfill waste, water consumption, oil and gas depletion, solid fuel depletion, deforestation, productive farmland lost, habitat, and ecosystems impacts). The study compared wood windows and aluminum-clad wood windows to PVC (polyvinyl chloride) and aluminum framing systems. The environmental LCA assessment considered the initial embodied performance, the life-cycle embodied performance (repair and maintenance) and the energy implications of the windows' performance.

"PVC poses serious threats to environmental health at every stage of its existence. Its production contributes to the ongoing contamination of fish and seafood with methylmercury. Its manufacture and assembly is linked to lung cancer, as well as liver cancer, in workers. PVC plants routinely poison neighboring communities. The use of PVC as a building material contributes to the degradation of indoor air and is linked to respiratory symptoms in children and office workers. The plasticizers with which it is treated pose clear threats, at background level, to fetal development of the male reproductive tract and may also damage sperm cells in adult males. At the end of its life, PVC waste creates intractable disposal problems because it is expensive and unsafe to burn, it releases hazardous chemicals into groundwater and air when buried, and is not cheaply or easily recycled."

—Dr. Sandra Steingraber[78]

The Australian study consistently found aluminum-clad wood windows to have the lowest environmental impact initially, over the life of the window or for energy implications, followed closely by wood windows, and less closely by PVC and aluminum. Aluminum-clad windows edged in front of all-wood models primarily because the ones tested used a softer wood that entailed shorter transport distances.

Windows were evaluated for service life of components, performance (including air leakage), and both initial and final life cycle impacts. The study found that insulated glass, with an assumed 20-year replacement cycle, did not always perform well enough, especially for cooling loads, to justify the extra environmental impact its manufacture created.

LCA evaluations are tied to geographic eccentricities, and their conclusions are not automatically transferable. LCA's usefulness lies in its capacity to challenge the perceptions of those advocating window replacement, as well as those advocating retention. LCA will expand the decision process to consider aspects beyond immediate or perceived reduction in operational energy. Beyond heritage considerations, existing windows—like existing buildings—offer the possibility of avoiding environmental impacts created by new products. Whether this will justify retention in any particular case remains to be seen.

Windows represent another example of the complexity of sustainable design. There are no simple rules, no invariably right or wrong approach that can be applied across the board to every building, much less every window.

"Some modern materials currently in use, especially for window manufacture, will make future repairs very difficult to achieve and often wholesale replacement will become the preferred option."

Mike Parrett[79]

5.5 AVOIDING SILOS

"A silo-based approach to energy policy that considers buildings separate from urban form, transportation infrastructure, and the communities they operate within will not maximize energy solutions in the long term."

—Geared for Change: Energy Efficiency in Canada's Commercial Building Sector[80]

Figure 5.8 Byerly Hall is one of several dozen historic buildings at Harvard University that have been registered under the U.S. Green Building Council LEED system. Energy-use reduction strategies include ground-source heat pumps, variable-speed pumps, CO_2 sensors, variable air volume (VAV) boxes, efficient indoor lighting, a combination of glass fiber insulation and polyurethane spray insulation in walls and the attic, weather-stripping around doors and windows, premium efficiency motors, submetering, commissioning and measurement, and verification by building managers. (Refer to Chapter 4 for a LEED Platinum project at Harvard and www.greencampus.harvard.edu for additional information.) © *Anton Grassl/Esto.*

Addressing energy reduction within individual buildings is essential, but buildings are part of a community. Making each building a self-contained "zero-energy" power station may not be as effective as addressing the shared opportunities of a neighborhood, city, or region. Smart, self-healing distribution grids can use electric meters to identify periods with high prices and high use of coal and, with computer software, curtail electricity use during those periods. Shared services allow energy to be routed and balanced. The U.S. Department of Energy estimates that digital monitoring and control technologies could save consumers $70 billion to $120 billion over the next 20 years and obviate the need to build 30 large coal-fired plants."[81]

Enactment of land-use policies that encourage thoughtful reuse of buildings and promote transit-oriented design could curtail greenhouse gas emissions by 3 to 8 percent by mid-century, because of reductions in vehicle miles traveled and efficiencies brought about by a shift to district integrated energy systems a diminished need for supporting municipal infrastructures.[82]

Imagine the carbon savings if the construction industry became a model of reuse instead of replacement. Because the renovation of buildings is labor-intensive, it creates 20 to 30 percent more jobs than new construction for every dollar spent. Repairing rather than replacing building components such as windows and doors would create even more jobs. The cost of a new product does not reflect the full cost of the environmental degradation it causes, which often makes replacing a product less expensive than repairing it. A low-carbon world values what already exists. A low-carbon world understands that energy-use reduction is not a one-time fix, but an ongoing process that touches every aspect of our lives.

Cambridge City Hall Annex
Cambridge, MA

Current Owner: The City of Cambridge

Building Type: Commercial Offices

Original Building Construction: 1871

Historic Designation: Part of the Mid-Cambridge Neighborhood
Conservation District, 1985

Restoration/Renovation Completion: 2004

Square Footage: 33,216 ft^2

Percentage Renovated: 100%

Occupancy: 109 people (40 hrs/week)

Recognition: LEED NC v2.0—Gold; Sustainable Buildings Industry Council
Beyond Green Award, First Place Exemplary Sustainable Building
2006; Massachusetts Historical Commission, Preservation Award
2005; Environmental Design and Construction, Excellence in Design
Award Finalist / Government Category 2005; Build New England
Award, Associated General Contractors 2005; Cambridge Historical
Commission, Preservation Award 2004; Massachusetts Municipal
Association, Innovation Award 2004; Building Design and Construction,
Innovation Award 2004

"When restored and reopened in 1899 following a fire, the press heralded the building as an example of innovation in ventilation, circulation and daylighting. Today, Cambridge City Hall Annex is again a showcase and sends the message that sustainable design is achievable and makes economic sense in historic preservation and municipal projects. The renovated annex became the oldest building certified under the USGBC LEED for New Construction (NC) program in 2005, earning the Gold rating."

—*William R. Hammer, AIA, HKT Architects, writing in
High Performing Buildings (Spring 2008)*[83]

Figure 5.9 The 1871 Cambridge (MA) City Hall Annex is a public showcase of renewable energy technologies, including roof-mounted photovoltaic panels, a ground-source heat pump, daylighting, and numerous energy-efficiency measures. Together, these measures reduce energy consumption by almost 50 percent below a conventional building. *Photo by Blind Dog Photo, Inc.*

Figure 5.10 The building was originally two stories high, with a third floor in a mansard roof. After a fire in 1899 destroyed the top floor, a new third story was added in brick. The recently restored parapet and chimneys were removed in the 1950s to create a flat roof. After partial renovations, the building was evacuated in 1999 due to a mold infestation. *Photo by HKT Architects Inc.*

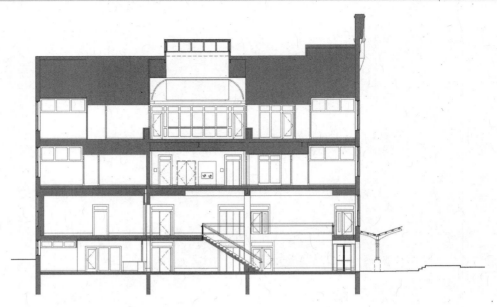

Figure 5.11 The building houses five city departments that receive visitors and do business with the public on a daily basis. The new double-height lobby serves as an active circulation and information hub. Six conference rooms, each infused with direct or borrowed light, host meetings with homeowners, residents, small businesses and developers. The building actively demonstrates the success of a "green" renovation. *Drawing by HKT Architects Inc.*

BUILDING DESCRIPTION

Constructed in 1871 as a grammar school, the Cambridge City Hall Annex became a municipal office building in 1942. The renovation completed in 2004 reduces CO_2 emissions from operations by slightly over 40 percent. Triggered by the need for mold and asbestos remediation, the project demonstrated the city's commitment to historic preservation, energy efficiency, renewable energy, and environmental responsibility.

The building exterior was restored using historic images as a guide. The interior was reconfigured to meet program needs. Wood paneling and lighting fixtures reflect the civic nature of the building while incorporating the latest technology: motion-sensitive lighting controls and, in the public hearing room, accommodations for a wide range of presentation modes and equipment. The building is completely handicapped-accessible, with a new main entry that includes a two-story lobby and elevator access to every floor.

Alternative Transportation

Located in a dense, compact urban community, the building—which houses many of the city's public agencies and hosts frequent community meetings—takes advantage of proximity to public transit to encourage alternative transportation use.

Employees are offered incentives for using public transportation, and indoor bicycle storage and shower facilities are provided for employees (outdoor bicycle racks serve visitors). Four bicycles are also housed in the building for use by employees during the workday. Limited parking is provided, and car poolers have reserved spaces.

Historic Preservation Review

The overall design process required approvals from the Mid-Cambridge Neighborhood Historic District Commission. Although supportive of the green aspects of the design, commission members opposed any adverse impact on the historic nature of the building, such as visible mechanical equipment or photovoltaic panels on the roof. The large double-hung windows match the original appearance but are thermally glazed with intermediate mullions and meet the state energy code. Historic detailing—both inside and out—respects the original building design.

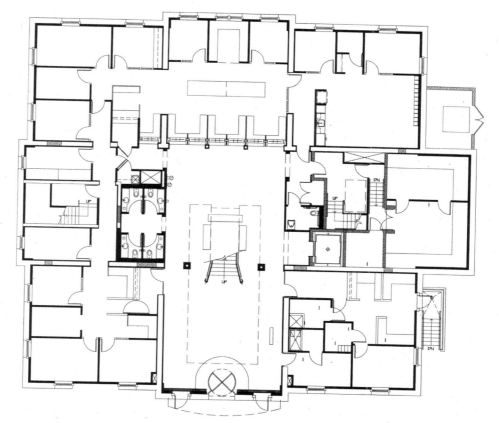

Figure 5.12 Closed for many years because of unhealthy indoor air conditions, the building now has low-emitting materials, operable windows, daylighting, and views for 90 percent of employees, as well as CO_2 monitoring as part of the indoor air quality monitoring. *Drawing by HKT Architects Inc.*

GREEN DESIGN ELEMENTS

Cambridge City Hall Annex

Sustainable Sites:
- Public transportation proximity
- Bicycle accommodation
- Highly reflective roof
- Xeriscaping

Energy and Atmosphere:
- Photovoltaic system
- Ground-source heat pumps
- Displacement and heat-recovery ventilation
- Natural ventilation
- Additional insulation
- Automatic daylight and occupancy sensors

Materials and Resources:
- Construction waste recycled
- Recycled content and recyclable materials (carpet)
- Forest Stewardship Council-(FSC) certified wood

Indoor Environment Quality:
- Skylights and interior glazing
- Operable windows
- Low-VOC materials and finishes
- CO_2 sensors
- Indoor air quality program

Energy and Envelope

- A 26.5-kW solar photovoltaic system on the roof provides about 10 percent of the building's electricity.
- Eight ground-source heat pumps meet all the building's heating and cooling needs.
- Variable air volume (VAV) air-distribution system. Make-up air in public meeting rooms is provided by displacement ventilation with outside air. A heat-recovery system minimizes heat loss by preheating incoming air with heat from outgoing air.
- Energy Star–rated roof, coated with a high-reflectance/low-emissivity material, minimizes heat absorption and lowers demand for cooling.
- System zoning allows meeting rooms used in the evening to be heated and cooled independently of the unoccupied building.
- Low-e double-glazed panes in operable wood windows reduce heat exchange and passage of infrared and ultraviolet radiation into the interior space; 90 percent of rooms have natural ventilation.
- Lighting controls adjust lighting in response to daylight levels and occupancy.
- 90 percent of the building interior receives daylight and has outside views. Original skylights were restored and a lightwell was created between the third and fourth floors. Borrowed light is provided by transoms and transparent sidelights.

PROJECT TEAM

The City of Cambridge
HKT Architects Inc. (Bill Hammer)
David Perry Architects, Inc.
Consigli Construction Co., Inc.
Arup
Weidlinger Associates, Inc.
Beals and Thomas, Inc.
Hammer Design
Sebesta Blomberg
Mike Glier, Public Artist

S.T. Dana Building
Ann Arbor, MI

Current Owner: Regents of the University of Michigan

Building Type: Higher Education

Original Building Construction: 1903

Restoration/Renovation Completion: 2003

Square Footage: 35,000 ft²

Percentage Renovated: 100%

Occupancy: 105 people (40 hrs/week) 550 visitors (20 hrs/week)

Recognition: LEED NC v2.0—Gold 2005; Michigan Chapter AIA Honor Award for Sustainability 2007; Maryland Society AIA Merit Award 2005; Washington, DC Chapter AIA Presidential Citation for Sustainable Design 2005

"Our building allows us to live what we teach: sustainability."
—*Rosina Bierbaum, Dean, University of Michigan School of Natural Resources and Environment (www.snre.umich.edu/greendana)*

BUILDING DESCRIPTION

Once known as the West Medical Building on the University of Michigan campus, the 1903 S.T. Dana building is home to the School of Natural Resources and Environment. To add much-needed office and classroom space without expanding the building footprint, the courtyard area in the center of the building was filled in and a fourth floor added, increasing usable space by 20 percent.

The project goals grew out of a philosophy that addressed both construction processes and lifetime performance of the building. Goals included:

- Increase energy conservation and efficiency.
- Use renewable energy (photovoltaics).
- Increase daylight use.
- Improve indoor air quality.

Figure 5.13 The School of Natural Resources and Environment received a LEED Gold certification from the U.S. Green Building Council for the Dana renovation. This made it the first major academic renovation to receive such a high rating for sustainable construction in the state of Michigan and put it among the first in the country. The school maintains an active website about "The Greening of Dana" (www.snre.umich.edu/greendana) and ongoing research and data collection about operations. © *Christopher Campbell 2003*

Figure 5.14 A photograph of the Samuel T. Dana Building c. 1910 shows the building without the new fourth floor and atrium roof. Used for almost 60 years as a medical training facility, the renovation completed in 2004 has achieved a 31 percent reduction in water use and a 30 percent reduction in energy even though building space and use increased. *Courtesy of QUINN EVANS / ARCHITECTS*

- Conserve water.
- Include operation costs in selecting mechanical equipment.
- Evaluate the life cycle of all products and materials used.
- Reuse and recycle components and materials for demolition.

Figure 5.15 The building section illustrates the decision to "build in and up" without expanding the building footprint. The renovation added a fourth floor to the building and covered and filled in the courtyard, providing about 20,000 square feet of much-needed office and classroom space. Both active and passive solar systems were added to the building. An active, roof-mounted system consists of a 30kW array of photovoltaic panels employing both Uni-Solar thin-film panels and Kyocera multicrystalline modules. A new 4,000-square-foot atrium skylight provides daylight to much of the building. © *QUINN EVANS / ARCHITECTS 2005*

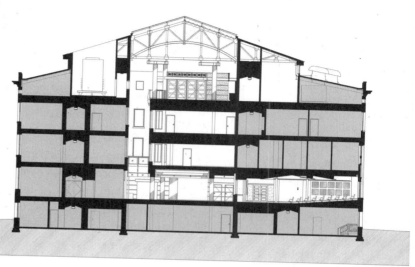

Over 60 percent of the existing interior materials were reused in different places in the renovated building; timbers from the attic were remilled for trim and furniture, old doors were refinished, casework and furniture were refinished. Chalkboards and whiteboards were salvaged and reused. Recycled materials include PET upholstery fabrics, recycled glass tile, high-density polyethylene (HDPE) countertops and partitions, and rubber flooring. Renewable materials such as biocomposites, wool, natural cork, bamboo, and all-natural linoleum received preference for finishes and appear throughout the building.

Low-flow and waterless plumbing fixtures reduce water use. Water faucets are sensor-activated, and the men's restrooms incorporate waterless urinals. Three composting toilets were installed. Composting toilets allow human waste to undergo microbial decomposition in a self-contained system, creating a safe-to-handle compost "tea" and solid compost that can be used as plant fertilizers and soil amendments, completing the nutrient cycle.

Energy Conservation
(excerpted from http://www.snre.umich.edu/greendana/conservation)

- *Solar power*—a 30kW array of photovoltaic panels employing both Uni-Solar thin-film panels and Kyocera multicrystalline modules sit atop the roof. The electricity they produce supplements the energy supplied by the campus co-generation plant.

GREEN DESIGN ELEMENTS

S.T. Dana Building

Sustainable Sites:
- Public transportation proximity
- Bicycle accommodation
- Xeriscaping
- Natural fertilizer

Water Efficiency:
- Composting toilets
- Waterless urinals
- Low-flow plumbing fixtures

Energy and Atmosphere:
- Additional insulation
- Photovoltaic system
- Radiant-cooling system in ceiling
- Natural ventilation
- Direct digital controls

Materials and Resources:
- Recycled materials
- Reclamation of exiting materials
- Renewable materials

Indoor Environment Quality:
- Skylight/clerestory windows
- Atria
- Operable windows
- Low-VOC materials and finishes

Additional Features:
- Building tours of eco-design

■ *Daylighting*—The 4,000-square-foot atrium skylight provides daylight to much of the building. Shades on the south side help keep the building cool in the summer months.

■ *Lighting*—Fluorescent fixtures with sensor-activated controls were installed throughout. The lamps are more efficient in converting electricity into light than incandescent or halogen fixtures and do not give off as much heat.

■ *Radiant cooling system*—The renovation added a radiant cooling system utilizing cold water in ceiling-level copper pipes. The cold water acts as a heat sink for warm air in the room, replacing the forced-air of a traditional system. This translates into substantial energy savings, as water is roughly three times more efficient than air as a heat-transfer medium. The radiant system is also healthier and quieter than traditional forced-air systems or less-efficient wall-unit air conditioners.

■ *Insulation*—Steel studs and insulation were added to the interior of the masonry walls.

■ *Controllability of systems*—All mechanical and electrical systems can be tailored to meet the needs of individual workspaces through direct digital control. These controls display the status of all systems and also call attention to any problems, leaks, shortages, etc.

PROJECT TEAM

Regents of the University of Michigan
University of Michigan School of Natural Resources and Environment (SNRE)
Quinn Evans | Architects
William McDonough + Partners
Ove Arup & Partners
Taylor Engineering, LLC
Timmons Design Engineers
JM Olson Corporation

Lion House at the Bronx Zoo
Bronx, NY

Current Owner: Wildlife Conservation Society

Building Type: Zoo/Assembly

Original Building Construction: 1903

Historic Designation: Historic District, New York City Landmarks
    Preservation Commission

Restoration/Renovation Completion: 2007

Square Footage: 40,865 ft²

Percentage Renovated: 100% + 25% addition

Recognition: LEED-NC v. 2.1–Gold; *Environmental Design & Construction
    Magazine* Excellence in Design 2009; The Municipal Art Society of New
    York Masterworks Award for Best Restoration Project 2009

"The building's sustainable features were integral to the overall restoration and design plan, and emblematic of the Wildlife Conservation Society's mission. This project certainly sets a precedent for other historic and existing buildings not only in New York, but across the country."

—*Sylvia J. Smith AIA, LEED, senior partner at
FXFOWLE Architects*

BUILDING DESCRIPTION

The 1903 Lion House embodies the Beaux Arts architectural principles of symmetry and formalism. The renovation integrated new public and private access within a constrained footprint, including accessible public exhibit space; semipublic multipurpose space for community meetings, staff lectures, educational activities, art exhibits, conservation conferences, and other events; and private, flexible, and secure animal holding and support spaces. The design passed reviews conducted by the New York City Landmarks Commission, the city's Design Commission, and the New York State Historic Preservation Office. It expanded usable area from 32,000 square feet to 40,000 by extending the width and depth of the basement and inserting an interior mezzanine.

Figure 5.16 Situated at the heart of the Bronx Zoo's early-twentieth-century Astor Court, the Lion House was designated a National Historic District by the New York City Landmarks Commission in 2000 in recognition of its aesthetic and historic distinction. Designed by Heins & LaFarge in 1903 as part of the original campus at Astor Court, the Lion House embodies the zookeeping paradigm of its time. The building's Beaux Arts architectural principles of symmetry, clarity, formalism, hierarchy, monumental scale, and articulation also reflect the social ideals of the late nineteenth century. The façade is an artful combination of limestone, Roman ironspot brick, copper roof, and a terra cotta roof cornice embellished with puma, jaguar, and leopard heads. Although a prominent building, the structure sat unused for decades after the lions were moved to a more natural environment, a clear indication of its unsuitability for the modern zoo experience. © *David Sundberg/Esto*

Integrated building systems are nearly invisible—roof vents are incorporated into existing building elements, and a ground-source heat pump system eliminates the need for a cooling tower. The contained, right-sized systems contribute to a healthy and sustainable environment for animals, handlers, and visitors, with high standards of interior environmental quality.

Energy Conservation

The building is projected to save 57 percent of energy costs, as compared to a building designed to comply with the energy code:

- *Geothermal heating and cooling:* Six modular, 28-ton water-to-water heat pumps provide chilled water for cooling in the summer and hot water for heating in the winter. A ground-source heat pump uses the principle that energy always flows from warmer areas to cooler ones. It takes advantage of the relatively constant temperature of the ground to provide heat in the winter and cooling in the summer. Five 1,500-feet standing column wells provide 34 tons of cooling and 304 MBTU/HR of heat each.

■ *Dynamic skylight:* The use of a three-layer ethylene tetrafluoroethylene (ETFE) dynamic skylight system with a movable center layer and staggered shading patterns balances the contradictory requirements of maximum natural light for the plants and animals of the exhibit with minimum heat gain and electrical and cooling load goals. This new technology, with an R-value of 3.3, rather than the typical 1.8 for a polyester film skylight, covers nearly 8,500 square feet of skylights.

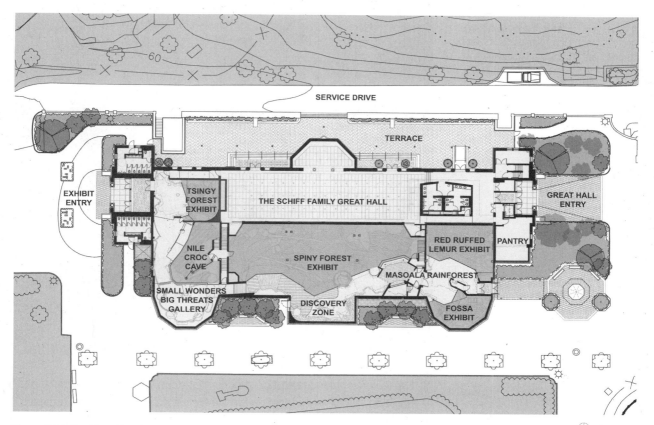

Figure 5.17 First Floor Plan. Programmatically, the project needed to integrate extreme degrees of public and private access within the original constrained footprint: accessible public exhibit space; semipublic multipurpose space for community meetings, staff lectures, educational activities, art exhibits, conservation conferences, and other events; and private, flexible, and secure animal holding and support spaces. The design also had to revive the west terrace as a semiprivate outdoor area and an extension of the multipurpose space. *FXFOWLE Architects*

Figure 5.18 View of the Schiff Family Great Hall after renovation. The renovation redefines the existing, rather than replicating an earlier look. The new functions within the building use a modern approach and materials. Restoration was only done when the interior use remained the same—at the entries, for example. The design of the new insertions employs functional, not decorative, elements, and materials are left exposed to maintain a sense of economy and essentiality. © David Sundberg/Esto

Figure 5.19 Historic view of the Great Hall. © Wildlife Conservation Society

■ *Fuel cell:* An inadequate underground electrical distribution system helped make a fuel cell an economical choice for the building. A fuel cell provides 200kW of energy an hour (approximately 50 percent of the electricity required), with excess electricity exported to the zoo grid. 650 MBtu/hr of waste heat from the fuel cell meets approximately 40 percent of the building heating load. The only use of fossil fuel is natural gas for the fuel cell.

- *Right-sized system:* Owner participation in the design process afforded the design team the opportunity to clearly communicate the advantages and disadvantages of various design decisions. The WCS agreed that a space temperature float of 2 or 3 degrees during peak loading was acceptable. Right-sizing the HVAC system included controlling exhibit lighting and the dynamic skylight shading through the building automation system (BAS) so as to limit peak loads.

- *Indoor air quality:* Quantities of outside air used for ventilation, which would normally reach about 6 ACH (air changes per hour) for the building volume, were reduced to 3 ACH by providing carbon filters and 95 percent particulate filtration in the air handlers.

- *VAV system and heat recovery:* Environmental quality controls for animal facilities normally approach the usage levels of a constant-volume reheat system. The high air-change rate needed to maintain indoor air quality in the exhibit and animal holding area would further exacerbate the energy penalty. A variable-volume system with a 50 percent minimum supply air rate and reheat coils was used, with heat recovered from the fuel cell, the air conditioning waste heat, and the campus cogeneration plant. These sources provide heating for the building, reheating, humidification, domestic water heating, and animal life-safety-filtration systems heating.

- *Building automation system:* In addition to controlling the dynamic skylight and lighting in concert with the HVAC system, the BAS controls the sources of heat and reheat for the building so as to provide the most energy-efficient configuration. In addition, the BAS controls the selection of heat sources so as to benefit the entire zoo campus, using local heat recovery (fuel cell and condenser water) before it recruits waste heat from the campus cogeneration plant. The BAS also controls the amount of outside air introduced for ventilation in the multipurpose/catering room, based on CO_2 levels, and provides for "night flushing" of the building as appropriate.

Water and Waste

The Lion House includes the zoo's main public toilet for the Astor Court area. The design incorporates a graywater storage/filtration system that recycles water from the lavatories for use in the water closet flushometers. Containing a 3,000-gallon underground filtered graywater storage tank, a 300-gallon dirty graywater indoor storage tank, and a filtration system and pumps, the graywater system is projected to save more than 141,000 gallons of water every year. The graywater system and low-flow fixtures will decrease potable water use by 53 percent and wastewater generated by 21 percent. The net reduction in sewage is expected to reach 251,500 gallons of water per year.

GREEN DESIGN ELEMENTS

Lion House at the Bronx Zoo

Sustainable Sites:
- Public transportation proximity
- Bicycle accommodation
- Carpool parking
- Reduced site disturbance
- Reduced paved area and increased shading
- Native, drought-resistant plants
- Reduced light pollution
- Site landscaping to reduce runoff

Water Efficiency:
- Wastewater output reduced
- No potable water for landscaping
- Low-flow plumbing fixtures
- Waterless urinals
- Graywater system for toilet use
- Recycled water for adjacent exhibit

Energy and Atmosphere:
- Optimized energy performance 60 percent
- Ground-source heat pumps
- Heat-recovery protocol
- Additional commissioning
- Underfloor air system
- Right-sized systems
- Ethylene tetrafluoroethylene skylights
- Fuel cell
- Computerized energy-conserving protocol
- Insulated glazing
- High-performance lighting
- High-efficiency variable-air-volume systems

Materials and Resources:
- Construction waste diverted/recycled
- Recycled content
- Local/regional materials
- Salvaged materials

Indoor Environment Quality:
- Low-VOC materials and finishes
- CO_2 monitors
- Low-emitting materials
- Daylight and views
- Operable windows

Additional Features:
- Green cleaning policy

PROJECT TEAM

- NYC Department of Design and Construction
- Wildlife Conservation Society
- FXFOWLE Architects
- Hill International
- Kallen & Lemelson
- Anastos Engineering
- Building Conservation Associates
- Langan
- Hayden McKay Lighting Design
- Quennell Rothschild
- Cerami
- DVI Communications

Scowcroft Building

Ogden, UT

Current Owner: Cottonwood Realty Services, LLP

Building Type: Commercial Office

Original Building Construction: 1906

Historic Designation: National Register of Historic Places

Restoration/Renovation Completion: 2003

Square Footage: 124,000 ft^2

Percentage Renovated: 100%

Occupancy: 1,100 people (40 hrs/week) no visitors

Recognition: LEED NC v2.1—Silver; GSA Environmental Excellence Award 2006; AIA Utah Merit Award 2006; Envision Utah, Governor's Quality Growth Award of Excellence for Implementation 2006; Utah Heritage Foundation Project Award 2004; Utah Masonry Council, Historic Restoration Award 2004; *Intermountain Contractor* Magazine's Best Renovation/Preservation Project 2003

"In addition to meeting historic preservation standards, the Scowcroft project utilized "green" building techniques. In fact, Scowcroft will likely be the first building in the United States to qualify for both federal historic rehab tax credits and Leadership in Energy and Environmental Design certification. Once a white elephant, Scowcroft now brings 1,100 employees to downtown Ogden each day."

—*Utah Heritage Foundation*

BUILDING DESCRIPTION

This innovative design/build project restored a historic warehouse—built in 1906 but long derelict—into Class A office space for a government tenant. The renovation enhanced the indoor environment by carving out two new full-height atria to bring daylight into the heart of the building. The design utilized 90 percent of the existing structural system, 100 percent of existing shell, and 95 percent of the existing interior materials. A raised-access floor system provides maximum flexibility for tenants.

Figure 5.20 The restoration of the long-derelict Scowcroft Warehouse—built in 1906 and listed on the Utah Historical Register—included extensive exterior restoration of the stone, brick, and metal façades. Missing and badly damaged units were replaced in kind. The masonry was cleaned and repointed. Metal cornices were restored. Metal windows were replaced with high-performance, matching units. Historic building tax credits helped make the project economically feasible. © *richerimages.com*

All existing glazing systems were replaced with energy-efficient windows that matched the appearance of the original to enable the project to achieve the 20 percent historic building tax credits. A seismic upgrade was accomplished by wall-coring the historic masonry.

Energy

Evaporative cooling—An indirect/direct evaporative-cooling (IDEC) system supplemented by chilled water furnishes 90 percent of the building's annual cooling requirements without mechanical refrigeration. The indirect evaporative-cooling stage circulates water from oversized cooling towers through six-row cooling coils to cool all of the outside air entering the building to within 7°F of the outdoor wet-bulb temperature. (Wet-bulb temperature is an indication of the amount of moisture in the air). Air leaves the indirect evaporative-cooling coils at 69°F and enters either a 4- or 8-inch-deep rigid evaporative medium for further cooling. Air leaves the medium at 62°F with no need for chiller operation. On the handful of days each year when the wet-bulb temperature reaches 68°F, a chiller lowers the temperature of the supply air as it passes through the chilled-water coils.

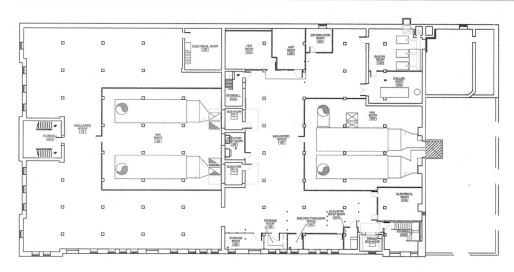

Figure 5.21 Basement floor plan. The central air-handling system relies on four built-up variable-air-volume (VAV) air handlers with a capacity of 106,000 cubic feet per minute, one propeller-type relief fans for each of the two atrium penthouses, indirect evaporative cooling coil banks, chilled-water coil banks, evaporative media, and one 140-ton chiller with dual screw-type compressors. *Cooper Roberts Simonsen & Associates*

BASEMENT FLOOR PLAN

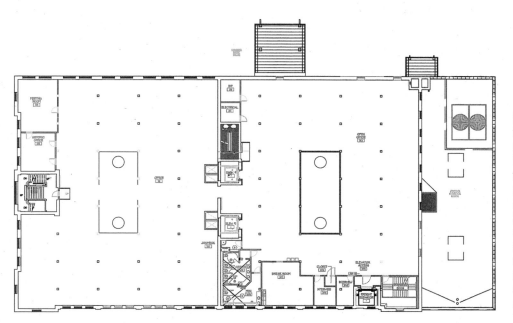

Figure 5.22 Second floor plan. Two large atria provide the majority of the building's daylight. Large windows at every level provide additional daylight and views. The daylighting in the building is effective enough that daytime overhead lighting is not required in 80 percent of the regularly occupied spaces. *Cooper Roberts Simonsen & Associates*

SECOND FLOOR PLAN

Air handling—The central air-handling system relies on four built-up variable-air-volume (VAV) air handlers with a capacity of 106,000 cubic feet per minute, one propeller-type relief fan for each of the two atrium penthouses, indirect evaporative-cooling coil banks, chilled-water coil banks, evaporative media, and one 140-ton chiller with dual screw-type compressors.

Baseboard heat—Hot-water radiant baseboard heat provides warmth in the winter.

Underfloor air system—Space temperature sensors adjust the volume of air flowing from the pressurized floor plenum through modulating floor diffusers. The underfloor air system gives occupants control over the temperature in their spaces and reduces energy use.

Figure 5.23 Two new atria were added for daylighting and mechanical systems. Extensive computer modeling of the historic building informed the design and confirmed the efficiency of the mechanical and electrical systems. As a result of the high-performance equipment used, the building is projected to provide a 23 percent yearly cost savings. © *richerimages.com*

Figure 5.24 The historic building has a thick massing and windows on all four sides. The structural masonry walls were retained and the developer employed an innovative, noninvasive "wall coring" technology to carry out a seismic upgrade without altering the exterior or interior of the perimeter masonry walls or the historic interior. All exterior glazing systems were replaced. Much of the interior lighting is indirect, with compact can-type fixtures in hallways and lobbies. © *richerimages.com*

GREEN DESIGN ELEMENTS

Scowcroft Building

Sustainable Sites:

- Public transportation proximity
- Car/vanpooling accommodation
- Energy Star–rated roof
- Xeriscaping
- Bioswales

Water Efficiency:

- Low-flow plumbing fixtures

Energy and Atmosphere:

- Renewable-energy certificates (wind)

- Raised-access floor
- Indirect/direct evaporative cooling
- Radiant baseboards
- Efficient window replacement

Materials and Resources:

- 75 percent of construction waste recycled
- Reuse of existing structure and materials

Indoor Environment Quality:

- Clerestory windows
- Atria
- Low-VOC materials and finishes

PROJECT TEAM

Cottonwood Partners
Cooper Roberts Simonsen Architects
Jacobsen Construction Company, Inc.
Spectrum Engineers
Colvin Engineering Associates
ABS Consulting
Reeve & Associates
Brent Morris Associates
Johnson Controls

John W. McCormack Federal Building
Boston, MA

Current Owner: General Services Administration

Building Type: Offices

Original Building Construction: 1933

Historic Designation: Eligible for individual listing on the National Register of Historic Places, Landmark petition filed with the Boston Landmarks Commission.

Restoration/Renovation Completion: 2009

Square Footage: 633,032 ft^2

Percentage Renovated: 100%

Occupancy: 1,150 people (45 hrs/week)

Recognition: Registered LEED-NC 2.2—Gold

"The renovation of the historic John W. McCormack Building at Post Office Square is expected to set the standard in the integration of historical preservation and modern day sustainability."

—*EPA website, Moving Region 1: EPA New England (www.epa.gov/ne/about/move/greenbuilding.html)*

PROJECT DESCRIPTION

The 22-story John W. McCormack Federal Building was constructed between 1931and 1933 as an expression of Boston's national stature and demanding growth. The building represents one of the finest art-deco style buildings in the region from the 1920s and 1930s. The Public Buildings Act of 1926, of which the courthouse is a product, represented the first congressional authorization for new federal construction programs since 1913. Construction of the building illustrated early efforts to use large federal projects to help offset the impact of the Great Depression and spur the economy.

The renovation restored the significant interior spaces, including lobbies, courtrooms, and a library, while creating flexible work areas and introducing amenities and new, energy-efficient systems. A green roof in the center of the building surrounded by 16 floors covers over 25 percent of the site footprint, providing both views and an important open space for occupants. The roof is planted with native species that, once established, should require no irrigation. Captured rainfall gathered from upper roof areas is stored in cisterns inside the building and will provide irrigation during drought condition.

Figure 5.25 The 22-story John W. McCormack building, built 1931–1933, opened during the worst of the Great Depression and is now a model of green renovation. The granite and limestone tower, incorporating elements of both art deco and stripped classical styles, was designed by the nationally known Boston firm of Cram & Ferguson in collaboration with the U.S. Treasury. *David Salvia photo, courtesy Goody Clancy*

Figure 5.26 The building section demonstrates the thin profile and lightcourt design of many historic buildings that make daylighting and views easilty achievable in renovations. The design plants a new green roof in the heart of the building and a skylight, which introduces natural light, into the staff cafeteria. *© 2009 Goody Clancy*

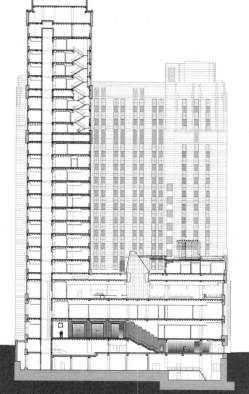

Figure 5.27 The grade-level lobby has been renovated to become the main entrance of the building. *© 2009 Goody Clancy*

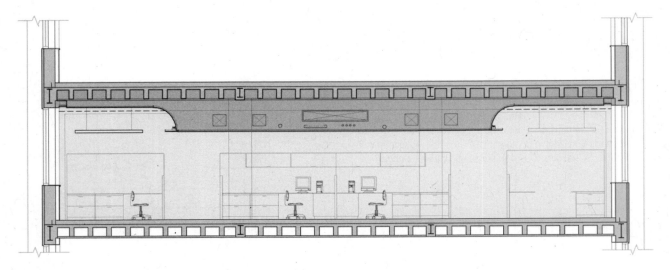

Figure 5.28 Green strategies in the renovation include clustering the mechanical systems in the center of the space to facilitate daylighting. An open office plan increases occupant density and long-term flexibility. Insulation was added to the walls, and the 70-year-old aluminum windows were replaced with units that have low-e, insulated glass. *© 2009 Goody Clancy*

GREEN DESIGN ELEMENTS

John W. McCormack Federal Building

Sustainable Site Selection:

- *Density:* Development in a high-density area (709,485 ft²/acre) and a landmark preservation project.
- *Brownfields redevelopment:* Abatement of asbestos and lead paint.
- *Alternative transportation:* The building lies close to public transit and provides indoor bike storage for over 15 percent of the building users as well as showers.

Water Efficiency:

- *Landscaping:* Native plant species populate the green roof, and 5,500 gallons of rainwater will be captured and stored within the building, should the plantings require irrigation.
- *Water use:* Reduction of 32 percent over code, 1.5 gallon/flush toilets, 2.5 gallon/minute showers and sinks.

Energy and Atmosphere:

- *Energy performance:* Designed to meet Energy Star; energy cost savings, but will be 20 percent better than required. Low-e spectrally selective and historically appropriate windows, R-11 insulation, variable-speed fans/pumps, occupancy sensors in offices and daylighting sensors near the windows.

- *Green power:* Purchased to offset electricity consumption at the building.

Materials and Resources:

- *Recycling:* Five materials from the offices are recycled: plastics, metals, paper, cardboard, and glass. Collection areas in the lounge on each floor and storage in the basement. Food waste collection in the cafeteria.
- *Construction waste:* Over 75 percent was diverted from disposal and recycle.

Indoor Air Quality:

- *Environmental tobacco smoke:* There is a no-smoking policy in the building, on the green roof, and within 25 feet of the entrances.
- *Daylighting:* Over 70 percent of the occupants have daylight.
- *Low-emitting materials:* These include paint, carpeting, and composite wood.
- *Sources of contaminants:* Such as copy rooms and janitors' closets are exhausted directly to the exterior.

Innovation

- *Education:* An educational kiosk describes the green features.
- *Green cleaning and integrated pest management.*

PROJECT TEAM

General Services Administration
Tishman Construction Co.
Goody Clancy Associates
Suffolk Construction Co.
Cosentini Associates
Weidlinger Associates Inc.
Heller & Metzger, Inc.
Rolf Jensen & Associates, Inc.
Brandston Partnership Inc.

Acentech Inc.
Andropogon Associates, LTD
Lerch, Bates & Associates Inc.
RDK Engineers, Inc.
Sako Associates
Gruzen Samton LLP
Veridian
ATC Associates Inc.
Hanscomb, Faithful & Gould

ENDNOTES

1. Fatih Birol, "World Energy Outlook 2008," Federal Ministry of Economics and Technology, Berlin, November 19, 2008.
2. United Nations Environment Programme, *Buildings and Climate Change; Status, Challenges and Opportunities* (Nairobi, Kenya, 2007), www.unep.org, p. v.
3. http://www.epa.gov/climatechange/emissions/downloads09/GHG2007-03-508.pdf.
4. U.S. Energy Information Administration, Emissions of Greenhouse Gases in the United States 2008 (December 2009), p. 2, ftp://ftp.eia.doe.gov/pub/oiaf/1605/cdrom/pdf/ggrpt/057308.pdf, DOE/EIA-0573 (2008).
5. Quoted at www.nrdc.org/energy/coalnotclean.asp. Accessed April 28, 2009.
6. Nathan S. Lewis, "Powering the Planet," *MRS Bulletin,* vol. 32 (October 2007), p.808, www.mrs.org/bulletin.
7. U.S. Energy Information Administration, *Annual Energy Review 2008* (June 2009), p. 38, http://www.eia.doe.gov/aer/pdf/aer.pdf, DOE/EIA-O384.
8. U.S. Energy Information Administration, *Emissions of Greenhouse Gases in the United States 2008*, pp. 2 and 5.
9. Marilyn A. Brown, Frank Southworth, and Andrea Sarzynski, "Shrinking the Carbon Footprint of Metropolitan America," Metropolitan Policy Program Brookings Institution (May 2008), www.blueprintprosperity.org.
10. U.S. Energy Information Administration, *Annual Energy Review 2008*, pp. xxxiii and xxxiv.
11. The National Research Council, "Environmental Impacts of Wind-Energy Projects," The National Academy of Sciences (2007), www.nap.edu.
12. The Center for Health and the Global Environment, Harvard Medical School, "Healthy Solutions for the Low Carbon Economy, Supporting Material" (July 2008), p. 26, http://chge.med.harvard.edu/programs/ccf/healthysolutions.html.
13. Keith Bradsher, "China: Earth-Friendly Elements Mined Destructively," *New York Times,* December 26, 2009.
14. Paul R. Epstein, William Moomaw, Christopher Walker, with Archie Kasnet and Mary B. Rice, "Healthy Solutions for the Low Carbon Economy; Guidelines for Investors, Insurers and Policy Makers," The Center for Health and the Global Environment, Harvard Medical School, (July 2008), p. 7, http://chge.med.harvard.edu/programs/ccf/healthysolutions.html.
15. U.S. Energy Information Administration, *Annual Energy Review 2008*, p. xix.
16. Centre National De La Recherche Scientifique Delegation for Scientific and Technical Information, "Focus: Energy," *CNRS* (February 2005), p. 4, Paris, France, www.cnrs.fr.
17. World Business Council for Sustainable Development, "Energy Efficiency in Buildings Transforming the Market" (April 2009), p. 10, www.wbcsd.org.
18. McKinsey Global Energy and Materials, *Unlocking Energy Efficiency in the U.S. Economy* (2009), www.mckinsey.com/clientservice/electricpowernaturalgas/downloads/us_energy_efficiency_full_report.pdf.
19. Victor Olgyay, "Sense and Response: A Bioclimatic Dialogue of Place," Rocky Mountain Institute (2009), http://www.rmi.org/?UrlName=LibraryandCat1=Built+EnvironmentandCat2=Built+EnvironmentandCatType=sharepoint accessed December 2010.
20. Amory B. Lovins, "Energy End-Use Energy Efficiency," Rocky Mountain Institute, www.rmi.org, InterAcademy Council, Amsterdam, www.interacademycouncil.net, part of 2005–2006 study, "Transitions to Sustainable Energy Systems" (September 19, 2005), ©2005 IAC.
21. Ibid., p. 15.
22. www.esbsustainability.com, accessed January 2009.
23. *Clean Air-Cool Planet, EnergyEfficiency, Renewable Energy and Historic Preservation: A Guide for Historic District Commissions* (2009), www.cleanair-coolplanet.org.
24. McGraw Hill Construction SmartMarket Report "Green Building Retrofit and Renovation" (October 2009), p. 14, www.construction.com.
25. Michelle Addington, "No Building Is an Island; A Look a the Different Scales of Energy," *Harvard Design Magazine* (Spring/Summer 2007).
26. Jon Wallsgrove, "Age Energy Research; A Study of the Energy Usage of Buildings Relative to Their Age," HMCS Estates Ministry of Justice (May 2007).
27. Ibid.
28. National Round Table on the Environment and the Economy and Sustainable Development Technology Canada 2009, Figure 7, *Geared for Change: Energy Efficiency in Canada's Commercial Building Sector*, www.nrtee-trnee.ca, www.sdtc.ca.
29. Office of Business Performance Public Buildings Service U.S. General Services Administration, "Financing Historic Federal Buildings; An Analysis of Current Practice" (May 1999).
30. Wallsgrove, p. 3.

31. Michael C. Henry, "The Heritage Building Envelope as a Passive and Active Climate Moderator: Opportunities and Issues in Reducing Dependency on Air-Conditioning," Contribution to the Experts' Roundtable on Sustainable Climate Management Strategies, held in April 2007, in Tenerife, Spain, www.getty.edu/conservation/science/climate/paper_henry.pdf. Accessed February 2010.

32. The Getty Conservation Institute, "Experts' Roundtable on Sustainable Climate Management Strategies." Edited transcript, Tenerife, Spain, April 2007, www.getty.edu/conservation/science/climate/roundtable_transcript.pdf. Accessed February 2010.

33. www.getty.edu/conservation/science/climate/index.html. Accessed February 2010.

34. Shin Maekawa, Vincent Beltran, and Franciza Toledo, "Testing Alternatives to Conventional Air-Conditioning in Coastal Georgia." *APT Bulletin,* vol. 38, no. 2-3 (2007), www.getty.edu/conservation/science/climate/hollybourne_cottage_APT.pdf. Accessed May 2010.

35. M. B. C. Aries, J. A. Veitch, G. R. Newsham, "Physical and Psychological Discomfort in the Office Environment." Paper presented at the Light and Health Research Foundation (SOLG) Symposium, Eindhoven, the Netherlands, November 8, 2007.

36. Benjamin Stein, John S. Reynolds, Walter T. Grondzik, and Alison G. Kwok. *Mechanical and Electrical Equipment for Buildings* (Hoboken, NJ: John Wiley and Sons, 2006), p. 86.

37. Marilyn A. Brown, Frank Southworth, and Therese K. Stovall, "Towards a Climate-Friendly Built Environment" (Arlington, VA: Pew Center on Global Climate Change, 2005), www.pewclimate.org, p. iii.

38. Many of the topics discussed in this section are drawn from "Proposed LEED Credit for Electrical Load Shedding," by Wayne Jensen, Tim Wentz, and Bruce Fischer, *Journal of Green Building* 4(3) (Summer 2009).

39. John Straube, Ph.D., P. Eng., "Insight: Why Energy Matters" (April 2009), www.buildingscience.com.

40. U.S. Energy Information Administration, *Annual Energy Review 2008,* p. 350.

41. Brown, Southworth, and Stovall, p. 2.

42. U.S. Energy Information Administration, *Annual Energy Review 2008,* p. 64.

43. Ibid., p.16.

44. RICS (Royal Institution of Chartered Surveyors) "Transforming Existing Buildings: The Green Challenge" (March 2007), www.rics.org.

45. Email correspondence with Adrian Tuluca, Viridian Energy and Environmental, www.viridianee.com, March 21, 2005.

46. ASHRAE Green Tip, www.engineeringforsustainability.org/docs/greentips_2006.pdf. Accessed November 2009.

47. Peter St. Clair and Richard Hyde, "Towards a New Model for Climate Responsive Design at the University of the Sunshine Coast Chacellery," *Journal of Green Building,* vol. 4 (3) (Summer 2009), College Publishing, Glen Avlen, VA.

48. ASHRAE Green Tip #6, www.engineeringforsustainability.org/docs/greentips_2006.pdf. Accessed November 2009.

49. Alliant Energy, "HVAC:Chillers" at http://www.alliantenergy.com/UtilityServices/ForYourBusiness/EnergyExpertise/EnergyEffiiency/012393. Accessed on February 7, 2010.

50. ASHRAE Green Tip #22, www.engineeringforsustainability.org/docs/greentips_2006.pdf. Accessed November 2009.

51. David Chandler, "Manufacturing Inefficiency; Study Sees 'Alarming' Use of Energy, Materials in Newer Manufacturing Processes," MIT Tech Talk (March 18, 2009).

52. Sandy Halliday, *Sustainable Construction,* © Gaia Research (Oxford, UK and Burlington, VT: Butterworth-Heinemann, Elsevier Linacre House, 2008), p. 282.

53. Vasilis M. Fthenakis, Hyung Chul Kim, and Erik Alsema, "Emissions from Photovoltaic Life Cycles," *Environmental Science and Technology,* vol. 42 (6) (February 6, 2008): 2168–2174, on http://pubs.acs.org.

54. www.energystar.gov/ia/business/EPA_BUM_CH1_Intro.pdf.

55. Steve Fredrickson, "Fabric Facades; New Sustainable Advantages Can Be Found by Wrapping a Building in Fabric," *Fabric Architecture,* vol. 20 (5) (September/October 2008).

56. Halliday, *Sustainable Construction.*

57. Caroline Alderson, "Technical Preservation Guidelines—Upgrading Historic Building Windows," Center for Historic Buildings, Office of the Chief Architect, Public Buildings Service, U.S. General Services Administration, March 2009. Available online at http://www.gsa.gov/Portal/gsa/ep/contentView.do?contentType=GSA_BASICandcontentId=14985.

58. 2000 European Commission Communication on the Precautionary Principle.

59. Royal Institution of Chartered Surveyors (RICS), *Transforming Existing Buildings: The Green Challenge* (March

2007). London: Royal Institution of Chartered Surveyors. Available at www.rics.org/site/download_feed.aspx?fileID=907&fileExtension=PDF. (Accessed May 2010.)

60. Elisabetta Rosina and Elwin C. Robison, "Applying Infrared Thermography to Historic Wood-Framed Buildings in North America," *APT Bulletin*, vol. XXXIII (4) (2002).

61. Michael J. Heule, Steve McGuire, Paul E. Totten, and Lew Harriman, "Richard Bolling Federal Building: Modernization and Energy Efficiency Upgrades," *Journal of Building Enclosure Design* (Winter 2009), National Institute of Building Science, www.nibs.org.

62. Paul Baker, "Improving the Thermal Performance of Traditional Windows," Technical Paper 1. Technical Conservation Group, Historic Scotland (October 2008), www.historic-scotland.gov.uk/gcu-technical-_thermal-effiency-traditional-windows.pdf, p. 2.

63. www.energysavers.gov/your_home/energy_audits/index.cfm/mytopic=11210.

64. Peter Yost, "Sustainability Requires Durability," *GreenSource* (2009), 01/200.

65. Paul Baker, "In situ U-value measurements in traditional buildings—preliminary results," Historic Scotland Technical Conservation Group, Technical Paper 2 (October 2008), http://www.historic-scotland.gov.uk/u-value_measurements_traditional_buildings.pdf.

66. Research Highlights, "Performance Evaluation of Retrofitted Solid Masonry Exterior Walls," Technical Series 07-105, Canada Mortgage and Housing Corporation (March 2007), www.cmhc.ca.

67. John Straube and Chris Schumacher, "Interior Insulation Retrofits of Load-Bearing Masonry Walls in Cold Climates," *Journal of Green Building*, vol. 2 (2).

68. J. Wilkinson, D. De Rose, B. Sullivan, and J. F. Straube "Measuring the Impact of Interior Insulation on Solid Masonry Walls in a Cold Climate," *Journal of Building Enclosure Design* (Summer 2009), www.nibs.org.

69. Ibid.

70. English Heritage, *Energy Efficiency in Historic Buildings: Insulating Solid Walls*, www.english-heritage.org.uk (February 2010), http://www.climatechangeandyourhome.org.uk/live/content_pdfs/779.pdf.

71. Ibid.

72. Unpublished study, completed March 2009 for the MIT Department of Facilities. Team led by Payette included Transsolar Energietechnik GmbH, Simpson Gumpertz,

and Heger, Energysmiths, Building Conservation Associates and Daniel O'Connell's Sons.

73. Lloyd Alter, "Why Old Windows are Green Windows: Installing New Windows Doesn't Necessarily Pay" (March 30, 2009), http://planetgreen.discovery.com/home-garden/green-windows.html?campaign=daylife-article. Accessed February 7, 2010.

74. Refer to the Web sites of the National Trust for Historic Preservation, http://www.preservationnation.org/issues/weatherization/windows/, and the California Office of Historic Preservation for Window Repair and Retrofit, Studies and Research, http://ohp.parks.ca.gov/?page_id=25935, as well as English Heritage, www.climatechangeandyourhome.org.uk/live/research_generic.aspx, and Historic Scotland.

75. *Energy Efficiency, Renewable Energy and Historic Preservation: A Guide for Historic District Commissions* (2009). Available at www.cleanair-coolplanet.org/for_communities/HDCGuide.pdf (accessed May 2010).

76. Unpublished studies of window alternatives completed by Goody Clancy for the General Services Administration.

77. Australian Government Forest and Wood Products Research and Development Corporation, "Comparative Service Life Assessment of Window Systems" (August 2007), www.fwprdc.org.au.

78. Sandra Steingraber, Ph.D, "Update on the Environmental Health Impacts of Polyvinyl Chloride (PVC) as a Building Material: Evidence from 2000–2004," Healthy Building Network (April 2, 2004), www.healthybuilding.net/pvc/steingraber.pdf.

79. Mike Parrett, "Window Performance and Sustainability," in Michael Tutton, Elizabeth Hirst, and Jill Pearce, eds., *Windows: History, Repair and Conservation* (Shaftesbury, UK: Donhead Publishing Ltd., 2007), p. 242.

80. National Round Table on the Environment and the Economy and Sustainable Development Technology Canada 2009, *Geared for Change: Energy Efficiency in Canada's Commercial Building Sector*, www.nrtee-trnee.ca, www.sdtc.ca.

81. The Center for Health and the Global Environment, *Healthy Solutions for the Low Carbon Economy: Guidelines for Investors, Insurers and Policy Makers* (Boston, MA: Harvard Medical School, Center for Health and the Global Environment, July 2008), p. 10.

82. Brown, Southworth, and Stovall, p. v.

83. William R. Hammer, "Old Is New Again," *High Performing Buildings* (Spring 2008).

chapter 6

INDOOR ENVIRONMENT—
LIGHT, AIR, AND HEALTH

6.1   INDOOR AIR POLLUTION

"Good indoor air quality is a human right!"

—*Fin Jorgensen, Norwegian Engineer*[1]

The Magnitude of the Problem

THE AIR INSIDE OUR BUILDINGS is almost always less healthy than the air outside. In developed countries, where people spend up to 90 percent of their time indoors, exposure to indoor pollutants becomes even more problematic when building envelopes are tightened in support of more efficient heating and cooling without ensuring adequate ventilation. This is not good news, and it should underline the need for caution in selecting materials and emphasize the importance of shunning "Red List" chemicals (refer to Chapter 7), which significantly contribute to unhealthy interior (and exterior) environments.

According to the U.S. EPA, "Known health effects of indoor pollutants include asthma, cancer, developmental defects and delays, including effects on vision, hearing, growth, intelligence, and learning, and effects on the cardiovascular system (heart and lungs). Pollutants found in the indoor environment may also contribute to other health effects, including those of the reproductive and immune systems." The report further notes, "Most chemicals in commercial use have not been tested for possible health effects."[2]

Elements contributing to indoor air pollution have changed dramatically in the last 50 years. Composite-wood, synthetic carpets, polymeric flooring, foam cushioning, plastic items, and scented cleaning agents have become common. Electrical appliances, including TVs and computers, emit chemicals. Levels of certain indoor pollutants (e.g., formaldehyde, aromatic and chlorinated solvents, chlorinated pesticides, PCBs) have increased and then decreased. Levels of other indoor pollutants have increased and remain high (e.g., phthalate esters and brominated flame-retardants, nonionic surfactants, and their degradation products). Many of the chemicals commonly found in indoor environments today were not present 50 years ago.[3]

Unfortunately, as the National Institute of Building Sciences notes, some measures considered good for the environment might actually increase indoor air pollution. For instance, motion sensors can create electromagnetic fields, and waterless urinals may require chemical treatments. Both citrus- and pine-based cleaners can react with even low levels of ozone to produce hazardous byproducts.[4] Holistic thinking and problem solving are as essential for interior air quality (IAQ) solutions as they are for every other part of sustainable design.

Volatile Organic Compounds (VOCs)

Green materials, renovations, and new projects almost always claim low levels of volatile organic compounds (VOC) emissions, which may (or may not) be true—but why does this category of gases receive so much attention? The simplest technical definition of VOCs is that they are organic compounds with one or more carbon atoms that have high vapor pressures and therefore evaporate readily to the atmosphere. Thousands of compounds meet this definition—from both man-made and natural sources, including trees and animals—but the VOCs generated by the transportation sector, by solvents, and from industrial sources are worrisome, both individually and as a group. According to Environment Canada, "VOCs are primary precursors to the formation of ground level ozone and particulate matter in the atmosphere which are the main ingredients of the air pollutant referred to as smog."[5] Smog has serious health effects and is harmful to vegetation.

In the United States, the annual cost of building-related sickness is estimated to be at $58 billion.[6]
—*Secretariat of the Commission for Environmental Cooperation*

Often potent in minute doses, VOCs are even more detrimental when they occur together. According to Environment Canada, consumer and commercial products such as domestic and commercial cleaning products, personal care products, paints, and printing inks produce the second largest volume of VOC emissions in Canada, accounting for 28 percent of the country's total.[7]

Indoor concentrations of many VOCs are consistently higher (up to ten times higher) than concentrations outdoors, according to the U.S. Environmental Protection Agency. The list of products that emit VOCs indoors include paints and lacquers, paint strippers, cleaning supplies, dry-cleaned clothing, moth repellants, air fresheners, pesticides, building materials and furnishings, office equipment such as copiers and printers, correction fluids and carbonless copy paper, graphics and craft materials (particularly glues and adhesives), permanent markers, and photographic solutions.[8] Typical VOC compounds released from building materials include formaldehyde, acetaldehyde, toluene, isocyanates, xylene, and benzene.[9]

VOCs directly affect the health of individuals, both through immediate discomfort and the long-term potential for cancer and damage to the liver, kidneys, and the central nervous system. Signs or symptoms of exposure to VOCs include eye, nose, and throat irritation, headaches, loss of coordination, nausea, allergic skin reactions, and fatigue and dizziness.[10]

> Minute levels of phthalates, which are used to make building materials, have been statistically linked to sperm damage in men and genital changes, asthma, and allergies in children.
>
> —The Wall Street Journal, *July 25, 2005*[11]

Semivolatile organic compounds (SVOC) are compounds with higher vapor pressures than VOCs, which means they emerge more slowly from materials and are likely to be transferred to humans by contact or by attaching to dust and being ingested. SVOCs used in building materials have shown up in increasing concentrations in humans, raising concern about short- and long-term health effects. SVOCs in building products include phthalates (softeners used in PVC plastic), halogenated flame retardants (added to products from fabrics to computers to inhibit ignition), and perfluorochemicals (added to products for stain resistance or water repellency).[12]

Material Selection

Material selection in terms of indoor air quality should favor products that are inert, nonporous, and offer no opportunity for mold or moisture. Materials that have the potential for off-gassing VOCs or that include questionable chemicals should be avoided. Keep in mind that many "miracle" products of the past—including lead paint, asbestos, and PCB-laden caulks—have become the toxic problems of today. Today's miracle products show every indication of continuing the pattern.

Figure 6.1 Plants in an office at Clipper Mill, an adaptive reuse project in Baltimore, Maryland, provide the connection with nature that biophilic design supports as an important part of human well-being. The evidence that plants can significantly improve indoor air quality, however, is inconclusive (see page 224). *Jo Ann Stallings photo, courtesy Struever Bros. Eccles & Rouse*

"At the end of a product's service life, it must be removed and replaced. The removal itself might result in pollutant emissions, either from chemicals used to aid in the removal or mechanical damage to existing materials.... It is obvious that the longer the service life of a product or material, the less often it must be replaced. Durability is important for indoor air quality as well as overall environmental sustainability. *The service life of a product is the denominator in any calculation of sustainability.*" [emphasis added]

—Hal Levin, president, Indoor Air Institute, Inc.[13]

Until recently, most fiberglass insulation was bound with formaldehyde, an eye, skin, and respiratory-tract irritant and a probable human carcinogen. PBDEs (polybrominated diphenyl ethers) were the fire-retardant chemical of choice for many years. (Stringent California flammability standards may be the reason that the blood levels of some PBDEs are significantly higher in California residents than the rest of the country.[14]) The European Union banned certain PBDEs as early as 2003 and continues to add to the list. Like PCBs, PBDEs are persistent in the environment and bioaccumulative, building up in people's bodies.

Controlling interior pollutant sources through material and finish selections requires life-cycle thinking. If the material choice for a wall is a gypsum wallboard with low-VOC paints, how cleanable will it be with plain water (as opposed to stronger chemical or natural cleaners), and how often will it require repainting? Over the lifetime of the wall, repainting may actually contribute more VOCs than would another material with higher early VOC emissions but greater durability, longer life, and easier cleaning.

6.2 AIR QUALITY AND VENTILATION

"The real challenge for sustainable buildings is to optimize the balance between an indoor environment that promotes occupant health and well-being and the use of energy and emission of greenhouse gases associated with maintaining that environment."

—Elia Sterling,[15] Living Futures 09 Conference

Airtight Buildings

When we tighten building envelopes to decrease energy consumption, we trap pollutants and moisture inside and become more dependent on mechanical systems and monitors to assure adequate ventilation or dilution of toxins and moisture. The lessons of the 1970s should stay clearly in front of us. The drive for energy efficiency created a new industry to combat sick building syndrome (SBS). The title SBS distracts from the reality that *people* become sick when building designs and retrofits ignore the rules of physics and address one problem while creating others. The more appropriate term is *building-related illness* (BRI), which remains an issue when tighter building envelopes inadvertently create moisture problems and unintentionally add toxic materials to spaces.

Moisture and Mold

Controlling moisture within any building, whether historic or not, is essential to protecting materials from deterioration and maintaining a healthy environment; trapped moisture sets the stage for mold and mildew. *Holding the Line: Controlling Unwanted Moisture in Historic Buildings,* National Park Service Preservation Brief No. 39, by Sharon Park, describes three forms of moisture transport particularly im-

"The concept of a wall 'breathing' should be considered as a condition that facilitates the transfer of moisture in liquid or gaseous phases more than the passage of air. Tests have indicated that ordinary walls of tufa, brick or sandstone of medium thickness, as used in domestic structures, allow the passage of 1 oz/sf of water daily...."

Bernard Feildon, Conservation of Historic Buildings[16]

portant to historic buildings— infiltration, capillary action, and vapor diffusion—and the design characteristics of many historic buildings that facilitated the movement of air and water to avoid condensation and entrapment.

These characteristics include passive ventilation strategies, cavity walls, the placement of heating elements to reduce condensation, and use of naturally hygroscopic materials such as wood, plaster, and unsealed textiles and stone. These materials can help regulate relative humidity by absorbing moisture when humidity rises and emitting it when air dries, smoothing out peaks and troughs.[17] Altering systems and features and changing materials and uses all affect moisture sources and moisture movement in buildings.

Hidden moisture always represents a potential problem in any structure, which is why a musty smell should never be ignored, and its source should be systematically pursued. Moisture might originate in leaking pipes, in exterior sources, or with inadequate exhaust fans in bathrooms, laundries, or kitchens. It is important to understand the building and physics. For instance, is a basement dehumidifier keeping a below-grade space dry or actually drawing moisture through the foundation wall? If new condensation is occurring on cold surfaces, what changes may have created the situation? Can natural ventilation be restored to facilitate dissipation?

Ventilation

Michelle Addington provides an informative and delightful description of the love affair that the industrial age had (and continues to have) with mechanical building ventilation in the essential text, *Indoor Air Quality Handbook*.[18] It is not surprising that both engineers and manufacturers have championed mechanical ven-

tilation for over 100 years.[19] The need, amount, and timing of mechanical ventilation are the subject of countless studies, which include discussions of how and what to test for to ensure acceptable indoor air quality.

The dirt and noise of urban environments encourage keeping buildings closed tight, with a resultant reliance on mechanical systems. That, in turn, contributes to the exterior noise level and intensifies both energy consumption, and the heat island effect. It is a slower version of the London Killer Fog of 1952, when the smoke from coal-burning fires was trapped by a cold mist that drove people indoors to stoke their coal fires—creating more smoke. An estimated 12,000 people died in four days from the air pollution.

"Pollutant source control is a far better, cost-effective option for good IAQ than is increasing the ventilation rate. Adding more outside air simply dilutes levels of indoor contaminants. The HVAC system itself may be a source of contamination (microbial amplification site, unbounded fiberglass, outdoor pollutant entrainment, etc.)."

—*Ted Nathanson, Indoor Air Quality Handbook*[20]

During building renovations, the entire team, not just the engineers, must address indoor air quality and ventilation. Rather than assuming that mechanical ventilation represents the only solution, especially in periods of mild weather, the design team should fully explore opportunities that the building and the site offer for decreasing mechanical needs and improving passive ventilation. Whole-system design considers heat island mitigation, potential shading, cross-ventilation strategies, and low-energy solutions such as ceiling and attic fans to draw air through spaces.

6.3 LIGHT AND CONNECTIONS TO NATURE

"The challenge is to find the technologies that will allow us to take advantage of beautiful views and daylight and the whole circadian quality of the change of light over time so that we can take advantage of being part of nature without having the problems of glare."

—*Vivian Loftness*[21]

Lighting uses energy and increases the heat load inside a building, which increases the need for cooling. Taking full advantage of natural light is desirable to reduce carbon emissions and support healthy interior environments. Historic buildings offer lessons and opportunities in how best to capture both daylight and views. Old technologies such as awnings, refractive lenses, glass floor inserts, shutters, and interior blinds are being rediscovered. New technologies being developed—such as light tubes, W-blinds, and various interior light shades—add more ways to enhance natural light's use in existing buildings.

Studies show that both physical and mental health benefit from increased daily light exposure and that

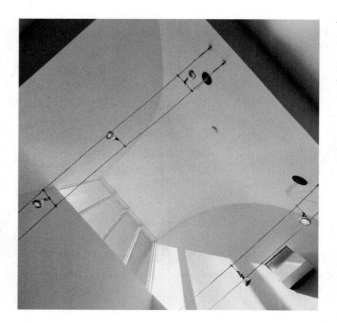

Figure 6.2 The interior of the light scoop: Daylighting is an important strategy for the well-being of building occupants and the reduction of electrical lighting loads (which also reduces air conditioning loads). A south-facing light scoop created by the design firm of Burt Hill at headquarters of the Friends Committee on National Legislation in Washington, D. C., increases the amount of light that penetrates into building. *Photography by Jim Morris*

Natural Light Benefits in Schools[23]

20 percent speed improvement on math tests

26 percent speed improvement on reading tests

Natural Light Benefits in Stores

40 percent more sales

Natural Light Benefits in Hospitals

Improved patient outcomes and reduced stays

---

small increases in daylight exposure improve mental well-being in healthy people. Being in a sunny hospital room has been linked to lower mortality rates among cardiac patients and faster symptom remission for depressive patients.[22]

Biophilia

Natural settings are particularly associated with restoration from stressful conditions. Hospital patients in rooms with windows that looked onto a nature view recovered more quickly from surgery than those with windows overlooking a brick wall. Even images of nature are more restorative than images of urban set-

Figure 6.3 The light scoop exterior sits adjacent to a green roof, which was one of the first in the District of Columbia. The project, which involved renovation of a historic townhouse, was approved by the district's Historic Preservation Review Board. To support healthy indoor environment—a priority in the design— natural light and views to the outdoors are provided in 100 percent of regularly occupied space. *Photography by Jim Morris*

Figure 6.4 Interior floor panels below the light scoop: A key design concept for the Friends Committee on National Legislation headquarters was "inner-light," the Quaker notion of the spiritual force that guides and directs our lives. The central light shaft created by the firm of Burt Hill has structural-glass floor panels across which building occupants pass several times a day. Daylight and connection to nature through the changing intensity of light are closely connected to health. *Photography by Jim Morris*

Connectivity to Nature—Biophilic Design Elements Across Scales

Regional
　Regional greenspace systems
Community
　Community forest/community orchards
　City tree canopy
　Urban creeks and riparian areas
Neighborhood
　Community gardens
　Neighborhood parks/pocket parks
Street
　Urban trees
　Vegetated swales and skinny streets
Block
　Green courtyards
　Clustered housing around green areas
Building
　Sky gardens and green atria
　Green walls
　Daylit interior spaces

Source: Cynthia Girling and Ronald Kellet, *Skinny Streets and Green Neighborhoods: Design for Environment and Community* (Washington, DC: Island Press, 2005).

tings and—not surprisingly—time spent in nature is better for well-being than time spent in built settings. Children's cognitive function and ability to cope with stressful life experiences are improved by having access to green space near their homes.[24]

Indoor Plants—Pros and Cons

Indoor plants are appealing and are often touted as a means of improving air quality. A few studies link indoor plants to improved work performance, and the Center for Building Performance and Diagnostics at Carnegie Mellon University places an economic value on plants that reflects that connection. Skeptical observers, however, contend that the science around both air quality and improved productivity is weak.

There is concern that indoor plants, especially hydroponic systems, may add to the risk of moisture-related problems, such as allergies and asthma, for building occupants. Plants can support insects, like mosquitoes, cockroaches, and aphids, which in the United States are often treated with chemicals.

Commenting on an article about indoor plants in *Environmental Building News* in 2009, Hal Levin, an indoor air quality consultant, writes, "Use of plants indoors to create a more pleasant environment is a great idea if it is done carefully. But assuming that it can clean the air or enhance productivity is unwarranted at this time."[25]

6.4 HEALTHY SPACES AND PRODUCTIVITY

Health is "…a state of complete physical, mental, and social well-being and not merely the absence of disease or infirmity."[26]

World Health Organization, 1947

It's just common sense to recognize that a healthy world avoids the costs of extensive healthcare and worker absences. A healthy world also generates greater income through improved worker performance. A world that supports physical and mental health should be non-negotiable.

The cross-connections between spaces we use and the effects on lifestyle are multiple. One study ties healthy workplaces to better sleep, and healthy environments in schools and homes have been connected to decreases in attention deficit disorder and asthma, as well as improved concentration for tasks. Hundreds of reports provide data and documentation that validate the cost effectiveness of healthy workplaces, residences, and schools as a result of decreased health costs and insurance, lower absenteeism, and longer retention of employees.

Resources that combine health research with design include the Canadian Building and Health Sciences Network, the online magazine *Research-Design Connections* (www.researchdesignconnections.com/), and the summarizing site, Informed Design, whose founders include the American Society of Interior Designers (http://informeddesign.com).[27]

The Center for Building Performance at Carnegie Mellon has evaluated reports and assembled data on the cost of doing business that is linked to healthy buildings. The cost of productivity at $200/ft^2/year overshadows the costs of rent, averaging $20/ft^2/year, and energy at $2/ft^2/year. Improvements in productivity, decreases in absenteeism, and satisfaction levels that reduce staff turnover all benefit employers financially. Salaries account for the majority of the cost of doing business (as much as 60 percent). Even a 1 percent increase in productivity adds $500 per employee per year if average annual compensation is $50,000.

Estimated Savings from Green Buildings in the United States (in 1996 $US)[28]

Reduction in respiratory disease:
$6 to $14 billion

Reduction in allergies and asthma:
$1 to $4 billion

Reduction in sick building syndrome:
$10 to $30 billion

Improved worker performance:
$20 to $160 billion

Energy savings:
$70 billion

Figure 6.5 Health and well-being are improved by ready access to natural areas, fresh air, and daylight. The sliver park adjacent to the Chicago Center for Neighborhood Technology (see Chapter 2), offers multiple amenities at the same time it reduces urban heat island effect (see Chapter 4), shades the building (reducing cooling loads), and allows natural filtration of stormwater. The renovation of the 80-year-old former textile factory in 1987 created the first nontoxic interior space in Illinois. © *2008 Center for Neighborhood Technology*

Cleaning Impacts

Of more than 70,000 chemicals in use daily, fewer than 2 percent have been thoroughly tested for their effects on human and aquatic life.[29] Every year over 6 billion pounds of chemicals are used to clean buildings. When raw materials and the processes involved in manufacturing are added in, the cleaning industry is responsible for 60 billion pounds of chemicals that contribute to the toxic waste stream in the U.S. In addition, cleaning consumes 45 billion pounds of paper products—requiring the pulp from 27 million trees—each year. Added to this are chlorine bleach, required to whiten paper, and dioxin, a byproduct of the bleaching process and a deadly poison. Thousands of pieces of cleaning equipment are discarded each year, to say nothing of 10 million plastic bags used daily.[30]

Cleaning materials and methods not only affect the larger environment but also have a very immediate effect on indoor air quality and the health of people in buildings. Between 1993 and 1999, the Sentinel Event Notification System for Occupational Risk (SENSOR) found connections to cleaning agents linked in 11.6 percent of all work-related asthma cases, making them second among all groups associated with work-related asthma.[31] A study funded by the EPA found that the average janitor in Santa Clara County, California, uses an estimated 28 gallons of chemicals per year, 25 percent of which contain extremely hazardous ingredients. The same study found that 27,000 janitors in Santa Clara County experience a total of about 1,200 chemical injuries each year.[32] A rough extrapolation of this figure to the national level suggests that medical expenses and lost time for chemical injuries cost about $75 million per year.[33]

The estimated cost in the United States of treating asthma in those younger than 18 years of age is $3.2 billion per year.

—Center for Health and the Global Environment
Harvard Medical School[34]

Green Cleaning for Health and Savings

Green cleaning identifies multiple strategies that can yield healthier ways of cleaning:

- *Source reduction:* Place 15 to 20 feet of multilevel mats on the outside and inside of buildings. The majority of all dust and dirt entering a building walks in through the doors.
- *Material choices:* Choose materials and finishes that have low or easy cleaning options.

- *Cleaning cloths:* Use microfiber mops and cloths. Microfiber captures dust and harmful microbes while reducing the use of paper products.
- *Spray cleaners:* Spraying cleaning products, even if nontoxic, irritates human airways and can trigger asthma.
- *Equipment choices:* Use equipment designed to prevent dirt and soil from contaminating surfaces, such as two-chamber mop buckets that keep dirt from being redeposited by the mop, and high-efficiency particulate air (HEPA) filtration vacuum cleaners.
- *Third-party certification:* Seek products that carry nonprofit, third-party certification from organizations such as Green Seal and EcoLogo.
- *Disinfectants:* Toxic by nature, disinfectants should be used only where absolutely necessary, such as health stations. Clarify the difference between areas needing disinfection and those needing to be sanitized, such as food-service areas. Clean before sanitizing or disinfecting.
- *Product reduction:* Use the minimum amount of cleaning product possible. Institutions can install automatic dilution equipment to the combat overconcentration from manual dilution.
- *Training:* Trained cleaning professionals stay current on environmentally preferable processes and methodologies and better understand the importance of the objectives.

Noise and Health

The word *noise* is derived from the Latin word "nausea," meaning seasickness. Noise is the single largest reason that people in the United States move from a neighborhood. Evidence that chronic noise exposure has adverse effects on cardiovascular health and other outcomes has led the World Health Organization to

▶ **C1** The Children's Museum of Pittsburgh (see Chapter 7) viewed at night, showcases a modern addition joining the former Post Office building, an 1897 structure on the National Register, and the elegant 1939 Buhl building. The vibrant facility, cloaked in a shimmering wind sculpture, revitalized the area and demonstrates in design, operations, and programs a commitment to environmental sustainability. © *Albert Vecerka/Esto*

▼ **C2** Part of the Throop Green Bungalow Block (see Chapter 9), a project launched by the Historic Chicago Bungalow Association in 2006, this house employs multiple features to ensure high energy efficiency while maintaining the historic character of the home. Spray-foam insulation in the attic and air sealing assist the efficiency of an Energy Star furnace and programmable thermostat. © *Historic Chicago Bungalow Association*

▶ **C3** The new entrance canopy at the Thoreau Center for Sustainable Design in San Francisco (see Chapter 3) includes photovoltaic cells as a demonstration of alternative energy options. This and similar energy-saving features did not preclude the building, which is part of a National Historic Landmark site, from qualifying for the highest level of historic tax credits, which required compliance with the Secretary of the Interior's Standards for Rehabilitation. (Refer to Chapter 3 for a discussion of preservation standards and green guidelines. *Richard Barnes photo, courtesy Leddy Maytum Stacy Architects*

C4 The new entrance to the Karges-Faulconbridge Office Building (see Chapter 10) in Roseville, Minnesota, leads to a modern light-filled space in what once was an uninspiring food store built in the 1970s. By reusing the existing building, KFI, an engineering firm with a strong commitment to the environment, saved an estimated $40 per square foot over new construction. © *Jim Gallop Photography*

C5 The 1913 Balfour-Guthrie building in Portland, Oregon, was the first reinforced concrete building on the West Coast and, after renovation in 2002, became the first architectural office in the United States to be certified LEED Silver by the U.S. Green Building Council (refer to Chapter 3 for a discussion of metric systems). As part of the renovation, Thomas Hacker Architects opened up the floor plan down to the basement level, exposing concrete aggregate, reinforcement, and other structural elements from the original construction. © *Thomas Hacker Architects*

C6 At the Alliance Center for Sustainable Colorado (see Chapter 3), a renovation introduced common spaces in order to reduce resource use. Shared services for tenants include conference rooms, telecom services, copiers, and catering kitchens. Furniture in lobbies and common areas had previous lives at a convention center as furniture or as entirely different objects, such as rubber tires or industrial pallets. Plastic walls molded into honeycombs provide a sound barrier without sacrificing light penetration. The wheatboard in the walls is a nontoxic fiberboard made from an agricultural waste, wheat chaff. *Courtesy Alliance for a Sustainable Colorado*

◀ C7 The 1903 S.T. Dana Building is home to the School of Natural Resources and Environment (SNRE) at the University of Michigan (see Chapter 5). A renovation completed in 2003 increased usable space by 20 percent without expanding the building footprint by adding new rooms in the courtyard, seen at the left, and a fifth floor, visible just beneath the skylight. The 4,000-square-foot skylight provides daylight to much of the building, while shades on its south side help keep the building cool during the summer months. © *Christopher Campbell 2003*

▼ C8 Renovation of Crown Hall at the Illinois Institute of Technology (see Chapter 10) reestablished and improved on original active and passive techniques for occupant comfort designed by architect Mies van der Rohe in the 1950s. The passive solar strategies, reliance on shading, and natural ventilation contradict the common belief that modernist architecture favored mechanical dependencies with disregard for the natural environment. *Photography by Todd Eberle*

▼ C9 Renovation of the 1903 Lion House at the Bronx Zoo combines preservation, exhibit design, and viable habitat creation with sophisticated sustainable features (see Chapter 5). Inadequate underground electrical distribution on the campus helped make a fuel cell an economical choice. Energy generated by the cell beyond the building's needs is exported to the zoo grid. In addition, waste heat from the fuel cell supplies some 40 percent of the building's heat. A new three-layer ethylene tetrafluoroethylene (ETFE) system with a movable center layer interacts with the environment to balance the goals of natural light and minimum heat gain. © *David Sundberg/Esto*

C10 The Clipper Mill development in Baltimore, Maryland, demonstrates "long life and loose fit" with creative new uses in a 150-year-old foundry complex. Commercial development of existing buildings addresses the holistic sustainability discussed in Chapter 2, with attention to social welfare, economic viability, and environmental-impact reduction. © *Struever Bros. Eccles & Rouse*

C11 The penthouse addition at the Capitol Hill House (see Chapter 9) in Seattle, Washington, provides access to a new roof terrace and serves as a light catch and solar chimney for the house. It also supports a photovoltaic canopy that provides about 50 percent of total electrical requirements. *Photo courtesy of Michael Moore*

C12 An extensive remodel of the Capitol Hill House (see Chapter 9) left the building's footprint intact. The only addition was a penthouse that carries out multiple functions and provides access to a roof terrace that serves to increase usable square footage without adding volume that requires tempered air. "Smart" whole-house monitoring connects all major systems and is calibrated to yield aggressive reductions in electricity use. The system allows alarm and security systems to communicate with lighting controls, and it supports ambient-light-level monitoring. *Photo courtesy of Michael Moore*

C13 Renovation of the 1899 Historic Academic Group at the U.S. Naval Academy (see Chapter 1) reestablished historic skylights and demonstrated whole-building sustainability by restoring durable original materials while integrating new systems. New energy-saving features introduced in the renovation included high-efficiency motors, variable-frequency drives, variable air-handling distribution, and low-temperature (high delta), low-pressure air supply that reduces fan requirements. *Richard Mandelkorn photo, courtesy Goody Clancy*

C14 The Gottfried Regenerative Home (www. gottfriedhome.com), a 1915 Craftsman bungalow in Oakland, California, received a LEED for Homes Platinum certification from the U.S. Green Building Council in 2008. Not least of the green features is the use of 1,460 square feet to house a family of four. The plan's efficient approach to space includes use of the enclosed old porch as a mudroom. Housing offers one of the greatest opportunities for reducing carbon emissions. After a period of ballooning house sizes in the U.S.—from the late 1970s to the early 2000s, average size increased 50 percent,—this home's compact footprint demonstrates that a dramatic reduction in carbon footprint does not require sacrificing comfort. (Refer to Chapter 9). *© 2008 Open Hones Photography*

C15 The primary design concept for the Friends Committee on National Legislation Headquarters was "inner light," the Quaker notion of a spiritual force that guides and directs our lives. The central light shaft created by the firm of Burt Hill has structural-glass floor panels, across which building occupants pass mutliple times each workday. Daylight and connection to nature—made evident through the changing intensity of light within the light shaft—are closely tied to health. *Photography by Jim Morris*

C16 The neon sign on top of the eight-story Montgomery Park Business Center recalls the 1920s, when this Baltimore landmark, now a model of innovative green office development, housed a Montgomery Ward retail store and regional distribution center (see Chapter 6). The building was Baltimore's first suburban department store and largest mercantile building; the Environmental Protection Agency recognized the renovated structure as a preeminent example of an environmentally compromised property returned to productive use. © Patrick Ross Photography

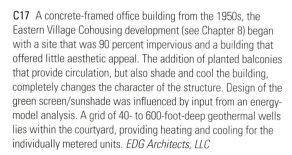

C17 A concrete-framed office building from the 1950s, the Eastern Village Cohousing development (see Chapter 8) began with a site that was 90 percent impervious and a building that offered little aesthetic appeal. The addition of planted balconies that provide circulation, but also shade and cool the building, completely changes the character of the structure. Design of the green screen/sunshade was influenced by input from an energy-model analysis. A grid of 40- to 600-foot-deep geothermal wells lies within the courtyard, providing heating and cooling for the individually metered units. *EDG Architects, LLC*

C18 New stairs at the heart of Harvard University's Barker Center for the Humanities provide opportunities for accidental meetings that build community, encourage walking instead of elevator use, and facilitate daylighting from a new skylight. Sustainable design seeks solutions that support social and physical health while reducing the environmental impact of buildings. (Refer to Chapter 2 for a discussion of holistic sustainability.) *Richard Mandelkorn photo, courtesy Goody Clancy*

TRANSVERSE BUILDING SECTION PRIOR TO RENOVATION

C19 Before renovation of Harvard University's Barker Center, many areas of the building were unused or underutilized. Efficient use of existing resources includes making the best use of building space. The greatest environmental gain in building design comes from avoiding the impacts of new construction entirely. (Refer to Chapter 1 for additional information about avoided impacts.) *Courtesy Goody Clancy*

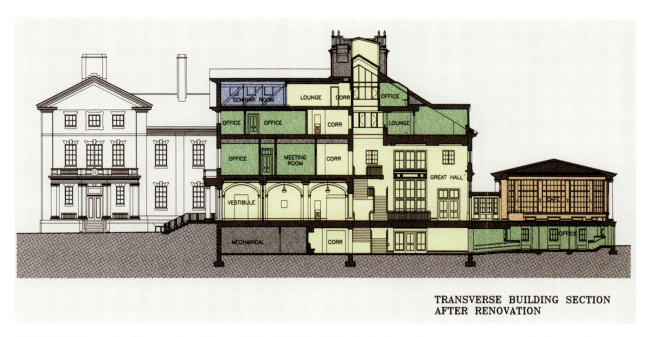

TRANSVERSE BUILDING SECTION AFTER RENOVATION

C20 This building section after renovation of Harvard University's Barker Center for the Humanities shows how reorganization increased the usable space in the building and improved natural daylighting to internal spaces. Occupant density and efficiency of space utilization are essential elements of resource management; focusing too intently on end-use energy per square foot can obscure their importance. *Courtesy Goody Clancy*

C21 At 700,000 square feet, the Lazarus Building in downtown Columbus, Ohio (see Chapter 4) is one of the largest renovation projects in the country to have achieved a LEED rating of Gold. Green features include the harvesting of rainwater from the roof for reuse; a "living roof" to reduce summer heat build-up and slow water runoff; energy-efficient fixtures, lighting, and windows; and the use of nontoxic interior finishes. *Photography © Brad Feinknopf 2007*

C22 A new seven-story sky-lit lightwell was added at the heart of the Lazarus Building (see Chapter 4). The new art deco lobbies include hotel-style concierge reception desks. The project was awarded the Green Development Award in 2007 by the National Association of Industrial and Office Properties. *Photography © Brad Feinknopf 2007*

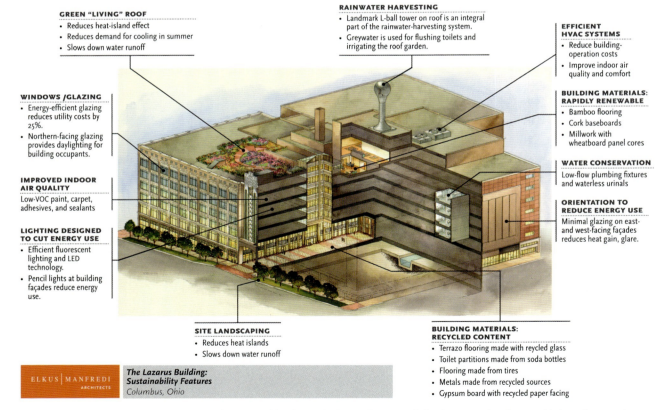

GREEN "LIVING" ROOF
- Reduces heat-island effect
- Reduces demand for cooling in summer
- Slows down water runoff

RAINWATER HARVESTING
- Landmark L-ball tower on roof is an integral part of the rainwater-harvesting system.
- Greywater is used for flushing toilets and irrigating the roof garden.

EFFICIENT HVAC SYSTEMS
- Reduce building-operation costs
- Improve indoor air quality and comfort

WINDOWS /GLAZING
- Energy-efficient glazing reduces utility costs by 25%.
- Northern-facing glazing provides daylighting for building occupants.

BUILDING MATERIALS: RAPIDLY RENEWABLE
- Bamboo flooring
- Cork baseboards
- Millwork with wheatboard panel cores

IMPROVED INDOOR AIR QUALITY
Low-VOC paint, carpet, adhesives, and sealants

WATER CONSERVATION
Low-flow plumbing fixtures and waterless urinals

ORIENTATION TO REDUCE ENERGY USE
Minimal glazing on east- and west-facing façades reduces heat gain, glare.

LIGHTING DESIGNED TO CUT ENERGY USE
- Efficient fluorescent lighting and LED technology.
- Pencil lights at building façades reduce energy use.

SITE LANDSCAPING
- Reduces heat islands
- Slows down water runoff

BUILDING MATERIALS: RECYCLED CONTENT
- Terrazo flooring made with reycled glass
- Toilet partitions made from soda bottles
- Flooring made from tires
- Metals made from recycled sources
- Gypsum board with recycled paper facing

ELKUS | MANFREDI
ARCHITECTS

The Lazarus Building:
Sustainability Features
Columbus, Ohio

C23 The building's vast scale provided multiple opportunities for employing environmentally benign strategies, from sophisticated approaches to daylighting (including glazing to block heat gain and the addition of an atrium that brings light into the building's heart) to materials chosen for construction and diversion of significant volumes of construction waste. *Courtesy Elkus Manfredil*

C24 Before renovation, the 12,000-square-foot basement of Trinity Church in the City of Boston (see Chapter 1) was a dirt-floored storage space that once housed large boilers used to heat the building through updrafting floor grills. Like many urban buildings, the church, a National Historic Landmark, could only expand by dramatically rethinking how it used below-grade space. *Courtesy Goody Clancy*

C25 After renovation, the new undercroft below Trinity Church in the City of Boston (see Chapter 1) provides a flexible space for the many community events hosted by the church. The design intentionally featured the building's stone foundations and introduced as few new materials as possible. Acoustic separation is achieved by pivoting panels of art glass when smaller spaces are needed. Supporting the role of the church in the community was considered as central to the sustainable design as environmental issues. *© Anton Grassl/Esto*

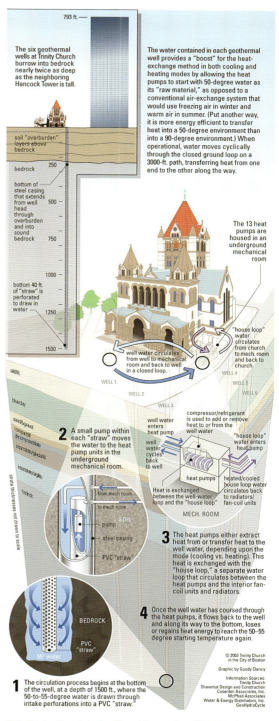

793 ft. —

The six geothermal wells at Trinity Church burrow into bedrock nearly twice as deep as the neighboring Hancock Tower is tall.

The water contained in each geothermal well provides a "boost" for the heat-exchange method in both cooling and heating modes by allowing the heat pumps to start with 50-degree water as its "raw material," as opposed to a conventional air-exchange system that would use freezing air in winter and warm air in summer. (Put another way, it is more energy efficient to transfer heat into a 50-degree environment than into a 90-degree environment.) When operational, water moves cyclically through the closed ground loop on a 3000-ft. path, transferring heat from one end to the other along the way.

soil "overburden" layers above bedrock

bedrock

250

bottom of steel casing that extends from well head through overburden and into sound bedrock

500

750

1000

bottom 40 ft. of "straw" is perforated to draw in water

1250

1500

The 13 heat pumps are housed in an underground mechanical room

"house loop" water circulates from church to mech. room and back to church

well water circulates from well to mechanical room and back to well in a closed loop.

WELL 1   WELL 4
WELL 2   WELL 5
WELL 3   WELL 6

2 A small pump within each "straw" moves the water to the heat pump units in the underground mechanical room.

well water enters heat pump

well water cycles back to well

compressor/refrigerant is used to add or remove heat to or from the well water

"house loop" water enters heat pump

heat pumps

heated/cooled house loop water circulates back to radiators/ fan-coil units

Heat is exchanged between the well-water loop and the "house loop"

MECH. ROOM

from mech room
to mech room
SOIL
pump
steel casing
PVC "straw"

3 The heat pumps either extract heat from or transfer heat to the well water, depending upon the mode (cooling vs. heating). This heat is exchanged with the "house loop," a separate water loop that circulates between the heat pumps and the interior fan-coil units and radiators.

BEDROCK
PVC "straw"
55° water

4 Once the well water has coursed through the heat pumps, it flows back to the well and along its way to the bottom, loses or regains heat energy to reach the 50–55 degree starting temperature again.

© 2003 Trinity Church in the City of Boston

Graphic by Goody Clancy

Information Sources:
Trinity Church
Shawmut Design and Construction
Cosentini Associates, Inc.
McPhail Associates
Water & Energy Distributors, Inc.
GeoHydroCycle

1 The circulation process begins at the bottom of the well, at a depth of 1500 ft., where the 50-to-55-degree water is drawn through intake perforations into a PVC "straw."

C26 Trinity Church in the City of Boston (see Chapter 1) ground-source heat-pump system. *Courtesy Goody Clancy*

C27 Two large atria added to the 1906 Scowcroft Building provide the majority of the structure's daylight (see Chapter 5). Large windows on all five levels bring in additional daylight and offer views to the outside. The daylighting is effective enough that daytime overhead lighting is not required in 80 percent of the regularly occupied spaces. The developer used federal historic preservation tax credits to help fund the renovation, which achieved a 23 percent yearly cost savings through extensive computer modeling that informed the design and selection of efficient mechanical and electrical systems. © richerimages.com

▲ C28 The Gerding Theater at the Armory in Portland, Oregon (see Chapter 3), was both the first National Register building and the first theater in the United States to achieve a LEED Platinum certification. The theater's lobby, a site of neighborhood activity, showcases the original trusses. The project is one of the earliest and largest to combine New Market Tax Credits with the Historic Preservation Tax Incentives program. *Josh Partee photo, courtesy of GBD Architects, Inc.*

◄ C29 The many materials in the Barn at Fallingwater (see Chapter 7) include existing, salvaged, and innovative new. The glazed-tile block walls, concrete floor, and glass-block windows date to the 1940s milking parlor. The red cedar was part of the 1960s ceiling. New wallboard material is made from sunflower-seed composite, and straw panels are used as sound-absorptive material in the ceiling. *Nic Lehoux photo, courtesy Bohllin Cywinski Jackson*

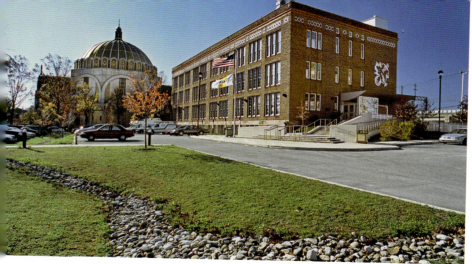

C30 Sustainable design addresses more than just the environment. North Philadelphia suffers from the highest murder rate in the city, concentrated poverty, and aging infrastructure. For these reasons a sustainability task force of the city's Capital Program Office selected an abandoned 1929 art deco school building in the heart of the community as the site for the police department's new Forensic Science Center (see Chapter 2). A "green" transformation of the lot—previously entirely paved over—introduction of an active 24-hour presence, and creation of an award-winning and environmentally responsible building have combined to provide a dramatic example of civic leadership. © 2009 Croxton Collaborative Architects, PC

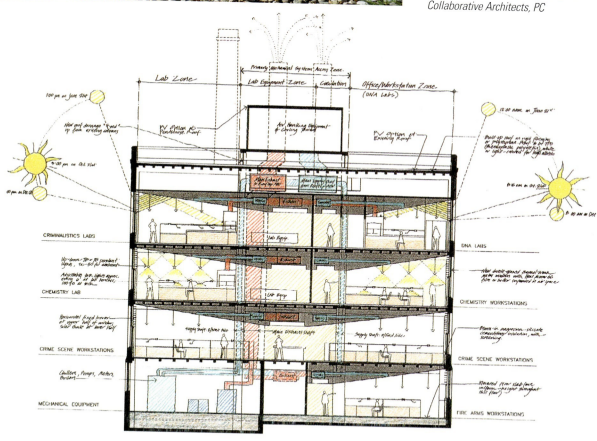

C31 A whole-building design (see Chapter 2) at the Philadelphia Forensic Science Center (see Chapter 2) resulted in a 72 percent reduction in total annual source energy, a 69 percent reduction in 25-year CO_2 (a global warming component), a 67 percent reduction in annual utility costs, a 65 percent reduction in SO_2 (contributor to acid rain) and NO^X (ozone-smog component), and a 61 percent reduction in annual peak electrical demand. The cumulative payback time of the combined strategies was 2.2 years. © 2009 Croxton Collaborative Architects, PC

▲ C32 The signature neon image of Natty Boh on the Baltimore skyline marks the location of the Brewers Hill Complex (see Chapter 2). The mixed-use redevelopment of the brewery that once produced National Bohemian beer includes offices, commercial, mini-storage, day care, and retail space. The 27-acre, 737,000-square-foot complex was the first project to combine Maryland Green Building tax credits with federal and state historic tax credits. Preserving historic symbols such as signage reinforces a sense of place essential to social sustainability. © 2006 Patrick Ross Photography

◀ C33 Nestled amidst a neighborhood of one- and two-story bungalows in Venice, California, the Solar Umbrella Residence (see Chapter 9) is inspired by Paul Rudolf's Umbrella House of 1953. Solar panels protect the body of the building from thermal heat gain by screening large portions of the structure from direct exposure to the intense southern California sun. Rather than deflecting sunlight, the solar skin treats it as a resource, absorbing and transforming it into usable energy, providing the residence with 95 percent of its electricity. Like many features at the Solar Umbrella, the solar canopy is multivalent and rich with meaning—performing several roles for functional, formal, and experiential effect. Marvin Rand photo, courtesy of Pugh + Scarpa

▲ C35 The fourth-floor roof of the John W. McCormack Federal Building in Boston, Massachusetts, offered views of air-handling units and exposure to the resulting heat and noise before renovation created a new green roof (see Chapter 5). *Courtesy Goody Clancy*

▲ C34 A new passage at St. Stephen's Episcopal Cathedral and School in Harrisburg, Pennsylvania, (see Chapter 8) creates an accessible corridor between the cathedral and chapter house, both listed on the National Register of Historic Places, and leads to the new school, located inside a renovated 1920s garage. *McKissick Associates Architects*

▶ C36 A new green roof at the John W. McCormack Federal provides urban wildlife habitat and allows workers from the building to enjoy fresh air (smoking is not allowed) (see Chapter 5). Environmental benefits of the roof include reduction of stormwater runoff and reduced heating and cooling demand within the building because the soil and plants provide more insulation and a cooler surface than a typical roof. Plantings feature species native to Cape Cod and the Berkshire Mountains in western Massachusetts that require little to no irrigation. When water is needed for the plants, solar pumps distribute it, drawing from cisterns that store up to 5,500 gallons of roof runoff and air-conditioning. *Courtesy Goody Clancy*

◀C37 The 1950s view of the Candler Library (see Chapter 8) Reading Room at Emory University shows a space divided in half horizontally with floors added after World War II to house expanding collections. *Photo courtesy of Emory University Archives*

▶C38 A 2004 view shows how restoration of the Candler Library (see Chapter 8) Reading Room returned it to its original two-story grandeur. The Reading Room is the centerpiece of an extensive renovation that restored one of the oldest buildings on the Emory University while using environmentally responsible green building principles. *Photo courtesy of Woodruff Brown Photography*

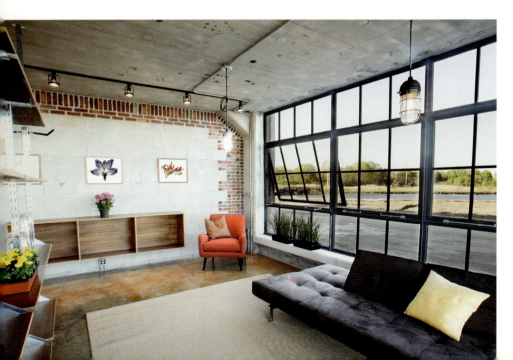

◀C39 A Forbes Park loft in Chelsea, Massachusetts (see Chapter 1), illustrates the durable finishes typical of many industrial buildings and the often-spectacular daylight and views. This waterfront development restored over ten acres of natural habitat and installed a wind turbine to provide 60 percent of the energy used by the 250 lofts. © Forbes Park LLC

▶ **C40** The Thoreau Center for Sustainable Design (see Chapter 3) in San Francisco utilizes natural daylight and ventilation in buildings constructed between 1899 and 1933 to create healthy workplaces. New materials (see Chapter 7) are biodegradable and recyclable, and have been manufactured in a way that does not damage the environment or contribute to social inequity. *Richard Barnes photo, courtesy Leddy Maytum Stacy Architects*

▶ **C41** The Alberici Corporation Headquarters achieved the highest possible certification under both the LEED and Green Globes™ metric systems (see Chapter 6). The project is a remarkable example of many aspects of sustainability, including reuse of industrial buildings, a regenerative approach to a brownfield site, systems thinking in energy management, water reuse and conservation, and a healthy daylighted work environment. *Vertegy*

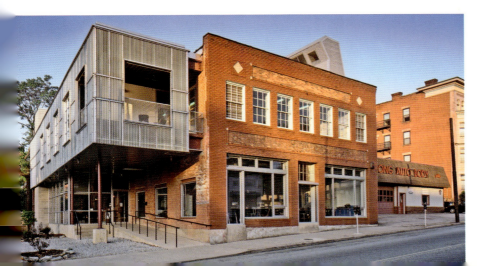

◀ **C42** The addition to the Pittsburgh Glass Center (see Chapter 7) uses a salvaged corrugated-glass panel wall system, including the original aluminum battens and custom-designed mounting hardware. The new design was shaped to require the least amount of panel cutting and let the panel system's module dictate all elements of the wall. Part of a neighborhood revitalization plan, the project was reviewed by the city's historic preservation planner. *© Ed Massery*

C43 The newly enclosed light well at the Howard M. Metzenbaum U.S. Courthouse (see Chapter 3) in Cleveland, Ohio, serves multiple functions, including secure court circulation. Temperature control in the atrium was addressed by a careful study of the shadows cast by adjacent buildings, use of high-performance glazing in the skylight, and installation of demand-control ventilation. Regularly occupied perimeter areas above the ground floor have access to lighting controls and numerous large, operable windows typically found in early–twentieth–century buildings. © *Kevin G. Reeves, courtesy of Westlake Reed Leskosky, Archiitect and Mechanical/ Electrical Engineeer*

C44 Glass awnings made from the salvaged hatchbacks of junked sports cars and benches and railings fabricated from a mix of colorful truck tailgates enrich the Adeline Street Urban Salvage Project (see Chapter 9). The project increases density in an existing building and creates modern, sun-filled spaces that use a minimum of new material. © *Ethan Kaplan Photography*

C45 At historic Fenway Park in Boston, Massachusetts, home of the Boston Red Sox, a new sub-field drainage system installed in 2005 has significantly cut irrigation needs. A sand-filtration layer moderates runoff into city storm drains, and the groundskeeping crew uses organic fertilizers and limited pesticides. Water supply and handling raises many issues—in this case, the stadium has reduced potable water use, stormwater runoff, and pollutants flushed into the water system—and it remains a central element of environmental sustainability, with wider implications for energy and infrastructure costs (see Chapter 4). *Photography: Jordan Wirfs-Brock, courtesy of Struever Bros. Eccles & Rouse*

formulate guidelines for urban noise levels[35] and to the formation of groups such as the Noise Pollution Clearinghouse (www.nonoise.org), whose mission is to "create more civil cities and more natural rural and wilderness areas by reducing noise pollution at the source."

Research has linked excessive noise and difficult speaking conditions to poor performance in schools. The American National Standards Institute publishes Standard 12.60, which provides acoustical performance criteria, design requirements, and design guidelines for classrooms where speech intelligibility is essential. Acoustics have no hard-and-fast rules because changes in the size and shape of rooms change the ideal combination and location of absorptive and reflective surfaces. The ANSI standard is 10 pages long, but the 26-page appendix offers design options.

In offices, noise is one of the most prevalent annoyances and leads to increased stress for occupants. Excessive noise in factories is linked to permanent loss of hearing, as well as increased accidents. Finishes, spatial layouts, mechanical systems, and equipment all contribute to interior noise levels. If possible, the design of an interior should provide sound and vibration isolation between different areas and should cluster equipment that produces noise. Quiet areas can be identified and, where possible, increased space between workstations provided.

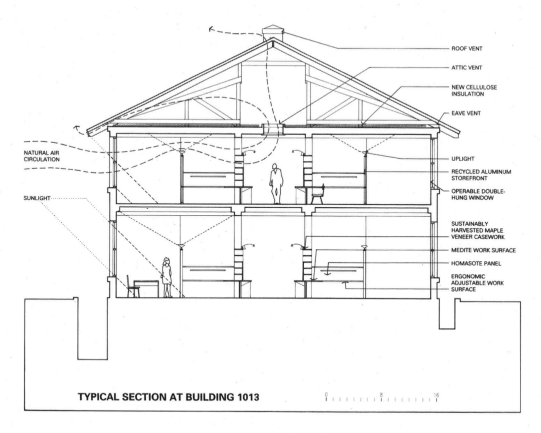

NATURAL AIR CIRCULATION

SUNLIGHT

ROOF VENT

ATTIC VENT

NEW CELLULOSE INSULATION

EAVE VENT

UPLIGHT

RECYCLED ALUMINUM STOREFRONT

OPERABLE DOUBLE-HUNG WINDOW

SUSTAINABLY HARVESTED MAPLE VENEER CASEWORK

MEDITE WORK SURFACE

HOMASOTE PANEL

ERGONOMIC ADJUSTABLE WORK SURFACE

TYPICAL SECTION AT BUILDING 1013

Figure 6.6 A typical section at the Thoreau Center for Sustainability (see Chapter 3) in San Francisco illustrates how the renovation by Tanner Leddy Maytum Stacy Architects utilizes original building features that provide light and cooling air, and added nontoxic and environmentally friendly new materials to create the best possible indoor environmental quality. *Leddy Maytum Stacy Architects*

Figure 6.7 Closed in 1999 because of mold infestation, the renovated City Hall Annex of Cambridge, Massachusetts (see Chapter 5), takes advantage of features designed for the 1871 building's original use as a school: large operable windows with views, high ceilings, and natural daylight. The daylight is shared between spaces through new clerestories. The design team chose paints, adhesives, carpets, and wood products for their low emission of volatile organic compounds, generally favoring water-based products. *Photo by Blind Dog Photo, Inc..*

Figure 6.8 The renovated City Hall Annex in Cambridge, Massachusetts (see Chapter 5), utilizes an open floor plan with cross views to large windows. Carbon dioxide sensors ensure air quality throughout the building. Indoor air-quality planning implemented during and after construction ensured that occupants were not exposed to dust and other contaminants. Ducts were sealed during construction to prevent dust accumulation. The contractor undertook a thorough cleaning afterward, which included a two-week airing out to allow "off-gassing" of any volatile compounds in building materials and furniture. *Photo by Blind Dog Photo, Inc..*

6.5 RENEWAL AND DELIGHT

"The project must contain design features intended solely for human delight and the celebration of culture, spirit and place appropriate to the function of the building."

—Prerequisite Fifteen—Beauty and Spirit, Living Building Challenge v.1.3 © 2008 Cascadia Region Green BuildingCouncil

"Durability, convenience, and beauty" is one translation of the universal architectural goals offered by a Roman, Marcus Vitruvius Pollio, over 2,000 years ago. Beauty required making a building "pleasing and in good taste" with "members in due proportion according to correct principles of symmetry."[36] Spaces at their best offer functional and aesthetic delight, provided through design and current technology. Technologies—lighting, mechanical systems, security measures,

information delivery—change many times over the life of a building, but the base design does not. The qualities and resultant satisfaction provided in a heritage building often elude the normal parameters of metric evaluation.

Occupant Satisfaction in Heritage Buildings

Post-occupancy studies evaluating occupant satisfaction within buildings have become more common, and they suggest that people are more willing to accept variable comfort requirements within heritage buildings, which facilitates reduced energy use. Noting that the pre-1900 buildings are the most energy efficient per square meter and per court, a study by the Ministry of Justice in the United Kingdom adds that "users are more tolerant of minor inconveniences due to higher quality of environment and greater space allowances."[37]

Figure 6.9 The Clipper Mill development in Baltimore, Maryland, possesses a charm and character that springs from the historic buildings and site. The residential spaces benefit from the rich natural materials of the original buildings and are designed to take full advantage fo the wooded Jones Falls Valley. The connection and celebration of culture, spirit, and place are intrinsic to both historic preservation and sustainability. *Photo by Patrick Ross, courtesy Struever Bros. Eccles & Rouse*

Several papers at the 26th Conference on Passive and Low Energy Architecture (PLEA 2009) addressed the comfort level in refurbished heritage buildings and the willingness of occupants to take advantage of passive comfort strategies when given the opportunity. One study of office spaces in reused historical palaces in Cairo, Egypt, demonstrated that emotional attributes such as "pride, status, historical value, and indoor décor attributes affect the overall perceived physical qualities of the environment in offices and workspaces." High environmental quality was perceived in richly decorated historical offices, even though measured temperatures and ambient light levels were below recommended comfort levels.[38]

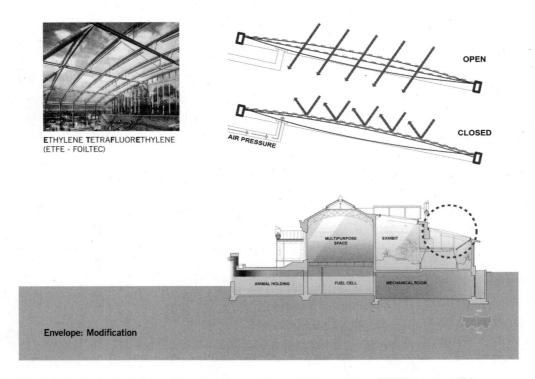

Figure 6.10 New technologies such as a three-layer ethylene eetrafluoroethylene (ETFE) dynamic skylight system at the Bronx Zoo Lion House (see Chapter 5) balance the often-contradictory requirements of encouraging maximum natural light, discouraging heat gain, and reducing electrical and cooling loads. The ETFE, with an R-value of 3.3 (rather than the typical 1.8 for a polyester-film skylight), adjusts for shading and temperature as the sun moves, admitting ultraviolet light for plants and animals but blocking excessive heat. At the end of its life, thought to be at least 50 and possibly 200 years, ETFE can be melted down and reused. *FXFOWLE Architects*

AIA Honolulu Office

Honolulu, HI

Current Owner: American Institute of Architects

Building Type: Commercial Office

Original Building Construction: 1901

Restoration/Renovation Completion: 2003

Square Footage: 1,676 ft^2

Percentage Renovated: 100%

Occupancy: 3 people (40 hrs/week)

Recognition: LEED CI Pilot—Gold; Honolulu AIA Award of Merit 2003; Sustainability Award of Merit 2003; Mayor's Choice Award

---

"Today, this space is a living model that serves to educate its members and the visiting public on sustainability issues and practices."

—*AIA Honolulu, www.aiahonolulu.org*

PROJECT DESCRIPTION

The American Institute of Architects' (AIA) Honolulu chapter occupies the fourth floor of the historic 1901 Stangenwald building. The six-story Italianate structure, designed by Charles W. Dickey, is considered one of Hawaii's first high-rise buildings and its first "fireproof" office building. The AIA office design takes advantage of the original sustainable features of the building and incorporates green materials and high technology whenever possible.

The design team removed dropped acoustical ceilings to increase natural daylighting and to restore the original architectural proportions. They restored original operable windows to allow for natural ventilation on cool days. The plan places interior circulation along the two perimeter walls to allow maximum daylight penetration, and interior views are maintained with full-height pocketed doors.

Figure 6.12 The AIA Honolulu offices on the fourth floor take advantage of 12-foot ceilings and operable windows for daylighting and natural ventilation. Sustainable features include reclaimed materials and low-toxicity finishes. *© 2008 Ferraro Choi And Associates Ltd.*

Figure 6.11 One of the first multistory buildings in Honolulu, the historic Stangenwald Building featured a vent shaft for access to maintenance pipes, an underground parking lot for bicycles, and the first shared law library in Hawaii, a feature that attracted lawyers as tenants for most of its life. A steel frame, concrete flooring, and brick construction, plus built-in fire hoses and flameproof vaults on every floor, defined the building as "fireproof." *© 2004, David Franzen*

Sustainable practices included:

- Sustainable material content and processes in new furniture.
- Existing materials, furniture, and fixtures whenever possible.
- Energy-efficient light fixtures with occupancy sensors.
- Drywall of 100 percent recyclable ash.
- Carpeting composed of recycled material that can be recycled again.
- Carpet adhesive and paints with low levels of VOCs.
- Cork flooring—a sustainable and renewable material.
- Wood shelves and counters, manufactured from certified or renewable forest products.
- Medium-density fiberboard (MDF) shelves with no formaldehyde.

GREEN DESIGN ELEMENTS

AIA Honolulu Office

Sustainable Sites:
- Public transportation proximity
- Pedestrian emphasis

Energy and Atmosphere:
- Natural ventilation
- Energy-efficient lighting
- Automatic occupancy sensors

Materials and Resources:
- Construction debris recycled
- Recycled/recyclable materials (carpet, furniture)
- 100 percent recycled-ash drywall
- Rapidly renewable materials (cork flooring)
- Sustainably harvested wood
- Locally produced materials
- Resource reuse (reusing existing furniture)

Indoor Environment Quality:
- Operable windows
- Low-VOC materials and finishes

PROJECT TEAM

- American Institute of Architects
- Alexander & Baldwin (A&B)
- Ferraro Choi and Associates LTD—Design Architects
- Lincoln Scott, Hawaii
- Cornair Remodeling

Boulder Associates, Inc. Offices

Boulder, CO

Current Owner: Pearl Street Mall Properties, Tenants: Boulder Associates Architects

Building Type: Commercial Office

Original Building Construction: 1906

Restoration/Renovation Completion: 2005

Footage: 13,323 ft^2

Percentage Renovated: 100%

Occupancy: 54 people (40 hrs/week)

Recognition: LEED CI v2.0—Gold; American Institute of Architecture Colorado North Chapter Merit Award 2005; American Society of Interior Design Award in Sustainability 2005

"The firm has created a healthy and inspiring office space that brings sustainable concepts to life for clients, consultants, and staff."

—Boulder Associates, www.boulderassociates.com

Figure 6.13 Boulder Associates' architectural offices on the Pearl Street Pedestrian Mall are located in the historic landmark Citizens National Bank Building. The 100-year-old structure housed a dance hall and jazz club, among other businesses, before becoming a model of environmental responsibility that protects the historic spaces. *Photo courtesy of Boulder Associates Architects*

PROJECT DESCRIPTION

Boulder Associates currently occupies part of the second and third floor of the 1906 Citizens National Bank Building. Although renovated a few years apart, both floors were certified LEED for Commercial Interiors at the Gold level. The office demonstrates sustainable practices that ensure high indoor air quality and reinforce a practice that focuses on healthcare and senior living.

Materials used throughout the space include nontoxic, environmentally friendly products and finishes such as clear-sealed laminated strand lumber, wheatboard, sunflower board, and re-cycled cotton-fiber insulation. Post-consumer or post-recycled materials, such as reclaimed pickle barrels and refurbished furnishings, are used throughout.

Installation of efficient fixtures, dual-flush toilets, waterless urinals, and low-flow showerheads reduced water usage by 43 percent. Micro hydro-powered turbines charge the batteries of the sensor faucets in the bathrooms, significantly extending battery life.

Indoor environmental quality was enhanced through wise use of daylight, individual task lighting, multilevel switching, and zoning of mechanical systems. Low-wattage light fixtures interact with lighting controls throughout and, in combination with Energy Star–rated appliances and electronics, substantially reduce the use of electrical power. To reduce greenhouse gas emissions, the office purchases 100 percent of its electrical power from renewable wind energy providers.

GREEN DESIGN ELEMENTS

Boulder Associates, Inc. Offices

Sustainable Sites:

- Public transportation proximity
- Bicycle accommodation
- Close community connection

Water Efficiency:

- Low-flow plumbing fixtures
- Dual-flush toilets
- Waterless urinals
- Automatic sensor faucets

Energy and Atmosphere:

- Renewable energy certificates (100 percent wind)
- Energy Star–rated appliances
- Occupancy and photoelectric sensors

Materials and Resources:

- Construction waste recycling
- Innovative recycled content materials (27 percent)
- 40 percent of materials manufactured locally
- 42 percent of furnishings relocated or donated
- Ceiling-tile recycling program

Indoor Environment Quality:

- Interior light shelves
- Low- or no-VOC materials and finishes
- Green Label Plus–rated carpeting
- One-month flush out

Additional Features:

- Occupant recycling program

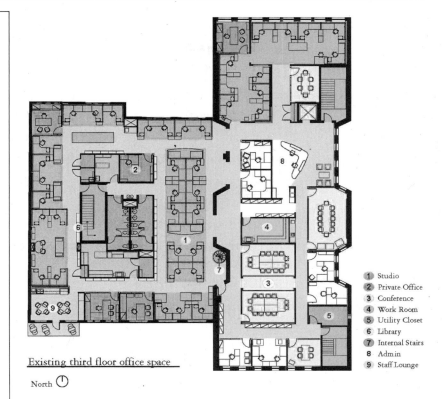

Existing third floor office space

North ⊕

1. Studio
2. Private Office
3. Conference
4. Work Room
5. Utility Closet
6. Library
7. Internal Stairs
8. Admin
9. Staff Lounge

Figure 6.14 Workstation layout takes as much advantage of daylight as possible and utilizes low, glass-topped partitions to increase views and a sense of openness. Interior light-shelves, reflective ceiling panels, and new roof monitors bring diffuse light into the inner workspaces while helping to manage direct light. Reflective-backed roller shades control glare and reduce heat gain. Indoor air quality was protected by specifying very-low-emitting materials, minimizing contaminants during construction, and flushing the space with high volumes of fresh air prior to occupancy. © *Boulder Associates Architects*

PROJECT TEAM

- Boulder Associates, Inc.
- Boulder Engineering
- David Nelson & Associates
- Faurot Construction
- Architectural Energy Corporation

Robert Redford Building—Natural Resources Defense Council

Santa Monica, CA

Current Owner: Natural Resources Defense Council

Building Type: Commercial Office/Interpretive Center/Retail

Original Building Construction: 1917

Restoration/Renovation Completion: 2003

Square Footage: 15,000 ft^2

Percentage Renovated: 100%

Occupancy: 36 people (35 hrs/week) 10–25 visitors (1–2 hrs/month)

Recognition: LEED NC v2.1—Platinum; Congress for the New Urbanism Charter Award 2004

"Using advanced but off-the-shelf technology, this building shows it's possible to protect our natural environment, achieve greater energy independence, and also save money."

—Robert Redford, a member of the NRDC Board of Trustees

PROJECT DESCRIPTION

The Natural Resource Defense Council's offices in Santa Monica, California, achieved Platinum certification under the LEED-NC (New Construction and Major Renovations) regime and serves as an important example of sustainable practices and adaptive re-use that demonstrates the feasibility of reducing environmental impact and creating a healthy workplace. The NRDC shares the building with the David Family Environmental Action Center and the Leonardo DiCaprio e-Activism Zone. Each of these organizations has a mission to boost ecological awareness within the community through interactive museum-quality exhibits that are open to the public.

The interior of the building was largely reconstructed, which allowed the addition of a series of atria for light and ventilation. These wells of light feature clerestory windows atop and open areas directly below to allow light to penetrate each floor. Daylight sensors balance the natural and artificial lighting in each space to minimize unnecessary electrical energy use.

Figure 6.15 NRDC's building uses plantings and light-colored roofing to reduce its contribution to heat islands. A 7.5 kW grid-connect solar electric array produces approximately 37.5 kWH of electricity daily, enough for approximately 20 percent of NRDC's needs. When the building's electrical consumption is low, the system puts power back into the grid, running the electricity meter in reverse. *Photo: Tim Street-Porter, courtesy of Moule & Polyzoides, Architects and Urbanists*

Operable windows provide natural ventilation that fills the offices with fresh air and supplements the HVAC system during agreeable weather. An air-quality and climate-control monitoring system maintains optimum indoor environmental conditions and continuously measures CO_2 levels within the building. Exhaust fans above each atrium are connected to this system and operate accordingly.

A 37.5kW photovoltaic system on the roof provides 20 percent of the building's electrical needs; the remaining energy needed is purchased through renewable energy certificate to promote wind-power development. Overall, the building saves over 50 percent on utility bills compared to a conventional building of equal size.

NRDC also dramatically reduced its water consumption by employing a graywater system that harvests and filters rainwater as well as wastewater from showers and sinks. Dual-flush toilets and waterless urinals are used throughout.

The materials and finishes within the building contain either no or very low levels of off-gassing chemicals. Green housekeeping techniques ensure that all cleaning products are free from harmful chemicals such as chlorinated solvents.

Figure 6.16 Lighting is the largest energy user in commercial buildings, and the building reduces the need for artificial lighting. Three multilevel light wells with rooftop monitors, as well as side-yard light wells, allow sunlight to reach three floors. Clerestories and architectural glass afford privacy while diffusing natural light throughout the building. Task lighting is used, and state-of-the-art fixtures with occupancy and photo-sensors dim lights when daylight is sufficient. *© Moule & Polyzoides, Architects & Urbanists*

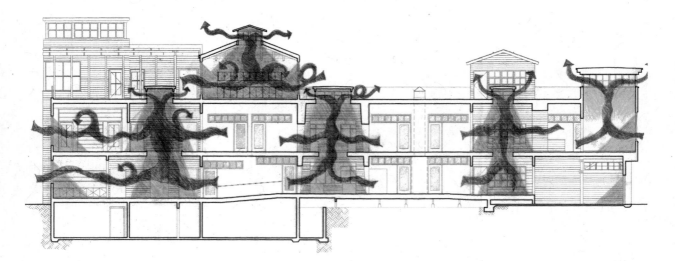

▲ **Figure 6.17** Natural ventilation cools offices through operable windows, transoms, and airflow out rooftop monitors. When needed, the building uses a high-efficiency, multistaged, low-velocity-displacement ventilation/air conditioning system with ozone-friendly refrigerants. Heating and cooling to an individual office shuts off automatically when windows are opened. *© Moule & Polyzoides, Architects & Urbanists*

▶ **Figure 6.18** Americans spend 80 to 90 percent of their time indoors, and the EPA estimates that poor environmental quality causes productivity loss and healthcare costs of more than $2 billion per year. NRDC used low- or nonemitting adhesives, paints, and materials. The building is free of urea formaldehyde and vinyl. Areas where harmful substances are present, such as copy rooms, are designed with negative pressure, and vented outside the building. Carbon dioxide levels are constantly monitored, and occupants have control over their office's temperature, ventilation, and lighting for optimal comfort and productivity. *Photo: Tim Street-Porter, courtesy Moule & Polyzoides, Architects & Urbanists*

GREEN DESIGN ELEMENTS

Robert Redford Building

Sustainable Sites:
- Public transportation proximity
- Bicycle accommodation
- Rooftop garden
- Energy Star–rated reflective roof
- Permeable paving material
- Xeriscaping

Water Efficiency:
- Graywater system (rainwater and wastewater)
- Dual-flush toilets
- Waterless urinals

Energy and Atmosphere:
- Photovoltaic system
- Hot-water heat-distribution system
- Displacement and natural ventilation
- High-efficiency T-5 and T-8 fluorescent lighting
- Occupancy and daylight sensors
- Renewable energy certificates purchased (wind)

Materials and Resources:
- 98 percent construction waste reused/recycled
- Salvaged materials (old movie sets)
- Recycled-content materials
- Rapidly renewable materials
- Forest Stewardship Council–certified wood
- Locally manufactured materials

Indoor Environment Quality:
- Clerestory windows/skylights
- Atrium
- Operable windows
- Low-/no-VOC materials and finishes
- CO_2 monitors

Additional Features:
- Green cleaning policy
- Environmentally friendly cleaning services
- Environmental education center/programs

PROJECT TEAM

Natural Resources Defense Council
Moule & Polyzoides Architects and Urbanists
TG Construction, Inc.
Syska Hennessy Group, Inc.
Nabih Youssef & Associates
Tishman Construction Corporation of California
CTG Energetics, Inc.
Solar Design Associates
Environmental Planning & Design, LLC
Equaris Corporation
GreenWorks

Alberici Corporate Headquarters

Overland, MO

Current Owner: Alberici Corporation

Building Type: Commercial Office

Original Building Construction: 1958

Historic Designation: None

Restoration/Renovation Completion: 2004

Square Footage: 110,000 ft^2

Percentage Renovated: 100%

Occupancy: 200 people (40 hrs/week) 150 visitors (2 hrs/week)

Recognition: LEED NC v2.1—Platinum; Green Globes™ for Continual Improvement of Existing Buildings (93 percent rating); AIA/COTE Top Ten Green Projects 2006; *Environmental Design & Construction* Magazine Excellence in Design Awards 2005; *Midwest Construction's* Best of 2005 Awards Project of the Year: Commercial; Associated General Contractors of St. Louis Keystone Award 2005

"The challenge came in getting everyone to understand that this project was different and we would use some different materials. It wasn't easy getting the trades people to understand that they couldn't just use the products they were currently using."

—*Thomas Taylor, vice president of special projects, Alberici Constructors Inc.*

PROJECT DESCRIPTION

The Alberici Corporation headquarters is an exceptional example of holistic sustainable design, construction, and operation that demonstrates the feasibility of achieving the highest ratings in two metric systems—the U.S. Green Building LEED-NC and Green Building Initiative Green Globes for Continual Improvement of Existing Buildings—with cost-effective strategies. Every aspect of the project provides lessons in the synergies of sustainability that contribute to the health of occupants and the wider world. Transformation of a large metal fabrication shed into a "green" Class A office created a sunlit, nontoxic workplace in a new natural setting while keeping construction waste to a minimum.

Indoor Environmental Quality

- *No smoking:* The entire property is a no-smoking zone.
- *Carbon dioxide:* The building management system monitors carbon dioxide levels and introduces additional fresh air into the building as needed.
- *Indoor pollutant control:* Copying and printing operations are consolidated into copy centers, which have separate, exterior ventilation.
- *Nontoxic materials:* Low-emitting adhesives, sealants, paints, carpet, and composite wood were used throughout.
- *Daylighting and views:* 100 percent of employees have a direct view to the outdoors while seated at their workstation.
- *Ventilation:* Employees can control airflow through floor vents located at each work station throughout the building's raised-floor distribution system.

Materials

- *Construction waste management:* Ninety-three percent of all construction and demolition waste was diverted from the landfill. Gypsum board, clean lumber, metal, glass, and cardboard were recycled.
- *Resource reuse:* Sheet pile salvaged from another Alberici project was used to build a permanent retaining wall on the south end of the property. Overhead crane rail beams were reused to support the structure for the second level of the parking garage.

Figure 6.19 A 65kW refurbished wind turbine, which meets 20 percent of the facility's energy needs, is part of a holistic energy strategy at the Alberici Corporation headquarters—and also contributes to creation of a pleasant workplace. The HVAC system uses a mix of under-floor air distribution and natural ventilation through operable windows, and the central utility plant is located in the parking garage for improved energy efficiency and reduced noise. The motorized clerestory windows are linked to a weather-monitoring system to determine when opening them will take advantage of natural stack ventilation. *Photo courtesy of Vertegy, an Alberici Enterprise*

Figure 6.20 The original warehouse skin was removed from a section that connects the office building to the parking structure to create an internal garden courtyard while increasing daylighting and views for the interior. The south façade of the existing building was modified to create a saw-toothed pattern that blocks the undesirable glare of the western sun and utilizes a true southern exposure. There are only five closed-wall offices in the building. Most employees work in an open area with low, 42-inch wall cubicles. Operable windows and the clerestory glazing system allow for an open, sun-lit work space where everyone has a view to the outdoors. *Photo courtesy of Vertegy, an Alberici Enterprise*

Figure 6.21 Taken before construction began, the aerial view shows the heavily paved site with a neglected landscape that encouraged excessive stormwater runoff. The company restored much of the campus to a natural prairie, added constructed wetlands for greater stormwater retention, and employed shading strategies to reduce the site's contribution to a heat island. Additional heat-island reduction was achieved with a new white roof made of an Energy Star®–rated and soybean oil–based polymer. The soy is harvested and the covering is manufactured in the region. *Photo courtesy of Vertegy, an Alberici Enterprise*

GREEN DESIGN ELEMENTS
Alberici Corporate Headquarters

Sustainable Sites:
- Public transportation proximity
- Bicycle accommodation
- Carpool parking
- Highly reflective roof
- Reduced paved area
- Strategic tree planting (for shade)
- Native prairie restoration
- Constructed wetlands

Water Efficiency:
- Graywater system (sewage conveyance/cooling equipment)
- Low-flow plumbing fixtures
- Dual-flush toilets
- Waterless urinals

Energy and Atmosphere:
- Modify south elevation (solar advantage)
- 65kW wind turbinet
- Flat-plate solar hot-water heating
- Natural ventilation
- Raised-floor air distribution system
- Heat recovery ventilation

Materials and Resources:
- Construction waste diverted/recycled
- Recycled materials
- Rapidly renewable materials
- Forest Stewardship Council–certified wood
- Locally manufactured materials

Indoor Environment Quality:
- Hazardous material decontamination (asbestos/lead)
- Low-VOC materials and finishes
- CO_2 monitors
- Motorized operable clerestory windows and skylights
- Operable windows

Additional Features:
- Green cleaning policy

- *Recycled content:* The entire project achieved close to 30 percent recycled content by cost. Recycled fly ash and furnace slag were used as a cement replacement in the concrete.
- *Local/regional materials:* More than 50 percent of the building materials used in the project came from sources within a 500-mile radius of the site.
- *Rapidly renewable materials:* A bamboo-derived plywood called Plyboo was used for the building's feature walls and baseboards. Casework at the coffee bars, copy centers, mail room, and training rooms is made from wheatboard.

Site and Water

- *Brownfield redevelopment:* The rejuvenation of the site into an organic native prairieland creates a campus of seasonal beauty that provides delight at the same time that it eliminates equipment-intensive lawn mowing and the need for irrigation.
- *Constructed wetlands:* The wetlands aid the natural stormwater management of the prairie by allowing water to absorb slowly into the ground, naturally filtering out harmful chemicals.
- *Rainwater* that falls on the roof is collected in a 38,000-gallon tank, filtered, and then used throughout the building for sewage conveyance and within the mechanical system's cooling tower.

Energy

- *Optimized energy performance:* The building is 60 percent more energy- efficient than a conventional building.
- The HVAC system uses a mix of under-floor air distribution and natural ventilation through operable windows.
- A passive-solar preheat system provides all of the building's hot water.
- An energy-recovery system incorporated into the HVAC extracts heat from the air without the need to recirculate stale air.

PROJECT TEAM, ALBERICI CORPORATE HEADQUARTERS

- Alberici Redevelopment Corp.
- Mackey Mitchell Associates
- Alberici Constructors, Inc.
- Vertegy
- Stock & Associates
- Intuition & Logic
- Alper-Audi, Inc.
- CDH Energy Corp.

- Corrigan Company
- Guarantee Electrical Company
- PayneCrest
- Colliers Turley Martin Tucker
- CDH Energy Corp.
- Shaw Nature Reserve

Montgomery Park Business Center

Baltimore, Maryland

Current Owner: Himmerlich Associates Inc.

Building Type: Commercial Offices

Original Building Construction: Between 1925 and 1927

Historic Designation: National Register of Historic Places

Restoration/Renovation Completion: 2002

Square Footage: 1.3 million ft^2

Percentage Renovated: 100%

Recognition: EPA Grand Prize Phoenix Award 2003; Green Roof Award of Excellence for Retrofit/Extensive Roof 2003

"Projects such as this are the type of successes we want to become commonplace. By reinvesting in an existing community and reusing an older building, we are making sound economic and environmental decisions that will benefit the surrounding community, city and state."

—*Secretary Kendl P. Philbrick, Maryland Department of the Environment*

Figure 6.22 Located on the edge of southwest Baltimore's commercial and industrial districts, the Montgomery Park sign on the roof of the eight-story landmark building is a dramatic fixture, visible from the nearby interstate highway. The complex is a model for innovative development, utilizing an historic landmark and providing a vision for ecologically minded revitalization for economic growth. © *Patrick Ross Photography*

Figure 6.23 Once the city's largest mercantile building, Montgomery Park received the Environmental Protection Agency's grand-prize Phoenix Award in 2003, recognizing the project as the preeminent property nationwide among outstanding green building development projects that have returned environmentally compromised properties to productive use. © *Patrick Ross Photography*

PROJECT DESCRIPTION

Montgomery Park is a design model for a green workplace. A former Montgomery Ward catalog house and retail store, it provides over one million square feet of flexible office space that offers both urban flair and suburban amenities. The 143,000-square-foot floors have lofty ceilings and large windows that provide generous ambient light throughout the building. 1,000 multipaned steel-framed windows offer panoramic views of the city.

The 56-acre project, located in Baltimore's West Side Empowerment Zone, incorporates a green roof, high-efficiency mechanical and electrical systems, a graywater-conservation system that captures stormwater runoff, recycled building materials, insulated glass, energy-saving lighting with photocell dimming and occupancy sensors, and energy-efficient high-speed elevators.

The project symbolizes Maryland's commitment to smart growth. Montgomery Park is the south anchor of an urban renewal plan that seeks to focus development in existing neighborhoods. Over 60 bus lines serve the location, which is connected to light rail service by a shuttle.

There are approximately 70,000 windows at Montgomery Park, and every third window cluster is operable. The steel windows were preserved, and reglazed with low-E, argon-filled glass panes. The new windows exceed the state's efficiency guidelines and retain sufficient light transmission (75 percent) to meet preservation guidelines.

Indoor Environmental Quality

- Acoustical ceiling tiles are formaldehyde-free and contain 79 percent recycled content.
- All primer and paints are vinyl acetate/acrylic latex paint that emits zero VOCs.
- Window shades have pinholes that allow natural light in, but still provide light deflection.
- Organic pigments contain no heavy metals.
- Homosote—used for workstations to dampen sound—is made from 100 percent recycled postconsumer newsprint and contains no asbestos or formaldehyde.
- No glues were used in manufacturing the workstations. UV curing of the sealant on work surfaces prevents off-gassing.

Materials and Resources

- All of the glass panes removed from the building were downcycled into "glassphalt," used to pave the parking lot entrance.
- Pavers at the building entrance are a reused floor from a nearby factory.
- 3 million pounds of metal, 5,800 cubic yards of wood, and 24,840 pounds of copper were recycled.
- 8,036 board feet of wood was reused.
- 80 percent of all materials removed during construction was recycled.

Site and Water

- The site is landscaped with native species that require no irrigation.

- Bioretention ponds are used to trap and filter stormwater runoff.
- Stormwater is collected and cleaned via a sand-filtration system; the treated graywater is pumped to a rooftop cistern, where it is held for use in toilets.

Energy and Systems

- The elevators use 66 percent less energy than standard models.
- LED exit lights provide an 87.5 percent savings over standard 40-watt fixtures.
- Floor plans are designed to maximize opportunities for natural lighting. Enclosed offices are concentrated in the center of each floor, and open workstations are placed along the perimeter of the building.
- High-efficiency lighting is combined with occupancy and ambient light sensors.
- An ice-storage tank on the roof allows use of off-peak electricity for cooling.
- An economizer system utilizes fresh air and monitors CO_2 levels within the building.

Figure 6.24 For more than three quarters of a century, the art deco edifice of the Montgomery Ward catalog store had been a familiar sight in southwest Baltimore. The main structure looks much as it did in the 1920s and is listed on the National Register of Historic Places. Designed by Montgomery Ward's in-house engineer of construction, W. H. McCaully, and built by Wells Brothers Construction Company, it was the seventh of nine industrial warehouses that Ward constructed around the country in the early twentieth century, when the mail-order industry was at its peak. © *Patrick Ross Photography*

GREEN DESIGN ELEMENTS
Montgomery Park Business Center

Sustainable Sites:
- Public transportation proximity
- Bicycle accommodation
- Carpool parking
- Green roof
- Reduced paved area
- Strategic tree planting (for shade)
- Indigenous plantings

Water Efficiency:
- Graywater system
- Low-flow plumbing fixtures
- Waterless urinals

Energy and Atmosphere:
- Ice storage for off-peak electrical use
- Natural ventilation
- Low-energy elevators
- Light sensor controls
- Economizer system

Materials and Resources:
- Construction waste diverted/recycled
- Recycled materials
- Rapidly renewable materials
- Forest Stewardship Council–certified wood

Indoor Environment Quality:
- Hazardous material decontamination (asbestos/lead)
- Low-VOC materials and finishes
- CO_2 monitors
- Operable windows

Additional Features:
- Green cleaning policy

Figure 6.25 The high ceilings and large floor plates of the historic building at Montgomery Park provide flexibility that accommodates diverse business requirements. Concrete floors provide floor-loading capacities well beyond the requirements of any office tenant. © *Patrick Ross Photography*

PROJECT TEAM

Himmelrich Associates
Terra Nova Ventures
Daniel, Mann, Johnson + Mendenhall
Notari Assciates, PA
RM Design
Inland Builders, Inc.
RMF Engineering, Inc.
Morabito Consultants, Inc.
Farrand & English, Inc.

ENDNOTES

1. Gaia Research and Gaia Architects, "Affordable Low Allergy Housing; A Guidance Note," © Gaia Research 2005, Edinburgh.

2. U.S. EPA, "Healthy Buildings, Healthy People: A Vision for the 21st Century," www.epa.gov/iaq/hbhp/hbhp_report.pdf.

3. Charles J. Weschler, "Changes in Indoor Pollutants Since the 1950s," *Atmospheric Environment,* vol. 43 (1), (2009): 153–169.

4. National Institute of Building Sciences (NIBS), "IEQ Indoor Environmental Quality," *NIBS IEQ Final Report,* July 14, 2005.

5. Environment Canada, www.ec.gc.ca/nopp/voc/en/bkg.cfm. Accessed July 25, 2009.

6. Secretariat of the Commission for Environmental Cooperation (CEC), (2008), *Green Building in North America: Opportunities and Challenges,* p.4, Montreal (Quebec) Canada, www.cec.org/greenbuilding

7. Environment Canada, www.ec.gc.ca/nopp/voc/en/bkg.cfm. Accessed July 25, 2009.

8. www.epa.gov/iaq/voc.html. Accessed July 25, 2009.

9. Healthy Building Network and Kaiser Permanente, (May 2008), "Toxic Chemicals in Building Materials; An Overview for Health Care Organizations," www.healthybuilding.net.

10. www.epa.gov/iaq/voc.html. Accessed July 25, 2009.

11. Peter Waldman, "Levels of Risk: Common Industrial Chemicals in Tiny Doses Raise Health Issue," *The Wall Street Journal* (July 25, 2005), Accessed online July 2009, www.WSJ_on_low_dose_EDCs[1].pdf.

12. Healthy Building Network and Kaiser Permanente, "Toxic Chemicals in Building Materials; An Overview for Health Care Organizations," (May 2008), www.healthybuilding.net.

13. Hal Levin, "Indoor Air Quality by Design," *Indoor Air Quality Handbook,* by John D. Spengler, Jonathan M. Samet, John F. McCarthy (New York: McGraw-Hill, 2001).

14. American Chemical Society, "Potentially Toxic Flame Retardants Highest In California Households," *Science Daily* (October 8, 2008). Retrieved July 25, 2009, from www.sciencedaily.com/releases/2008/10/081006170710.htm.

15. Elia Sterling, "We Are What We Build: A New Paradigm for Sustainable Healthy Buildings," Powerpoint presentation at Living Future 09 conference, Portland, Oregon, May 2009, http://cascadiapublic.s3.amazonaws.com/LF09%20Presentations/ThursAM/LF09_WeAreWhatWeBuild.pdf.

16. Bernard Feilden, *Conservation of Historic Buildings,* Third Edition; First published in 1982 (London Architectural Press, 2003), p.173.

17. Sandy Halliday, *Sustainable Construction,* © Gaia Research (Oxford, UK, and Burlington, VT: Butterworth-Heinemann, Elsevier Linacre House, 2008), p. 128.

18. John D. Spengler, Jonathan M. Samet, John F. McCarthy, *Indoor Air Quality Handbook* (New York: McGraw-Hill, 2001).

19. D. Michelle Addington, "The History and Future of Ventilation," *Indoor Air Quality Handbook,* by John D. Spengler, Jonathan M. Samet, John F. McCarthy (New York: McGraw-Hill, 2001).

20. Nathanson, Ted, "Prevention and Maintenance Operatons," *Indoor Air Quality Handbook,* by John D. Spengler, Jonathan M. Samet, John F. McCarthy (New York: McGraw-Hill, 2001), p. 639.

21. Penny Bonda, "Vivian Loftness: Quality of Place Matters," *Interior Design* (September 7, 2005), www.interiordesign.net/artitlcle/CA6255165.html. Accessed July 27, 2009.

22. J. A. Veitch, "Investigating and Influencing How Buildings Affect Health: Interdisciplinary Endeavors," NRCC-50073, National Research Council Canada (2009), http://irc-nrc-cnrc.gc.ca.

23. The Center for Health and the Global Environment, "Healthy Solutions for the Low Carbon Economy: Guidelines for Investors, Insurers and Policy Makers," Harvard Medical School (July 2008), p.11.

24. Veitch.

25. Allyson Wendt, "Bringing Nature Indoors: The Myths and Realities of Plants in Buildings," *Environmental Building News* EBN:17:10 (March 2009), www.buildinggreen.com.

26. Preamble to the Constitution of the World Health Organization as adopted by the International Health Conference, New York, June 19–22, 1946; signed on July 22, 1947, by the representatives of 61 States (Official Records of the World Health Organization, no. 2, p. 100); and entered into force on April 7, 1948.

27. Veitch.

28. The Center for Health and the Global Environment, p. 11.

29. "Cleaning Chemicals and the Environment," Harvard Medical School Green Cleaning Program, www.green .harvard.edu/node/132. Accessed October 11, 2009.

30. David R. Holly, *Green Cleaning, What it Can Mean for You and Your Customers,* The Canadian Sanitation Supply Association and The Ashkin Group, LLC (May 4, 2005), www. ashkingroup.com/cleaners.html. Accessed October 2009.

31. NIOSH. Worker Health Chartbook, 2004. NIOSH Publication No.2004-146. Available at: www2a.cdc.gov/ NIOSH-Chartbook/ch2/ch2-10.asp. Accessed October 30, 2005.

32. Santa Monica Improves Custodial Environmentally Preferable Purchasing. The Ashkin Group, LLC—Case Study. www.ashkingroup.com/pdfs/casestudies/stmonica4.pdf.

33. BOMA International, "Reduce, Reuse, Reinvent: How to Revitalize Your Janitorial Procedures Using Green Cleaning Techniques" (2009), http://www.boma.org/Site CollectionDocuments/Org/Docs/ReduceReuse%20 Reinvent%20FINAL.pdf.

34. Paul R. Epstein and Christine Rogers, "Inside the Greenhouse: The Impacts of CO_2 and Climate Change on Public Health in the Inner City" (April 2004), The Center for Health and the Global Environment, Harvard Medical School, www.med.harvard.edu/chge, p. 4.

35. Veitch.

36. Morris Hicky Morgan, *Vitruvius: The Ten Books on Architecture* (Cambridge: Harvard University Press. London: Humphrey Milford. Oxford University Press. 1914). Accessed at http://old.perseus.tufts.edu October 18, 2009, Chapter 1.3.1.

37. Jon Wallsgrove (2007), "Age Energy Research: A Study of the Energy Usage of Buildings Relative to Their Age," www.glasgow.gov.uk/NR/rdonlyres/C043FCA4-0678-4035-BC1E-DDA444467205/0/OPHSHeritagedesign 141207.pdf. Accessed November 2008.

38. Ihab Elzeyadi, Ph.D., FEIA, "Architectural Pride and Environmental Prejudice: The Effect of Personal Status, Historical Value and Indoor Décor on Occupants Indoor Environmental Quality in Offices," PLEA2009—26th Conference on Passive and Low Energy Architecture, Quebec City, Canada, June 22–24, 2009, www.plea2009 .arc.ulaval.ca/Papers/2.STRATEGIES/2.3%20Post-Occupancy%20Evaluation/ORAL/2-3-01-PLEA2009 Quebec.pdf. Accessed November 2009.

chapter 7

MATERIALS AND RESOURCES— REDUCE, REPAIR, REUSE, RECYCLE

"A solution at the economic and technological level can be found only if we undergo, in the most radical way, an inner change of heart, which can lead to a change in lifestyle and of unsustainable patterns of consumption and production."

—Pope John Paul II and Patriarch Bartholomew I of Constantinople, "Declaration on the Environment," June 10, 2002

7.1 CONSUMPTION AND WASTE— A THROWAWAY CULTURE

"If everybody consumed at U.S. rates, we would need three to five planets."

—*The Story of Stuff with Annie Leonard, www.storyofstuff.com*

NO DESCRIPTION of a sustainable world can avoid addressing the completely unsustainable way in which "developed" countries carelessly use and dispose of materials. Throwaway cultural norms apply as directly to buildings and their components as they do to plastic bottles. Current economic structure and cultural attitudes support new over old, replacement over repair. A sustainable approach takes an entirely different tack. A sustainable world values stewardship, repairability, and durability, because a sustainable world recognizes that every new object has substantial but hidden environmental costs, including health impacts, that may be irreversible. It is against the framework of consumption and waste that every decision about new materials and the importance of sustaining existing materials must be made.

251

Figure 7.1 Repurposing discarded materials, such as Volvo station wagon tailgates, at the Adeline Street Urban Salvage Project, is the most environmentally friendly way of keeping materials out of landfill because no reprocessing or downcycling is required. As described by Leger Wanaselja Architecture, "The reuse and salvage in the project infuses it with a sense of connection, history and narrative. Every detail comes alive with a story of origins, disposal, and rebirth." © Ethan Kaplan Photography

Consumption Statistics

Planetary use and depletion of resources and the resulting waste have steadily increased since the middle of the twentieth century, with the citizens of North America leading the way. The United States is notable for containing a small part of the world's population, less than 5 percent, yet for driving a large part of the consumption-and-waste pattern. The United States uses 30 percent of all raw resources in the world,[1] of which the U.S. Geological Society estimates 60 percent are directed to construction.[2] That means that every year the United States uses 18 percent, or almost a fifth of the entire world's resources—billions of tons of material—to construct buildings, roads, bridges, and other structures. The aggregate investment in the U.S. built environment is reported by the National Research Council to be around $22 trillion.[3]

The portion of this vast stream of raw resources that actually winds up in a product is depressingly small, reported as between 5 and 10 percent in the book *Cradle to Cradle* by William McDonough and Michael Braungart.[4] According to L. Hunter Lovins, founder of Natural Capitalism Solutions, less than 1 percent of raw materials is embodied in a product and still there six months after sale.[5] The other 99 percent has become waste somewhere in the chain of extraction, fabrication, transportation, and use. At each step, environmental (and often social) impacts occur as energy is consumed and effluent, pollution, and toxic materials are produced.

The design and production of products and processes that reduce or eliminate substances hazardous to human health—or *green chemistry*—is not yet the norm. In the United States alone, 4.1 billion pounds of toxic chemicals were reported in 2007, of which 12 percent was identified as persistent bioaccumulative toxic (PBT) chemicals. Quoting the EPA, "PBT chemicals are of particular concern not only because they are toxic but also because they remain in the environment for long periods of time, are not readily destroyed, and build up or accumulate in body tissue. The TRI (Toxic Report Inventory) PBT chemicals include dioxin and dioxin-like compounds, lead and lead compounds, mercury and mercury compounds, polycyclic aromatic compounds (PACs), polychlorinated biphenyls (PCBs), and certain pesticides, among other chemicals."[6]

Only 10 percent of extracted materials make up final products. 90 percent of natural resources extracted for consumer use are disposed of as waste.[7]

Increasing consumption in the construction industry reflects changing demographics and a trend in industrialized nations that dedicates consumption of greater volumes of material to achieving buyer satisfaction. New houses in the United States were 38 percent bigger in 2002 than in 1975,[8] and thanks to this increased volume, they used an estimated three times more construction materials. Bigger houses tend to have more appliances and consume more resources for both operation and maintenance. Regardless of dwelling size, low-density development requires about 2.5 times more materials than high-density development.[9]

Changing demographics mean that even when populations stabilize, more housing units are required. The number of people living under one roof fell from 5.1 in 1975 to 4.4 in 2002 in developing countries and from 3.2 to 2.5 in industrial countries in the same years, even as the total number of households increased.[10] More housing units mean less sharing of resources and higher individual consumption. A one-person household in the United States uses 17 percent more energy per person than a two-person household does and requires duplication in other shared resources such as furniture, appliances, and automobiles.[11]

"[C]onsumers in industrial countries are indirectly responsible for a significant proportion of China's carbon emissions."

—*The Worldwatch Institute*[12]

The Brookings Institution estimates that in the next 20 years, the United States will increase the square footage of all built space from 300 billion square feet to 427 billion square feet. The largest component of this added space will be homes.[13] The environmental impact of this expansion will be exacerbated by the fact that 82 billion square feet will involve replacement of existing space,

Figure 7.2 The tower stone restoration of the 1857 Lafayette Avenue Presbyterian Church in Brooklyn, New York, demonstrates the durability of stone as a material. 100 percent of the existing stone was salvaged and reused in the restoration to avoid waste. Work included stone replacement, salvage, and retooling of stone for use in new locations. Excess stone was donated to a local mason-training and apprenticeship program and for the manufacturing of restoration mortar mixes requiring stone dust. © *Walter Sedovic*

creating approximately 6.2 billion tons of waste from demolition and requiring consumption of new materials to match the original square footage.

Waste Production

Because of current systems, increased consumption increases waste, and the United States leads the way, creating 30 percent of all waste in the world,[14] including 254 million tons of municipal solid waste,[15] 170 million tons of building construction waste in 2003,[16] and *15 billion tons* of industrial waste.[17] Both United States consumption and waste continue to climb. Individual consumption has doubled in the last 50 years[18] and individual waste, now equal to 4.6 pounds a day,[19] has doubled in the last 30 years.[20] Construction and demolition waste in the United States increased 25 percent between 1996 and 2003.[21]

"Wasting directly impacts climate change because it is directly linked to global resource extraction, transportation, processing, and manufacturing.... When we minimize waste, we can reduce greenhouse gas emissions in sectors that together represent 36.7 percent of all U.S. greenhouse gas emissions."

—Stop Trashing the Climate[22]

The Impact of Waste

Waste is the physical evidence of the heedless way we utilize natural resources, creating environmental and social impacts at every stage of the process. The direct environmental impacts of waste as the ultimate product are sobering by themselves. As Heather Rogers points out in her 2005 book *Gone Tomorrow: The Hidden Life of Garbage,* more waste means more collection trucks and more transport. "Incinerators release toxics into the air and spawn ash that can contaminate soil and water. Landfills metastasize like cancer across the countryside, leaching their hazardous brew into nearby groundwater, unleashing untold environmental problems for future generations."[23]

Recovery from the United States waste stream for recycling (25 percent) and composting (85 percent) has increased, and a little over 12 percent of waste is incinerated for energy, but 54 percent of waste still ends up in landfill. By volume this is almost twice the total of 1960, when 94 percent of all waste went to landfill.

"Wastes, including extremely hazardous radioactive material, toxic heavy metals, and poisonous PCBs, are routinely transported around the world on the path of least economic resistance."

—The ARUP Journal[24]

Removal of waste is big business that more and more commonly involves trucking materials hundreds of miles to giant landfills that can meet the increasing cost of regulations through economies of scale.[25] The EPA estimates the U.S. currently counts fewer than 2,000 landfills; 30 years ago more than 20,000 existed. Regulations focus on preventing the leaching of dangerous metals and chemicals into groundwater,[26] but landfills are also the largest source of methane gas, which is 21 times more potent than carbon dioxide as a contributor to planetary warming. Regulation to capture methane is not universal and in the United States only addresses landfills operating after 1993.[27]

Incineration of waste, which creates carbon dioxide but produces electricity, is preferable environmentally to landfill,[28] but it hardly represents a panacea for the linear path of resource extraction to production to consumption to waste. Even if energy were the only consideration, the amount created by incineration equals only a fraction of the energy required to create the waste in the first place. Groups, such as the Global Anti-Incinerator Alliance/Global Alliance for Incinerator Alternatives (GAIA, www.no-burn.org), argue that incinerators emit more CO_2 per megawatt-hour than coal-fired, natural-gas-fired, or oil-fired power plants.[29] The necessary solution is consumption and waste reduction, not less-bad methods for making garbage disappear.

7.2 DIVERTING WASTE—REUSE, RECYCLE, DOWNCYCLE

"Within the zero waste approach, the most beneficial strategy for combating climate change is reducing the overall amount of materials consumed and discarded, followed by materials reuse, then materials recycling."

—Stop Trashing the Climate[30]

The waste management hierarchy proposed by the EPA includes the following components listed in order of preference:

- Source reduction, including the reuse of products and on-site composting
- Recycling, including off-site (or community) composting
- Combustion with energy recovery
- Disposal through landfilling

Recycling and Downcycling

Diverting waste from disposal for recycling, which is almost always downcycling, involves the reclamation of used materials to create new materials. The reclaimed products are broken down, melted, smelted, or extruded into new forms and/or used as a part of another material. Preferably, the quality is high enough that the reclaimed material can be *recycled*—that is, used again in the same application, such as aluminum cans.

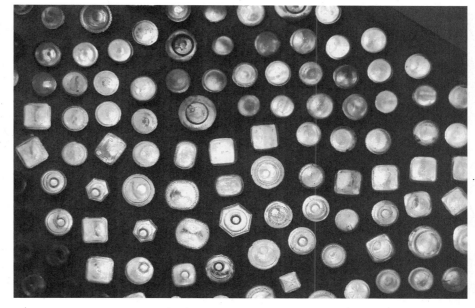

Figure 7.3 A mosaic of bottles set into the wall at the People's Food Co-op (see Chapter 1) increases thermal storage while adding light and interest. A combination of local indigenous material and salvage, the wall was constructed with volunteer labor out of straw, sand, and mud (cob). South-facing, the mass absorbs heat in the winter and is shaded in the summer to help cool the interior space. Natural materials such as earth, wood, plaster, and unsealed textiles can help regulate relative humidity in the indoor climate by absorbing moisture when humidity rises and emitting it when air becomes dry, smoothing out peaks and troughs. *Cheyenne Glasgow photo, courtesy People's Food Co-op*

More commonly, the material is *downcycled,* becoming a component of something else—such as plastic bottles that are incorporated into benches and crushed glass that makes up bathroom tile—which may not have the potential to be downcylced again.

Although recycling does keep materials out of a landfill, it does not address the root problem of consumption and it cannot always be assumed that recycling is better for the environment than waste. A large amount of processing is still required to remake materials. Most materials, other than some metals, lose molecular integrity during reprocessing. For instance, paper fibers degrade in quality each time they are recycled and eventually will not hold together. Glass loses workability and durability. Plastic, if it is a type that can be recycled, loses flexibility. Contamination of synthetics such as plastic with a different type of resin renders an entire lot unusable. Plastics also require large portions of virgin resin to create a useful new substance.[31]

Consumer recycling has been wholeheartedly embraced as the trademark of environmental action, but it suggests, falsely, that excessive consumption and the design and use of short-lived products is acceptable. Even dropping products into a recycling container does not guarantee that they will actually be reprocessed. Some are merely transported to another area of the globe with fewer regulations, and some go straight to landfill if market demand is weak or the volume of incoming waste exceeds sorting capacity.

Extended Producer Responsibility

Critics of recycling point out that the very industries most enthusiastic about the public's bearing the cost and responsibility for recycling and trash management are those that produce the waste in the first place, whether through products or packaging. An extended producer responsibility (EPR) regime, which started in Germany in 1991, shifts responsibility back to the manufacturers. Full EPR theoretically imposes accountability over the entire life cycle of a product, including upstream and downstream impacts.

"Whenever we can reuse a product instead of producing a new one from raw materials, we save resources and energy. From an environmental standpoint, a salvaged product is usually better than a recycled-content product, because significant energy did not need to be invested in re-manufacturing it."

Alex Wilson[32]

Managed Construction Waste

The USGBC's LEED metric system (see Chapter 3) has helped publicize the need for diverting many tons of construction debris—which include wood, masonry, glass, and metals—from landfills and out of the waste stream. Although some observers have suggested that the LEED system encourages building demolition (see Chapter 3), it is important to realize that renovation typically creates more direct construction waste per square foot than new construction, although using fewer new materials for the final product. The EPA estimates that 41 percent of construction debris in 2003 came from renovations. The most environmentally appropriate course of action may be rethinking gut rehabs and accepting less flexibility in a floor plan in order to reduce both waste and new material use, but the redirection of building debris away from landfill remains important regardless of source.

Regulations that prohibit disposal of construction waste help trigger new industries that focus on reclaiming and repurposing waste. Depending on location and available markets, renovation projects can achieve as much as 90 percent waste diversion, but the complete environmental effect is hard to evaluate. It's not uncommon for diverted materials to be

Figure 7.4 Materials at the Thoreau Center for Sustainability San Francisco (see Chapter 3) reflect a commitment to an environmentally friendly and healthy workplace. Sustainably harvested EcoPanels are from Architectural Forest Enterprises, and maple veneers are from the Menominee Tribe. Homosite fiberboard panels are made from 100 percent recycled paper. Diverting paper from landfill is especially important because the decomposition of organic materials creates methane gas, which is 21 times more harmful than CO_2. *Photography: Richard Barnes*

transported significant distances for reprocessing, and many materials are downcycled in some way.

The Institute for Local Self-Reliance, www.ilsr.org, developed a "Waste to Wealth" program that offers guidance and resources for salvaging and reusing building materials. The EPA site that addresses recovery of construction debris links to The ReUse People of America, www.thereusepeople.org, as a resource with additional links. Regional opportunities for material salvage vary considerably, but case studies from one part of the country or world can inform another.

7.3 IDENTIFYING BETTER PRODUCTS

"[E]nvironmental claims based on single attributes, such as recycling, should be viewed with skepticism. These claims do not account for the fact that other impacts may indeed cause equal or greater damage."

—*Barbara Lippiat and Amy Boyles*[33]

Product Certification

A big challenge for owners, designers, and contractors is determining which new products are less harmful to the environment. According to Scot Case, executive director of the EcoLogo Program, more than 400 environmental labels are in use, and "some are completely meaningless."[34] To add to the confusion, an environmental label does not help one choose between materials—for instance whether to use carpet or tile—or between choices like virgin local materials and recycled content that may have traveled some distance for reprocessing. A label rarely addresses comparative issues that include durability, cleaning, and maintenance requirements, as well as final disposal. Nor does a label necessarily address how a product may contribute to a healthy environment by avoiding situations that encourage mold, harbor dust, create uncomfortable acoustics, or facilitate eyestrain.

A good source for understanding the product certification labels that currently exist is BuildingGreen.com,

Figure 7.5 A bedroom at Forbes Park (see Chapter 1) demonstrates the durable long-lived materials common in many adaptive reuse projects. Finishes that require little maintenance and are easy to clean reduce consumption throughout a long service life and dilute the environmental effects of fabrication by delaying replacement. © *Forbes Park LLC*

the home of *Environmental Building News* and a source of editorial guidance for *GreenSource* magazine, the member magazine of the U.S. Green Building Council published by McGraw-Hill Construction. The March/April 2009 issue of *GreenSource,* available online, provides a chart that explains the scope of different certification systems, the managing organization, and the program name such as Energy Star, Green Seal, and Forest Stewardship Council.[35]

Green Material Directories

The BuildingGreen website hosts the GreenSpec® Directory, which lists descriptions for environmentally preferable products and explains their green attributes. Listing in the GreenSpec® cannot be purchased by the manufacturer. Another example of a green material directory is the Oikos® Green Building Source—

Green Product Information, www.oikos.com/green_products/index.php.

> "Keep up the search for green products, but understand that labels, at least the current crop, are only part of the search, not the final answer."
>
> *Tristan Roberts, "Searching for Clarity Amid Green Certificates"*[36]

Essays about evaluating and selecting green products can be found at the Whole Building Design Guide website, www.wbdg.com (refer to Chapter 3 for a description of this resource). At this site, an article by John Amatruda, a partner at the consulting firm of Viridian Energy and Environmental, lists the variety of attributes that define green products:

- They promote good indoor air quality (typically through reduced emissions of VOCs and/or formaldehyde).

- They are durable and have low maintenance requirements.
- They incorporate recycled content (post-consumer and/or postindustrial).
- They have been salvaged for reuse.
- They are made using natural and/or renewable resources.
- They have low "embodied energy" (the energy required to produce and transport materials).
- They do not contain CFCs, HCFCs, or other ozone-depleting substances.
- They do not contain highly toxic compounds, and their production does not result in highly toxic by-products.
- They are obtained from local resources and manufacturers.
- For wood or bio-based products, they employ "sustainable harvesting" practices.
- They can be easily reused (either whole or through disassembly).
- They can be readily recycled (preferably in a closed-loop recycling system).
- They are biodegradable.[37]

Materials Red List

The Cascadia Region Green Building Council, as part of the Living Building Challenge (refer to Chapter 3), has adopted a Red List of materials that should be phased out of production due to health/toxicity concerns. A Living Building project cannot contain any of the following materials or chemicals (although temporary exceptions are made for certain products like fluorescent lights, for which no satisfactory substitute is readily available):

- Cadmium
- Chlorinated polyethylene and chlorosulfonated polyethelene
- Chlorofluorcarbons (CFCs)
- Chloroprene (Neoprene)
- Formaldehyde (added)
- Halogenated flame retardants
- Hydrochlorofluorocarbons (HCFCs)
- Lead
- Mercury
- Petrochemical fertilizers and pesticides
- Phthalates
- Polyvinyl chloride (PVC)
- Wood treatments containing creosote, arsenic, or pentachlorophenal

Rapidly Renewable

The concept of using *rapidly renewable materials* is promulgated in some green building metric systems. It promotes the use of materials such as bamboo or soy that grow quickly and, because of this theoretically have, a reduced environmental impact. Yet no single attribute is really adequate as a full evaluation of a material. Although a plant may grow quickly, the manner in which it is grown, harvested, and processed may not be at all sustainable. If harmful chemicals are used in cultivation or manufacturing, or natural habitat is destroyed to produce unsustainable and polluting plantations, than the product is not environmentally preferable, regardless of the speed with which the source crop regrows.

"There have been many examples of the disastrous, unintended effects of human actions."

—*Complex Environmental Systems: Synthesis for Earth, Life, and Society in the 21st Century*[38]

Life Cycle Assessment

The holy grail of environmental evaluation is *life-cycle assessment* (LCA), which strives to evaluate the impacts of a product or process from the first acquisition of materials through to the end of life. Ideally, LCA yields an understanding of complete health and environmental impacts, but it is a complex undertaking, and the usefulness of its outcomes depends on both chosen parameters and available data.

Comparison of the environmental and economic performance of several hundred building products is possible with Windows-based software system known as BEES® (Building for Environmental and Economic Sustainability), which was developed by the National Institute of Standards and Technology Building and Fire Research Laboratory. BEES includes economic performance such as the costs of initial investment, replacement, operation, maintenance, repair, and disposal.

The National Renewable Energy Laboratory maintains a publicly available database known as the U.S. Life-Cycle Inventory (LCI) database. The Athena Institute, a nonprofit organization with offices in Canada and the United States, helps maintain the NREL database and offers two software tools for life-cycle assessment of whole buildings and assemblies, the ATHENA® Impact Estimator and the EcoCalculator for Assemblies. Developed in association with the University of Minnesota and Morrison Hershfield Consulting Engineers, the EcoCalculator was commissioned by the Green Building Initiative™ (GBI) for use with the Green Globes™ environmental assessment and rating system. The GBI also supported creation of a free generic version available at the Athena Web site, www.athenasmi.org.

7.4 RESOURCE OPTIMIZATION— EXTENDING SERVICE LIFE

"[A] large number of buildings are being demolished before the end of their technical service life..."

—*Organization for Economic Co-operation and Development/ International Energy Agency*[39]

The objects around us embody significant use of raw resources and resulting impacts to the environment. Yet most consumer objects have a service life of only six months,[40] and every year in the United States we tear down and replace 44,000 commercial buildings and demolish an estimated 100,000 homes so that larger homes can be constructed.

The limited evidence about why buildings are torn down indicates that it is not because they have reached the end of their service life but because of development opportunities for new construction and the perception that an existing building cannot support a proposed use. A more environmentally sound strategy is to extend the life of existing buildings and seek the creative reuse opportunities demonstrated in the case studies.

Embodied Properties— Energy, Carbon, Water

Discussions about the embodied properties of buildings or materials recognize that no product comes without an environmental price. In the 1970s, this then-emerging field focused narrowly on the embodied energy of a material. The American Council for Historic Preservation estimated in 1979 that the existing buildings in the United States had an embodied energy greater than the world's total annual energy production. Today, carbon and water footprints for construction materials are only beginning to be discussed. The calculator at www.

buildcarbonneutral.org projects that 13 to 18 percent of the total embodied carbon of any construction project is released the year the project is built. Studies in Australia show that a structure's embodied water equals 10 to 20 times its enclosed volume, "representing decades of operational water and centuries of potential rooftop water collection."[41]

Avoided Impacts

Embodied elements of an existing building have no inherent value unless juxtaposed against negative actions such as replacement. Reuse of a building avoids the impacts of new construction, and avoided impacts are

Figure 7.6 The many materials used in renovating the Barn at Fallingwater (Case Study 9-2) include existing, salvaged, and new. The glazed-tile block walls, concrete floor, and glass block windows all date from the structure's 1940s milking parlor. The red cedar was part of a 1960s ceiling. New wallboard is made from sunflower-seed composite, and straw panels are used as sound-absorptive material in the ceiling. *Nic Lehoux photo courtesy Bohlin Cywinski Jackson*

CO$_2$ Impacts Avoided by Building Reuse

In the spring of 2009, the Athena Institute and Morrison Hershfield Limited used the ATHENA® Impact Estimator and utility data to compare the environmental impact of renovating four historic buildings to the impact of demolishing them and replacing them with new construction. Completed for Parks Canada, the study found that the physical constraints of the heritage buildings, which are three- and four-story masonry structures, did not appear to limit the potential for high operational energy performance and that the avoided environmental impacts of reuse over replacement were significant. The calculated whole building global warming potential (GWP) results from each building case study were entered into the EPA's Greenhouse Gas Equivalencies Calculator (http://www.epa .gov/solar/energy-resources/calculator.html). The avoided CO$_2$ was the equivalent of one year of energy use for 85.2 homes for the smallest building and 1,591 homes for the largest.

---

of great importance when environmental degradation and climate change are at a crucial tipping point. All new construction creates a carbon balloon, a water impact, an energy cost, and a mountain of industrial waste. Can we really afford this? Scientific reports increasingly point toward the conclusion that immediate reduction of greenhouse gas emissions is essential. If the environmental benefit of new green buildings is 10 to 20 years away because of the construction impacts, then seeking to avoid these impacts and limit carbon emissions now through building reuse should be the highest priority.

Extending Service Life—Maintenance and Repairability

The Environmental Protection Agency pursues a targeted strategy of lengthening the service life of products, which includes encouraging manufacturers to design products to have longer service life and allow for repair.[42] The older a building, the more probable that it already has these attributes. Durability and repairability are common to many historic buildings and their component parts.

Durability has drawn increasing attention as an element of new green design because, as Peter Yost pointed out in a 2009 article, when you double the life of a building you halve the environmental impact of its construction in relation to its service life.[43] Low-maintenance materials are also a goal because they reduce added environmental impacts from cleaning requirements—although as Sandy Halliday cautions in her 2008 book *Sustainable Construction*, "maintenance-free" often describes components that are simply "non-maintainable" and must be disposed of in total when one part fails.[44]

"We have grown used to a culture in which we expect minimum maintenance of our habitat-buildings and gardens. In truth, this is unrealistic and not just in the field of ecological design. However, a consequence of our expectation is reduced life of many components—which is wasteful—and the substitution of polluting materials such as PVC and timber treatments and coatings in place of regular care."

—Sandy Halliday, Sustainable Construction[45]

7.5 CHANGING PRIORITIES AHEAD—RESPECTING BOTH PAST AND FUTURE

"Sustainability offers design the biggest problem of all: how to create more stuff without the impact of creating more stuff."

—Sam Grawe, Dwell *magazine*[46]

A sustainable society respects and learns from its past and plans for its future. Long-lived institutions, such as universities, understand that the investments made today in building renovations and repairs will benefit future generations. An organization that has already existed for hundreds of years and expects to exist for hundreds more makes decisions that have multigenerational timeframes, such as paying a higher initial cost for a tile roof knowing that it might last 100 years and consequently cost less per year of functional life than a roof requiring more frequent replacement. Removing several cycles of new material installation and waste disposal or reclamation is a greater benefit to the environment as well.

"There is tremendous impact to the environment when we construct something new, so avoiding new construction may be the most eco-conscious approach to our environment."

—"A Life Cycle Assessment Study of Embodied Effects for Existing Historic Buildings"[47]

Achieving more sustainable solutions is not a reliably straightforward undertaking, and it involves shifting values, priorities, and especially economics to reflect the true cost of decisions. In construction, replacement often costs less than repair, and the initial cost of a more-sustainable system or product often forces a less-sustainable choice.

The Case for Regular Maintenance

"The most significant contribution to sustainability must come from the education and training of practitioners in the processes and techniques of preservation as well as a more holistic and pathological understanding of the investigative processes (independent of vested commercial interests) required to identify the causes of building failures, and how the failure of one element of the building may be interrelated with another. The case for regular maintenance to stave off decay in buildings, made by William Morris (the founder of the Society for the Protection of Ancient Buildings in 1877), could not be more relevant today, and the impact upon energy conservation could not be greater for tomorrow."[49]

Few, if any, incentives exist to encourage property owners to practice regular maintenance and to incorporate products that allow repair rather than replacement, yet this is the greenest and most important part of resource management. Programs that give preference to renovation and repairs generate more jobs than new construction—approximately 20 to 30 percent for an equal expenditure. This is good news for the bulk of the construction industry, which is dominated by small establishments averaging ten employees each.[48] Building repairs offer an endless market and direct more money to the local economy, reinforcing holistic sustainability.

Figure 7.7 The off-grid site of the Block Island, Rhode Island, North Light built in 1867 takes advantage of two renewable energy strategies—solar and wind—and highly durable and repairable materials. Restoration techniques for the cast iron lantern included melting original corroded elements into new castings to ensure that the restored components of the lantern maintained the original's metaphorical DNA. Durable paint coatings, slate roofing, and lime mortars ensure long-term performance, and the project incorporated an exemplary construction-site management program, situated on active dunes and within the nesting grounds of an endangered species of tern.
© Walter Sedovic

1537 Webster Street

Oakland, CA

Current Owner: StopWaste.Org

Building Type: Public Agency Office

Original Building Construction: 1926

Restoration/Renovation Completion: 2007

Square Footage: 14,000 ft^2

Percentage Renovated: 100%

Occupancy: 31 people (30–40 hrs/week)

Recognition: LEED NC v2.2—Platinum

"In March 2007 the StopWaste.Org team moved into a building we renovated in downtown Oakland. We're proud of the effort we put into transforming a rundown, run-of-the-mill structure into a beautiful, green and healthy workplace."

—*www.stopwaste.org*[50]

PROJECT DESCRIPTION

StopWaste.org is the Alameda County Waste Management Authority and the county's Source Reduction and Recycling Board operating as one public agency "dedicated to achieving the most environmentally sound solid waste management and resource conservation for the people of Alameda County." Using the USGBC LEED Green Building Rating System (refer to Chapter 3) as a benchmarking tool, StopWaste.org, renovated a rundown 1920s urban building into a day-lit, spacious office that successfully incorporates a sophisticated set of interconnected strategies of environmental, social, and economic sustainability.

Site and Water

The rear courtyard of the building, which also functions as an emergency access lane, provides a 550-square-foot garden that models the seven principles described

▲ Figure 7.8 The architectural details on the exterior of 1537 Webster Street include decorative metal panels that were discarded by a sign fabricator. Discovered at a local salvage yard by Komorous-Towey Architects, they were customized to fit between the windows on the façade. © 2008 Komorous-Towey Architects

▶ Figure 7.9 The new connecting stairwell and skylight bring daylight to workspaces. Exposing materials like steel beams provides design impact, but it also eliminates the need for drywall and paint. Eliminating superfluous building materials reduces current resource use and reduces the burden on landfill when the building undergoes renovations in the future. © 2008 Komorous-Towey Architects

in StopWaste.Org's *Bay-Friendly Gardening Guide* and *Bay-Friendly Landscape Guidelines,* including:

- *Landscape locally*—45 percent of the plants selected to thrive in the shady garden are local natives, 30 percent are other California natives, and the remainder are from similar Mediterranean climates.
- *Landscape for less to the landfill*—plants at maturity will fit the space comfortably. Over time, the larger perennials will fill in and out-compete the shorter-lived plants.
- *Nurture the soil*—the existing sandy loam was aerated and amended with compost and organic fertilizers and then protected with a 2-inch layer of mulch made locally from ground tree limbs and branches.
- *Conserve water*—with drought-tolerant plants, drip irrigation monitored by an onsite weather-station controller and utilizing captured rainwater.

Figure 7.10 Seventy-five percent of the workspaces are daylit and 95 percent have views of the outdoors. Furnishings meet California's and the U.S. Environmental Protection Agency's guidelines for indoor air emissions, as well as the state's Green Specification for Office Furniture. Workstations have been certified at the Indoor Advantage Gold level by Scientific Certification Systems, an independent certification organization. © 2008 Komorous-Towey Architects

Inside the building, low-flow plumbing fixtures such as dual-flush toilets and waterless urinals further reduce the building's water consumption to 60 percent of a conventional building's potable water use.

Materials and Resources

Strategies for furnishings and finishes had the multiple goals of creating a healthy place to work, reducing waste, preventing pollution, and saving money. These goals complied with an environmental purchasing policy already in place.

- The ground-floor concrete slab is topped with stained epoxy concrete to eliminate the need for other finishes and reduce cleaning.
- Countertop materials include granite miscuts from local building-material salvage companies.
- Work stations have a high recycled content, including 100 percent recycled polyester fabric; 25 percent post-consumer recycled steel components; and between 20 and 90 percent post-consumer and post-industrial content in most other components, including hardboard, aluminum, glass, and zinc. Work stations were certified to the Indoor Advantage Gold level by Scientific Certification Systems, an independent certification organization.
- Ceramic tiles in the shower were left over from nearby installations and are locally manufactured with 50 percent recycled content.
- Window shades are free of polyvinyl chloride, which was avoided throughout the building because of concerns about the environmental and health impacts its manufacturing creates.
- Forest Stewardship Council (FSC)-certified wood materials were used and formaldehyde was avoided in composites.

GREEN DESIGN ELEMENTS
1537 Webster Street

Sustainable Sites:
- Public transportation proximity
- Bicycle accommodation
- Highly reflective white roof
- Permeable paving materials
- Native and drought-tolerant plants

Water Efficiency:
- Rainwater-catchment system
- Low-flow plumbing fixtures
- Dual-flush toilets
- Waterless urinals

Energy and Atmosphere:
- Renewable power certificates
- Photovoltaic system
- Natural ventilation
- Automatic light sensors
- Building commissioning

Materials and Resources:
- Construction waste diverted/recycled
- Extensive reuse of existing structure
- Fly-ash concrete substitute
- Reduction of finish materials needed
- Recycled content and reused materials
- Forest Stewardship Council-certified wood

Indoor Environment Quality:
- Skylights and 75 percent daylighting
- Operable windows
- Low-VOC materials and finishes
- CO_2 monitors

Additional Features:
- Occupant recycling and composting program
- Green cleaning policy
- Solar patio bricks

- Furnishings meet the State of California's and the U.S. Environmental Protection Agency's guidelines for indoor air emissions, as well as the State of California's Green Specification for Office Furniture standards.

Energy and Education

The building is 40 percent more energy-efficient than a comparable building based on California's Title 24–2005 energy code. A 5.2kW photovoltaic system provides over 10 percent of the building's electrical needs, and renewable-energy power certificates were purchased to encourage the development of these technologies. Kiosks in the lobby provide real-time energy data so occupants and visitors can view the building's energy performance, water use, and moisture levels of the soil.

PROJECT TEAM

Placeworks LLC
Komorous-Towey Architects
BBI Construction
Four Dimensions Landscape Company
OLMM Consulting Engineers
Rumsey Engineers, Inc.
Integrated Design Associates, Inc. (IDeAs)
Treadwell & Rollo
Charles Salter Associates, Inc.
Consolidated Engineering Laboratories
KEMA Green
Taylor Engineering

The Barn at Fallingwater

Mill Run, PA

Current Owner: The Western Pennsylvania Conservancy

Building Type: Interpretive Center

Original Building Construction: 19th-century

Restoration/Renovation Completion: 2003

Square Footage: 13,876 ft²

Percentage Renovated: 100%

Occupancy: 12 people (40 hrs/week) 100 visitors (4 hrs/week)

Recognition: LEED NC v.2.0—Silver Rating/U.S. Green Building Council 2006; 10,000 Friends of Pennsylvania Commonwealth Design Awards 2006—Bronze Award; Chicago Athenaeum American Architecture Award 2005; AIA/COTE Top Ten Green Projects 2005; AIA Pittsburgh Silver Award 2005; AIA Pittsburgh Green Design Citation 2005

"Sensitive, sincere and sustainable—the Barn at Fallingwater articulates connections between our bucolic heritage and the natural environment."

—*Bohlin Cywinski Jackson*

PROJECT DESCRIPTION

The renovation for the Western Pennsylvania Conservancy not only houses administration for the organization but also reminds the community of Pennsylvania's agrarian heritage and sets an example of good stewardship of the environment. The original nineteenth-century structure is a traditional "bank barn," a common type built into a hill to provide wagon access at two floor levels. Because the building type provides limited lower-level ceiling clearance, the renovation excavated floor and foundations to provide space suitable for offices and environmental systems. In addition the entire building was cleaned and treated to make it ready for human habitation.

A colony of brown bats was displaced in the renovation, so the designers built a bat house on site to relocate the creatures. No existing vegetation was removed from the site, and more than 30 native trees were added. During construction, the team was also careful not to store materials or excess soil near trees to avoid damaging their root systems.

Attention was paid to the historic integrity of the structure; in keeping with the original design of the slatted walls, the upper level of the barn is used only as a seasonal assembly space. Since this space does not require year-round climate control, the building requires less energy to function than a conventional building of similar size.

Materials and Construction

The interior is filled with recycled and salvaged materials that celebrate the barn's history and the site's agrarian heritage. A twentieth-century dairy barn addition was converted into an open, multipurpose exhibit and conference area that boasts a tapestry of materials. Utilitarian glazed block walls discovered during demolition, glass-block windows, and the site-built roof trusses were left exposed. Contrasting with these existing materials is a lattice screen of site-recycled tongue-and-groove fir from an old ceiling, new sunflower-seed composite panels, and natural straw panels installed on the ceiling for sound absorption. Contrasting the barn's existing heavy timber structure are new, sustainable wood paralam members used as beams and columns in the lower barn.

The wooden floor of the assembly space was recovered from a nearby convent that had recently remodeled its gym floor. Recycling the wood reduced the volume of convent construction waste that would have ended up in a landfill and minimized the amount of new materials needed for the barn.

Figure 7.11 The Barn at Fallingwater was built in 1870 as a part of the Tissue Farm. It is a "bank barn," built into a hillside with a back entrance at the second floor level. In 1940 the owners added a milking parlor. Fallingwater and the Barn were entrusted to the Western Pennsylvania Conservancy in 1963 and the Barn was transformed into a nature center. © *Ed Massery*

Figure 7.12 A wood screen with hydraulic jacks extends over the windows of the private offices to control light and blend with the barn's rustic exterior. Maintaining the rustic character was a key part of the design concept. *Nic Lehoux photo courtesy Bohlin Cywinski Jackson*

Figure 7.13 The original heavy timber-frame construction was retained and is visible in the office suite. *Nic Lehoux photo courtesy Bohlin Cywinski Jackson*

Material selection was influenced by local availability. Wood products, stone, and millwork all came from within a 500-mile radius of the project. The project contains more than 25 percent regional resources and material. The construction process also recycled 81 percent of construction debris.

Water and Energy

A graywater system—paired with indigenous vegetation chosen for site landscaping (xeriscaping) and low-flow plumbing fixtures—helped reduce potable water use by over 70 percent. Energy needed to heat and cool the building was reduced by the use of ground-source heat pumps, a heat-recovery ventilation system, and the addition of Icynene insulation that is both highly efficient and contains no VOC materials. As a result of these

GREEN DESIGN ELEMENTS

The Barn at Fallingwater

Sustainable Sites:

- Xeriscaping
- Bioswales

Water Efficiency:

- Graywater system
- Low-flow plumbing fixtures

Energy and Atmosphere:

- Renewable-energy certificates (wind)
- Ground-source geothermal heat pumps
- Heat-recovery ventilation
- Solar shading devices
- Occupancy and photoelectric sensors
- Seasonal assembly space

Materials and Resources:

- Over 80 percent of construction waste recycled
- Recycled wood floor (gym)
- Icynene insulation
- Innovative materials (straw and sunflower-seed composite panels)

Indoor Environment Quality:

- Operable windows
- Low-VOC materials and finishes
- Hazardous material decontamination (guano)

Figure 7.14 The Fireplace Room is the original milking parlor from the time when the barn served an active dairy farm. Although it has been renovated to serve as event space it retains the unique, organic feel of the original space. *Nic Lehoux photo courtesy Bohlin Cywinski Jackson*

techniques, along with other smart building principles, the barn surpasses by 38 percent the ASHRAE 90.1-1999 requirements for energy efficiency. Fifty percent of the grid-supplied energy is purchased with American Wind Energy certificates (a renewable energy source).

PROJECT TEAM

Western Pennsylvania Conservancy
Clearview Project Services Company
Bohlin Cywinski Jackson
Civil and Engineering Consultants, Inc.
Atlantic Engineering Services
H.F. Lenz Company
The Weavertown Group
Marshall Tyler Rausch, Inc.

Pittsburgh Glass Center

Pittsburgh, PA

Current Owner: Pittsburgh Glass Center

Building Type: Classrooms/Gallery/Glass Working Studios/Offices

Original Building Construction: 1920s

Historic Designation: None

Restoration/Renovation Completion: 2002

Square Footage: 17,600 ft^2

Percentage Renovated: 85% + 15% addition

Occupancy: 8 people (40 hrs/week) 70 visitors (28 hrs/week)

Recognition: LEED NC v2.0—Gold; AIA/COTE Top Ten Green Projects 2005

"One of the top public access glass facilities in the U.S., Pittsburgh Glass Center is a nonprofit, glass studio and gallery dedicated to teaching, creating and promoting glass art. Pittsburgh Glass Center...is a cornerstone of the Penn Avenue Arts Initiative's redevelopment of an underutilized part of the city through the arts...helping the city connect its history as a major producer in glass to its creative future through the innovative use of glass as art. Building elements such as garage doors, glass paneling and exposed brick are not only recycled elements, but also give PGC its unique urban/industrial edge."

—*Pittsburgh Glass Center Fact Sheet www.pittsburghglasscenter.org*

PROJECT DESCRIPTION

The renovation of the existing 16,000-square-foot, two-story masonry and concrete structure, along with a 2,500-square-foot addition, provides studios and shops for glass-working, as well as offices, a gallery space, classrooms, and seminar rooms. Due to the nature of glassworking, heat management, adequate ventilation, and quality of light were primary issues to address in order to provide a healthy and comfortable working environment. Alterations in the shell of the building increased daylight and views and broadened opportunities for natural ventilation. As a result, most occupied spaces do not require artificial lighting during daytime hours.

Figure 7.15 The Pittsburgh Glass Center, located on commercial Penn Avenue in the Friendship neighborhood, followed the local standards of the Urban Redevelopment Authority's "Streetface" program on the street façade in order to receive grant funding for a portion of the work. The URA's standards are not based on Secretary of the Interior's Standards for the Treatment of Historic Properties, but the City's historic preservation planner reviews the design/proposed work prior to approval of the grant application, and the Streetface project manager performs a post-construction inspection. © *Ed Massery*

The Pittsburgh Glass Center renovation project was part of a neighborhood revitalization plan, and the neighborhood is a now thriving art district with over a dozen galleries and theaters. The building is part of ongoing education and public awareness programs.

Resource Reduction

The addition to the building utilizes a corrugated-glass panel wall system, including aluminum battens and custom-mounted hardware salvaged from another building renovation 40 miles away. The new design was shaped to require the least amount of panel cutting and allowed the panel system module to dictate all elements in the wall.

Other materials salvaged from the existing building and purchased from recycling vendors were used throughout the renovation. These materials include doors, windows (reused to send borrowed light to the interior), sinks, brick, and stone. Concrete from the demolition of portions of the existing building was crushed and recycled.

All metals, plastics, gypsum, and plaster materials, glass, carpet, and ceiling tiles from demolition were separated and delivered to recycling centers. A plan to minimize construction waste was established and all remaining materials recycled.

2nd Floor

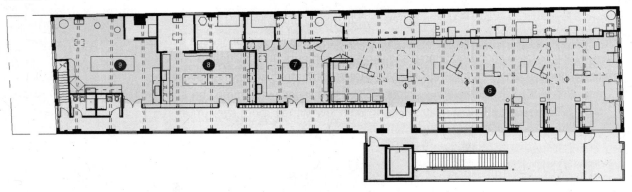

1st Floor

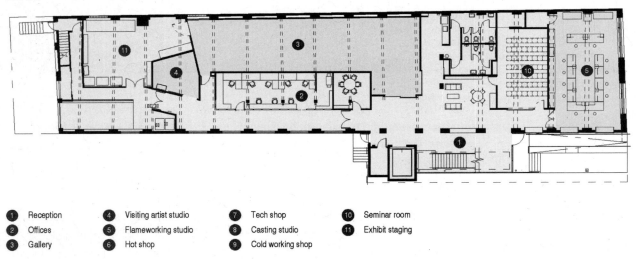

① Reception		④ Visiting artist studio		⑦ Tech shop		⑩ Seminar room
② Offices		⑤ Flameworking studio		⑧ Casting studio		⑪ Exhibit staging
③ Gallery		⑥ Hot shop		⑨ Cold working shop		

Figure 7.16 The Pittsburgh Glass Center is a nonprofit arts organization devoted to teaching and promoting glass art. The project consists of the renovation of an existing 16,000-square-foot, two-story masonry and concrete structure, along with a 2,500-square-foot addition. Alterations in the shell of the building were made to increase daylight, views, and opportunities for natural ventilation. As a result, most occupied spaces do not require artificial lighting during the daytime. *FortyEighty Architecture with Bruce Lindsey AIA*

All new construction materials were evaluated and specified for recycled content, locally sourced manufacturing, and raw materials. Wood used for the project is certified sustainable, and in many cases plywood and framing lumber was reused several times for barricades and formwork before being installed in permanent locations in the building (for blocking and rough carpentry elements).

Energy

The intent of the energy-efficiency strategy is to make the most efficient use of the fuel provided to the glassmaking processes and collect tempered air before exhausting it. Heat from the tempered air is transmitted to a water-loop system that supplies the concrete radiant floors, helping to reduce energy use by 27 percent. The thermal mass of the concrete floors also maintains an even temperature in the building by slowly releasing heat. When ventilation is needed, the garage doors can be opened selectively to allow the appropriate amount of fresh air to enter the spaces. The existing boiler was refurbished and serves as a backup and supplements the heating system.

Landscaping and surface treatments were selected to increase shading of the parking lot and the building, as well as for high reflectance and evaporative cooling to reduce the heat-island effect.

Figure 7.17 The intent of the energy-use strategy for the building is to make the most efficient use of the fuel provided to the glassmaking processes and collect heat from the tempered air before exhausting it. The collected heat is distributed to smaller air-handling units in a water loop. *FortyEighty Architecture with Bruce Lindsey AIA*

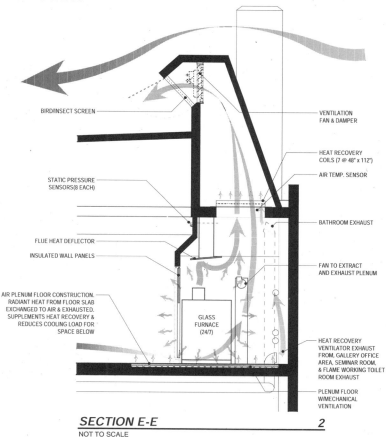

BIRD/INSECT SCREEN

STATIC PRESSURE SENSORS(8 EACH)

FLUE HEAT DEFLECTOR

INSULATED WALL PANELS

AIR PLENUM FLOOR CONSTRUCTION. RADIANT HEAT FROM FLOOR SLAB EXCHANGED TO AIR & EXHAUSTED. SUPPLEMENTS HEAT RECOVERY & REDUCES COOLING LOAD FOR SPACE BELOW

VENTILATION FAN & DAMPER

HEAT RECOVERY COILS (7 @ 48" x 112")

AIR TEMP. SENSOR

BATHROOM EXHAUST

FAN TO EXTRACT AND EXHAUST PLENUM

GLASS FURNACE (24/7)

HEAT RECOVERY VENTILATOR EXHAUST FROM, GALLERY OFFICE AREA, SEMINAR ROOM, & FLAME WORKING TOILET ROOM EXHAUST

PLENUM FLOOR W/MECHANICAL VENTILATION

SECTION E-E
NOT TO SCALE

2

GREEN DESIGN ELEMENTS
Pittsburgh Glass Center

Sustainable Sites:
- Multiuse parking area
- Permeable paving materials
- Xeriscaping
- Highly reflective roof

Water Efficiency:
- Low-flow plumbing fixtures
- Pressure-assisted toilets
- Waterless urinal

Energy and Atmosphere:
- Waste-heat recovery
- Radiant floors
- Thermal massing
- Natural ventilation
- "Best practice" commissioning

Materials and Resources:
- Construction waste recycled
- Recycled-content materials
- Materials supplied by recycling vendors

Indoor Environment Quality:
- Large exterior windows (garage doors)
- Operable windows

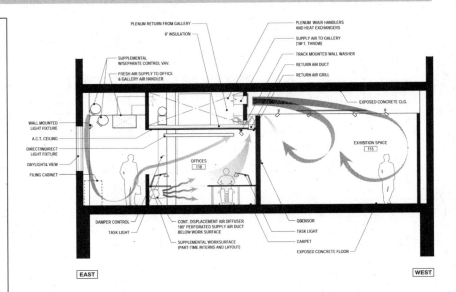

SECTION F-F
NOT TO SCALE

Figure 7.18 The building has reduced cooling demand due to selective use of mechanical cooling, increased natural ventilation, use of thermal mass, and program distribution. *FortyEighty Architecture with Bruce Lindsey AIA.*

PROJECT TEAM

Pittsburgh Glass Center
FortyEighty Architecture (formerly dggp)
Bruce Lindsey, AIA
Michael Kokayko, P.E.
Q-Dot, Inc.
Apex Plumbing
Tudi Mechanical Systems, Inc.
Clearview Project Services Company
LaQuatra Bonci Associates
Sustainaissance International, Inc.

Renaissance Hall—NDSU Visual Art and Architecture
Fargo, ND

Current Owner: North Dakota State University

Building Type: Higher Education

Original Building Construction: 1903

Historic Designation:

Restoration/Renovation Completion: 2004

Square Footage: 70,000 ft^2

Percentage Renovated: 100%

Occupancy: people (hrs) visitors (hrs)

Recognition: LEED NC Certification (2.0); National Preservation Honor Award 2006; AIA North Dakota Design Award Grand Prize 2005; Preservation ND Success Story Award 2005

"Renaissance Hall, a 100-year-old building, formerly a farm implement warehouse and dealership, is now a state-of-the-art facility."—www.ndsu.edu "The historical character of this building plays an important role in its design for sustainability. Maintaining the exterior facades and interior structural elements not only reflect on the history of the building, but also teach us about architectural style and construction methodology. Keeping these elements as unaltered as possible show us that building and material reuse benefit the environment by limiting use of virgin materials."

—*The Greening of NDSU Downtown*

PROJECT DESCRIPTION

The conversion of the former warehouse to the Visual Arts and Architecture/Landscape Architecture School utilized both historic tax credits and North Dakota Renaissance Zone tax credits. In 1981, the building was listed as a pivotal building in the Downtown Fargo Historic District on the National Register of Historic Buildings. Vacant from 1997 to 2001, the building was slated for demolition until a local business owner purchased it and donated it in 2001 to the university's development foundation.

Figure 7.19 A pivotal building in the Downtown Fargo Historic District, but targeted for demolition, the 1903 warehouse was donated to North Dakota State University in 2001 and was successfully renovated to house the Visual Arts and Architecture/Landscape Architecture School. It was the first project in North Dakota to receive LEED certification (refer to Chapter 3 for a description of green metric systems). It utilized federal historic tax credits. © *Saari & Forrai Photography*

The new plan provides a variety of studio spaces and classroom settings for about 360 students, numerous faculty offices and studios, a centralized Tri-College Office, a museum-grade gallery, public meeting and gathering areas, a wood shop, and necessary ancillary spaces. Visual arts studios include state-of-the-art sculpture with forge, ceramics with various kilns, printmaking, painting, drawing, and photography. Three large design studios with adjacent "break out" rooms for architecture/landscape architecture are provided on the upper four floors. The fifth floor was added above the bottom chords of the original roof to preserve the original appearance of the building.

Material Reuse

The design combines visible celebration of historic elements and reuse of materials to intentionally establish a connection to the past. Retained features include the ragged masonry and partially wallpapered entrance wall; sawn-off floor joists in the masonry walls, and extensive exposed-brick surfaces throughout the building. Original wooden windows on the west, north and south sides were restored, retaining original glass and attaching interior storms to increase their energy efficiency.

Reused materials include salvaged steel trusses that were removed from several floors of the eastern half of the building to support the gallery ceiling. Wood joists were re-used as ceiling structure for the conference room and university offices, and they extend over the reception desk for lighting support.

To further enhance the historical connections and creatively meet necessary functional and budget requirements, old wood doors from a freight elevator were used as a dropped ceiling in the main conference room; the elevator cab became both part of the wall and the floor of one of the faculty prep areas; and sections of the damaged wood floor were dried and reinstalled wherever possible—stains and all. Wood columns, joists, and other pieces were left with various colors of paint on them, and the original roofline—highlighted by the tar and rafter pockets in the former masonry parapet—now forms part of the addition.

▲ Figure 7.20 As an intentional design strategy, keeping the interior structural elements visible and as unaltered as possible served two purposes. It benefitted the environment by limiting use of virgin materials and it educates students about construction methodology. © *Saari & Forrai Photography*

▶ Figure 7.21 To enhance historical connections and creatively meet functional and budget requirements, wood doors from the building's old freight elevator were used as a dropped ceiling in the main conference room. © *Saari & Forrai Photography*

GREEN DESIGN ELEMENTS

Renaissance Hall—NDSU Visual Art and Architecture

Sustainable Sites:
- Alternative transportation
- Erosion and sedimentation control
- Urban redevelopment
- Reduced heat-island effect
- Light pollution reduction

Water Efficiency:
- Water-efficient landscaping

Energy and Atmosphere:
- Adaptable HVAC system
- (DOAP) ventilation system
- "Duct Sox" for low-velocity air
- Ventilation fan power minimized

Materials and Resources:
- Low-emitting carpet
- Existing building exposed without finishes
- Reuse of steel trusses
- Reuse of columns, beams, and floor joists
- Local materials—casework, brick, concrete
- Reuse of freight elevator cab walls

Indoor Environment Quality:
- Daylight and views
- Indoor pollutant source control at entries
- Interior glazing for daylight penetration

Energy

Energy demands on the building were met by:

- Adaptable HVAC system to meet diverse and constantly changing demands on the ventilation system. Some systems supply conditioned air to offices and classrooms while providing a high volume of conditioned outside air on demand for printmaking and welding studios and the gallery.

- Central Dedicated Outdoor Air Path (DOAP) system to handle ventilation needs independent of air-conditioning needs, reducing the amount of ductwork needed and permitting local control of humidity and temperature in individual spaces.

- Use of inexpensive fabric air ducts (sold as "Duct Soc") to evenly distribute air at very low velocities throughout their lengths across the studio spaces.

- Ventilation fan power was minimized using perimeter finned-tube radiation with DOAP consolidating the ventilation air requirements in one high-quality air handler.

- The building's rooftop chiller was placed in front of the building relief air louvers, enhancing energy efficiency and reducing the building's relief air temperature by 15 degrees.

PROJECT TEAM

North Dakota State University
Michael J. Burns Architects, Ltd.
Meinecke-Johnson Company

Children's Museum of Pittsburgh
Pittsburgh, PA

Current Owner: Children's Museum Pittsburgh

Building Type: Interpretive Center

Original Building Construction: 1897

Restoration/Renovation Completion: 2004

Square Footage: 85,000 ft^2

Percentage Renovated: 83% + 17% new construction

Occupancy: 167 people (50 hrs/week) 630 visitors (1–7 hrs/day)

Recognition: LEED NC v2.0—Silver; Mid-Atlantic Association of Museums Buildy Award 2009; PennFUTURE Platinum Green Power Award 2008; Western, Pennsylvania Environmental Award 2008; Rudy Bruner Award Gold Medal 2007; AIA National Honor Award 2006; AIA California Council Honor Award 2006; AIA Los Angeles Honor Award 2006; AIA Pittsburgh Honor Award and Green Design Citation 2006; *I.D.* Magazine Annual Design Review 2006; Design Distinction Award, MBA Building Excellence Award/ Best Project Over $5 million 2005; Chicago Athenaeum American Architecture Award 2005; AISC IDEAS Merit Award 2005

"We're proud there's been so much attention. Our next generation will inherit our progress, disasters, cities, and buildings.... Is there really an acceptable reason not to be healthy, productive, and environmentally sound? We pass these standards on as a legacy."

—*Rebecca Flora, Design Competition Advisor*[51]

PROJECT DESCRIPTION

The Children's Museum received the 2007 Rudy Bruner Gold Medal Award for Urban Excellence as the year's top urban place distinguished by quality design and social, economic, and contextual contributions to the urban environment. The museum was cited for its historic preservation, innovative architecture, and unique partnerships created

Figure 7.22 The new entry to the Children's Museum is cloaked in a shimmering wind sculpture that creates a focal point between the two historic buildings. Goals of the expansion project included environmental sustainability, utilization of the LEED Green Building Rating System, protection of the historic nature of the existing buildings, improved access to adjacent neighborhoods, cost effectiveness, and integration of innovative technology and design. © Albert Vecerka/Esto

Figure 7.23 The expanded Children's Museum created a unique "town square" for nearby residents and now serves as a revitalizing agent of change in an historic community. A new collaborative effort among the museum, Pittsburgh officials, community representatives, artists, architects, and designers focuses on transforming the public square into a new green space that serves as a shaded gathering place for farmers' markets, art shows and other festival events. © Albert Vecerka/Esto

Figure 7.24 Before being joined to the Children's Museum housed in the 1897 Post Office building, the 40,000-square-foot 1939 Buhl Planetarium building on the right sat vacant for more than ten years. An urban renewal project of the 1960s truncated the street grid and added the Allegheny Center shopping mall, with the intent of bringing consumers to the area. *Aerial photo provided by Children's Museum of Pittsburgh*

as part of its expansion completed in November 2004. The museum's role as a catalyst for urban redevelopment in its neighborhood was also cited.

Housed in three buildings whose architectural styles represent three centuries—the old Allegheny Post Office (a registered Historic Landmark), the Depression-era former Buhl Planetarium, and the new connecting structure referred to as the Lantern building—the museum incorporated environmental sustainability into every aspect of the renovations. Educational programs and facility-maintenance strategies carry on the commitment to sustainable practices.

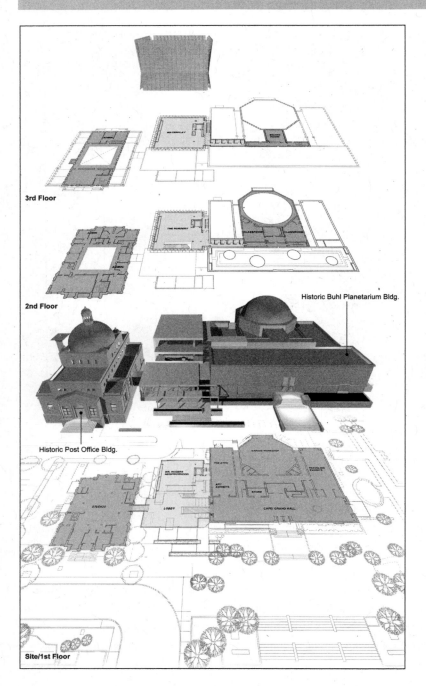

3rd Floor

2nd Floor

Historic Buhl Planetarium Bldg.

Historic Post Office Bldg.

Site/1st Floor

Materials and Resources

The renovations utilized 100 percent of the two historic building shells and more than 50 percent of the interior walls and ceilings. More than 60 percent of construction waste was diverted. During the construction, "items of value" (things such as marble panels, doors, and light fixtures.) were salvaged from the existing historic buildings and made available to the community at large through a third-party nonprofit organization. Building materials use high quantities of recycled materials and are locally manufactured and/or locally harvested.

All adhesives, sealants, paints, carpets, and composite wood are certified low-emitting—that is, they are formaldehyde-free and have low levels of volatile organic compounds. Much of the wood in the project is certified.

Examples of environmentally benign operations include "green cups" in the café made from NatureWorks™ PLA, a corn-based, 100 percent renewable

Figure 7.25 The exploded axonometric shows how the addition connects the two historic buildings. The project maintained 100 percent of the existing buildings' shells and more than 50 percent of the non-shell (interior walls and ceilings). In addition, 60 percent of construction waste was diverted. *Koning Eizenberg*

resource and a compostable, eco-friendly alternative to OPS and PETE. plastics. A facility-wide recycling program accepts white and mixed-use paper, newspaper, cardboard, glass, plastic, cans, computer equipment, batteries, copier and printer toner, phone books, and light bulbs.

Educational

The museum welcomes more than 220,000 visitors a year. This offers many opportunities to communicate a message of sustainability to children, families, school groups, and educators. The museum does so through ongoing programs, partnerships, and practices:

- *Everything Green,* a field trip that shows children how natural light, recycled materials, green building products and creative thinking combine to make a green building. Children also explore what they can do to create a greener environment at home and in school.

- The museum uses *recycled* paperboard, wood, plastic containers, and small appliances for art projects in two exhibit areas: the Studio and the Garage Workshop.

- An outdoor *worm compost bin* custom-made by the Pennsylvania Resources Council provides the focus for Worms Are Wonderful, a program that allows the public to feed food scraps from the café to 30,000 red wiggler worms and learn about worm life science and vermicomposting.

- *Child Development Series* sessions on healthy and energy-efficient homes are presented by Conservation Consultants, Inc., Healthy Homes Resources, and the Rachel Homestead Association.

- Outdoor *Tot Hikes* are offered in collaboration with Venture Outdoors.

- *Earth Day programs* include plays and puppet shows with environmental themes, plantings, and a green scavenger hunt.

- *The Green Table* serves a resource site for information from local environmental and conservation groups.

- *Teacher training programs:* Green Building as a Teaching Tool is a professional-development course that has been offered in collaboration with *Conservation Consultants, Inc.,* and the *Green Building Alliance* since 2005. The *Environmental Stewardship Awareness Workshop* is offered in summer in collaboration with Conservation Consultants, Inc.

GREEN DESIGN ELEMENTS
Children's Museum of Pittsburgh

Sustainable Sites:
- Public transportation proximity
- Bicycle accommodation
- Carpooling incentive program
- Small green roof (trial)
- White reflective roof

Water Efficiency:
- Low-flow plumbing fixtures
- Dual-flush toilets
- Faucet aerators

Energy and Atmosphere:
- Photovoltaic system
- Renewable-energy certificates (100 percent)
- Occupancy sensors
- Digital systems monitor
- Commissioned building

Materials and Resources:
- Over 60 percent construction waste salvaged or recycled
- Recycled content materials
- Forest Stewardship Council (FCS)-certified wood
- Locally manufactured materials

Indoor Environment Quality:
- Low-VOC materials and finishes
- CO_2 monitors
- Green cleaning policy
- Walk-off mats

Additional Features:
- Occupant recycling program
- Vermiculture composting bin
- Sustainable café products ("green cups")
- Environmental education programs

PROJECT TEAM

Children's Museum Pittsburgh
Koning Eizenburg Architecture
Perkins Eastman Architects, PC
Mascaro Corporation
Steeb Associates
Ned Kahn, environmental artist
Elwood S. Tower Corporation
Atlantic Engineering Services
Gateway Engineers
LaQuatra Bonci Landscape Designers
Pentagram Design
Vortex Lighting

ENDNOTES

1. J. Bogner et al., "Waste Management," In *Climate Change 2007: Mitigation*. Contribution of Working Group III to the Fourth Assessment Report of the Intergovernmental Panel on Climate Change (Cambridge, United Kingdom and New York: Cambridge University Press, 2008), p. 600.

2. USGS Factsheet FS-068-98, "Materials Flow and Sustainability" (June 1998), http://greenwood.cr.usgs.gov/pub/fact-sheets/fs-0068-98/fs-0068-98.pdf.

3. Committee on Business Strategies for Public Capital Investment, "Investments in Federal Facilities: Asset Management Strategies for the 21st Century," National Research Council (2004), http://www.nap.edu/catalog/11012.html. Accessed April 2009.

4. William McDonough and Michael Braungart, *Cradle to Cradle* (New York, Northpoint Press, 2002), p. 27.

5. Lovins, L. Hunter, "Rethinking Production," *State of the World 2008: Innovations for a Sustainable Economy* (New York: W.W. Norton, 2008), p. 32.

6. U.S. Environmental Protection Agency (EPA), "2007 Toxics Release Inventory (TRI) Public Data Release Report," EPA 260-R-09-001 (2009). Available at www.epa.gov/tri/.

7. William McDonough and Michael Braungart, *Cradle to Cradle* (New York, Northpoint Press, 2002), p. 27.

8. Gary Gardner, Eric Assadourian, and Radhika Sarin, "The State of Consumption Today," in *State of the World 2004, Special Focus: The Consumer Society* (New York: W.W. Norton & Company, 2004), p. 4.

9. Ibid., p. 5.

10. Ibid., p. 5.

11. Keilman, Nico, (2002), "The Threat of Small Households," Nature, vol. 421 (30) (January 2003): 489–490.

12. Brian Halweil and Danielle Nierenberg, "Watching What We Eat," Chapter 4 in *State of the World 2004, Special Focus: The Consumer Society* (New York: W.W. Norton & Company, 2004), p. 88.

13. Arthur C. Nelson, "Towards a New Metropolis: The Opportunity to Rebuild America," The Brookings Institution Metropolitan Policy Program (2004).

14. Bogner et al., "Waste Management," p. 600.

15. U.S. Environmental Protection Agency, "Municipal Solid Waste Generation, Recycling and Disposal in the United States: Facts and Figures for 2007," EPA-530-F-08-018 (November 2008). Available at www.epa.gov/osw.

16. U.S. Environmental Protection Agency Office of Resource Conservation and Recovery, "Estimating 2003 Building-Related Construction and Demolition Materials Amounts," EPA530-R-09-002 (March 2009), p. 19. Available at www.epa.gov/epawaste.

17. NRDC, "The Past, Present and Future of Recycling: Recycling's up, but So Is Trash," www.nrdc.org/cities/recycling/fover.asp. Accessed June 2009.

18. Betsy Taylor and Dave Tilford, "Why Consumption Matters," in *The Consumer Society Reader*, ed. by Juliet B Schor and Douglas Holt, (New York: The New Press, 2000), p. 467.

19. EPA, "Municipal Solid Waste Generation."

20. U.S. Environmental Protection Agency, *Office of Solid Waste and Emergency Response, Municipal Waste in the United States: 2001 Facts and Figures* (2003), pp. 3–4.

21. Achieved by comparing the EPA 1998 and 2005 reports on Construction and Demolition Waste.

22. Brenda Platt, David Ciplet, Kate M. Bailey, and Eric Lombardi, *Stop Trashing the Climate* (Washington, DC: Institute for Local Self-Reliance, June 2008), p. 6. Available at www.stoptrashingtheclimate.org/fullreport_stoptrashingtheclimate.pdf (accessed May 2010).

23. Heather Rogers, *Gone Tomorrow; The Hidden Life of Garbage* (New York The New Press, 2005), p. 4. Available at www.thenewpress.com.

24. Rachel Birch, "Waste as a Driver of Change," *The Arup Journal* 43(1) (1/2008), p. 18.

25. Richard C. Porter, *The Economics of Waste* (Washington, DC: RFF Press, 2002), p. 54.

26. Ibid., p. 58.

27. Ibid., p. 62.

28. Ibid., p. 78.

29. *Stop Trashing the Climate*, p. 30.

30. Ibid., p. 45.

31. Rogers, p. 177.

32. Alex Wilson, *Your Green Home: A Guide to Planning a Healthy, Environmentally Friendly New Home* (Gabriola Island, Canada: New Society Publishers, 2006), p. 112.

33. Barbara C. Lippiat and Amy S. Boyles, "Building for Environmental and Economic Sustainability (BEES) Software for Selecting Cost-Effective Green Building Products," CIB World Building Congress, April 2001, Wellington, New Zealand, Paper number 15.

34. Tristan Roberts, "Searching for Clarity Amid Green Certifications," GreenSource (March/April 2009). Available at http://greensource.construction.com/features/other/2009/03_Green-Certifications.asp. Accessed May 2010.

35. Ibid.

36. Ibid.

37. John Amatruda, "Evaluating and Selecting Green Products," www.wbdg.org/resources/greenproducts.php (2007). Accessed July 2009.

38. S. Pfirman and the AC-ERE *Complex Environmental Systems: Synthesis for Earth, Life, and Society in the 21st Century,* A report summarizing a 10-year outlook in environmental research and education for the National Science Foundation, 2003, p.16,

39. Organization for Economic Co-operation and Development, JT00164573, OECD/IEA Joint Workshop on Sustainable Buildings: Towards Sustainable Use of Building Stock," Working Party on Territorial Policy in Urban Areas, May 19, 2004, p. 9.

40. Paul Hawken, *Natural Capitalism* (Self-published, 1999), p. 81.

41. Graham, Treloar, "Water Embodied in Construction," http://www.abp.unimelb.edu.au/aboutus/events/research-seminar-series/archive-2007/treloar.html (March 2007). Accessed July 2009.

42. U.S. Environmental Protection Agency Office of Solid Waste. *Municipal Solid Waste in the United States 2007 Facts and Figures,* EPA530-R-08-010 (November 2008), p.137. Available at www.epa.gov.

43. Peter Yost, "Sustainability Requires Durability," *GreenSource* (January 2009).

44. Sandy Halliday, *Sustainable Construction,* © Gaia Research (Oxford, UK, and Burlington, VT: Butterworth-Heinemann, Elsevier Linacre House, 2008), p. 132.

45. Ibid., 132.

46. Sam Grawe, "A Deadline for Design," Editor's Note, *Dwell* (July/August 2008).

47. Athena Sustainable Materials Institute in association with Morrison Hershfield Limited, "A Life Cycle Assessment Study of Embodied Effects for Existing Historic Buildings," Prepared for Parks Canada, March 30, 2009.

48. U.S. Environmental Protection Agency Office of Resource Conservation and Recovery, "Estimating 2003 Building-Related Construction and Demolition Materials Amounts," (March 2009), EPA530-R-09-002, p. 2. Available at www.epa.gov/epawaste.

49. Michael Tutton, Elizabeth Hirst, and Jill Pearce, Windows: *History, Repair and Conservation* (Shaftesbury, UK: Donhead Publishing Ltd., 2007), p. 245.

50. http://www.stopwaste.org/home/index.asp?page=926. Accessed April 2009.

51. Candi S. Cross (2006), "Working with Nature: Children's Museum of Pittsburgh Salutes the Elements," *Industrial Engineer* (November 1, 2006).

PART III

OF SPECIAL NOTE

chapter 8

BEST PRACTICES—OPERATIONS, MAINTENANCE, AND CHANGE

"The built environment in the United States is the result of several centuries of investment decisions about buildings and infrastructure. Generations of individuals and multitudes of public and private organizations have contributed to this evolving environment by making investments in the buildings . . . and infrastructure systems. . . . This built environment and the services it provides directly affect the quality of life for more than 280 million U.S. residents as well as the strength of the national economy. The magnitude of this investment is large. In 2000 the value of structures and utilities in the United States amounted to almost $22 trillion."

—*Investments in Federal Facilities: Asset Management Strategies for the 21st Century*[1]

8.1 OPPORTUNITIES—ESSENTIAL AND IMMEDIATE

THERE ARE *300 billion square feet* of existing buildings in the United States, most of which will still be standing in 2030. Existing buildings outnumber new construction by 99 to 1. We cannot build our way to climate neutrality. We must change the resource consumption of existing buildings, and we must do it *now*. We do not have time to renovate fully (which is resource-intensive) or replace (which is even more resource-intensive) this square footage. Significant reductions in resource use are possible through changes in operations, changes in user behavior, and selective upgrades of equipment. Operations and maintenance

291

costs represent 60 to 85 percent of the expenditures over a building's lifetime.[2] Long-term savings as a result of lower electricity, water, and heating and cooling costs can be significant. Consistent maintenance of materials extends service life and reduces major renovation and replacement costs. Healthier buildings—from healthier cleaning practices to non-toxic pest control—benefit everyone.

The opportunities to stabilize escalating energy demands and carbon emissions—and the importance of stabilizing them—are staggering and include not only direct end-use energy consumption but the interwoven strategies discussed in previous chapters that address community infrastructure, water and site, material choices, and indoor environmental quality. Each of the chapters in Section II includes targeted maintenance strategies specific to the topic, many of which can be implemented without a major renovation.

Continuous Process of Sustainability

The foundation of environmental sustainability is a recognition that it is a continuous process, not a one-time action. That understanding makes it easier to see that sustainability does not require substantial renovation, and a renovation that does *not* include an ongoing maintenance and operational review will not reach or maintain meaningful green goals. Sustainability requires continuous education and review of user actions, either of which may need to change as new information and opportunities become available.

Operational cost reductions are possible by capturing available opportunities and investing in the future with maintenance, smart purchasing, and long-term planning. Some organizations and property owners quantify the savings from immediate easy actions and systematically use these funds to implement larger, more expensive actions that have longer economic

payback periods, even (or especially) benefiting future generations as well as current users. Current rewards in terms of improved occupant performance and health with lower absenteeism are also substantial and quantifiable (refer to Chapter 6).

Figure 8.1 The Solar Umbrella Residence (see Chapter 7) in Venice, California, was designed to reduce operation and maintenance costs significantly. Most of its constituent materials such as Homasote, oriented-strand board, concrete, natural stone, and natural solid woods, have a homogenous solid core. When scratched or damaged, these materials are easy to repair, or the damage is unnoticeable. *Marvin Rand photo, courtesy of Pugh + Scarpa*

In the first five months of its new Energy Education program, Grand Rapids Community College, with a student enrollment of 28,000, reduced its energy use by 16.25 percent, saving $224,000 and 1.2 million kWh of electricity. A trained energy manager works closely with GRCC's energy-conservation partner, Energy Education, a national consulting company, to monitor and analyze energy use, inspect boilers, test air-handling units, and study water and room temperatures, leaks and usage patterns.[3]

In 2009, the U.S. General Services Administration identified low-cost strategies for saving 300 million kWh/year across 176 million square feet that also improved workplace conditions. Partnering with the Center for Building Performance and Diagnostics (CBPD) at Carnegie Mellon University, the GSA developed the targeted saving strategies after surveying more than 6,000 federal workers and measuring environmental conditions at 624 workstations in 43 workplaces across 22 separate buildings. The study projected more than $30 million in annual savings for very little investment. Simple strategies identified in the study, *Energy Savings and Performance Gains in GSA Buildings*, include:

- Adjust workplace temperature for the summer months, saving 18.7 million kWh/year and $1.87 million per year.

The study found that federal workers report that overcool indoor air in summer is uncomfortable. The solution is, during the summer, to set the ambient indoor temperature between 74°F and 78°F. The California Energy Commission estimates a 1 to 3 percent energy savings for each degree a thermostat is set above 72°F.

- Replace HVAC filters on schedule and with high-performance filters, saving 10.8 million kWh/year and $1.08 million.

The study found that expired filters reduced indoor air quality and increased building energy use by up to 10 percent. The solution is implementation of a regular plan for filter replacement that incorporates filters with a minimum efficiency reporting value (MERV) rating of 13 or greater to remove particulates while improving delivered air quality at the lowest energy cost.

Figure 8.2 The materials used at the University of Michigan School of Natural Resources and Environment, S. T. Dana Building (see Chapter 5), include bathroom tile composed of more than 55 percent recycled glass, primarily from airplane windshields, and HDPE (high-density polyethylene) bathroom partitions and countertops. HDPE is a plastic-sheet material manufactured from 100 percent post-consumer plastic. The school chose materials that were environmentally friendly, both in source and use, with green cleaning strategies as part of the selection process. © *Christopher Campbell 2003*

■ Consolidate and reduce the number of printers and copiers, saving 55 million kWh/year and $5.5 million.

Consolidating printers saves energy and supports collaboration. The study recommends providing distributed printer/copier rooms with a 1:25 equipment/user ratio—a significant change from the current ratio (1:5) and distribution pattern, with many copiers located in workstations or circulation areas. Clustering copiers in separate rooms provides a healthier, less-distracting work environment, encourages collaboration, and discourages unnecessary printing.

Despite digital communications, paper use is on the rise. Paper production uses one-third of the wood harvested in the United States and is the third-most energy-intensive of U.S. manufacturing industries, using 11.5 percent of all energy in the industrial sector.

■ Replace CRT monitors with LCD monitors, saving 39 million kWh/year and $3.9 million.

The cathode ray tube (CRT) monitors create glare and are needlessly bright and energy-consuming. A CRT monitor draws at least three times the energy of a liquid crystal display (LCD) monitor—75 watts versus 20 to 25 watts. Replacing the 200,000 still on federal desks with flat screen LCDs is expected to improve performance of visual tasks.

■ Upgrade ambient and task lighting in the workplace to save 199.1 kWh/year and $19.9 million.

Lighting needs differ, depending on the work being performed; technology has changed, and upgrading ambient and task lighting supports new work situations. Research shows that lighting that is too bright or dim can cause headaches and negatively affect user performance and productivity.[4]

8.2 IMPLEMENTATION TOOLS

"How things are kept and cared for demonstrates their significance not just as objects, buildings or landscapes, but in terms of how much value we place on them."

—*It's a Material World; Caring for the Public Realm*[5]

Figure 8.3 StopWaste.Org, in Oakland, California's joint waste-management/recycling agency (see Chapter 5), monitors building energy performance and water usage and uses the data to analyze whether the building continues to meet performance expectations. Building systems take advantage of both natural and mechanical ventilation. © *Kamorous-Towey Architects*

The metrics tools discussed in Chapter 3, such as Green Globes® and USGBC LEED, are valuable in providing a framework for implementing operations and processes that facilitate best practices and change. Both programs offer systems specifically for existing buildings that are intended to jump-start improvements and provide a continuous framework for ongoing improvements—USGBC's LEED for Existing Buildings: Operation and Maintenance and the Green Globes® Continual Improvement of Existing Buildings.

"Remember that a Green Action Plan is never complete. As new information, improved measurement tools and technological solutions continually evolve, an organization's plan will respond accordingly. The organization will then be able to keep up with the emerging process of creating a sustainable footprint."

—Christopher Ratcliff, "A Green Action Plan for Sustainable Buildings"[6]

Organizations that focus on facilities management of specific building types, such as offices or schools, also offer tools and guidelines that are often easily available online. BOMA, Building Owners and Managers Association International, offers Web resources and the 7-Point Challenge toolkit (www.boma.org). The federal government provides case studies, information, and resource links at the Whole Building Design Guide (www.wbdg.org) that tie to agencies such as the Federal Energy Management Program, the National Park Service, and the Environmental Protection Agency. Local environmental groups and energy suppliers are further sources of assistance that may focus on regional opportunities and issues.

Building Maintenance Plans

Tools intended to promote "green" performance may neglect guidance on the overall maintenance of build-

"LEED-EB starts with implementing green practices, then green recycling, a building operating plan, analyzing water use, etc."—not necessarily a retrofit or remodel.

—Katherine Watenschutz, "Greening Existing Buildings to Address Climate Change"[7]

ings and building materials. A maintenance plan that addresses the regular review of the exterior envelope and interior finishes is an important and overlooked aspect of sustainability, regardless of the age or significance of the building. Repairing a broken downspout always costs less than remdiating extensive water damage or water infiltration into the building. Becoming a culture that values maintenance is essential to achieving sustainability.

The historic preservation community excels at preventive maintenance and repairs. Building owners and managers can modify the available checklists to address buildings of the recent past; the concept of regular inspection of building components and ongoing, manageable repairs that forestall major repairs later applies to every structure, regardless of size, period, or style.

The main reason for a maintenance plan is that it is the most cost-effective way to maintain the value of an asset. . . . When buildings are neglected, defects can occur which may result in extensive and avoidable damage to the building fabric or equipment

—NSW Heritage Office[8]

The Illinois Historic Preservation Agency (www.illinoishisotory.gov) offers simple checklists for building owners and a good online presentation about building inspections and the importance of maintenance that correlates with the management of moisture. (The National Park Service Preservation Brief #39, *Holding the Line: Controlling Unwanted Moisture in Historic Buildings*, by Sharon Park FAIA can also serve as a maintenance checklist.) The Illinois checklist identifies problems and connects these to the applicable National Park Service Preservation Briefs that provide additional information about specific topics or materials. The site also offers a calendar to remind property owners of the seasonal importance of actions such as removing debris from roofs, especially at valleys or behind chimneys.

The town of Steamboat Springs, Colorado, offers a historic-properties maintenance checklist that is also applicable to nonhistoric buildings. A maintenance manual, prepared by Humphries Poli Architects, P.C., and available online, uses five historic buildings owned by the city as models. Funded by a grant from the State Historical Fund of the State of Colorado, research for the project was conducted nationwide and examined successful building-maintenance programs for large and small historic buildings.

The Episcopal Diocese of New York posts a resource page with many links organized by subject matter, including accessibility, bird deterrence, energy, flooring, graffiti, graveyards, landmarking, lead hazards, routine inspections, masonry, moisture, painting, plaster, roofing, siding, stained glass, and windows. Most articles are available online (http://propertysupport.dioceseny.org/res.htm).

Commissioning Existing Buildings

The focus on sustainability has helped to promote the practice of *commissioning* to ensure optimum performance of building systems. The Building Commissioning Association defines existing building commissioning, EBCx, as "a systematic process for investigating, analyzing, and optimizing the performance of building systems through the identification and implementation of low/no cost and capital intensive facility improvement measures and ensuring their continued performance. The goal of EBCx is to make

building systems perform interactively to meet the Current Facility Requirements and provide the tools to support the continuous improvement of system performance over time."[9] The association defines EBCx to include such practices as retrocommissioning, recommissioning, and ongoing commissioning. More to the point, it treats the commissioning process not as a one-time event but as an activity that continues throughout a facility's useful life.

EXISTING BUILDING COMMISSIONING SHOULD:

- Verify that a facility and its systems meet the current facility requirements (CFR).
- Improve building performance by saving energy and reducing operational costs.
- Identify and resolve building-system operation, control, and maintenance problems.
- Reduce or eliminate occupant complaints and increase tenant satisfaction.
- Improve indoor environmental comfort and quality and reduce associated liability.
- Document system operation.
- Identify the operations and maintenance (O&M) personnel training needs and provide such training.
- Minimize operational risk and increase asset value.
- Extend equipment life cycle.
- Ensure the persistence of improvements over a building's life.
- Assist in achieving LEED for existing buildings (www.usgbc.org/LEED).
- Improve the building's ENERGY STAR rating (www.energystar.gov/).

Source: Building Commissioning Association[10]

Ideally, EBCx is a *whole-building process* performed by a third party not directly involved in operating the subject building. This ensures an objective and critical evaluation. Looking at the entire building is important to ensure an understanding of the interaction among systems and the impact systems might have on the building envelope—and vice versa.

Commissioning is not a panacea for everything, as a 2007 NCARB monograph on "The Hidden Risks of Green Buildings: Avoiding Moisture and Mold Problems" cautions. The monograph notes that the current industry approach to building commissioning "is unlikely to prevent moisture and similar building failures in almost any climate, except for the most forgiving," adding that "any good energy management plan must be subservient to adequate moisture control." [11] Whole-building thinking and evaluation are essential in both design and operation, but commissioning is an important tool for ensuring that systems continue to function as intended.

Energy savings of 5 to 20 percent are typical for EBCx with modest capital expense. Documentation in 2008 by Portland Energy Conservation, Inc. (PECI) of 27 million square feet of EBCx shows a typical project payback of less than two years for costs that range from $0.05 to $1.25 per square foot, depending on the size of a building and the complexity of its systems. The larger the facility, the lower the EBCx costs, but the largest savings by percentage were most often found in the smallest facilities. [12]

Commissioning typically helps to ensure good indoor environmental quality, reduce energy and water consumption, and improve how well the building is operated.

—*ASHRAE's Sustainability Roadmap* [13]

Understanding sustainability as a continuing process tips the balance in favor of *continuous commissioning*, which builds commissioning into operating and maintenance processes so that no separate recommissioning process is required. Even under a continuous commissioning program, however, periodic review by a third party is important to ensure that operating and maintenance processes are appropriate.

"Commissioning is critical to long-term performance, especially for large buildings. 'A mediocre building commissioned properly will be more energy-efficient than a well-designed building that's not commissioned.'"

—*Adrian Tuluca, Principal,
Viridian Energy and Environmental* [14]

8.3 HOUSEKEEPING—CONTINUAL IMPROVEMENT

"When we try to pick out anything by itself, we find it hitched to everything else in the Universe."

—*John Muir* [15]

What we do in and around buildings on a daily basis must, like everything else, be considered holistically. Decisions about purchasing, cleaning, and building management should address ways these activities can help limit water use, reduce site pollutants and chemicals in stormwater runoff, improve indoor environmental quality, promote the most efficient use of mechanical systems, employ healthy materials in building construction, and reduce waste—all topics discussed in previous chapters. An awareness of the impact of decisions creates a cycle of review and change as change becomes possible. Checklists help. Continual education and motivation of everyone in a building, regardless of their function in

Figure 8.4 The conversion of a 1928 garage into classrooms at St. Stephen's Episcopal School reduced the amount of electricity needed for lighting by taking full advantage of daylight. The project achieved a 22 percent reduction in energy consumption beyond the base ASHRAE 90-1 standard. *McKissick Associates Architects*

the building, are also essential. The goals of green housekeeping are multiple and overlapping but can follow simple rules:

- *Reduce material consumption*—whether energy, water or products.
- *Purchase responsibly*—buy materials and products with less environmental impact.
- *Reduce waste of all sorts*—in resources and physical materials, even materials being recycled.
- *Avoid introducing chemicals*—whether for cleaning, pest control or landscape management.

Think upstream and downstream. Where did a material come from, and where is it going? What actions lead to reactions—for instance, in addition to introducing green cleaning, introduce practices that reduce cleaning requirements like walk-off mats and durable materials. In addition to a pest-control program, address habits such as cluttered work stations

and eating at desks that may be contributing to the problem.

Reduce Material Consumption

This involves everything in the office, whether a cup for coffee or a new filing cabinet. Think about the opportunities to reduce material use, whether that entails offering guests a mug instead of a Styrofoam cup, printing on both sides of paper (or not printing at all), or avoiding the purchase of new filing cabinets by reorganizing instead of adding. This kind of thinking is, for many people, tedious and irritating, but there are almost 7 billion people on this planet, and less than 5 percent of them live in the United States—consuming 30 percent of the all resources worldwide. This level of consumption triggers all of the upstream and downstream consequences discussed in Chapter 7. If each one of us takes responsibility for our actions, collectively we will change the world.

The Pennsylvania Green Building Operations and Maintenance Manual

This manual is used as a tool for everyday operations in Commonwealth buildings. With recommendations for green landscaping, roofing, parking garage, HVAC and lighting maintenance, and cleaning procedures and product selection, the manual was developed with Green Seal (www.greenseal.org) and the expertise of General Services' employees for the maintenance of state government buildings and grounds. While published in April 2002, lessons learned from field tests early on and ongoing fine-tuning continue to make this manual a widely used and valuable resource in any location.

Green Seal's criteria for Green Facilities Operation and Maintenance require substantial compliance with the procedures and products recommended in the Pennsylvania manual.

From *A Guide to Green Maintenance and Operations*, http://www.stopwaste.org/docs/greenmaintguide.pdf, p. 19.

Waste Management

Each person in the United States makes 4.5 pounds of garbage a day, which is twice what we generated 30 years ago. For every trashcan of waste, 70 trashcans were filled upstream to make the products, which are often so quickly disposed of. Reducing waste is the first step; ensuring that waste is diverted from landfill for either reuse or recycling is the next. More and more communities and companies are making this possible, with programs that collect paper, plastic, aluminum, and electronic products. (Of course, arranging for removal does not always ensure recycling.)

Office furniture can often be given to nonprofits or second-hand stores. As we move toward a zero-waste world (likely a reality within most of our lifetimes), new opportunities for reuse and recycling of everything from paper clips to couches will be created.

Green Purchasing

The purchasing power of institutions, governments, and businesses is immense. State and local governments spend more than $400 billion and universities spend more than $300 billion on products and services every year.[16] If this purchasing power is targeted toward environmentally preferable products, it shifts the market and makes these products more available and affordable. Regardless of the size of an organization or office, buying things like 100 percent recycled-content paper means buying a product whose manufacture used 44 percent less energy, created 37 percent less greenhouse gas, and used 50 percent less water and practically no new wood.

"[A] focus on waste reduction and materials efficiency can lead to important cost savings. Reusing materials or selecting highly durable products means that few new products need to be purchased..."
—*Collaborative for High-Performance Schools*[17]

Many organizations have green purchasing guides, which are available online with a little searching. It's good to find a guide that is from a particular geographic region, because part of green purchasing is to reduce the impact of packaging and shipping. Products of all types are registered with organizations such as Green Seal, EcoLogo, Energy Star, Scientific Certification Systems and EPEAT, to name a few. The U.S. Environmental Protection Agency has online guidance on environmentally preferable purchasing (EPP). The government of Canada, which established the Ecologo Program in 1988, also offers guides for green procurement, operations and events at the Greening Government website, www.greenin government.gc.ca.

Food Service

Each food item in a typical U.S. meal has traveled an average of 1,500 miles. If every U.S. citizen ate just one meal a week that utilized only local, organically raised meat and produce, our national oil consumption would drop by 67.6 billion barrels a year—the equivalent of the oil carried by about 30 supertankers.[18] Food provided for meetings and events should be as local as possible and served with a minimum of packaging and plastic. If possible, food waste should be composted rather than being sent to a landfill, where it will create about 20 times more greenhouse gas than if composted. Yard trimmings and food residuals together constitute 24 percent of the U.S. municipal solid waste stream, according to the U.S. Environmental Protection Agency.

Integrated Pest Management

Food and food waste may contribute to pests, so active policies for managing waste and avoiding situations that encourage pests are important.

Green Cleaning

Green cleaning seeks to avoid toxic and harmful chemical cleaners and cleaning practices, which may contribute to airborne particulates and potential mold from excessive use of water. Ample documentation exists to show the importance of clean indoor environments, but a growing body of research also demonstrates that current cleaning practices contrib-

ute to indoor air pollution and poor health of both cleaning staff and building occupants.[19] Recognizing the impact of a healthy workplace on employee satisfaction and productivity, the U.S. General Services Administration developed green cleaning policies as early as 1992.[20]

Planning for Clean

Stephen Ashkin, founding executive director of the Green Cleaning Network (www.greencleaningnetwork.org), points out that green cleaning is not just about products but about changing the way things are done—like source control of dirt. For example:

- Drain exterior areas away from the entrance
- Avoid messy plants at entrance ways
- Place spigots to allow for cleaning of exterior areas
- Hardscape the entry to scrape material off shoes

Cleaning costs (and the related use of water and materials) can be reduced by adequate walk-off mats that capture soils. Durable materials (common to historic buildings) that reduce frequency of cleaning and the installation of new materials with an eye to cleaning ease can reduce cleaning costs as much as 25 to 30 percent a year.[21]

"Green maintenance is an approach to the maintenance and operation of buildings with the aim of increasing the life of products, reducing exposure to chemical and toxic substances, and reducing the cost to operate equipment.... Green maintenance practices make the buildings... last longer, cost less to operate, and feel more comfortable."

—A Guide to Green Maintenance and Operations[22]

Figure 8.5 Educational kiosks provide real-time information on energy use and onsite energy generation, as well as detailed information for visitors about the building and site-sustainable features. Many such kiosks are interactive and allow building occupants to track and compare energy use in individual offices or spaces. *Courtesy Shawmut Design and Construction, Boston, Massachusetts*

8.4 O&M—THE USER IMPACT

"We envision well informed and more participatory society as a fundamental means in the building of a more sustainable model."

—*Cultura Ecológica*[23]

Engagement of facility occupants in maintenance and operations is important for two reasons: (1) building users can have a dramatic impact on the success of conservation measures through individual actions and (2) understanding the interconnection of actions and their impact on the environment can catalyze change in other places.

Figure 8.6 Schools such as the California College of the Arts, which adaptively reused a 1950s bus maintenance garage (see case study at the end of the chapter) as an art facility, have active and evolving educational programs for students that foster a cross-disciplinary understanding of sustainability and the positive impact that design can have on resource use and social well-being. *Richard Barnes photo*

Behavior Change Benefits

Schools, colleges, and universities, in particular, have recognized that an informed and motivated user group can significantly lower operational costs with no capital costs. The fourth Student Energy Waste Watch Challenge at the University of New Hampshire in 2008 saved more than $16,000 in energy costs in resident halls and on-campus apartments over an eight-week winter period. The intent is for long-term incorporation of environmental awareness into daily habits and lifestyles. A campuswide campaign to "power down" by turning off computers, lights, office equipment, and electronics for the 2008 Thanksgiving holiday saved the university $10,000 in energy costs.[24]

Harvard University has targeted behavior change programs that include "Shut the Sash" in the medical school and chemistry departments. The goal is to encourage researchers to close fume hood sashes to reduce energy waste. The campaign uses prompts, incentives, and various communication techniques. The results, which include ongoing monitoring and improvements, are saving the university an estimated $188,000 per year in energy costs.[25]

Energy Star—Green Team Strategies
Recruit from A to Z—Encourage coworkers from different levels and parts of your organization—from senior management and interns to facility managers and human resources personnel—to get involved. A team approach improves buy-in from all levels of the organization, which helps to ensure greater support and success.

The Danville, Illinois, school district has reduced utility bills by over $1.2 million in a three-year energy conservation program. The program, managed by Jack Harrier—who works part-time as a building custodian in addition to running the energy-conservation program—involves training custodial staff in all buildings about smart operations and working with teachers and staff to make sure they turn off lights, computers, copy machines, and other equipment when not in use. The district teamed up with Energy Education, Inc., a firm based in Wichita Falls, Texas, to design the program with a goal of saving $1.9 million in seven years.[26]

"The education component of our [Energy Education] program is critical because education affects human behavior and that can create long-term change."
—Thomas Smith, Grand Rapids Community College[27]

Targeted energy savings are an important motivator for landlords, companies, and institutions, but the entire greening effort requires the involvement of facility staff, building management, and users. Training programs for the LEED EB (O&M) stress that building users must be willing to incorporate the system into their daily practices to make it successful.

Spillover Effect

It is a common premise that knowledge about environmental issues will result in changed behavior. The National Environmental Education and Training Foundation (NEETF) reports that people with even cursory environmental knowledge are:

- 10 percent more likely to save energy in the home
- 50 percent more likely to recycle
- 10 percent more likely to purchase environmentally safe products
- 50 percent more likely to avoid using chemicals in yard care[28]

It is appealing to believe that education will, in and of itself, serve as an impetus for change, because as author and environmentalist Paul Hawken has said, "If you look at the science about what is happening on earth and aren't pessimistic, you don't understand the data."[29] Ideally, pessimism translates into action, or at least an understanding of the need for action. Most of the significant environmental benefits that accrue from improved operations and management are low in cost and involve changes in habit but not lifestyle, and consequently can and should be implemented immediately.

8.5 BEST PRACTICE—FACILITATING CHANGE

"[Sustainability is] about taking a well-rounded approach to making personal, government and business decisions that put environmental awareness and social responsibility on par with sound economics."

—*Gerald Farias, Executive Director, Fairleigh Dickinson University Institute for Sustainable Enterprise*

Figure 8.7 The Boston Red Sox have systematically reduced environmental impact and operating costs at Fenway Park with strategies such as the 28 Heliodyne solar hot water collectors and four 400-gallon storage tanks tied to the historic ballpark's water system. The solar-heated water is used by both the ballpark and restaurants on its lower level and is projected to reduce natural gas consumption by about one-third. Carbon dioxide reduction is about 18 tons every year, or the equivalent of planting 5 acres of trees. The installation is part of a citywide initiative launched by the City of Boston to increase solar power output to 50 times its current level by 2015. *Photography: Jordan Wirfs-Brock, courtesy of Struever Bros. Eccles & Rouse*

Figure 8.8 The Boston Red Sox teamed with the Natural Resources Defense Council in 2007 to help make Fenway Park more environmentally responsible in operations. With the help of Waste Management, recycling for staff and fans has been increased. ARAMARK, the concessionaire at Fenway Park, is making more environmentally friendly food products available, including locally grown organic produce. *Photography: Jordan Wirfs-Brock, courtesy of Struever Bros. Eccles & Rouse*

Simple "Green" Tips for Your Building, Neighborhood and Community

By Joe Lawniczak, design specialist, Wisconsin Main Street

For individuals

- Reuse and recycle whenever possible.
- Use alternative transportation whenever possible (walk, bike, bus, carpool, etc.).
- Unplug unused electronics.
- Turn lights off when you leave a room (or add a motion sensor).
- Buy local, organic, or recycled products.
- Use nontoxic cleaning products.
- Long term: Purchase a fuel-efficient car, support alternate/renewable energy sources, support new green technologies that create many new "green collar" jobs.

For individual buildings

- Add weatherstripping and caulk to doors and windows, chimneys, electrical outlets, etc.
- Add insulation where needed (attic, basement, crawl space).
- Install a programmable thermostat.
- Inspect and properly maintain the building's heating and cooling system.
- Install Energy Star–qualified appliances, light fixtures, light bulbs, etc.
- Install retractable awnings on storefronts and windows where appropriate.
- Repair, reglaze, recaulk existing windows.
- Install interior or exterior storm windows.
- Install self-closing device on all storm doors.
- Schedule an overall energy audit of your building.
- Utilize operable windows for natural ventilation in temperate months.
- Use "green" materials indoors (carpet, tile, paints with low volatile organic compounds [VOCs], etc.).
- Install faucet aerators (and low-flow or dual-flush toilets when possible).
- Long term: Install solar system, redo landscaping to improve shading and create windbreaks.
- Install a green roof.

For the office

- Utilize electronic communication, such as e-mail blasts, enewsletters, blogs, etc.
- Only print necessary documents.
- Purchase products that contain recycled material.

For a neighborhood or commercial district

- Provide pedestrian amenities and bike racks.
- Encourage upper-floor housing.
- Provide opportunity for residents to "buy local" (farmer's markets, etc.).
- Provide easy access to recycling programs.

For the Community

- Install bike lanes.
- Provide pedestrian amenities.
- Improve mass transit.
- Implement comprehensive recycling program.
- Limit sprawl, determine growth boundaries.
- Limit demolition of existing structures (residential and commercial).
- Encourage rehab and reuse of existing structures (provide financial incentives).
- Recruit new "green" industries.

Source: Joe Lawniczak, "Historic Preservation and Sustainable Development: What Does It Mean for Main Street?" *Wisconsin Main Street News*, vol. 2 (4) (Fall 2008).

Best practices for operations and maintenance must incorporate the ability to change. Leith Sharp, founding director of Harvard University's Green Campus Initiative, speaking at the GreenBuild conference in 2008, stressed that "the global environmental imperative requires us to change the way in which we do almost everything. The end goal, environmental sustainability, is a moving target. Therefore, any organization or individual that is serious about addressing the environmental imperative needs to expand their capacities for engaging in the process of change itself."

The National Science Foundation says the same thing. "Imagination, diversity, and the capacity to adapt quickly have become essential qualities for both institutions and individuals, not only to facilitate research, but also to ensure the immediate and broad-based application of research results related to the environment."[30] Checklists and metric systems can help but must also change as new information becomes available.

The LEED metric systems developed by the U.S. Green Building Council (USGBC) have expanded and evolved steadily since their introduction and show no sign of reaching a static plateau. The growth rate of the organization and endorsement of the systems have been exponential. However, Rick Fedrizzi, president, CEO, and founding chairman of the USGBC, wisely states in the council's 2008 annual report that the "USGBC's most important achievement isn't measured in LEED-certified buildings—it's measured by changing minds."[31] The changing of minds supports USGBC's mission of moving the culture toward energy independence, climate change mitigation, affordable green housing, and green jobs.

Sustainability involves more than the environment (refer to Chapter 2), as demonstrated by many of the case studies, which describe buildings that

Facilitating Change—Isles in Trenton, New Jersey

Isles is a nonprofit community development and environmental organization that supports personal and community change, offering an array of services and training that empower people to improve their lives, families, and communities—while they restore the environment. Isles addresses immediate challenges such as food, shelter, jobs, and toxic environments in an entrepreneurial way that impacts future generations. Isles helps people to reimagine and redevelop older communities.

www.isles.org

house organizations committed to both education and social change. To facilitate change, best practice in operations and maintenance must reach beyond traditional guidelines to address the ideal of complete sustainability. Solutions can be surprising and entrepreneurial.

The Rhode Island firm Durkee, Brown, Viveiros & Werenfels Architects donates scrap materials to RRIE.org (Resources for RI Education), where the materials can be used for educational projects. This solution prolongs the useful life of materials before recycling and supports social sustainability. The firm supports social sustainability through volunteer activities that address stewardship, such as painting a church or collecting litter from a riverbank. A culture expresses values through the objects it decides to care for; engaging the community in that care sustains the commitment.

Respecting the Past While Planning for the Future

The high turnover rate in commercial buildings (and housing; refer to Chapter 7) makes future-thinking investments difficult. According to the Energy Information Administration, nearly three-quarters of commercial energy users require a payback on energy-saving initiatives of less than two years.[32] In a sustainable world, incentives would reward all decisions based on long-term benefits, not short-term rewards. This includes design that acknowledges and embraces a diverse and aging population. As we make adjustments in our building stock, fewer future alterations will be needed if we are inclusive and forward-thinking about universal design or strategies that help buildings work for all types of people. This can represent a challenge with existing buildings, but modifications become easier to make each year. New technologies spawned by access laws and the Americans with Disabilities Act are assisting in the same way that the current surge in new green technologies will make it easier to be environmentally responsible.

Universal Design

Design is only one part of the solution to a more inclusive world in which all people have equal opportunity for independence, autonomy and participation. But design matters. Understood as the work of "changing existing situations into preferred ones" [Simon, 1967], and expanded to embrace solutions that include everyone, Universal Design is a framework that accepts diversity of ability and age as the most ordinary reality of being human and evaluates strategies and solutions based on how well they meet the needs of the widest possible group of potential users and enhance everyone's experience. It demands a quality of creativity and invention that can energize generations of designers to become partners with users in a revitalized appreciation of design as intrinsic to social sustainability.

Institute for Human Centered Design, www.adaptenv.org

St. Stephen's Episcopal K–8 School

Harrisburg, PA

Current Owner: St. Stephen's Episcopal Cathedral

Building Type: K–8 Education/Assembly

Original Building Construction: 1840s/1920s

Historic Designation: National Register of Historic Places (cathedral and chapter house)

Restoration/Renovation Completion: 2003

Square Footage: 37,300 ft^2

Percentage Renovated: 97% + 3% addition

Recognition: LEED NC (2.0)—Pending; *American School and University* Magazine 2004; Green Building Association Design Awards for Overall Sustainable Design, Design Innovation, and Sustainable Sites 2007; selected for *Learning by Design* annual review of green design schools by the National School Board Association 2009.

"We see it as an expression of what the stewardship of God's creation is all about.... We start with the premise that creation is blessed, and we have to raise that up."

—*Very Rev. Malcolm McDowell, dean of St. Stephen's Episcopal Cathedral, speaking about the commitment to environmentally responsible design*[33]

PROJECT DESCRIPTION

In pursuit of St. Stephen's mission of environmental stewardship, the building project converted a four-story 1920s-era parking garage into classrooms and multipurpose spaces and maintained the integrity of the abutting historic properties. The full project encompassed five existing buildings on a city block—including the 177-year-old cathedral and its 158-year-old chapter house, both on the National Register—and an internal circulation spine that connects the campus while providing handicapped access. The congregation's undercroft gathering area in the basement of the cathedral was rebuilt, and the cathedral itself received a new displacement-ventilation cooling system.

▶**Figure 8.9** Converting the 1928 parking garage behind the church into an addition with classrooms, restrooms, cafeteria, and administrative offices accommodated an additional 120 students without increasing building footprint. Water-source heat pumps take advantage of waste heat and cool sinks created by the complementary schedules of school and church, thus reducing heating- and cooling-equipment loads. *McKissick Associates Architects*

▼**Figure 8.10** A new stair tower links two of the five buildings that form the complex. St. Stephen's Episcopal Cathedral was the first church in the United States to register its facilities with the USGBC LEED system. *McKissick Associates Architects*

Interfaith Works, a nonprofit organization that collaborates with religious organizations to do good works by integrating environmental stewardship with community outreach, provided technical services for the project, including energy modeling, daylighting studies, materials consulting, project management, and LEED documentation.

Water, Energy, and the Atmosphere

- Landscaping is designed to be *water-efficient*.
- Plumbing fixtures are designed for *water-use reduction*. This includes toilets that use less water with each flush and wash sinks that reduce flow.
- The *building systems are being commissioned* to ensure that all features are installed and run efficiently as an integrated system.
- *Optimized energy use* through super-insulation, triple-glazed windows, and a heat pump system that minimizes the need for outside fuel (in this case, utility steam). Energy-saving features include:

- Triple-glazed windows: two layers of clear glass with outer pane of low-E glazing on the #2 side along with aluminum-clad wood frames for maximum durability and thermal isolation (used in the school portion of the project).

- Double-glazed curtainwall with $R = 3.5$ and $R = 5+$ for the skylight in the cloister. Particular glass by PPG, Solarban 60, provides high ratio of visible light transmittance to highest thermal performance characteristics currently available.

- Thick exterior walls filled with cellulose insulation made from recycled newspapers.

- Roof insulation of 7 inches of CFC-free and HCFC-free polyisocyanurate with an aged R value = 40 on the main roof, R value = 30 on the roof assembly of the small school entrance.

- 22 heat pumps throughout the buildings are linked to share energy and controlled by a computer.

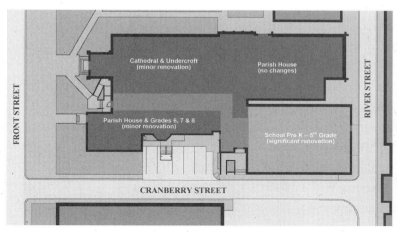

▲ Figure 8.11 The parish renovated five existing buildings, two of which—the nineteenth-century cathedral and chapter house—are designated historic structures. The largest building, an unoccupied 1920s parking structure, was converted into classrooms. Also included in the project are renovations of the 1840s school building and an internal circulation spine that connects the campus while providing handicapped access. *McKissick Associates Architects*

▶ Figure 8.12 The new passage creates an accessible corridor between the cathedral and house, both listed on the National Register of Historic Places, and leads to the new school in the renovated 1920s garage. *McKissick Associates Architects*

GREEN DESIGN ELEMENTS

St. Stephen's Episcopal K–8 School

Sustainable Sites:
- Water-efficient landscaping

Water Efficiency:
- Water-efficient fixtures

Energy and Atmosphere:
- Water-source heat pump
- Waste-heat-recovery ventilation

Materials and Resources:
- Recycled-content ceramic tile
- Recycled-content ceiling tiles
- Recycled-content floor tile
- Recycled-cellulose tack boards

Indoor Environment Quality:
- Original roof vents restored to provide natural stack-ventilation

Operations and Maintenance:
- Ongoing education

- Energy model found the building to be 30 percent more efficient than the base case study. Actual operation has shown the constructed building to outperform the energy model by close to 30 percent for electricity. Evaluation of the steam system continues.
- All heating and air conditioning systems, as well as drinking fountains, are designed *without CFC refrigerants* (freon-type substances) *to reduce ozone depletion*.
- Interior *lighting is controlled* with motion sensors, so lights are on only when rooms are occupied *to reduce electric power use*.

Materials

- There is a *recycling program* and storage space for materials.
- The classroom *building* was "recycled" by reusing not only the exterior but also the flooring. Features include:
  - Maintaining existing window openings
  - Locating elevator and utilities in garage's original car elevator shaft
  - Use of strong concrete floors, which can be seen in ceilings of classrooms
  - Use of original wood-domed roof in the upper room on the third floor
- *Recycled content* materials were used throughout the project:
  - The tack boards under the fabric walls in each classroom are made from recycled cellulose.
  - The third-floor tile is recycled rubber.
  - The ceiling tiles are recycled cellulose.
  - The ceramic tile has recycled glass content.

PROJECT TEAM

St. Stephen's Episcopal Cathedral Parish

McKissick Associates

Caldwell, Heckles and Egan

Interfaith Works (www.interfaithworks.org)

Candler Library Renovation

Atlanta, GA

Current Owner: Emory University

Building Type: Higher Education/Library

Original Building Construction: 1926

Restoration/Renovation Completion: 2003

Square Footage: 53,540 ft²

Percentage Renovated: 82% + 18% new construction

Occupancy: 398 people (20–40 hrs/week) 1,120 visitors (1–2 hrs/day)

Recognition: LEED NC v2.0—Silver; AIA Connecticut Citation for Design Award 2004; SCUP/AIA-CAE Award 2006

"The new design creatively adapts and recycles what had become an obsolete facility, giving it new life. The original building itself lends strong character to its new multi-use function, giving a building without a distinguishing function a distinguished character."

—*Emory College—project mission statement*

PROJECT DESCRIPTION

As part of Emory University's vision to achieve positive transformation in the world, environmental sustainability in construction and operations is considered a responsibility that helps "restore the global ecosystem, foster healthy living and reduce the University's impact on the local environment. Progress is assessed using environmental, economic and social impact measures."[34]

The renovation and expansion of the 1920s Candler Library reestablished the character of interior spaces altered in the 1950s and integrated sustainability standards measured by the LEED metric system.

Figure 8.13 Designed in 1926 by noted library architect Edward Tilton as Emory's first free-standing library building, the Asa Griggs Candler Library was, for decades, the center of the university's academic and intellectual community. The mission of the renovation was to restore the architectural character of the building, as well as add much-needed office and classroom space near the heart of the campus. *Photo courtesy of Woodruff Brown Photography*

Figure 8.14 Along with construction of a two-story addition, the building's renovation provided state-of-the-art classrooms and office space. The addition was created to replenish usable square footage lost as a result of bringing the building up to code and to fulfill the need for new space on the college Quadrangle. *Image courtesy of The S/L/A/M Collaborative*

Alternative Transportation

This building is served by Emory's alternative transportation system, which relies on clean-burning natural-gas and electric buses. This reduces local emissions and results in no net increase in vehicle parking. Occupants have access to eight bus routes within a quarter-mile of the building. Bike racks and a changing/shower room were installed to support those who bike or walk to work, a particularly useful feature during Atlanta's humid summers.

▶Figure 8.15 Restored to its original two-story grandeur, the William L. Matheson Reading Room houses Emory's current periodicals collection. *Photo courtesy of Woodruff Brown Photography*

▼Figure 8.16 This 1950s view of the reading room shows the space divided horizontally by floors, added to increase usable area in the building. *Photo courtesy of Emory University Archives*

Water-Efficient

Low-flow aerators were added to water fixtures, resulting in a 30 percent reduction in water consumption. This reduces the burden on municipal water supply and wastewater systems.

Optimizing Energy Performance

Heating and cooling requirements were reduced by over 30 percent by careful selection of building system components, insulation, and building automation and control devices. Energy savings were also realized by utilizing variable-speed motors and occupancy sensors.

Materials

Of the new building materials used in constructing Candler Library, 60 percent comprised recycled materials. Forty-three percent of new raw building materials used in the project were manufactured within 500 miles of the job site, thus reducing transportation costs and supporting the regional economy. More than 50 percent of those locally manufactured materials were harvested regionally.

GREEN DESIGN ELEMENTS

Candler Library Renovation

Sustainable Sites:
- Public transportation proximity
- Bicycle accommodations
- Relocation of four large and historic holly trees

Water Efficiency:
- Low-flow plumbing fixtures

Energy and Atmosphere:
- Variable-speed motors
- Automatic occupancy sensors

Materials and Resources:
- Construction waste recycled
- Original materials replaced
- Recycled content materials
- Locally manufactured and harvested materials

Indoor Environment Quality:
- Restored original ceiling height
- Restored copper-plated skylight
- Interior windows
- Low-VOC materials and finishes

Additional Features:
- Green cleaning policy

About 15,000 ft² of 1.5-inch-thick marble, weighing approximately 130 tons, were removed from the original library floors. The bulk of the marble remains in storage for use in future campus projects. Some of it returned to Candler in the form of signage plaques, computer kiosk surfaces, reading room furniture tops, and accent walls.

Tree Relocation

Prior to construction, four exceptionally large holly trees were relocated. The holly trees were considered to have historic value. The process for moving the trees (the largest weighed over six tons) required hand-digging a rootball, wrapping the rootball with burlap, lifting the tree from the ground using a crane, and moving it to a new site for careful replanting.[35]

DESIGN TEAM

Emory University

The S|L|A|M Collaborative

Holder Construction

Sutton Kennerly & Associates

Nottingham Brook Pennington

Estes Shields

Waveguide Consulting

HagerSmith Design, PA

Ch2M HILL

Jean Vollum Natural Capital Center

Portland, OR

Current Owner: Ecotrust

Building Type: Commercial Office/Restaurant/Retail

Original Building Construction: 1895

Restoration/Renovation Completion: 2001

Square Footage: 70,000 ft^2

Percentage Renovated: 83% + 17% addition

Occupancy: 230 people (20–40 hrs/week)

Recognition: LEED NC v2.0—Gold

"Ecotrust's mission is to inspire fresh thinking that creates economic opportunity, social equity and environmental well-being."

"We wanted an old building to help anchor us in the region's history—to take a building from the time of westward expansion (and a frontier economy) and redeploy it as a hub for the new conservation economy."

www.ecotrust.org

PROJECT DESCRIPTION

Ecotrust, a unique organization dedicated to new business models based on interconnected economic, social, and environmental principles, documented the creation of the Jean Vollum Natural Capital Center in *Rebuild Green: The Natural Capital Center and the Transformative Power of Building* (2003 © Ecotrust), which Paul Hawken calls "the first book to explore the true meaning and social dimensions of building green."[36]

The rehabilitation of the vacant 1895 warehouse into a thriving place of commerce clearly demonstrates Ecostrust's mission and offers a case study for the application of the LEED metric system to an historic building—the first in the country to achieve a LEED Gold rating. An integrated design process used the synergy of building to best advantage, with strategies such as recovering heat from the pizza shop's exhaust fan to help warm

Figure 8.17 The janitorial service for the Jean Vollum Natural Capital Center is committed to eliminating the use of environmentally hazardous products and chemicals associated with the maintenance of commercial facilities. The cleaning materials are biodegradable, all-natural, phosphate free, and contain no animal byproducts or perfumes. Proceeds from the cleaning products support environmental education in schools and the work of various environmental organizations. *Phil Goff photo, courtesy Goody Clancy*

Materials

The design team conscientiously conserved and reused existing materials in the build-ing, deconstructing a small side addition and using the constiuent materials to create the third-floor addition. Approximately two-thirds of the new wood used in the build-ing—including lumber, plywood, particleboard, decking, and window components— was certified under Forest Stewardship Council (FSC) standards. The project team took care to retain the original fir floorboards on the main floor; these boards were eventually sanded and finished with a low-emission sealer and finish. The wood floor-ing in the third-floor lobby is FSC-certified, Bolivian-sourced guariuba, a teak alterna-tive not commonly marketed but used here to promote the maintenance of natural forest diversity. Other areas on the third floor boast more conventional FSC-certified wood species, some of it a lower grade than would normally be used, a choice in-tended to enhance the aesthetics of the building. Douglas fir truss members, plywood, and wood wainscoting salvaged from the warehouse's deconstruction have taken on new life in the building's coat racks and hooks, stools, pedestals, building directories, tenant signs, a podium, and a workstation.

The countertop of the Ecotrust reception desk, near the second-floor main en-trance, has locally obtained glass scraps and ceramic aggregate cast into it. This area also features a collection of artifacts from the original building, including door

Figure 8.18 Long, narrow strips of landscaping in the parking lot are part of the Natural Capital Center's stormwater management system. All of the rainwater the bottomless swales receive from the parking lot and the roof's downspouts filters through the vegetation and soil to seep into the groundwater table or evaporate into the atmosphere. Native plants were carefully selected for their ability to tolerate seasonal fluctuations between inundations of water and intense heat. Once established, these plants require little maintenance, and will receive irrigation from rainwater alone. *Image provided by Holst Architecture*

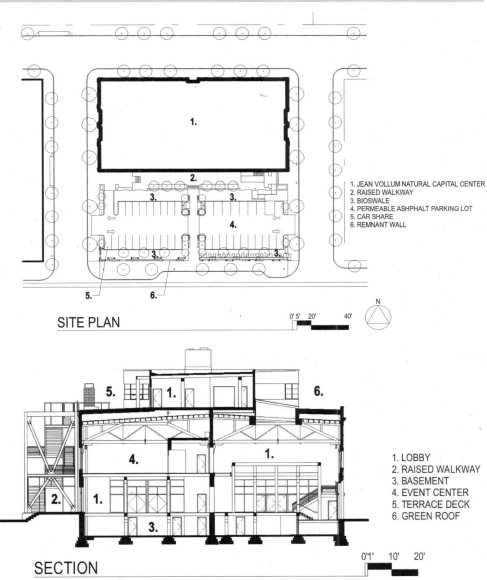

SITE PLAN

1. JEAN VOLLUM NATURAL CAPITAL CENTER
2. RAISED WALKWAY
3. BIOSWALE
4. PERMEABLE ASHPHALT PARKING LOT
5. CAR SHARE
6. REMNANT WALL

0' 5' 20' 40'

N

SECTION

1. LOBBY
2. RAISED WALKWAY
3. BASEMENT
4. EVENT CENTER
5. TERRACE DECK
6. GREEN ROOF

0'1' 10' 20'

Figure 8.19 At the Jean Vollum Natural Capital Center, customers and visitors encounter a wide range of environmentally and socially responsible goods, services, and ideas. The building community includes governmental, business, and nonprofit groups gathered around the themes of sustainable forestry, farming, fishing, green construction, community building, and socially responsible investing and financial services. Retail tenants surround a public atrium. Second-floor tenants share a public mezzanine space and a conference center for business and community events. Two offices on the third floor overlook a terrace and "ecoroof" planted with hearty vegetation to absorb and filter stormwater. *Image provided by Holst Architecture*

pulleys obtained from that same floor. Fabric for the armchairs in the Eco-trust waiting area and window-drapery fabric in the second-floor conference center contain 78 percent post-industrial recycled polyester. Much of the office furniture on the second and third floors, including conference-room tables and chairs, contains between 40 percent and 100 percent recycled content, and many of the materials used for construction, such as steel, aluminum, and polypropylene, are readily recyclable.

▲ Figure 8.20 Tenants and visitors to the building's roof can enjoy city views and fresh air year round with an outdoor fireplace. The fireplace builds on a long tradition in the Pacific Northwest of gathering around the fire to share stories and resolve conflicts. The wood for the patio is Ipe, an Amazonian hardwood that was grown and harvested sustainably from a Forest Stewardship Council (FSC)-certified forest in Bolivia. The decking came in shorter lengths to increase log utilization, a process that reduces wood waste, a serious problem in many Latin American milling operations. The durable wood requires no protective finish. *Rebekah Johnson photograph, courtesy of Eugene and Amelia Monteiro (www.rebekahjohnson.com)*

▶ Figure 8.21 The Natural Capital Center building renovation respects the character of the original structure, a warehouse built in 1895, while incorporating environmentally innovative materials and techniques. The floors on the main level are the original Douglas fir planks milled for the warehouse over a century ago. The planks were sanded and refinished with products that are low in volatile organic compounds; joints were filled with colored cork shavings. *Phil Goff photo, courtesy Goody Clancy*

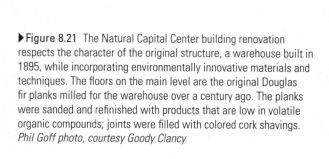

GREEN DESIGN ELEMENTS

Jean Vollum Natural Capital Center

Sustainable Sites:
- Public transportation proximity
- Bicycle accommodation
- Permeable paving materials
- Green roof
- Xeriscaping
- Bioswales

Water Efficiency:
- Low-flow plumbing fixtures

Energy and Atmosphere:
- Waste-heat recovery
- Natural ventilation
- Additional roof insulation
- Occupancy and photoelectric light sensors

Materials and Resources:
- Existing structure exposed
- Original windows restored

Indoor Environment Quality:
- Atrium
- Operable windows
- CO_2 monitors

Additional Features:
- Hybrid car share program
- Multiuse permeable parking surface
- Farmer's market

Floor tiles made from recycled tires with added color granules are used in the building. Due to their interlocking configuration, these tiles required no adhesives for installation. Marbleized linoleum—made from natural, renewable resources, including linseed oil, wood flour, pine rosins, and jute fiber—cover floors and countertops in certain locations. Carpet tiles in the building include recycled fibers, permitting the replacement of only those tiles that become stained or worn, and can ultimately be returned to the manufacturer for recycling. Porcelain tile, made largely from unfired scrap generated during the manufacture of conventional tile, was also used for flooring.

Several hinged wood doors were salvaged from the warehouse deconstruction and used as a partition in one of the tenant office spaces. Other massive wood-and-steel barn-type hanging doors salvaged from the original warehouse were used as conference-room dividers.

Diversion of Construction and Demolition Waste

To encourage recycling of construction and demolition waste, recycling containers were clearly labeled, neatly maintained, conveniently located close to the work site, and frequently emptied. The team located recycling facilities that accepted polystyrene foam insulation board and polyethylene sheeting, as well as more typically recycled materials. Overall, 2,331 tons of waste, 98 percent of all construction and demolition debris generated on site, was diverted from landfills.

Stormwater

A green roof reduces stormwater runoff and heat islands. Most new vegetation species are indigenous to the site and relatively maintenance- and drought-free. Onsite bioswales achieve 95 percent diversion of stormwater.

Public Transportation

The building site is close to public transportation systems (including a trolley line that abuts the property), and bike racks are provided for visitors. Bike storage, lockers, and showers are provided for building employees, and two hybrid cars are available to rent on a short-term basis to run errands.

PROJECT TEAM, JEAN VOLLUM NATURAL CAPITAL CENTER

- Ecotrust
- Holst Architecture
- Naito Development, LLC
- Walsh Construction Company
- KPFF Consulting Engineers
- Interface Engineering
- Edelman Soljaga Watson
- Nevue Ngan Associates
- Green Building Services
- Gregory Acker Architecture

Eastern Village Cohousing Condominium

Silver Springs, MD

Current Owner: Eastern Village Cohousing Homeowners' Association

Building Type: Multiunit Residential/Assembly

Original Building Construction: 1957

Historic Designation: None

Restoration/Renovation Completion: 2004

Square Footage: 92,600 ft²

Percentage Renovated: 85% + 15% new construction

Occupancy: 100 people (168 hrs/week) 20 visitors (4 hrs/week)

Recognition: LEED NC v2.1—Silver 2002; Green Roofs for Healthy Cities Award/Extensive Residential 2006; Excellence in Design Award for Multi-Use Residential 2005; NAHB Green Project of the Year 2005; Smart Growth Award 2003

Eastern Village Cohousing is committed to inclusive decision-making through consensus and the following principles:

- We cherish and support diverse ages, ethnicities, interests, abilities, relationships, and spiritual beliefs.
- We value ecological responsibility, sustainable design, and a balance of aesthetics and affordability.
- We foster interconnectedness, growth, care, communication, and respect among our membership.
- We engage responsibly with our neighborhood and the wider world.

—Mission Statement, www.easternvillage.org

◀Figure 8.22 Balconies, added to the original structure, provide circulation, and their shade helps cool the building—and they completely alter the appearance of the run-of-the-mill structure, giving it great character. Conversion of the central parking court to a garden and the addition of a green roof reduce site impermeability by 54 percent. Design of the green screen/sunshade took shape with input from the energy model. *EDG Architects, LLC*

▼ Figure 8.23 A concrete-framed office building from the 1950s, the Eastern Village Cohousing development began with a site that was 90 percent impervious and a building that offered little aesthetic appeal. *EDG Architects, LLC*

PROJECT DESCRIPTION

This reuse of a mundane and vacant 1950s office building demonstrates multiple principles of sustainable development, including planning for the future aging of cohousing residents. Cohousing communities are small-scale neighborhoods created with the active involvement of residents. The Eastern Village Cohousing created 56 condominiums with shared community spaces that include a dining hall, living room, kids playroom, game room, yoga room, library, workshop, hot tub, green roof, and garden areas.

Figure 8.24 A grid of 40- to 600-foot-deep geothermal wells under the courtyard area provides heating and cooling for the individually metered units. Energy Star appliances were used throughout. Eastern Village is designed to be fully accessible and adaptable for the future needs of residents, allowing them to age in place. Door widths and access aisles accommodate wheelchair users, and bathrooms include blocking for future installation of grab bars. *EDG Architects, LLC*

Figure 8.25 The common area on the roof forms part of the building's extensive shared community spaces. Cohousing is a unique form of multifamily housing in which the future residents participate actively in the design and development of the community. Their direct involvement in the design of common areas and individual units ensures a close fit between end product and end user. *EDG Architects, LLC*

GREEN DESIGN ELEMENTS

Eastern Village Cohousing Condominiums

Sustainable Sites:
- Public transportation proximity
- Bicycle accommodation
- Permeable paving materials
- No parking onsite
- Green roof
- Xeriscaping

Water Efficiency:
- Low-flow plumbing fixtures

Energy and Atmosphere:
- Ground-source heat pumps
- Additional insulation
- Low-E windows
- "Green screen" shading
- ENERGY STAR appliances

Materials and Resources:
- Over 50 percent of construction waste recycled
- Recycled-content materials
- Rapidly renewable materials
- Locally manufactured and harvested materials

Indoor Environment Quality:
- Abundant daylight
- Asbestos containment
- Low-VOC materials and finishes
- Walk-off mats

Additional Features:
- Occupant recycling program

Future Thinking

Eastern Village is designed to be fully accessible and adaptable for the future needs of its residents as they age in place. Door widths and access aisles are designed to accommodate wheelchair users. All unit bathrooms include blocking for the future installation of grab bars, and kitchens are easily adaptable for future use by nonambulatory users.

Gardens, Stormwater, and Green Screens

Prior to construction, more than 90 percent of the site was impervious. Conversion of the central parking court to a garden and provision of a green roof decreases permeability by 54 percent. The existing storm drainage system was repaired, with the green roof acting as a filtration and detention device. Rain barrels collect water used for watering plants in the courtyard and on the roof.

New exterior walkways provide access to the units. A galvanized-steel "green screen" with climbing plants provides shading that decreases the need for air conditioning.

Energy Efficiencies

Residential units and common areas are heated and cooled by a ground-source heat pump system. A grid of 40- to 600-foot-deep geothermal wells has been installed in the courtyard area. The results of energy modeling directly influenced the choice of a high-efficiency hot-water heating system and the design of the "green screen"/sunshade. Energy Star appliances are used in all units. As a result of these and other measures, the building uses 44 percent less energy than a comparable building based on the ASHRAE 90.1-1999 baseline.

PROJECT TEAM

EDG Architects

R K Consulting (MPE)

Sustainable Design Consulting

Architectural Support Group, Inc.

Lila Fendrick Landscape Architects

Eco Housing Corporation/Poretsky Building Group Cohousing

Ann Zabaldo

Meridian Construction Company, Inc.

Felician Sisters Convent and School

Coraopolis, PA

Current Owner: Felician Sisters of Pennsylvania

Building Type: Special Needs/K–12 Education

Original Building Construction: 1932 and 1960s

Restoration/Renovation Completion: 2003

Square Footage: 161,000 ft^2

Percentage Renovated: 100%

Occupancy: 64 full-time residents, a student body of 345, and 37 full-time staff. Number of Visitors: Approximately 50 visitors tour the facility each week for an hour; 2,600 visitors tour the premises annually.

Recognition: LEED NC (2.0)—Gold Rating (39/69 points); 2003—Finalist in the green design category of the annual Western Pennsylvania Environmental Awards sponsored by Dominion and the Pennsylvania Environmental Council; Associated Builders and Contractors Western Pennsylvania Chapter Award of Merit for Historical Renovation 2003; *Environmental Design and Construction* Magazine Excellence in Design Awards 2004; Northeast Sustainable Energy Association Northeast Green Building Design Awards First Place—Places to Live 2004; AIA Pittsburgh Green Design Citation 2004; Boston Society of Architects Sustainable Design Award 2005; National Association of Home Builders Green Project of the Year/Affordable Multifamily 2005; Citizens for Pennsylvania's Future Green Building Award 2006

PROJECT DESCRIPTION

As followers of Saint Francis of Assisi, the patron saint of the environment, the Felician Sisters view environmental stewardship as a responsibility. They were strongly committed to making the renovation environmentally responsible while preserving the building's historic architectural character. Education is an important aspect of the environmentally sustainable design implemented in the renovation of their motherhouse and school. Educational programs have been established for the residents of the convent, students, and staff of the high school, and for the general public. These include composting, recycling, green cleaning, and energy conservation.

▶ Figure 8.26 Total renovation of the Felician Sisters provincial house, built in 1932, included restoring seven acres of the campus to native meadow, planting trees to provide natural shading, and instituting green, pesticide-free outdoor maintenance. © *denmarsh 2008*

▼ Figure 8.27 New energy-efficient, low-E-glazed windows were installed throughout the building, and six inches of additional insulation were added to the building envelope to promote heat retention in the winter and offset heat gain in the summer. © *denmarsh 2008*

Operations and Education

A vermi-composting system converts preconsumer kitchen waste and postconsumer cafeteria waste to provide nutrient-rich soil for the site. There is a compost heap for grass clippings, weeds, and other yard waste. Green, pesticide-free outdoor maintenance is practiced. A comprehensive recycling plan is in place in the convent and adjoining school; materials recycled are newspapers, office paper, magazines, catalogs, glass, plastic, and aluminum. Purchases of food, cleaning products, and other supplies utilize bulk packaging from local distributors and vendors whenever possible.

Permanent signs around the school point out the project's sustainable features, promoting and encouraging environmentally responsible behavior. The school has formed a "Green Guys" Club for

GREEN DESIGN ELEMENTS

Felician Sisters Convent and School

Sustainable Sites:
- Restored natural meadows
- Reduced hardscape
- Natural shading established
- Reduced heat island effect with white roofing
- Composting and vermi-composting

Water Efficiency:
- Rainwater collection for cooling make-up
- Rainwater collection for irrigation
- Low-flow fixtures and automatic sensors
- Xeriscape planting

Energy and Atmosphere:
- Low-E insulated windows
- Building insulation added
- Solar hot water
- Demonstration photovoltaic panels
- Daylighting

Materials and Resources:
- Use of salvaged materials
- Recycled content
- Natural materials
- Hand dryers to reduce paper waste

Indoor Environment Quality:
- Green cleaning

students interested in environmental issues. A campus clean-up day is held on the Saturday closest to Earth Day for students, sisters, and associates. The provincial newsletter features an "EcoFact" each month. The sisters continue to administer tours to groups interested in green renovations or new buildings.

The province is developing a program of support for small farmers, purchasing local meats, produce, and dairy products. The Felician Sisters are members of the Building in Good Faith group, a national ecumenical effort to devise green guidelines and standards for churches and other properties owned and operated by religious organizations.

PROJECT TEAM

Perkins Eastman Architects, PC

Sota Construction Services, Inc.

Elwood S. Tower Corporation

The Kachele Group

Clearview Project Services Company

The Gateway Engineers, Inc.

Rolf Sauer & Partners, Ltd.

ENDNOTES

1. Committee on Business Strategies for Public Capital Investment, *Investments in Federal Facilities: Asset Management Strategies for the 21st Century* (Washington, DC: The National Academies Press, 2004), www.nap.edu/catalog/11012.html. Accessed April 2009.

2. Ibid.

3. News release, "GRCC Energy Savings Hit 16.25 Percent After Only Five Months Under New Program" (November 18, 2008), www.grcc.edu/prenergysavings. Accessed December 15, 2008.

4. GSA Public Buildings Service, "Energy Savings and Performance Gains in GSA Building; Seven Cost Effective Strategies" (March 2009), www.gsa.gov.

5. Samuel Jones and John Holden, *It's a Material World; Caring for the Public Realm* (London: Demos, 2008).

6. Christopher Ratcliff, "A Green Action Plan for Existing Buildings" (January 29, 2009), www.greenerbuildings.com/feature/2009/01/29/green-action-plan-existing-buildings. Accessed April 21, 2009.

7. Katherine Watenschutz, webcast, "Greening Existing Buildings to Address Climate Change," *Building Design+Consruction* (December 6, 2007).

8. NSW Heritage Office, Information Sheet 1.1, "Preparing a Maintenance Plan," March 1998, online edition 2004, www.heritage.nsw.gov.au/docs/maintenance1-1_preparingplan.pdf. Accessed May 2009.

9. Building Commissioning Association, "Best Practices in Commissioning Existing Buildings" (2008), www.bcxa.org/downloads/bca-ebcx-best-practices.pdf. Accessed April 2009.

10. Ibid.

11. J. David Odom, Richard Scott, and George H. Dubose, "The Hidden Risks of Green Buildings: Avoiding Moisture & Mold Problems," *Direct Connection: A Publication of NCARB,* vol. 10 (2) (2007): 32–41.

12. Lia Webster, "Results and Insights from the Largest Existing Building Commissioning Effort Yet," Portland Energy Conservation Inc. (PECI), Building Commissioning Association Convention and Exposition, October 2008, www.bca-expo2008-webster.pdf. Accessed April 2009.

13. ASHRAE, ASHRAE's Sustainability RoadMap (2006), http://images.ashrae.biz/renovation/documents/sust_roadmap.pdf. Accessed April 2009.

14. As quoted in Douglas E. Gordon, Hon. AIA, and Stephanie Stubbs, Assoc. AIA, "Four Shades of Green," *The AIA Journal of Architecture* (October 2005), p. 15.

15. John Muir, *My First Summer in the Sierra* (New York: Barnes & Noble, 1911), p. 110.

16. www.responsible purchasing.org/about/rpnfaq.php. Accessed June 2009.

17. *Collaborative for High-Performance Schools, Best Practices Manual, Volume IV: Maintenance and Operations* (San Francisco: Collaborative for High-Performance Schools, 2006). www.chps.net/dev/Drupal/node/288.

18. Barbara Kingsolver with Steven L. Hopp and Camille Kingsolver, *Animal, Vegetable, Miracle: A Year of Food Life* (New York: Harper Collins Publishers 2007), p. 5.

19. Air Quality Sciences, Inc., "Cleaning Chemicals and Their Impact on Indoor Environments and Health," Marietta, Georgia (2008), www.aqs.com.

20. U.S. General Services Administration, *Sustainability Matters* (Washington, DC: Public Buildings Service, Office of Applied Science, 2008) p. 10.22.

21. Stephen P. Ashkin, "Green and Clean: The Designer's Impact on Housekeeping and Maintenance," *Environmental and Economic Balance: The 21st Century Outlook* (Washington, DC: The American Institute of Architects, 1997).

22. StopWaste.org, *A Guide to Green Maintenance and Operations* (Oakland, CA: StopWaste.org, 2009), p. 2; www.stopwaste.org/docs/greenmaintguide.pdf.

23. Cultura Ecológica, www.accessinitiative.org/partner/cultura-ecologica. Accessed May 2009.

24. Sara Cleaves, "Fall Initiatives Save Energy, Money, Emissions," *Campus Journal,* University of New Hampshire (December 10, 2008), http://unh.edu/news/campus journal/2008/Dec/10fall.cfm. Accessed December 15, 2008.

25. Jaclyn Emig, "Shut the Sash: Behavior Change Programs in Labs at Harvard," Presentation at Labs21 Conference October 2006.

26. Noelle McGee, "Energy Program Brings Big Savings for Danville Schools," The News-Gazette.com, Monday, May 4, 2009.

27. News release "GRCC Energy Savings Hit 16.25 Percent After Only Five Months Under New Program" (November 18, 2008), www.grcc.edu/prenergysavings. Accessed December 15, 2008.

28. Kevin Coyle, *Environmental Literacy in America; What Ten Years of NEETF/Roper Research and Related Studies Say About Environmental Literacy in the U.S.* (Washington, DC: The National Environmental Education and Training Foundation, 2005), www.neetf.org.

29. Paul Hawken, "Healing or Stealing?" The Commencement Address to the Class of 2009, University of Portland, May 3, 2009, http://www.paulhawken.com/multimedia/UofP_Commencement_05.03.09.pdf. Accessed May 2009.

30. S. Pfirman and the AC-ERE 2003, *Complex Environmental Systems: Synthesis for Earth, Life, and Society in the 21st Century,* A report summarizing a 10-year outlook in environmental research and education for the National Science Foundation, p. 1.

31. USGBC, Annual Report, 2008. Available at www.usgbc.org/DisplayPage.aspx?CMSPageID=1923&.

32. McKinsey Global Institute, "Wasted Energy: How the U.S. Can Reach its Energy Productivity Potential," McKinsey & Company (June 29, 2007), p. 16. Available at www.mckinsey.com/mgi.

33. Quoted in Mary Warner, "An Easy-on-the-Earth Expansion," *The Patriot News,* November 4, 2001.

34. www.environment.emory.edu/who/mission.shtml. Accessed April 5, 2009.

35. www.college.emory.edu/candler/LEED/index.html. Accessed April 6, 2009.

36. www.ecotrust.org/publications/rebuilt_green.html. Accessed April 5, 2009.

chapter 9

HOUSES

9.1 HOUSES—THE IMPACT OF OUR CHOICES

"U.S. households account for about 38 percent of national carbon emissions through their direct actions, a level of emissions greater than that of any entire country except China and larger than the entire U.S. industrial sector."

—*Gerald Gardner and Paul Stern, "The Short List: The Most Effective Actions U.S. Households Can Take to Curb Climate Change"[1]*

OF MORE THAN 100 million households in the United States, 59 percent occupy single-family detached homes, consume 73 percent of all residential energy, and contribute to additional carbon emissions with transportation choices and product purchases. According to researchers at Oak Ridge National Laboratory, the greatest potential for carbon dioxide reduction in the country lies with the single-family residence.[2]

It is not within the purview of this chapter or book to provide the definitive text for residential-scale green

Figure 9.1 The Adeline Street House (Case Study 9-4) in Berkeley, California, creatively avoids the use of new materials. Kitchen countertops are slabs sliced from nearby trees felled by storms, and terrazzo tile is made of recycled glass. Cabinet doors were built from salvaged redwood wainscot. Original Victorian trim, windows, and doors, as well as old framing lumber, were carefully saved, sorted, and restored. © *Ethan Kaplan Photography*

Figure 9.2 Small is the greenest of all. The Gottfried Regenerative Home (www.gottfriedhome.com) counters the national trend of expanding space requirements for each member of the family with a house size of 1,460 square feet for a family of four. A LEED Platinum renovation, this house has achieved net zero energy performance, but on a national level, a 1,500-square-foot house with even mediocre energy-performance standards (R-13 walls and R-19 ceilings) will use far less energy for heating and cooling than a 3,000-square-foot house of comparable geometry with much better energy detailing (R-19 walls and R-30 ceilings). © 2008 Open Homes Photography

renovations and modifications, but rather, to establish the importance of the issue and offer key statistics, resources, and examples of how existing homes, both historic and nonhistoric, and our domestic habits can have a significantly reduced impact on the environment at the same time that we increase our quality of life through the reinforcement of walkable, memory-rich neighborhoods.

New house size has *increased* about 50 percent in the last 30 years, while family size has *decreased* about 25 percent. The average new house is now 2,300 square feet, up from 1,500 square feet in the 1970s.

While household size has decreased in the last 50 years, both house size and the number of vehicles per household have steadily risen. The average household now has 2.28[3] cars for an average family size of 2.62. Floor area has tripled since 1950 to almost 1,000 square feet per family member, with a related increase in number of bathrooms and garage area. Air conditioning, once relatively rare, is now found in 87 percent of single-family homes.[4]

Expanding use of resources and land for housing multiplies the environmental effect, with a nonlinear impact on resources—a house that is twice as big as the average house built in 1975 often uses three to four times more materials to make, and larger houses with bigger volumes—even when designed to be energy-efficient—often use more energy than smaller, less efficient homes. In addition, there is greater storm-water runoff from impermeable surfaces.[5] Beginning in the 1990s, new supersized houses have frequently replaced existing homes, altering the character of neighborhoods and removing green space while placing a heavier burden on infrastructure. In 2002, the National Trust for Historic Preservation identified 100 communities in 20 states affected by teardowns. By March 2008, that number had increased to nearly 500 communities in 40 states.[6]

Every building project has environmental impacts, but as Alex Wilson reminds us in *Your Green Home,* "If you start with an existing building—even if you carry out an extensive gut-rehab, where almost everything is removed down to the structural frame, then rebuilt," you will eliminate many of the extensive environmental impacts of excavating for foundation walls and erecting new exterior walls and roofs.[7] The greenest home may be the one that already exists even if it can't match the square-foot energy consumption and high-tech solutions of a new green home. The mantra of *reduce, reuse, recycle* continues to serve as a solid guideline for sustainable choices—particularly when we remember that recycling still uses energy and often pushes materials closer to becoming waste.

9.2 ENERGY CONSERVATION, ENVELOPE, AND ALTERNATIVE ENERGY

"By changing their selection and use of household and motor vehicle technologies, without waiting for new technologies to appear, making major economic sacrifices, or losing a sense of well-being, households can reduce energy consumption by almost 30 percent—about 11 percent of total U.S. consumption."

—*Gerald Gardner and Paul Stern "The Short List: The Most Effective Actions U.S. Households Can Take to Curb Climate Change"*[8]

In their 2008 paper identifying the most-effective actions for U.S. households to take in reducing greenhouse gas emissions, Gardner and Stern criticize the random and inclusive manner in which most lists for greening your life or home are presented, creating confusion about what the priorities should be and fueling assumptions that green actions require sacrifice and discomfort. Comparing the success of public health commercials to the failure of energy conservation campaigns, the authors conclude that it is much more effective to focus on a small number of very specific actions and disseminate the message repeatedly. Analysis of multiple lists and recommendations led them to "The Short List of Effective Actions" that juxtaposes specific solutions against the areas of major energy use—specifically, for motor vehicles, space conditioning, water heating, and lighting.

Electricity Losses

Of the electricity used in a home, 89.3 percent is lost in transmission, so even small reductions in use have a magnified effect on the amount of electricity that needs to be produced.[9]

Household Energy Conservation

Most of the energy consumed in a home is for space heating (30 percent) and air-conditioning (11 percent), an additional 12 percent is used for water heating and a further 12 percent is for lighting. The remainder of the energy consumed in homes goes for appliances, electronics, and other purposes.[10]

Ranking the actions required from no cost to more expensive, Gardner and Stern estimate the following:

Most Effective Actions	Estimated Percent Total Energy Saved
Reduce heat from 72°F to 68°F during the day and to 65°F at night. Change AC from 73°F to 78°F (ceiling fans will assist with comfort)	3.4
Clothes washing: use warm/cold or cold/cold cycle	1.2
Replace 85 percent of incandescent bulbs w/fluorescent	4.0
Caulk/weatherstrip home	up to 2.5
Install/upgrade attic insulation and ventilation	up to 7.0
Install a more-efficient water heater	1.5
Install an Energy Star refrigerator/freezer	1.9
Install a heating unit w/92 percent efficiency	2.9
Install efficient A/C (SEER 13 or EER 12 units)	2.2
Total Potential Savings	Up to 26.6 percent

Technology Improvements

Compact fluorescent lamps are 70 percent more efficient than incandescent lamps. Modern refrigerators use 75 percent less energy and clothes washers are 50 percent more efficient than models from 30 years ago.[11]

Smart Efficiency Upgrades

- Check to be sure you have adequate insulation in the attic and crawl space. Attic insulation may be the single most effective means for conserving energy in an older home.
- Insulate your water-heating tank.
- Seal around doors and windows with caulk and ensure they close tightly. (Avoid sealing your house so tightly that indoor air quality suffers.)
- Install energy-efficient lighting.
- Install a programmable thermostat.
- Replace worn-out heating and air conditioning equipment, appliances, and electronics with energy-efficient models.
- Close off rooms that are seldom used and block off the heating and air-conditioning to those rooms.
- Check to see if solar hot water heating makes sense and can work on your house at www.FindSolar.com.
- Check for financial incentives and rebates at www.dsireusa.org .

From "Home Energy Upgrades That Pay," *Solar Today* (March 2009)[12]

Walls and Windows

For those committed to aggressive house-by-house deep retrofitting as a means to achieve carbon neutrality, questioning the appropriateness and cost-effectiveness of wall insulation, replacement windows, and air-tight envelopes is heresy. However, multiple documents describing the most cost-effective strategies for energy conservation in single-family houses do not list either wall insulation or window replacement. They do repeatedly list attic and crawl space insulation and the importance of reducing (but not necessarily stopping) air infiltration, as well as checking for leaking ducts. These are effective actions, which can be taken relatively easily across a wide spectrum of housing stock and which carry minimal risk of creating moisture problems and consequent health and maintenance concerns.

"Increased thermal insulation changes wall-system performance (dewpoint location) with possible condensation in the wrong location. Modifying heating, ventilating, and air conditioning (HVAC) can also impact moisture control."
—*"The Hidden Risks of Green Buildings: Avoiding Moisture and Mold Problems"*[13]

Decisions about more invasive or dramatic insulation of an existing house must be made with an eye to age, style, historic importance, and climate. Many retrofits do not or cannot utilize the expertise of building science experts who can analyze and predict how changing a building's envelope and mechanical systems may also change the way moisture interacts with the building. Nor are there currently life-cycle analysis comparisons that allow a complete understanding of the environmental effects of actions such as replacing 100-year-old windows with new windows that may be vinyl or aluminum and have a life span of only 20 to 30 years (best case) and no cradle-to-cradle capacity. If widespread energy conservation is the goal, the actions required should be achievable and risk-free. Building owners should have the option of choosing less-extreme envelope modifications and balancing them with better energy conservation, the use of renewable systems, and adoption of holistic lifestyle changes.

Should the Walls of Historic Buildings Be Insulated?

"The mandate to conserve energy in all buildings, including historic buildings, does not automatically translate into an imperative for wall insulation.... In most historic structures, other strategies for energy conservation should be considered to have higher priority than wall insulation. These include forgoing air-conditioning, reducing infiltration, allowing float in interior temperature and humidity settings, using energy-efficient equipment, and operating windows effectively. Attic insulation is easier to install and contributes more effectively to reducing heat loss than adding wall insulation."

—*William B. Rose, Building Research Council, University of Illinois–Urbana*[14]

Cost-effective strategies for existing windows combine retrofitting, weathersealing, quality exterior and interior storm windows (with warnings about condensation), applied window films, and low-tech solutions such as awnings, shutters, reflective window shades, blinds, and heavy curtains, depending on climate. Strategies for blocking air infiltration at weight pockets in double-hung windows include creating an isolated track for the weights and filling voids around the track with insulation.

Alternative Energy

Alternative energy strategies for existing houses can include ground-source heat pumps, small wind or solar collectors, and solar hot water, depending on house configuration and site. (Solar hot water heating can provide up to 75 percent of a house's hot water needs and save 10 percent on a the utility bill.)[15] Alternative fuels such as wood pellets and corn are also available in some areas of the country.

Figure 9.3 The renovation of the Gottfried home (www.gottfriedhome.com) maintained the historic details and character of a 1915 Craftsman bungalow but removed walls and interior hallways to create more openness and efficiency in spaces. Care was taken to improve the structure's energy performance by blowing cellulose insulation, recycled from newsprint, into the existing walls through small holes without disturbing the existing wood paneling. © 2008 Open Homes Photography

Figure 9.4 The small size of the Gottfried Regenerative Home (www. gottfriedhome.com) is supplemented by a 10-foot-by-12-foot steel structure (called the "LifePod") in the rear yard that houses a home office. Eight solar panels on the slanted roof help to cut the family's electricity bill by half. Eight more panels on the roof of the main house are designed to bring the bill down to net zero, in part by sending electricity back to the grid on sunny days. *© 2008 Open Homes Photography*

Historical commissions around the country are moving quickly to address the need for new energy strategies in existing neighborhoods, but they often bemoan that the need for dramatic interventions before pursuing common-sense, lower-cost strategies, such as attic insulation, caulking, and wrapping of hot water heaters.

Smart Building and Site Strategies

Both the National Association of Home Builders and the National Trust for Historic Preservation recommend using xeriscape landscaping to reduce water consumption and introducing or protecting site trees for shading and wind breaks. Covered entries and ves-

tibules reduce water infiltration and provide weather breaks. Routing rainwater away from the foundation keeps the soil dry; a thick cushion of dry soil provides significant thermal resistance.

"**Renewable Energy and Heritage Buildings**
Cutting demand for energy is as important as finding alternative means of generating it. Before deciding whether to install a renewable energy technology in a building, all available energy-saving measures—including low-energy light bulbs, heating controls, and improved insulation—should already have been taken. An English Heritage guidance document, *Energy Conservation in Traditional Buildings*, looks at methods of improving insulation and introduces other methods for saving energy."
—English Heritage, "Small Scale Solar Electric (Photovoltaics) and Traditional Buildings"[16]

9.3 HOLISTIC WATER CONSERVATION

"**The amount of freshwater on earth is finite....**"
—The United Nations[17]

Prior to 1994, toilets typically used between 3.5 and 7 gallons per flush. New toilets now use 1.6 gallons per flush or less. Advanced shower and sink faucets aerators provide the same flow regardless of pressure to reduce water use and the energy required to heat it. Front-loading washers use about 40 percent less water and half the energy of conventional models. Conserving water in the home is easier than ever and reduces demands on fresh water supplies, for wastewater treatment centers, and for energy used in creating and moving potable water.

The same strategies for water-use reduction in commercial and institutional work apply in houses, as does

Energy Costs in an Old House: Balancing Preservation and Energy Efficiency

Sally Zimmerman, Preservation Specialist Historic Homeowner Membership, Historic Program, Historic New England (September 2008)

This winter rising energy costs will challenge owners of old and/or historic homes to improve home energy usage, and this challenge poses some particularly difficult questions about balancing historic preservation and energy efficiency. Articles in the popular media focus either on energy enhancements in new construction or on generic retrofits for improved efficiency. Recommended approaches can be incompatible or even inappropriate for the traditional older, historic house. Certain energy upgrades, such as blown-in or spray foam insulations that are now standard for new construction, can seriously damage or compromise the fabric and significance of a historic house. Following are some observations and tips on improving energy efficiency in old houses without damaging their historic character.

BEWARE OF INSULATING WALLS

Often the first recommendation made to old house owners looking to conserve energy usage is to add insulation to the exterior walls of the house. Rarely is it feasible, let alone advisable, to insulate the walls of an old house: this is because installing wall insulation requires permanently altering the historic fabric of the building or introducing potentially destructive forces the house was never engineered to manage. While the newest insulation materials and techniques achieve significant energy efficiencies with few or none of the health and moisture-related problems associated with forms of insulation promoted after the oil crises of the 1970s, these products are primarily designed for new or recently constructed houses. They are generally not suited for use in historic houses, and the older the house, the greater is the potential that significant features will be adversely affected by their installation.

The two most common wall-insulating materials homeowners encounter for use in existing homes are loose-fill and spray foam (or foamed in place) insulation. Loose-fill insulation, most often composed of cellulose, fiberglass, or mineral wool, is generally blown into cavities in existing walls using hoses to pack the material in tightly and infrared monitors to ensure that insulation reaches irregular or obstructed areas in the walls. Sprayed or foamed in place insulation uses a variety of plastics that expand to completely fill wall cavities with a highly thermally-resistant foam (usually polyurethane or polyisocyanurate). Additionally, spray foam insulation creates superior air sealing and has good moisture controlling properties when installed in conjunction with other ventilation and vapor retarding systems, and achieves a high standard of energy efficiency in new construction.

But foam insulation, which is easily sprayed over the open framing of a house under construction, can only be added to existing finished spaces if the interior wall surface is removed. In a historic home, this could require the removal of original plaster or other potentially significant original or historic finishes. Furthermore, the sprayed foam forms a continuous layer over the entire structural frame, which obscures historic construction details. Most troublesome from a preservation standpoint is the irreversibility of this procedure: a core tenet when adding any new material or feature to a historic structure is that it be capable

(continued)

of being removed without damaging the historic fabric. Once installed, foam insulation cannot be removed, short of scraping it off of the frame.

The other major wall insulation, blown-in loose-fill insulation, only requires drilling small holes in the exterior walls, a relatively easily repaired intervention, but with blown-in materials, a series of other variables must be addressed to prevent problems. The U.S. Department of Energy's Energy Efficiency and Renewable Energy website[2] advises that a home's energy efficiency depends on maintaining a balance between four elements: air sealing, insulation, moisture control, and ventilation. Installing any wall insulation without at the same time sealing for air leakage, providing properly installed vapor barriers to control moisture, and adequately ventilating for interior air quality can cause serious structural and health problems.

Old houses by their nature reflect a host of alterations made by various owners over the life of the structure, alterations that create unforeseeable conditions within that structure. The extent to which the Energy Department's recommended balance can be maintained in an old or historic house is questionable and probably shouldn't be tested by adding blown-in insulation.

INSULATING WALLS FROM OUTSIDE . . .

Another approach to wall insulation recommends adding insulation to the outside of the house. This involves removing all of the exterior siding and trim down to the sheathing boards, applying an exterior housewrap (such as Tyvek or Typar, two typical housewraps on the market) to provide a drainage plane, and then installing one or two layers of two-inch polyisocyanurate insulating rigid foam panels on the exterior wall surfaces. For the owner of a

historic or traditional older house, this approach presents some critical drawbacks, among them the necessity of removing original siding and trim. Wholesale removal and replacement of these materials destroys historic fabric and even when the intent is to reproduce the detailing, the dimensions, workmanship, and appearance of the original is rarely matched, even by conscientious carpenters.

Once the original walls have been encased in 2 to 4 inches of foam panel insulation, other problems arise from the standpoint of retaining historic character: windows, which cannot be moved forward to the new outer plane of the wall, will sit farther back than intended, new trim elements will meet the roof in a different plane, and proportions of other architectural features, such as bays or porches, will meet the thickened walls in unintended ways. The Department of Energy warns that achieving "maximum performance from foam board insulation depends heavily on proper installation"[3] to avoid trapping moisture in the wall cavity. Finally, foam insulation, though hard to ignite, emits toxic gases when burnt. Adding wall insulation, either in the wall cavity or over the building exterior, adversely impacts the historic, architectural, and structural integrity of an old or historic house. For all of these reasons, the most prudent option is to avoid insulating walls.

FOCUS ON THE MAIN LIVING SPACE

Even without insulating walls, old house owners can still achieve important gains in energy efficiency (and comfort) by concentrating on those systems and aspects of the old house structure that can be easily accessed and modified without detriment: First focus on enhancing the energy use within the main living space.

In new construction, the entire interior envelope (attic, main floors, basement) is treated as a single "conditioned" (i.e., heated and cooled) space, within which air sealing, insulation, moisture control, and ventilation have been engineered into one comprehensive, integrated, energy-efficient volume. In historic houses, where attics and basements often function solely as service spaces, conditioned space is almost always confined to the main floors. Focusing on these primary living spaces is the key to achieving a higher standard of energy efficiency in an older or historic house.

"Conditioning" the main living spaces requires minimizing air leakage and reducing heat flow (from the interior to the outdoors in heating season and to the interior from outdoors in cooling season). Minimizing air leakage means caulking and sealing both inside and outside the house; reducing heat flow involves containing heat within the living area by adding insulation to attic floors and sometimes to basements and crawlspaces. Both are relatively easy and inexpensive to complete.

Two different types of caulk or sealant are needed to air seal the house. On the interior, use a water-based latex caulk to seal the perimeters around window and door casings, baseboards, and other moldings. Latex caulk is inexpensive, adheres well, and is paintable. Outside, new hybrid modified-silicone polymers, which combine water-base, silicone and polyurethane products, are more costly but provide the best sealant for exterior joints around windows, doors, and moldings. While the lower edge of clapboards should never be sealed, all other construction joints need to be caulked against air leakage. Seal large gaps and cracks at foundations with expanding polyurethane foam, cutting back any excess once it cures (in exterior applications, polyurethane foam needs to be painted to remain weather resistant).

Adding insulation to basements and attics reduces heat flow between main living spaces and these areas and the outdoors. Again, advice on how and where to add insulation varies when dealing with an older or pre-modern house. The Department of Energy advises insulating basement walls rather than ceilings for a better payback in energy savings, but in most historic houses, "basements" are cellars, unfinished spaces with brick or unmortared fieldstone foundations. It is generally not feasible to insulate this type of wall. Instead, consider sealing gaps (to the outside and first floor), sealing and insulating ductwork, and wrapping hot water pipes to minimize heat loss and air infiltration.

Far more effective is insulating the attic. Heat loss through the roof accounts for a major component of overall heat loss and insulating an attic floor quickly repays the effort. In the attic, floorboards are often loosely laid on top of the joists and can be taken up along with any existing loose-fill or batt insulation laid in the joist spacing.[4] Check for evidence of air infiltration (dirt marks on old batt insulation) and seal gaps with caulk or expanding foam before relaying insulation. Install insulation in joist spacing to the top of the joist and relay flooring; loose-fill insulation is cheaper and easier to install than batts.

KEEP YOUR OLD WINDOWS BUT REPLACE YOUR OLD FURNACE

Keep your existing windows and get them repaired or restored and weather-stripped by one of the many preservation carpenters now specializing in this area. Then, invest in new, heavy-duty storm windows.[5] Spring-bronze weather-stripping,

(continued)

a v-shaped metal strip attached to the sash (or door) using copper-plated steel nails, provides a further seal against air leakage. You'll be saving a valuable architectural resource, one that contributes immeasurably to the authenticity and appearance of your historic house, "reinvesting" the embodied energy of the existing windows, reducing your carbon footprint, *and* saving money on heating and cooling.

Another cost-effective way to "green" your historic house is to update the heating system with a highly efficient new furnace or boiler. All furnaces and boilers are now measured by their annual fuel utilization efficiency (AFUE) and must operate at or above 75% AFUE. Condensing furnaces and boilers, which use the heat generated in combustion condensation to further enhance efficiency, can operate at 90–97% efficiency, saving fuel costs and reducing carbon emissions. Discontinuing use of the heating system flue in a historic chimney and direct-venting a high-efficiency system through the foundation, an existing cellar window, or an unobtrusive wall location will also help to preserve the chimney by eliminating the build-up of destructive creosote and combustion byproducts.

FOR FURTHER INFORMATION

- The most reliable general information source on energy efficiency comes from the Department of Energy's Energy Efficiency and Renewable Energy Building Technologies Program, online at http://www1.eere.energy. gov/buildings/. Remember that the information and advice it contains does not account for historic buildings or significant architectural resources.
- The best technical discussion of the pros and cons of wall and window upgrades for historic buildings is contained in the Association for Preservation Technology's *Special Issue on Sustainability and Preservation,* available at http://www.apti.org/publications/PastBulletin-Articles/bulletin-PR-36-4.pdf.

- The most comprehensive and detailed practical source on energy-related installations in the old or historic house is *Renovating Old Houses: Bringing New Life to Vintage Homes* (Taunton Press, 2003) by George Nash.

- Still useful though it is not recent is *The Old-House Journal Guide to Restoration* (Dutton Adult, 1992), edited by Patricia Poore.

- The National Park Service's Technical Preservation Brief Number 3 "Conserving Energy in Historic Buildings" (1978) by Baird M. Smith (available on line at http://www. nps.gov/history/hps/tps/briefs/brief03.htm) continues to provide relevant information for the old house owner.

- For historic preservation efforts underway to address sustainability in old buildings, see the National Conference of State Historic Preservation Officers website, http:// www.ncshpo.org/current/leed.htm or the Sustainability page of the National Trust for Historic Preservation's website, http://www. preservationnation.org/issues/sustainability/.

---

[2] See http://www.eere.energy.gov/consumer/your_home/insulation_airsealing/index.cfm/mytopic=11220.

[3] See http://www.eere.energy.gov/consumer/your_home/insulation_airsealing/index.cfm/mytopic=11620.

[4] Check http://www.eere.energy.gov/consumer/your_home/insulation_airsealing/index.cfm/mytopic=11390 for warnings on vermiculite insulation or heat sources such as recessed lights, chimneys, fans or flues.

[5] See www.windowrestorationne.org, the Northeast Window Restoration Alliance for repair information.

Source: www.historicnewengland.org/preservation/regional-resources/PRE-regionaltopicsEnergy%20Costs.pdf

Another source of groundwater pollution comes from the common use of commercial fertilizer (made with fossil fuels, every 40-pound bag of lawn fertilizer contains the equivalent of 2.5 gallons of gasoline[18]) and chemical pesticides. Sixty-five percent of the fertilizer put on each yard will end up in runoff.

Homeowners use 20 times more pesticides per acre than farmers.

—U.S. Environmental Protection Agency[19]

According to www.SafeLawns.org, the average American lawn uses about 18 gallons of gasoline per year to power the mower, run the sprinkler system, and transport materials, for an accumulated total of 2.2 billion gallons of gasoline. Yard waste is close to 20 percent of our landfill debris, and landscaping accounts for about half of our residential water use. Avoiding pollutants, conserving water, and using water responsibly are all inextricably linked to environmental, social, and economic sustainability on a global scale.

Figure 9.5 At the Gottfried Regenerative Home, (www.gottfriedhome.com), graywater from the bungalow's bath and sinks, along with captured rainwater, are funneled into nine 50-gallon storage tanks called Rainwater Hogs. Seven feed one of the toilets, as well as providing water to the mostly native plantings. The other two contain graywater that is filtered prior to supplying an automated water system for the grounds. Surplus runoff replenishes groundwater via a shallow basin lined with stone and gravel. © 2008 Open Homes Photography

9.4 MATERIALS—REDUCE, REUSE, RECYCLE, REPAIR, AND RENEW

"1,800 new chemicals are still being introduced in North America each year with little or no toxicity testing. We are the testing laboratory for these chemicals, and most of us have little opportunity for opting out of this experiment."

—Alex Wilson, Your Green Home[20]

the recognition of the overlapping impacts of decisions. Like air, water carries pollutants great distances. Chapter 4 noted that the largest current source of pollution of water in the United States is stormwater runoff contaminated by motor vehicles. Lifestyle decisions that decrease the use of cars benefit watersheds, as does the protection of open land and permeable surfaces. One of the unintended consequences of replacing existing houses in urban neighborhoods with larger residential units that provide for more cars and have more hardscape has been the increase in stormwater runoff.

The precautionary principle comes naturally to those used to dealing with historic buildings. Miracle products of past generations, such as asbestos and lead, are the problems of today. It is quite likely that many of the new miracle products of today will be the problems of tomorrow. Determining what materials to in-

Types of Insulation

Types of insulation that are commonly used include fiberglass batting or rigid-foam panels, but fiberglass, in addition to having microfibers of glass, may contain formaldyhyde. Rigid foam produces chlorofluorocarbon (CFC) in the manufacturing process, damaging the ozone, and may continue to outgas chemicals after installation. Cellulose insulation is made from recycled paper, mostly newspaper, and treated with fire-retardant borate chemicals that also prevent mold and mildew. It can be poured or blown into walls, and a spray-on version is available. Rock wall or mineral wool comes from melting and spinning iron slag, a waste product of pig iron manufacturing which may also be a recycled material. Essentially spun metal, it is fireproof, does not support mold and mildew and is considered to be noncarcenogenic. Cotton batting uses recycled denim scraps thermally bonded without glue.

—SolarToday[23]

troduce into a home is essential to immediate health, and long-term health of our society requires that we consider service life and the requirements of maintenance and renewal.

Calculations completed by the Brookings Institution Metropolitan Policy Program on the loss rates of housing "implies that the typical residential unit lasts about 170 years."[21] The average period of home ownership, however, is from 11 to 14 years per dwelling.[22] The contrast between a continuous change of ownership and buildings that will have a service life of many generations creates a disconnect in how we care for and change our houses.

There are currently few incentives for making regular repairs or using materials that extend the life of the house and benefit future owners, unless the investment has an immediate return in sales value. Prolonging the service life of products, including buildings, is an essential concept of a sustainable world. The longer an object can effectively be in service, the lower the environmental impact from waste management and replacement with new or recycled materials, all with upstream and downstream consequences.

Repairability and product life lie at the heart of many of the perceived conflicts between green advocates and the historic preservation community, both of which believe their position to be best for the environment. Windows are a case in point. Many of the objections about replacement windows by the historic preservation community are not just about aesthetics, but about the quality and service life of the replacement window. Does it make sense to replace a wood window that is very repairable and can last for over a hundred years with a new window that will, in the very best of cases, need to be replaced in 30 years (or quite often, sooner)? What are the upstream and downstream environmental consequences of replacing significant building components, like windows, every 20 to 30 years?

New materials—The use of many new building products often have the unintended consequence of performing in unexpected ways, sometimes encouraging significant moisture accumulation and mold growth. Since wall and roof assemblies have historically been high-risk areas, it should be no surprise that the increased use of new products in these areas can dramatically increase the overall potential of moisture problems within the envelope.

—The Hidden Risks of Green Buildings: Avoiding Moisture and Mold Problems[24]

9.5 CHANGING BEHAVIOR AND OPTIONS—LIVING SUSTAINABLY

"The bottom line is that the way you live in your house can have a tremendous impact on your energy use, regardless of how well built the home is or what energy-saving features you have put into it."

—*Ken Sheinkopf, author of "Ask Ken: Energy-Saving Q&As"*[25]

The results of a survey conducted in the fall of 2008 by researchers at Yale and George Mason universities about American's energy saving behaviors and motivations "suggest that most Americans believe that climate change is a solvable problem if everyone contributes in some way to the solution." Barriers to saving energy are primarily identified as cost, but also include not knowing what to do and not having time to research the options and do the work.[26]

Strategies for educating people about the feasibility and impact of actions are springing up on campuses and in communities utilizing real-time building-energy monitors, carbon challenges, and lively intracampus (refer to Chapter 8) and intracommunity competitions. In the suburbs of Boston, three teams—from Cambridge, Arlington, and Medford—competed in 2008 to see which could make the biggest energy reduction in 12 months in an Energy Smackdown. At the six-month report, 102 households averaged a 33 percent reduction in carbon emissions, a 14 percent reduction in electricity use, and a 37 percent reduction in heating. Strategies and inquiries were shared on a website.

Transportation

The single biggest action that most Americans can take to reduce carbon emissions involves automobile use. Using cars less and more effectively through combined errands, carpooling with only one other person, avoid-

Increase Your Comfort Range with Fans

With fans creating breezes, air conditioning can be comfortably set at 78°F (unless humidity is high). Each increased degree on the thermostat saves approximately 3 to 5 percent on operating costs.

The American Council for an Energy-Efficient Economy[27]

ing sudden acceleration and stops, reducing highway speed by 10 miles per hour, and maintaining tire pressure has the potential of reducing the energy use of a household or individual by 17.6 percent.[28] According to the U.S. Environmental Protection Agency, driving a private car is likely a typical citizen's most polluting daily activity[29] especially since driving 1 mile in the United States uses 37 percent more fuel on average than in Europe, due to larger vehicle size and less-efficient engines.[30]

Good Energy Behavior

Once the car is put away, the water heater is wrapped in insulation and air infiltration has been stopped, good habits that maintain efficiency and a healthy lifestyle include common-sense strategies. Change doesn't require sacrifice, but simply not using energy when it's not needed. Unplug appliances and entertainment units when not in use. Turn off fans and lights when leaving a room. Close and don't fully heat or cool rooms that aren't in use. Line or rack dry clothes if possible, both to save energy and prolong the life of fabrics. Think holistically about ways to decrease chores and increase heath—walk-off mats at doors help keep dust and dirt out of the house (two-thirds of indoor dust is tracked in from the outside).[31]

Hanvey House

North Vancouver, British Columbia, Canada

Current Owner: Kevin Hanvey and Helen Goodland

Building Type: Single-Family Residential

Original Building Construction: 1970

Historic Designation: None

Restoration/Renovation Completion: 2004

Square Footage: 1,620 ft^2

Percentage Renovated: 75% + 25% new construction

Occupancy: 4 people (90 hrs/week) 5 visitors (1 hr/day)

Recognition: Canadian Home Builders' Association of British Columbia Georgie Awards/Best Residential Renovation $200,000 to $400,000, 2005; finalist for Best Kitchen/Great Room Renovation; finalist for Best Environmental Consideration and Energy Efficiency

BUILDING DESCRIPTION

The Hanvey House, built in the 1970s, is the typical age of single-family housing in North America and consequently representative of a vast quantity of housing ready for renovation. The elegant simplicity of a small 300-square-foot addition created an open floor plan to allow natural light and fresh air to flow freely throughout the main living spaces.

Materials

All new materials, appliances, and furnishings introduced into the design were evaluated for their environmental impact and durability. Construction waste was kept to a minimum, and over 50 percent of the demolition debris was reclaimed or recycled. Recyclable materials such as metal scraps, drywall, cardboard, and yard waste were sorted and sent to their respective facilities. Masonry on the original chimney was meticulously removed, cleaned, and reused to form a new brick patio. Dimensional lumber was reused for framework and cedar paneling from the living room was sent to a local park to help construct a new concession stand. All new lumber was Forest Stewardship Council (FCS)-certified to ensure that the wood had been responsibly harvested. The

foundation was constructed of a 35 percent flyash concrete mixture poured over aggregate made from a crushed concrete footpath previously removed from the site.

Water and Site

Inefficient plumbing fixtures were replaced with low-flow faucets and showerheads. New dual-flush toilets were installed utilizing a local rebate incentive. Potable water consumption was reduced by 50 percent and stormwater is now collected and stored for irrigation needs.

Site changes included replacing concrete areas with crushed stone and adding bioswales to allow stormwater runoff to soak into the earth, recharging the groundwater basin as opposed to overflowing the city sewer system.

▲ Figure 9.6 New doors lead to the garden area. Crushed stone and rain garden techniques (Refer to Chapter 4) capture stormwater and allow it to percolate into the ground. Rainwater is also captured in a rain barrel for irrigation of the landscaping, which uses native vegetation. During construction, efforts were made to control erosion and reuse excavated soil. *Photo courtesy of Kevin Hanvey and Helen Goodland*

▶Figure 9.7 The Hanvey House—built in 1970 and shown here before renovation—is similar to the average U.S. housing stock, the majority of which is 35 years old and ready for remodeling (NAHB Housing Facts, Figures and Trends, 2007). The bricks from the chimney were salvaged and reused in the garden terrace. *Photo courtesy of Kevin Hanvey and Helen Goodland*

Figure 2: Proposed site plan
Hanvey House, North Vancouver, BC (builder: T.Q. Construction)

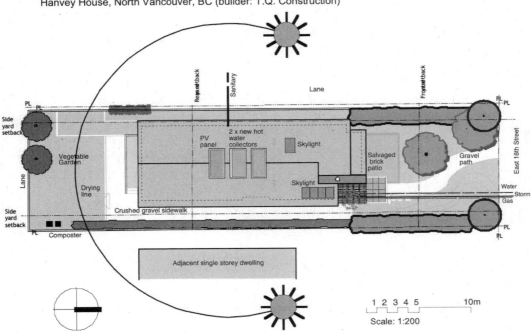

▲ Figure 9.8 Photovoltaic panels, solar hot water, and skylights all contribute to the 35 percent reduction in energy costs. Other strategies included a new, high-efficiency condensing gas furnace. Insulation was added between floor joists at the perimeter. Double-glazed windows were used in the addition, along with draft-proofed or dampered vents, doors, and windows, new weatherstripping at all doors, and an outdoor clothesline in the south-facing yard. *Photo courtesy of Kevin Hanvey and Helen Goodland*

▶ Figure 9.9 The 300-square-foot addition increased the building footprint by less than 20 percent but combined with a more open floorplan, views, and access to the garden, it significantly increases the sense of space and openness. *Photo courtesy of Kevin Hanvey and Helen Goodland*

GREEN DESIGN ELEMENTS

Hanvey House

Sustainable Sites:
- Public transportation proximity
- Permeable paving materials
- Xeriscaping
- Bioswales

Water Efficiency:
- Graywater system
- Low-flow plumbing fixtures
- Dual-flush toilets (rebate program)

Energy and Atmosphere:
- High-efficiency condensing gas furnace
- Natural ventilation
- Additional insulation
- Dual-glazed windows
- New weatherstripping

Materials and Resources:
- Over 50 percent construction waste diverted
- Salvaged materials (bricks, wood)
- Recycled content materials
- 35 percent flyash concrete
- Forest Stewardship Council (FSC)-certified wood
- Locally manufactured materials

Indoor Environment Quality:
- Skylights
- Operable windows
- Low-VOC materials and finishes
- Occupant recycling

PROJECT TEAM

- Kevin Hanvey & Helen Goodland
- Brantwood Design
- T.Q. Construction, Ltd.
- Omicron AEC, Ltd.
- Jeff Vaughn

Solar Umbrella House

Venice, CA

Current Owner: Angela Brooks and Lawrence Scarpa

Building Type: Single-Family Residential

Original Building Construction: 1923

Historic Designation: None

Restoration/Renovation Completion: 2005

Square Footage: 1,790 ft^2

Percentage Renovated: 35% + 65% addition

Occupancy: 3 people (105 hrs) 15 visitors (3 hrs)

Recognition: AIA/COTE Top Ten Green Projects 2006; AIA California Design Merit 2005; *Building Design & Construction* Magazine/Excellence in Residential Home Design 2005; AIA Honor Award for Architecture 2007; AIA Housing PIA Award/Innovation in Housing Design 2006; AIA Los Angeles Honor Award for Design 2005; *Architectural Record* Magazine Record Houses 2005

BUILDING DESCRIPTION

"You can't have a really sustainable building if it's not good design. People won't want to live in it. Playful elements are as important as avoiding waste and living responsibly."

—*Angela Brooks and Lawrence Scarpa*

The Solar Umbrella House reuses an existing 600-square-foot tract home that in many communities would have been a "tear down." The architect/owners took advantage of the architectural diversity of the surrounding neighborhood to create a thoroughly modern and elegant 1,200-square-foot addition that increases lot coverage by only 400 square feet. Winner of multiple awards, including a national AIA Honor Award and a National AIA Committee of the Environment Award in 2006, the design is a compelling demonstration of holistic sustainability where design features perform several roles for functional, formal, and experiential effect.

Figure 9.10 Nestled amid a neighborhood of single- and two-story bungalows, the renovation takes advantage of the through lot to reorganize the residence toward the south. This move creates a new entry and facilitates exposure to the sun with the new solar canopy that meets 95 percent of the electricity needs of the house. *Marvin Rand photo, courtesy of Pugh + Scarpa*

Figure 9.11 What was formerly the front and main entry at the north has become the back. The existing single-story structure located along Boccaccio Avenue was retained and remodeled. A variance was granted for a 13-foot-wide carport (charging ports were provided for the owners' electric car) in lieu of a code requiring an enclosed two-car garage that would have dominated the small, 40-foot-wide street frontage. *Marvin Rand photo, courtesy of Pugh + Scarpa*

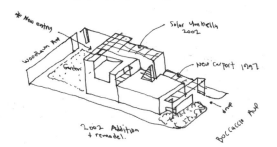

Descriptions of how the house meets the COTE award criteria can be found at www.aiatopten.org/hpb/ in the following categories:

- Sustainable Design Intent and Innovation
- Regional/Community Design and Connectivity
- Bioclimatic Design
- Light and Air
- Water Cycle
- Energy Flows and Energy Futures
- Materials and Construction
- Long Life, Loose Fit
- Collective Wisdom and Feedback Loops
- Project Economics
- Process and Results

Figure 9.12 The existing 600-square-foot structure built in 1923 was retained and remodeled, despite being considered a tear-down. The existing garage was replaced with a smaller carport. Even though the completed structure is three times its original size, the net increase in lot coverage is less than 400 square feet. *© 2008 Pugh + Scarpa Architects, Inc*

Figure 9.13 The orientation and shape of the building and the placement of windows maximized natural daylighting and natural ventilation and provided shading where needed. The building's design and technologies allowed it to achieve a level of energy efficiency that exceeds by more than 50 percent both the California Title 24 Energy Code and local standards set by the city of Santa Monica's Green Building Design and Construction Guidelines, resulting in annual energy bills of less than $300. © 2008 Pugh + Scarpa Architects, Inc.

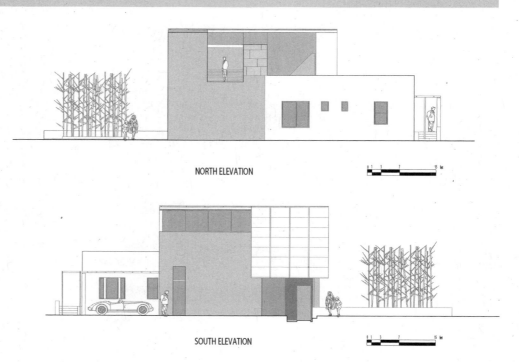

NORTH ELEVATION

SOUTH ELEVATION

Energy Use

A large part of the design of the house is the solar canopy. This solar canopy provides 95 percent of the building's electric load through 89 amorphous silicon solar panels. For the existing house, new insulation was blown into the walls and the roof, and batt insulation was provided under-floor.

Heat is provided through a radiant in-floor heating system (integrated with the solar electricity) for the concrete floors of the new addition. In-floor heating offers a more efficient mode of heating than forced air; air temperatures can be lower and energy uses reduced. 100 percent of the house is daylit and requires no electric light except at night and on overcast days. Lighting control systems are used inside and out to further reduce consumption. Because of the very low power demand of the building, thousands of feet of wire were saved.

Three roof-mounted solar hot-water panels are used: one preheats domestic hot water before it gets to the gas-fired water heater and the other heats the pool. The domestic hot water solar panel has halved the house's natural gas use. Payback for all energy systems is anticipated in approximately ten years.

GREEN DESIGN ELEMENTS
Solar Umbrella House

Sustainable Sites and Water:

- Xeriscaping, minimal turf
- Minimal site coverage and 65 percent permeability
- Minimal construction impact
- Water-efficient appliances, fixtures and irrigation
- 90 percent of precipitation managed on site

Energy and Atmosphere

- Electric vehicle-charging station
- 92 percent naturally ventilated
- 100 percent daylighting
- 90 percent of glazing on south and north elevations
- Building orientation for passive solar heating
- 95 percent of energy from on-site photovoltaic
- Solar hot-water collector
- Energy Star–rated appliances
- Whole-wall R-value of 15

Materials and Resources:

- Cellulose insulation
- Reuse of existing building
- Durable, low-maintenance materials
- Salvaged and recycled materials
- Formaldehyde-free materials
- Locally sourced materials

Indoor Environment Quality:

- Large, high-performance windows
- Natural cross ventilation
- Water-based natural finishes
- East–west axis controls daylighting

Materials

Materials were selected for their effects on indoor air quality; for durability; for low- or no-maintenance characteristics; for absence of formaldehyde content; and for ease of local availability and minimal shipping. Rigid or blown foam insulation made with an HCFC blowing agent was avoided.

BOCCACCIO AVE. ELEVATION

WOODLAWN AVE. ELEVATION

Figure 9.14 Numerous environmental considerations were incorporated in the early design stages of the project. The architects and energy consultant collaborated from the outset to minimize energy use and to find the best ways to use natural features such as sun and prevailing winds. © 2008 Pugh + Scarpa Architects, Inc.

PROJECT TEAM, SOLAR UMBRELLA HOUSE

Pugh + Scarpa
Above Board Construction
Helios International, Inc.
IBE Consulting Engineers
SQLA, Landscape Design
Waste Systems, Inc.

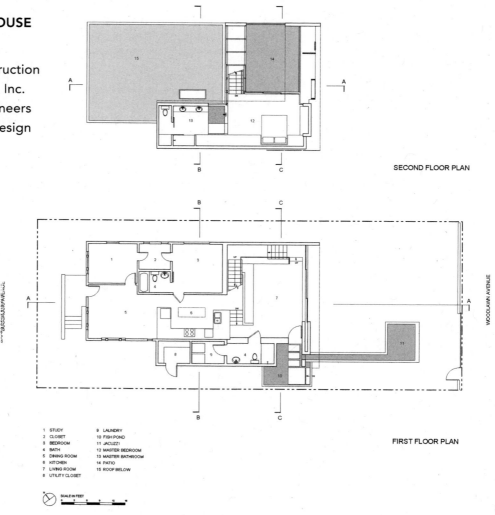

SECOND FLOOR PLAN

FIRST FLOOR PLAN

1	STUDY	9	LAUNDRY
2	CLOSET	10	FISH POND
3	BEDROOM	11	JACUZZI
4	BATH	12	MASTER BEDROOM
5	DINING ROOM	13	MASTER BATHROOM
6	KITCHEN	14	PATIO
7	LIVING ROOM	15	ROOF BELOW
8	UTILITY CLOSET		

SCALE IN FEET

Figure 9.15 The surrounding neighborhood has a density of about 14 dwelling units/acre, and most of the lots and houses are very small compared to the national average. Efficient use of space was seen as important: Some of the furniture is built-in, as in the children's bedroom and the living room, where some furniture incorporates storage). The living room couch is sized so that a portion of it can be used as a queen-sized bed for overnight guests. In the master bedroom on the second floor, a built-in wall of cabinets conceals clothes and drawers and individually controlled lighting for the bed. The design also incorporates a relatively large garden space for such a small lot. © 2008 Pugh + Scarpa Architects, Inc.

Capitol Hill House

Seattle, WA

Current Owner: Ophir Rohen and Io Salant

Building Type: Single-Family Residential

Original Building Construction: 1912

Restoration/Renovation Completion: 2003

Square Footage: 4,200 ft^2

Percentage Renovated: 90% + 10% addition

Occupancy: 3 people (128 hrs) 6 visitors (2 hrs)

Recognition: Master Builders Association of King and Snohomish Counties Built Green Seattle Design Competition/Remodeler Award 2005; Master Builders Association of King and Snohomish Counties Built Green (three stars) 2004

BUILDING DESCRIPTION

The Capitol Hill House demonstrates creative rehabilitation of an existing house on a tight urban site that leaves the footprint of the house unchanged. A new penthouse provides access to a new roof terrace and serves as a light catch and solar chimney for the house while supporting a photovoltaic canopy.

Energy Conservation and Management Systems

Multiple interconnected strategies are used to reduce initial energy needs and maintain optimum operating efficiencies:

- Photovoltaic modules are set up in a "net-metering" format, where the power generated is fed back into the grid, to earn credits, providing about 50 percent of need.
- Solar hot-water collectors coil through the water tank—the boiler is used only for make-up heat for domestic hot water.
- CeBus "smart" whole-house systems monitoring interconnects all major systems (lighting/electrical, HVAC, A/V, PV, security, ventilation, etc.) through the house wiring. All of the systems in the house are integrated into the server room to allow

Figure 9.16 Renovation of the existing 1912 building, previously renovated in 1980, updated the modern look and incorporated "smart" whole-house systems monitoring, hydronic radiant-floor heating, rainscreen siding, wastewater heat recovery, rainwater collection for reuse, bamboo flooring, and efficient lighting, appliances, and systems. The penthouse addition serves multiple purposes, providing access to a new roof deck, chimney ventilation, daylighting, and supporting a photovoltaic system that provides about 50 percent of electricity requirements. *Photo courtesy of Michael Moore*

interaction among them. The alarm and security systems communicate with the lighting controls for energy-use reduction. The audio/visual systems communicate with the security system for enhanced security and monitoring. The PV panels, solar hot-water system, and electrical consumption monitor continually measures inputs and outputs to lessen energy consumption.

- Additional electrical conservation is achieved using ambient light-level monitoring. Electrical consumption is reduced when outside light increases, providing efficient and consistent light levels throughout the house. The home security motion detectors interact with the lighting controls to show occupancy. The "smart" home management system communicates with the lighting control system to turn off lights in unoccupied areas.

- With ever-changing home efficiencies, future-proofing has been a focus. An extensive optical fiber network has been overlaid in the house for future growth. Gigabit communication and interactive coaxial links are provided in every room. Additional future-proofing is provided by the intelligent home manager—new products or systems are integrated into the home using the auto-detect features of the manager.

- A low-tech ventilation system, with fresh-air intake at the server room in the basement (which preheats

Figure 9.17 Capitol Hill House before renovation. *Photo courtesy of Blip Design*

the air at the same time as it cools the computers), and exhaust fans at bathrooms and laundry room act as a whole-house fan.

- Warm wastewater at the showers preheats water supplying the water heater.
- A super-tight, super-insulated envelope uses Icynene blown-in foam.
- New rain-screen siding minimizes heat gain through the walls and allows any moisture that does get behind the siding to evaporate (discouraging moisture build-up behind the drain plane, which can lead to mold and mildew and associated IAQ problems).
- All windows are new double-glazed and argon-filled, with low-E glass.
- Five-eighths-inch drywall is used throughout house to increase thermal mass, and predominantly light-color paints and finishes are used to decrease the need for lighting.

Figure 9.18 The renovation added multiple windows, almost all of them operable. All of the windows use low-emissivity glass, and are double-paned and gas-filled. Rainscreen siding minimizes heat gain through the walls and allows any moisture that does get behind the siding to evaporate. By discouraging moisture build-up behind the drainage plane, the siding reduces the growth of mold and mildew and the indoor-air-quality problems it can cause. *Photo courtesy of Michael Moore*

Figure 9.19 The rear of the house before renovation. *Photo courtesy of Blip Design*

GREEN DESIGN ELEMENTS

Capitol Hill House

Sustainable Sites:
- Public transportation proximity
- Permeable pavement
- Xeriscaping

Water Efficiency:
- Graywater system
- Low-flow plumbing fixtures

Energy and Atmosphere:
- Photovoltaic system
- Solar hot-water collector
- Hydronic radiant floors
- Wastewater heat recovery
- Solar chimney ventilation effect

Indoor Environment Quality:
- Operable clerestory windows
- Low/no-VOC materials and finishes
- Onsite recycling
- Green cleaning policy

PROJECT TEAM

- Ophir Rohen and Io Salant
- BLIP Design
- McGinnis Construction
- Swenson Say Faget
- Northwest Solar Center
- Advanced Radiant Technology, LLC

Adeline Street Urban Salvage Project
Berkeley, CA

Current Owner: Leger Wanaselja Architecture

Building Type: Commercial Office/Multiunit Residential

Original Building Construction: 1906

Historic Designation: None

Restoration/Renovation Completion: 2000

Square Footage: 4,500 ft^2

Percentage Renovated: 95% + 5% addition

Occupancy: 12 people (168 hrs/week)

Awards: AIA/COTE Top Ten Green Projects 2001; *Sunset* magazine Western Home Award 2001

PROJECT DESCRIPTION

"Recombining building elements with discarded auto parts and recycled materials, we created a modern, sun-filled architecture that uses a minimum of new material. The extensive reuse and salvage in this project infuses it with a sense of connection, history, and narrative. Every detail comes alive with a story of origins, disposal and rebirth."

Leger Wanaselja Architecture

The Adeline Street Urban Salvage Project demonstrates the importance of material re-use in objects as large as a house and as small as the bottles repurposed into light fixtures. Raising the 100-year-old house increased the density and functionality of the site by providing two street-level commercial spaces with two living units above.

Figure 9.20 In this project, Leger Wanaselja Architecture remodeled and added to a 100-year-old house and adjacent concrete block shop. All of the existing single-pane aluminum windows were replaced with double-pane wood windows. New triple-glazed skylights on the south added needed solar heat gain and daylighting. Exterior walls and both roofs were insulated. *Photo by Linda Svendsen, courtesy of Leger Wanaselja Architecture*

Figure 9.21 The increase in density and addition of mixed uses, improved energy performance, innovative architectural salvage, minimized construction waste, and nontoxic, low-impact materials used throughout the project demonstrate the compatibility of ecological responsibility and design. © Ethan Kaplan Photography

- Compound curved glass awnings are salvaged hatchbacks from junked sports cars.
- Benches and railings were fabricated from a mix of colorful truck tailgates.
- Discarded road signs satisfied code requirements for wall covering in a bathroom.
- Countertops are either slabs sliced from nearby storm-downed trees or terrazzo tile made of recycled glass.
- Pendant lamps were custom-made from recycled French vinegar bottles.
- Cabinet doors were built from redwood wainscot salvaged from the original house.
- An old water heater was cut in half to create a pair of sculptural water catchment basins.
- During construction, Victorian trim, fixtures, windows, and doors, as well as framing lumber, were carefully saved, sorted and restored as the buildings were stripped, gutted, and transformed.
- Several tons of debris were sorted and reused or recycled—material that typically ends up in a dump.
- Where needed, new wood was sustainably harvested.
- The insulation is blown-in cellulose made from recycled newspapers and phonebooks.
- The new foundation and first floor slab were made with 25 percent fly ash, reducing the use of portland cement.

Figure 9.22 The third floor, originally chopped up into awkward attic rooms, is now an open, sculptured residential space with views to San Francisco Bay. Salvage parts from automobiles are used for guardrails at the stairs. © *Ethan Kaplan Photography*

GREEN DESIGN ELEMENTS

Adeline Street Urban Salvage Project

Sustainable Sites:
- Public transportation proximity
- Permeable paving materials
- Xeriscaping

Water Efficiency:
- Low-flow appliances and plumbing fixtures

Energy and Atmosphere:
- Single-pane windows replaced with double-pane windows
- Additional insulation

- Natural ventilation

Materials and Resources:
- Construction waste recycled
- Extensive use of recycled materials
- Existing building raised (addition below)
- Blown-in cellulose insulation
- 25 percent flyash concrete
- Refurbished existing millwork

Indoor Environment Quality:
- Triple-pane skylights
- Operable windows
- Green cleaning policy

PROJECT TEAM

Leger Wanaselja Architecture

Melissa McDonald Metalworks

Santos and Usrurita

Wake and Bake Landscape

Cliff Niaderer

Chicago Bungalows (Multiple Property Listings)

Chicago, IL

Current Owners: Multiple

Building Type: One-and-one-half-story brick residences, rectangular in shape, with low-pitched roofs with overhang, large windows, stone trim, and central heat, electricity, plumbing, and a basement.

Original Building Construction: Between 1910 and 1940

Historic Designation: Six neighborhoods are listed on the National Register of Historic Places. Bungalows that are certified by the Historic Chicago Bungalow Association must comply with established guidelines in order to receive financial incentives for alterations/improvements.

Restoration/Renovation Completion: Ongoing

Dates of renovation: Ongoing

PROJECT DESCRIPTION

The Historic Chicago Bungalow Association—formed in 2000 by Mayor Richard Daley—provides affordable housing, creates green housing stock and revitalizes Chicago's neighborhoods. There are an estimated 80,000 houses, representing about one-third of Chicago's single-family housing, located between 4 and 8 miles from downtown in the c. 1920s "bungalow belt." Owners certify their houses with the Association for free, although frame structures or bungalows with compromised historic integrity are not eligible. Once a house is certified, owners can apply for low-interest loans or grants of up to $5,000 to help green and restore their homes. There are currently 9,000 certified bungalows.

The bungalows of the 6400 block of South Fairfield, renovated in 2002, serve as models for what can be done to update the houses for contemporary use and environmentally responsible design. This case study combines elements used in all four of the bungalows (classic bungalow, accessible bungalow, home office, dormer loft).

Figure 9.23 Owners who want to "green" a historic bungalow through HCBA have multiple funding opportunities, including the Bungalow energy$avers Program, which can be used for restoration of original wood windows and doors, weatherstripping, insulation, and solar attic fans, among other things. © *Historic Chicago Bungalow Association*

Figure 9.24 A small drilling unit creates a "well" that allows tubing to be inserted in the ground for a residential ground-source heat pump system at several of the model homes. The system either collects heat from the ground and pumps it to a coil inside the ductwork to provide air heating, or it collects heat from the same coil in the ductwork and rejects it into the ground to cool the house. © *Historic Chicago Bungalow Association*

Figure 9.25 Insulating the attic is one of the single most important actions in reducing the energy required to heat and cool a home. Care should be taken to install nontoxic insulation materials (refer to the Healthy Building Network, www.healthybuilding.net) in a manner that does not increase ice dams at the roof's edge and provides proper ventilation to prevent moisture build-up. © *Historic Chicago Bungalow Association*

Figure 9.26 The Historic Chicago Bungalow Initiative provides Design Guidelines that respect the architectural integrity of the existing building. Preserving or restoring original features maintains the integrity of the bungalow and the neighborhood and helps to sustain property values. New landscaping utilizes drought-tolerant indigenous plants in rain gardens (refer to Chapter 4). © *Historic Chicago Bungalow Association*

GREEN DESIGN ELEMENTS

Chicago Bungalows

Sustainable Sites:

- Site Selection: Reuse of an existing building
- Sustainable Site: Redevelopment of four previously vacant buildings
- Landscape: Rear-yard compost recycles biodegradable waste

Water Efficiency:

- Landscape: Use of native plants reduces need for irrigation
- Water Use Reduction: Downspout connected to French drain in sidewalk to collect rainwater and reuse for landscape irrigation

Energy and Atmosphere:

- Heat Island Reduction: Landscaped garage roof absorbs heat (Dormer Loft Bungalow)
- Windows: Front casement and transom windows were replaced with double pane insulated low-E glass. All windows are operable, increasing natural air circulation. Replaced windows match original profile, but replacement material (wood or metal) varies depending on the original design of the bungalow. Wood storm windows were added.
- Energy Conservation: 87 percent high-efficiency sealed combustion, a through-the-wall vented water boiler, and tankless "on-demand" hot-water heaters for the kitchen, bathrooms, and laundry were installed. A combination of insulation (fiberglass batt, rockwool, and spray foam) retains heat between rafters, sidewalls, floor joists, and

exterior walls. A high-velocity air conditioning system was utilized (Classic Bungalow). BioBase, a soy-based insulation, was used and air infiltration between the subfloor and exterior wall was eliminated with fiberglass sheets.

- Renewable Energy: Solar photovoltaic panels were placed on south-facing roof (Dormer Loft Bungalow).

Materials and Resources:

- Building Reuse: Reuse of an existing building
- Resource Reuse: Refurbished vintage lighting fixtures and hardware
- Plumbing fixtures were salvaged and reused.
- Recycled Content: Materials were recycled wherever possible.
- Restoration of existing wood doors, trim, window casements, and floors.
- Recycled materials were used for insulation in the walls, floors, and roof, and recycled content was used for drywall.

Indoor Environmental Quality:

- Daylight and views: Shared light from living room windows into dining room.
- South-facing living rooms introduce natural light to homes to reduce artificial illumination.
- Raised and set-back gable roof addition introduces additional light (Dormer Loft Bungalow).
- Air Quality: Energy-efficient exhaust fans were used in kitchens and bathrooms.
- Low-emitting paints, wood products, and flooring were specified for low emissivity of volatile organic compounds.

ENDNOTES

1. Gerald T. Gardner and Paul C. Stern, "The Short List: The Most Effective Actions U.S. Households Can Take to Curb Climate Change," *Environment* (September/October 2008); http://www.environmentmagazine.org/Archives/Back%20Issues/September-October%202008/gardner-stern-full.html (accessed June 2010).

2. Marilyn A. Brown, Frank Southworth, and Therese K. Stovall, Oak Ridge National Laboratory "Towards a Climate-Friendly Built Environment," Pew Center on Global Climate Change, Arlington, VA (2005), p. 3. Available at www.pewclimate.org.

3. Experian Automative as reported on Auto Spies, www.autospie.com/news/Study-Finds-Americans_Own-2-28-Vehicles-Per-Household-26437/. Accessed March 16, 2009.

4. Alex Wilson and Jessica Boehland, "Small Is Beautiful: U.S. House Size, Resource Use and the Environment," *Journal of Industrial Ecology*, vol. 9 (1–2) (2005): 278.

5. Ibid, p. 278.

6. Adrian Scott Fine, "Approaches to Managing Teardowns," Model Public Policies Forum (March/April 2008), p. 3.

7. Alex Wilson, *Your Green Home* (Gabriola Island, BC: New Society Publishers, 2006), p.18.

8. Gardner and Stern.

9. Energy Information Administration, Annual Energy Outlook 2008, referenced in *National Geographic,* vol. 215 (3) (March 2009): 67.

10. Ibid, p.10.

11. Brown, Southworth, and Stovall, p. 3.

12. Richard Crume, "Home Energy Upgrades That Pay," *Solar Today,* vol. 23 (2) (March 2009); www.ases.org/index.php?option=com_content&view=article&id=517&Itemid=23 (accessed June 2010).

13. J. David Odom, Richard Scott, George H. DuBose, Liberty Building Forensics Group, "The Hidden Risks of Green Buildings: Avoiding Moisture & Mold Problems," NCARB Mini-Monograph 2007, Volume 10 Issue 2 (2007), *Direct Connection: A Publication of NCARB,* Washington, DC.

14. William B. Rose, "Should the Walls of Historic Buildings Be Insulated?" *APT Bulletin,* vol. XXXVI (4), (2005), p. 18.

15. Crume.

16. English Heritage, "Small Scale Solar Electric (Photovoltaics) and Traditional Building" *Energy Conservation in Traditional Buildings* (London: English Heritage, 2008).

17. World Water Assessment Programme, *The United Nations World Water Development Report 3: Water in a Changing World.*(Paris: UNESCO, and London: Earthscan, 2009), p.xix.

18. www.SafeLawns.org. Accessed March 18, 2009.

19. As cited by Misty McNally in "Sustainable Landscaping and Chemical-free Yards: The Earth-Friendly Grass Is Always Greener," *Natural Home* (July/August 2007); www.naturalhomemagazine.com/Garden/2007-07-01/earth-friendly-grass.aspx (accessed June 2010).

20. Wilson, p. 209.

21. Arthur C. Nelson, "Toward a New Metropolis: The Opportunity to Rebuild America," Paper prepared for The Brookings Institution Metropolitan Policy Program, December 2004.

22. Paul Emrath, "How Long Buyers Remain in Their Homes," Report available to the public as a courtesy of HousingEconomics.com (February 11, 2009), www.nahb.org/generic.aspx?sectionID=734&genericContentID=110770. Accessed March 16, 2009.

23. "New Products," *Solar Today* (November/December 2008), p. 56. For more information on cellulose, see www.greenfiber.com; for more information on rock wool, see www.thermafiber.com; for more information on cotton batting, see www.bondedlogic.com.

24. Odom, Scott, and DuBose, p.3.

25. Ken Sheinkopf, "Wasting Energy in a High-Efficiency House," *Solar Today* (March 2009).

26. Yale Project on Climate Change, George Mason University Center for Climate Change Communications "Saving Energy at Home and on the Road: A Survey of Americans' Energy Saving Behaviors, Intentions, Motivations, and Barriers" (2009).

27. American Council for an Energy-Efficient Economy, Consumer Guide ot Home Energy Savings Condensed online version, Cooling Equipment, Step 4; www.aceee.org/consumerguide/cooling.htm#improve, accessed June 8, 2010.

28. Gardner and Stern, p.18

29. www.epa.gov/epahome/trans.htm. Accessed March 17, 2009.

30. McKinsey Global Institute, "Wasted Energy: How the U.S. Can Reach Its Energy Productivity Potential" (June 2007), www.mckinsey.com/mgi.

31. Asthma Regional Council, "Building Guidance for Healthy Homes" (2002). Available at www.asthmaregionalcouncil.org.

chapter 10

THE RECENT PAST

10.1 The Recent Past—Modern Architecture, Boomer Buildings

10.2 Preservation Challenges

10.3 Environmental Dilemmas

10.4 Strategies for Renewal

10.5 Lessons Learned

10.1 THE RECENT PAST— MODERN ARCHITECTURE, BOOMER BUILDINGS

"From futuristic coffee shops and soaring airport terminals to the homes of the postwar suburbs, twentieth-century architecture embodies the aspirations, priorities, challenges and successes of our recent history."

—*The National Park Service Recent Past Initiative*[1]

OF THE APPROXIMATELY 63 billion square feet of existing commercial space in the United States, about 80 percent has been constructed since World War II[2] and is loosely defined by the term "recent past," although the same term is sometimes limited to architecture less than 50 years old[3] and stretched to encompass "modern architecture." Theodore H. M. Prudon, in his book *Preservation of Modern Architecture*, defines modern architecture as "the architecture of the recent past" and sets the timeline as the "preservation of building stock dating from the beginning of the twentieth century to about 1975."[4] The firm of Mitchell | Giurgola Architects used the term "boomer buildings" in a 2005 book of the same name to describe the designs created in the three decades after WWII in the heyday of cheap oil.[5]

Whatever the exact title or calendar limits, the spectrum of building type and style built in the twentieth century—and particularly post-WWII—is vast, ranging from the mundane strip shopping center to high-rise glass office towers and concrete buildings created for education, religion and government.

Figure 10.1 An example of architecture of the "Recent Past," the Dreyfus Chemistry Laboratories Building, dedicated in 1970, was the first of three major structures designed by I. M. Pei at the Massachusetts Institute of Technology. Built to house most of the MIT Chemistry Department, it still serves as the university's largest single research facility, comprising 14 faculty lab groups. Designated 2004 Renovated Laboratory of the Year by *R&D* magazine after a thorough interior reconfiguration, the building appears unchanged on the exterior. © *Anton Grassl/Esto*

Often facilitated by wide-scale urban redevelopment, which required the demolition of large tracts of existing buildings, late twentieth-century architecture and landscape is frequently the product of tremendous idealism, a fact often ignored by New Urbanists, who brand the designs as "unlovable."

"One should recall," writes Maristella Casciato, chairwoman of Docomomo International, "that the main objectives of the majority of the Modern Movement was to build projects that were rational, functional, innovative, and rich, with strong political and cultural identities—futuristic in all senses, and at all costs, and bathing in an optimistic faith in progress."[6] Docomomo is the abbreviated acronym for The International Working Party for Documentation and Conservation of Buildings, Sites and Neighborhoods of the Modern Movement, an international organization established in 1988 out of concern for the increasing demolition of buildings not deemed "historic" by age.

An optimistic faith in technical progress encouraged dependence in the twentieth century on mechanical and electrical systems for user comfort. Nevertheless it is just as erroneous to assume that all buildings of the recent past lack passive-design attributes as it is to assume that all buildings of the nineteenth century are well-constructed or durable. The sandstone cladding widely used in the nineteenth century hasn't proven as long-lived a building material as desirable; in a similar vein, the new technologies and materials of the twentieth century haven't always succeeded. The same complaints are now being recorded about new "green" materials (refer to Chapter 7).

Given the vast inventory of twentieth-century buildings, the challenges and importance of reuse or preservation for both cultural and environmental reasons is immense. The framework of the physical problems, however, might not differ very much from that encountered in the stewardship of "historic" properties.

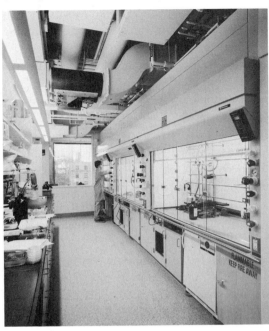

◀ **Figure 10.2** Buildings are most vulnerable to demolition around 30 years after construction, when a renovation is needed and the character of a space or building has been lost and/or no longer functions well. Renovations, such as the Dreyfus Chemistry Laboratories Building (see Figure 10.1) illustrate a change from a dark, crowded, claustrophobic interior to one that is open and bright and fully functional. Shown is a typical modular laboratory, reconfigured to improve access, flexibility, and daylight penetration. © *Anton Grassl/Esto*

▼ **Figure 10.3** Renovation of the Dreyfus Chemistry Laboratories Building (see Figure 10.1) provided 40 percent more chemical fume-hood space for each researcher while maintaining existing supply-air volume and reducing building floor area dedicated to supply and exhaust shafts. Reconception of the interior layout used interior glazing to open up the central lab zone, previously deprived of daylight, to extensive visual connections with the outdoors. Replacement of the existing glass with insulated low-E glazing in an unobtrusive frame has improved thermal comfort along walls where student desks and offices are located. Creative and knowledgeable design plays as valuable a role in the renewal of buildings as it does in the creation of new buildings—and renovation is far better for the environment. © *Goody Clancy*

Buildings built for one purpose often need to be renewed for another; values such as universal design not considered originally must be accommodated; materials manufactured years ago must be replaced, restored, or re-created; standards for environmental performance must be implemented or restored (see the case studies at the end of this chapter); and, as always, materials once thought to be benign but now understood to be toxic must be removed.

The biggest challenge that confronts the use of the recent past is a loss of cultural memory and appreciation for the reasons the buildings were created in the first place. We risk continuing the same attitude of throw-away consumerism that spawned many of the very buildings now in need of renovation and/or rehabilitation.

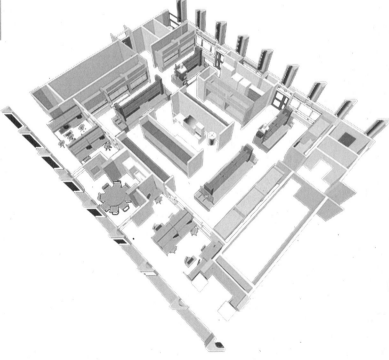

10.2 PRESERVATION CHALLENGES

"One of the greatest challenges currently facing us is persuading others that post-war architecture and landscapes do have historic significance and therefore are worth saving. It's not a new problem: Many nineteenth-century Parisians thought the Eiffel Tower was an eyesore, and it hasn't been long since Victorian buildings were considered ugly and Art Deco wasn't worth noticing, much less preserving. It takes time for people to fully appreciate historic significance and artistic merit— but while art, music, and literature can simply wait for their day to come, unappreciated buildings tend to disappear."

—*Richard Moe, President Emeritus, National Trust for Historic Preservation[7]*

Ada Louise Huxtable describes historic preservation as "a maverick movement begun by little old ladies in tennis shoes fighting bulldozers in the urban renewal demolition wars of the 1960s."[8] It should not surprise us that a movement born of reaction to "progress"— then defined as the destruction of historic urban architecture and the loss of huge tracts of farmland to make way for new schools, suburbs, strip centers, malls, factories, and offices[9]—has not moved quickly to protect "new" buildings as they age. The advocacy of the 1960s and 1970s spawned an anti-modern bias[10] in the preservation community that persists.

The anti-modernist bias ignores the fact that the post–World War II period enjoyed strong economic growth; that its architecture emphasized social values of modernity, industry and economy; and that it relied on new industrial techniques, processes, and products that were part of the times. The real challenge in renovating these buildings is to promote the values that shaped the forms, not just the forms themselves.[11]

This applies to not just the iconic structures, such as Paul Rudolf's 1963 Art and Architecture Building at Yale, recently restored to "its original intention,"[12] but also to the large-scale planned landscapes and urban areas that often accompanied these buildings. A challenging example is the 9 acres of brick paving that serve as a plaza for the 1969 Boston City Hall. Both plaza and City Hall were part of an urban-renewal project that demolished 90 acres of vernacular buildings considered part of a colorful but undesirable entertainment district. Architectural and landscape

---

Docomomo Mission

In the last past few decades, the architectural heritage of the modern movement appeared more at risk than during any other period. This built inheritance glorifies the dynamic spirit of the Machine Age. At the end of the 1980s, many modern masterpieces had already been demolished or had changed beyond recognition. This was mainly because many were not considered elements of heritage, their original functions had substantially changed, and their technological innovations had not always endured long-term stresses.

DOCOMOMO'S MISSION IS TO:

- Act as watchdog when important modern movement buildings anywhere are under threat.
- Exchange ideas relating to conservation technology, history and education.
- Foster interest in the ideas and heritage of the modern movement.
- Elicit responsibility toward this recent architectural inheritance.

www.docomomo.com

historians consider both building and plaza worth saving: The Cultural Landscape Foundation named the plaza to its 2008 list of endangered Marvels of Modernism, and the National Trust for Historic Preservation has joined the groups working to protect the once internationally celebrated City Hall, which was hailed as a symbol of a "New Boston" but is now considered an eyesore by many Bostonians.[13]

The 40-year-old City Hall has never been renovated, and like every aging building, it no longer performs either as designed or as it might with improvements. Ada Louise Huxtable describes it as being "systematically and willfully destroyed by abusive neglect, aggravated malfunction, and spreading bureaucratic blight,"[14] a situation common to other buildings of similar age but far less noteworthy. Lack of maintenance and stewardship is symptomatic of a "throwaway" culture (see Chapter 7).

10.3 ENVIRONMENTAL DILEMMAS

"Even on their best days, Boomer Buildings were not easy to love. They had (and in many cases continue to have) substandard heating and air conditioning systems, poor lighting, minimal chase space, drafty exterior walls, asbestos and other toxic materials, crumbling concrete exposing rusting rebar, not to mention hostile urban manners, contextual indifference, and monumental invulnerability."

—*Michael J. Crosbie, PhD, AIA*[15]

Boomer Buildings comprise the vast group of buildings built between 1953 and 1974 that, statistically, show a complete disregard for operational energy. If identified by period, however, the poorest energy performance occurs in commercial buildings constructed between the world wars and from 1960 through

Energy Consumption for Commercial Buildings (Other Than Shopping Malls)

Construction Date	Average Energy UseBtu/ft²	Approximate Square Feet
Before 1920	80,127	4 billion
1920–1945	90,234	7 billion
1946–1959	80,198	7 billion
1960–1969	90,976	8 billion
1970–1979	94,968	11 billion
1980–1989	100,077	10.5 billion
1990–1999	88,834	12.5 billion
2000–2003	79,703	2.5 billion

Source: US Energy Information Administration, 2003

1999, peaking in the 10.5 billion square feet built between 1980 and 1989. Buildings of the 1980s use 20 percent more energy per square foot than buildings built either in the twenty-first century, immediately after WWII, or before 1920, all of which have an energy intensity of about 80,000 Btu a square foot.

Not only are many of the twentieth-century buildings poor performers in terms of energy but the construction materials often contain, in addition to asbestos, toxic materials, metals, and chemicals that were considered benign miracle products (refer to Chapter 5). The concentration of PCBs is ten times higher in buildings dating from 1950 to 1979 than in buildings built after 1980, when polychlorinated biphenyls (PCBs) were banned. The level is four times higher than pre-1950.[16] Used in caulking, grout, paints, and sealants, and as additive to concrete, PCBs are persistent bioaccumulative toxicants that do not break down naturally and can last for decades, building up in living organisms and increasing in concentration as they move up the food chain.

Sustainability, A Modern Movement

According to Nina Rappaport, the early Modern Movement incorporated "back to nature," "light and air," and "Life Reform" philosophies while integrating many untested "sustainable" technologies as building elements, such as airflow systems, and lighting and shading devices, with structure and form. Architects such as Le Corbusier often made comparisons of the flow of the city to the body, and buildings' internal systems were anthropomorphized as holistic organisms. Paul Scheerbart stressed the importance of glass that would "remove the sense of enclosure from the space in which we live." And Rudolph Schindler focused on bringing the outside in to improve the mind.

—*Nina Rappaport, "Sustainability, A Modern Movement"*[17]

United Nations Renovations

The United Nations is beginning renovations on both its New York City complex, opened in 1952, and its historic office in Geneva to achieve large energy-savings and a reduced carbon footprint. The Geneva complex includes the original home of the League of Nations, now 80 years old.[20]

Renovations of the 39-story glass-and-steel curtain wall of the UN's Secretariat will replace asbestos-insulated panels with a new efficient envelope that will also be completely blast-proof. A range of planned green features is expected to reduce energy consumption by at least 40 percent and serve as a model for other buildings.[21]

10.4 STRATEGIES FOR RENEWAL

"In an age of diminishing natural resources...architects and their clients need to know about an environmentally sustainable alternative to new construction: new life for old buildings, especially boomer buildings. It's a more sustainable approach...that builds on the past and makes the old better than new.

Michael J. Crosbie and Mitchell/Giurgola Architects[18]

Strategies for renewal of twentieth-century buildings, like all renewal, must respond to the cultural importance of the building. For example, the restoration of New York City's Lever House, considered one of the first and most beautiful of modern skyscrapers, re-

quired replacement of the original glass curtain wall with a modern wall that meets energy codes but matches the original appearance. Renovation of the less culturally important 1964 fourteen-story headquarters of The Lighthouse was accomplished by stripping the building back to its structural frame and installing a new, high-performance envelope that also admits more natural light.[19]

In an exploration of Canadian Modernism, Susan Ross, former co-chair of the Technical Committee on Sustainable Preservation of the Association for Preservation Technology, and a senior conservation architect with Heritage Conservation Directorate, Public Works and Government Services, outlined potential strategies for improving the environmental sustainability of typical twentieth-century buildings:

Sustainable Site Design

Issue—Dark-colored flat roofs contribute to urban heat island, with hard-surfaced site planning evacuating rainwater to storm sewers.

Solution—New reflective roofing and/or green roof and site modifications will utilize pervious pavement and stormwater-retention techniques.

Issue—Low-density monofunctional development has high proportions of roads and parking lots.

Solution—Intensification through infill and additions, and incorporation of new services and amenities, including pedestrian and bicycle circulation.

Issue—Limited use of vegetation, building orientation and topography for natural cooling/ventilation.

Solution—Addition of shade trees and additions to buildings to improve wind, sun, etc.

Energy Conservation

Issue—Single glazing, thermal bridging, inadequate insulation or vapor barriers, and lack of shading.

Solution—Overcladding, partial or complete envelope replacement, and additional solar controls.

Issue—Inefficient heating, cooling and ventilation, and interior and exterior light design and control systems.

Solution—Mechanical system and light-fixture and control adaptation or replacement, change in use patterns.

Issue—Building design and systems rely on the use of transported fossil fuels.

Solution—Adaptation of systems to renewable energy and power sources such as ground-source heat pumps, solar and wind sources.

Water Conservation

Issue—Inefficient plumbing fixtures use high levels of water for flushing.

Solution—Plumbing-fixture adaptation or replacement to reduces consumption and waste.

Issue—Building design and systems rely on treated water for all plumbing needs.

Solution—Development of graywater-storage and distribution capacity.

Issue—Landscape water features or irrigation use potable water.

Solution—Use of graywater and recirculating systems for vegetation and integration of cisterns.

Materials and Resources

Issue—Complex assembly details involve multiple materials, dependent on the durability of the weakest (e.g., sealants, coatings, and other synthetic surface finishes intended to be low-maintenance but degraded by UV and other atmospheric conditions).

Solution—Monitor, maintain, and repair the weakest to prolong life-cycle improvement of these materials when replacement is considered (e.g., by developing strategies for disassembly and repair). May also lead to overcladding and other envelope changes.

Issue—Use of experimental materials or materials in combinations that have poor service quality (e.g., plastics), and some use of materials that require massive amounts of transportation and manufacturing energy for construction (e.g., aluminum).

Solution—Repair and continued use of these materials to make best use of previous investments, but consider alternatives where replacements are required, or use of salvaged materials where available.

Issue—Use of exotic materials from endangered tree species, or sites of exploitation, have devastated habitats and traditional uses of land (e.g., teak in Africa).

Solution—Repair and continue use of these materials to make best use of previous investments, but also consider alternatives where replacements are required, or ensure that new sources of same materials are sustainably managed.

Reduction of Waste

Issue—Poor durability, short life cycle, or poor re-pairability of building materials and elements.

Solution—Replace existing or new materials and elements with longer-life materials.

Issue—Building service spaces are based on garbage collection.

Solution—Adapt building service spaces to recycling services.

Issue—Obsolescence of large-scale structure intended to be adaptable but actually suited to a single function.

Solution—Zoning and planning adaptation to allow for alternative uses of spaces, including mixed uses.

Exterior Effluents and Pollution

Issue—Use of materials whose manufacturing or assembly processes involve adhesives, preservatives, and other toxic chemicals, such as glues in wood composites or creosote on exposed wood.

Solution—Where materials used on the interior have previously off-gassed, carry out repair and continue to make best use of previous investments, but also consider alternatives where replacements are required.

Issue—Use of asbestos for finishes and insulation or other problem building materials.

Solution—Encapsulate or remove, depending on use, and replace with compatible substitutes.

Issue—Use of materials that have poor durability in reaction to acid, gases, sulphates, and salts.

Solution—Monitor, maintain, and investigate potential protective measures, or strategies for replacement in part or completely. Might also lead to overcladding solutions.

Healthy Indoor Environments

Issue—Lack of operable windows, and related dependence on mechanical equipment for ventilation.

Solution—Provide alternative sources of natural ventilation (atriums, overcladding with double-skin walls), or retrofit existing windows to make operable where feasible.

Issue—Inadequate sources of daylight means dependence on artificial lighting.

Solution—Provide new sources for daylighting (atriums, light wells, skylights).

Issue—Poor control of solar radiation.

Solution—Add compatible solar controls, including architectural and plant solutions.[22]

Figure 10.4 Harvard University renovated a 1960s reinforced-concrete structure (see Figure 10.5) for student housing in Cambridge, Massachusetts. An eight-foot structural grid and low floor-to-floor dimensions are countered by large operable windows with views into an exterior courtyard. *Richard Mandlekorn photo, courtesy of Goody Clancy*

National Geographic Society Building Improvements

In 2003, the National Geographic Society completed upgrades on its 835,000-square-foot complex of buildings in Washington, D.C., which range in age from 1902 to 1984 and include the "17th Street Building" designed by Edward Durell Stone, which opened in 1963.

Upgrades included chiller replacements, generator upgrades, and boiler replacement after a comprehensive energy audit. Other upgrades included:

- Low-E window films for solar control.
- Integration of all HVAC controls into one direct-digital control system.
- A comprehensive lighting upgrade, including electronic ballasts, T-8 lamps, and LED exit signs.
- Occupancy- and daylight-based lighting controls.
- Variable-frequency drives on fans, motors, and pumps throughout the facility.
- Zone-isolation dampers, allowing control over which areas are conditioned during after-hours use of the facility.
- Upgrade of seven older traction elevators to electronic controls and drives.

- Elimination of CFCs from numerous chiller and refrigeration applications.
- Replacement of halon-based fire-suppression systems with environmentally friendly alternatives.
- Moisture sensors on all irrigation systems.
- Ultraviolet and filtration systems and sophisticated monitoring to reduce chemical biocide usage in HVAC systems.
- Installation of a white EPDM reflective roof membrane.
- Use of environmentally friendly cleaning products and HEPA-type vacuum cleaners.
- Upgrading of air filters in all air-handling units to 95 percent efficiency.
- CO_2-based monitors and controls for outside air to avoid excessive ventilation while ensuring safety

The National Geographic Society expects to save 1,850 MWh of electricity and 13,600 therms (1,400 GJ) of natural gas annually. The project used the LEED-EB system.[23]

Figure 10.5 The 1960s buildings shown before renovation shows the lack of daylight. It is not always appropriate in an historic building to remove the exterior skin, but reusing the structure and frame in this case avoided the environmental impacts of the construction waste and the upstream degradation and carbon bubble created by new materials. © Goody Clancy

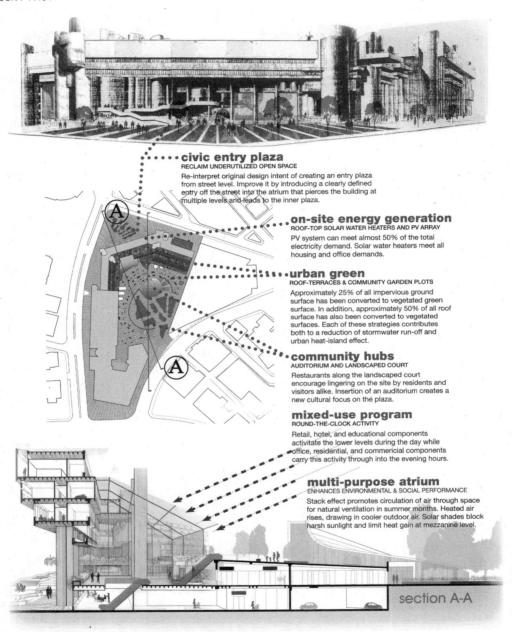

civic entry plaza
RECLAIM UNDERUTILIZED OPEN SPACE
Re-interpret original design intent of creating an entry plaza
from street level. Improve it by introducing a clearly defined
entry off the street into the atrium that pierces the building at
multiple levels and leads to the inner plaza.

on-site energy generation
ROOF-TOP SOLAR WATER HEATERS AND PV ARRAY
PV system can meet almost 50% of the total
electricity demand. Solar water heaters meet all
housing and office demands.

urban green
ROOF-TERRACES & COMMUNITY GARDEN PLOTS
Approximately 25% of all impervious ground
surface has been converted to vegetated green
surface. In addition, approximately 50% of all roof
surface has also been converted to vegetated
surfaces. Each of these strategies contributes
both to a reduction of stormwater run-off and
urban heat-island effect.

community hubs
AUDITORIUM AND LANDSCAPED COURT
Restaurants along the landscaped court
encourage lingering on the site by residents and
visitors alike. Insertion of an auditorium creates a
new cultural focus on the plaza.

mixed-use program
ROUND-THE-CLOCK ACTIVITY
Retail, hotel, and educational components
activate the lower levels during the day while
office, residential, and commericial components
carry this activity through into the evening hours.

multi-purpose atrium
ENHANCES ENVIRONMENTAL & SOCIAL PERFORMANCE
Stack effect promotes circulation of air through space
for natural ventilation in summer months. Heated air
rises, drawing in cooler outdoor air. Solar shades block
harsh sunlight and limit heat gain at mezzanine level.

section A-A

Figure 10.6 Ideas for the greening of Paul Rudolph's 1970 Lindemann Mental Health Center in Boston,
Massachusetts, illustrate the many opportunities available in existing buildings regardless of style. Team "Redo
Rudolph" won 1st place and the People's Choice Award in the 2008 USGBC Talent Design Competition in the
Boston Region and received Honorable Mention at the national level. *Design and diagram by Priya Jain, Marta
Morais-Storz, Matt Morong, and Dana Ozik*

10.5 LESSONS LEARNED

> "...maybe we can also learn something from this past, its optimism, and its interest in improving the quality of life, not just for a few but for everybody."
>
> —*Theodore H. M. Prudon,*
> *Preservation of Modern Architecture*[24]

The buildings of the twentieth century do not represent an easy problem. Whether iconic or pedestrian, they are not always "lovable," but they do exist—and they constitute the bulk of our building stock and account for most of the energy consumed and carbon created in this country. Rife with controversy within the historic preservation community and using once-inventive new materials that are now challenging to restore, they offer lessons in humility as well as demanding even more creative design and respect for reuse.

The protection and reuse of this building stock, both iconic and mundane, poses myriad challenges for cultural and environmental sustainability, but to continue the pattern of demolition and new construction that the recent past represents seems obviously unsustainable and remarkably similar to the path that brought us to the current crisis in climate change.

The case studies demonstrate the reuse and rehabilitation of buildings constructed in the latter half of the twentieth century, including an iconic glass building of modern design. See case studies in Chapter 2 (The Chicago Center for Green Technology, originally built in 1952), Chapter 8 (Eastern Village Co-housing Condominiums, built in 1957), and Chapter 6 (Alberici Corporate Headquarters, built in 1958).

> "The preservation of buildings, structures, or sites in any form is about much more than merely saving their material existence. In contrast to the heritage of earlier periods, architecture and design of more recent vintage represents the ideals and philosophy of the original architects, their clients and subsequent occupants, many of whom are well-known and still alive. Capitalizing on those visions is far more complex than ever before, but is as much a part of the preservation process as the preservation of the physical fabric. These intentions are the most difficult to capture, the hardest to interpret, and the most complicated to defend for an architecture that is often so much more the result of theoretical concepts than the buildings of earlier periods. At the same time, maybe we can also learn something from this past, its optimism, and its interest in improving the quality of life, not just for a few but for everybody."
>
> —*Theodore H. M. Prudon,*
> *Preservation of Modern Architecture*[25]

> "Many modern buildings now represent a degree of restraint and modesty that provides a welcome, not to say urgent, lesson today in the age of the McMansion."
>
> —*Paul Goldberger*[26]

Karges-Faulconbridge Office Building
Roseville, MN

Current Owner: Bill Karges and Jim Faulconbridge

Building Type: Commercial Office

Original Building Construction: 1972

Restoration/Renovation Completion: 2003

Square Footage: 33,400 ft^2

Percentage Renovated: 99% + 1% new

Occupancy: 100 people (40 hrs/week) 10 visitors (1–2 hrs/day)

Recognition: LEED EB Pilot—Gold; Minnesota Governor's Award for Excellence in Waste and Pollution Prevention 2006; Seven Wonders of Engineering Award 2005

PROJECT DESCRIPTION

The Karges-Faulconbridge offices demonstrate the creative and cost-effective reuse of a mundane but prevalent building type. A major engineering firm with a commitment to sustainable practices, Karges-Faulconbridge, Inc. created a modern, light-filled office out of a derelict 1970s Jubilee Foods store on a four-acre paved lot. By reusing the building's existing shell, KFI estimated a savings of $40 per square foot over new construction, significantly reduced the consumption of new materials, and recycled 80 percent of deconstruction debris, mostly asphalt removed from the heavily paved site.

Site and Water

The project shrank site parking and restored formerly paved areas to a natural prairie-style landscape. The combination of added vegetation, swales, and retention ponds increased green space by 54 percent, reduces the heat island effect, and retains stormwater on site. Waterless urinals and sensor-triggered faucets lower water use by 51 percent. At the time of construction, waterless urinals were not legal in Minnesota, but KFI won a variance for a trial installation.

Figure 10.7 The lobby features recycled rubber flooring, natural daylighting, and an antique air compressor. Substantial use of environmentally responsible materials included postindustrial waste structural steel, acoustical ceilings, acoustical sound panels, ceramic tile, and carpeting, as well as natural linoleum. *Jim Gallop Photography*

▲ **Figure 10.8** The original building had no windows. KFI's reconfiguration features windows for all exterior offices and provides daylighting to the interior spaces with north-facing vertical monitors on the roof. The landscaping around the building employs native prairie grasses, wildflowers and an "eco-grass" rather than the traditional but high-maintenance bluegrass. *Jim Gallop Photography*

◄ **Figure 10.9** Typical of commercial buildings from the 1970s, the Jubilee Foods site presented a vast expanse of parking with minimal green space. The building reuse, which served as a LEED for Existing Buildings pilot project, recovered about 800 tons of recycled materials—more than 90 percent of which was recycled asphalt. Greenspace was increased 54 percent on the site. *Photo courtesy of Pope Architects*

GREEN DESIGN ELEMENTS

Karges-Faulconbridge Office Building

Sustainable Sites and Water Conservation:
- Energy Star–rated roof
- Hardscape surface removal
- Xeriscaping (native prairie plantings)
- Stormwater-management ponds
- Bioswales
- Automatic sensor faucets (self-charging)
- Waterless urinals

Energy & Atmosphere:
- Ground-source heat pumps
- Infrared heating
- Radiant ceiling panels (bathroom)
- Displacement and heat-recovery ventilation (desiccant wheel)
- Transient-voltage surge-suppression system

Materials and Resources:
- Over 80 percent of construction debris recycled
- Post-consumer recycled content
- Recyclable materials
- Locally manufactured materials

Indoor Environment Quality:
- Added/enlarged windows
- Vertical monitors/clerestory windows

Additional Features:
- Occupant recycling program
- Green cleaning policy (Green Seal 37 products)
- Environmental tours

Energy

The KFI offices utilize a ground-source heat pump coupled with both infrared and radiant heating systems. Infrared heating utilizes the masonry building's thermal-massing properties to maximize efficiency. The ventilation system combines displacement and waste-heat recovery techniques with a desiccant wheel that manages humidity levels within the building. Lighting levels can be adjusted to take full advantage of natural daylight, which has been augmented with new clerestory monitors and exterior windows.

Green Cleaning and Recycling

The firm adopted a green cleaning policy in an effort to keep harmful chemicals out of the office and employs Green Seal 37 products with automatic dispensers that ensure the correct amount of solution for each job at hand. Recycling of all office materials is standard.

Figure 10.10 The central location of the plotting and catalog area makes it easily accessible from all offices within the building. The building core also features infrared heating and daylighting. Multilevel switching of lighting cuts light wattage by one-third. The bright and vibrant atmosphere for employees and visitors is intended to increase productivity and decrease absenteeism. *Jim Gallop Photography*

PROJECT TEAM, KARGES-FAULCONBRIDGE OFFICE BUILDING

Karges-Faulconbridge, Inc.

Pope Associates

Clark Engineering

Sunde Land Surveying Inc.

Roof Spec

Kvernstoen Kehl Associates

Hilscher Design & Ecology Inc.

VAC Systems Inc.

Crown Hall (Illinois Institute of Technology)
Chicago, IL

Current Owner: Illinois Institute of Technology

Building Type: Higher Education/Offices

Original Building Construction: 1956

Restoration/Renovation Completion: 2005

Square Footage: 52,800 ft^2

Percentage Renovated: 100%

Occupancy: 15 people (20-40 hrs/week), 500 visitors (40+ hrs/week)

Recognition: Chicago Architecture Foundation Patron of the Year 2007; AIA Chicago Citation of Merit 2006; Landmarks Preservation Council of Illinois Project of the Year 2006; Commission of Chicago Landmarks Award of Preservation Excellence 2005

PROJECT DESCRIPTION

The renovations of S.R. Crown Hall at the Illinois Institute of Technology reestablished and improved upon the original active and passive techniques designed by architect Ludwig Mies van der Rohe in the 1950s, which were themselves altered during build-

Figure 10.11 The original design of Crown Hall used monolithic sandblasted glass to diffuse incoming light. Sandblasting diffuses light but does not absorb it, resulting in no significant increase in surface temperatures over the ambient condition. Because the appearance is crucial to the experience of Crown Hall, the design team evaluated a wide number of potential glazing alternatives to re-create the original experience while incorporating lamination, now required by code, and improving thermal performance. *Photography by Todd Eberle*

ing "upgrades" in the 1970s and 1980s. The design team for the renovations describes the intended operation of the building as equivalent to sailing a fine yacht, with knowledgeable participation of building users throughout the day to adjust blinds, lights, and louvers. The passive-solar strategies and natural ventilation incorporated in the original design contradict the common belief that modernist architecture favored mechanical dependencies with disregard for the natural environment.

Integrated Design
The original landscape design at Crown Hall was integral to a cooling strategy for the building, with trees planted on the western side so that long shadows would stretch across the structure and significantly reduced solar gain. Operable interior blinds were actively utilized, and the windows incorporated monolithic sandblasted glass panels that diffused natural light without absorbing heat. Operable vents at the perimeter of the building, combined with an open floor plan, allowed fresh air to flow through the space during the day and brought cool air in at night. A zoned radiant floor system for heating addressed each section of the building separately and efficiently.

Reduced Performance with Early Renovations
The building was modified in the 1970s and 1980s to accommodate an increase in occupancy. The "updated" building decreased the effectiveness of sustainability strategies in the interior and removed trees that shaded the building naturally. The operable vents were sealed, and a mechanical air conditioning system was installed. The new HVAC system eliminated multiple zones and created one uniform zone for the entire building.

Dual-paned laminated glass windows with a white vinyl interlayer replaced the sand-blasted glass in the name of energy efficiency. This created an unintended countereffect because of the high solar gain of the vinyl.

Restoration

Restoration has reestablished zones for the radiant floor system and incorporated a new cooling function that uses tempered water in subfloor pipes to draw heat out of building spaces. Both original internal blinds and operable vents have been restored; both rely on occupants to control solar gain and natural ventilation throughout the building. Window replacement was an important issue in both the earlier changes

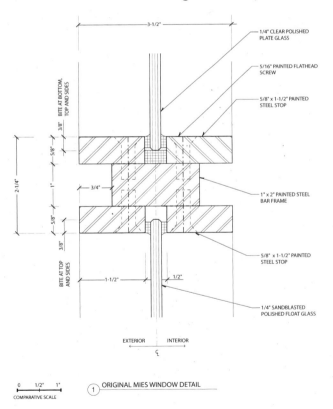

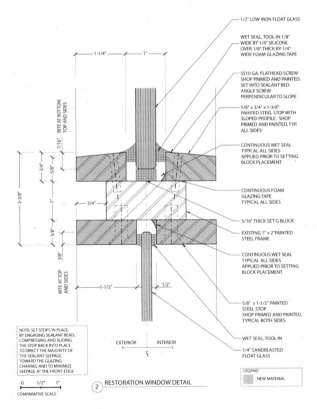

Figure 10.12 The original upper panels were enormous— 9 foot 8 by 12 foot 9— not tempered, and only ¼-inch thick. Great expanses of crystal-clear glass poured daylight into the studio and created a "barely there" effect. *Krueck & Sexton Architects*

Figure 10.13 To meet building codes yet maintain the effect of the original design, the new glazing relied on ½-inch low-iron glass. To hold the new, larger panels, new stops had to be enlarged from 5/8 inch to ¾ inch; sloping the stops allows them to maintain the same profile. *Krueck & Sexton Architects*

Figure 10.14 Crown Hall was conceived as a drawing studio, and the quality and quantity of diffuse light in the space was critical to the design and experience of the building. Off-white internal blinds were originally installed to reduce glare and direct solar radiation, but by the time of the renovation, most were broken in a closed and lowered position. *Photography by Todd Eberle*

and the most recent renovation. The current configuration reinstates Mies's original designs, with a slight modification. Sandblasted glass was restored in the bottom tier of windows for historic integrity and the "glow" that Mies had intended the design to create, but the upper windows were doubled in thickness to increase their efficiency. The trees surrounding the building are being replanted.

The original Crown Hall successfully integrated a beautiful design aesthetic with functionality of operation and use. The restoration builds upon the intelligence and elegance of the original design with new technologies and products that include sophisticated analytical tools, waste-heat recovery, improved window design, and occupancy and photoelectric sensors.

GREEN DESIGN ELEMENTS

Crown Hall (Illinois Institute of Technology)

- Replanted original trees

Energy and Atmosphere:
- Radiant floors
- Zoned heating and cooling
- Waste-heat recovery
- Natural ventilation
- Additional insulation
- Efficient window substitution
- Occupancy and photoelectric sensors

Materials and Resources:
- Extreme durability of new exterior paint, projected to last 25 years

Indoor Environment Quality:
- Operable vents and blinds

PROJECT TEAM

Illinois Institute of Technology

Krueck & Sexton Architects

McClier Preservation Group (now Austin AECom)

Fujikawa Johnson Gobel Architects

Cotter Consulting

Clune Construction Company

Thorton Tomasetti Group

Chandra Goldsmith Landscape Architect + UrbanLab

Atelier Ten

TransSolar

North Boulder Recreation Center

Boulder, CO

Current Owner: City of Boulder

Building Type: Recreation

Original Building Construction: 1973

Restoration/Renovation Completion: 2003

Square Footage: 61,000 ft^2

Percentage Renovated: 57% + 43% addition

Attendance (2006): 290,936

Recognition: LEED NC (2.0)—Silver (33/69 points); Colorado Renewable Energy Society Award for Sustainablity

PROJECT DESCRIPTION

An expansion of the North Boulder Recreation Center utilized an existing 1973 building and introduced to the region application of the U.S. Green Building Council LEED system for new construction and major renovations. With year-round, extended operating hours and energy-intensive swimming pools, recreation centers are high consumers of energy. The NBRC was the first municipal recreation center in the United States to be LEED-certified and demonstrates holistic strategies for reducing environmental impact.

Energy

In terms of size and cost, the most significant energy-conservation measure incorporated into the center is a $265,000 solar water-heating system. Thought to be one of the largest solar units installed in the United States with 5,700 square feet of collector surface, the system reduced natural gas consumption by 50 percent. The City of Boulder buys local wind-generated power to supply 50 percent of the center's electricity requirements.

Double-paned, low-E insulating windows were installed to limit gain from solar radiation and reduce air conditioning requirements. New, precision boilers operate at 20 percent greater efficiency than the old boilers.

Figure 10.15 Outside the center, liberal planting of drought-resistant species significantly reduces water use. A large detaining pond behind the center contains and reduces stormwater runoff from the property. Exterior lighting was designed to keep "waste" light out of the night sky and be minimally visible to residential neighbors. Six recharging outlets in the parking area accommodate electric cars, and the size of the parking area was limited to encourage use of alternative and public transportation for travel to and from the center, which is located on a bus route and near a bike path. © 2003 *Banker Rinker Seacat Architecture*

Figure 10.16 The building before renovation. To minimize use of material resources, the design reused significant portions of the original shell and emphasized recycled and environmentally sustainable materials throughout the building. More than 80 percent of construction waste was diverted from landfills. Salvaged materials from the existing building were reused at other facilities, and displaced trees from the addition footprint were transplanted to Boulder parks. © *Banker Rinker Seacat Architecture*

Construction Waste Management and Materials

Asphalt from the old parking lot was recycled, and old air conditioning and heating units were either reused, reinstalled in other city facilities, or salvaged for parts. The large, aesthetically pleasing structural beams located throughout the center are made from waste-reducing, compressed-wood strips known as parallel strand lumber. New benches and lockers in the locker rooms are made of durable recycled plastic materials that are particularly resilient to damage caused by moisture and humidity. The carpet binding is made from recycled materials.

Interior Environmental Quality

In order to improve indoor air quality and reduce levels of volatile organic compounds, low-emission paint, carpet, and adhesives were used

GREEN DESIGN ELEMENTS

North Boulder Recreation Center

Sustainable Sites:
- Reduce heat island effect with reflective roof
- Minimized site disturbance
- Access to public transportation
- Electric car charging
- Carpool parking
- Bicycle parking and changing rooms

Water Efficiency:
- Xeriscaping
- Drip irrigation

Energy & Atmosphere:
- DOE-2 energy model
- Solar hot-water heating
- Purchased wind energy
- Natural daylighting

Materials and Resources:
- Reused 83 percent of existing building shell
- Diverted 82 percent of construction waste
- 64 percent local materials
- Low-emitting materials
- All urea-formaldehyde-free

Indoor Environment Quality:
- CO_2 sensors and controls
- Nonsmoking facility
- Construction IAQ management plan
- Low-VOC adhesives and sealants
- 95 percent of space w/outside views

throughout the renovated building. Sensors automatically control carbon dioxide levels, and thermostats in every room allow for the efficient use of heat and air conditioning.

Site

A large detaining pond that was dug behind the center contains and reduces stormwater runoff. Exterior lighting was designed to minimize "light pollution"—ambient light common in urban areas that prevents viewing of the night sky—and to remain unobtrusive to residential neighbors.

Local Materials

The sandstone used on the exterior and interior of the center was quarried in Lyons, about 15 miles from Boulder. The concrete blocks used throughout the center were also manufactured locally.

Figure 10.17 The solar hot-water system, with 5,700 square feet of collector area, reduces natural-gas consumption by 50 percent and provides year-round heating for the two indoor swimming pools. High-efficiency boilers, high-performance glazing, a white roof, and tight envelope construction all contribute to an overall energy savings of roughly 37 percent annually over a minimally compliant ASHRAE 90.1-1999 building. © 2003 Banker Rinker Seacat Architecture

PROJECT TEAM, NORTH BOULDER RECREATION CENTER

City of Boulder

Everett/Zeigel Architects–original building

Barker Rinker Seacat & Partners, PC–expansion

Winston & Associates

Martin/Martin

JVA Inc.

ABS Consultants

Firm-Flatirons Company 1973–original building

Rhoads Construction–expansion

Water Technology Inc.

California College of the Arts (Carroll Weisel Hall)
San Francisco, CA

Current Owner: California College of the Arts

Building Type: Higher Education

Original Building Construction: 1951

Restoration/Renovation Completion: 1999

Square Footage: 91,000 ft²

Percentage Renovated: 100 percent

Recognition: AIA San Francisco Honor Award 2002; AIA/COTE Top Ten Green Projects 2001; AIA Portland Architecture + Energy Program Award 2001; Pacific Energy Center/San Diego Gas & Electric/Southern California Edison, Savings by Design Award 2000; AIA California Council, Honor Award 2000; California Preservation Foundation, Preservation Design Award

Figure 10.18 Originally a Greyhound bus maintenance facility designed by Skidmore Owings and Merrill in the 1950s, the renovated arts building retains original 30-foot-high industrial sash windows with dramatic views of downtown San Francisco. California codes requiring that a building envelope be improved for energy efficiency did not have to be met because solar heating was used. The structure is one of the largest solar-heated facilities in Northern California. *Photo by Richard Barnes*

PROJECT DESCRIPTION

The California College of the Arts, Montgomery Campus, reused a 30-foot-high clear-span bus maintenance garage for a new art facility that harnesses both passive and active solar energy. Over 70 percent of the building is heated with solar power and, in turn, the building uses 60 to 70 percent less energy than a conventional structure of the same size.

Energy

Heated water from flat-plate solar collectors on the roof is stored in a 15,000-gallon tank and utilized in a radiant floor system. The coils for the system were placed directly on the existing concrete floor, then covered with another layer of concrete to exploit thermal massing properties. Students often occupy the building 24 hours a day, and the thermal-mass system allows the building to remain comfortable, even after the sun goes down, by slowly releasing heat and maintaining an even temperature throughout. With original glass curtain walls on three sides, all interior spaces are daylit.

Materials

Finishing materials are simple to display the original structural beauty of the building, minimize cost, and provide maximum durability. Though most of the existing structural elements were left exposed, the ceiling was fitted with a recycled cellulose acoustical treatment. Formaldehyde-free fiberboard panels were used to create offices and class-rooms within the giant open floor plan.

Figure 10.19 Heating for the building is provided by a rooftop solar system and cooling by natural ventilation. A large rooftop array of hydronic solar collectors functions as the primary heating source for the large studio spaces, feeding a radiant-slab distribution system. A large tank located within the café area provides additional hydronic heat storage and becomes an interesting object in and of itself. *Image by Arup*

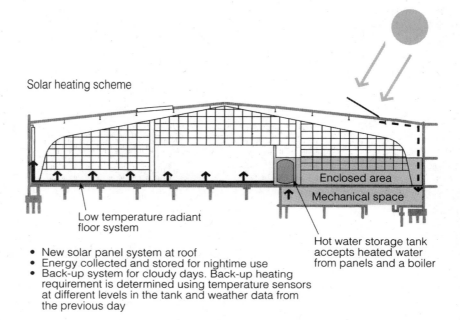

Solar heating scheme

Low temperature radiant floor system

Enclosed area

Mechanical space

Hot water storage tank accepts heated water from panels and a boiler

- New solar panel system at roof
- Energy collected and stored for nightime use
- Back-up system for cloudy days. Back-up heating requirement is determined using temperature sensors at different levels in the tank and weather data from the previous day

Figure 10.20 The original long-span concrete roof structure has new steel bracing as a seismic upgrade. The roof is punctuated by large skylights and rows of clerestories. The building's exaggerated height allows classrooms to stand as buildings within a building, an arrangement that supports selective conditioning. A concrete topping slab encapsulates toxics from prior use as a bus maintenance facility, while providing thermal mass. *Photo by Richard Barnes*

GREEN DESIGN ELEMENTS

California College of the Arts

Sustainable Sites:
- Bicycle accommodation

Energy and Atmosphere:
- Solar-powered hydronic coil heating
- Radiant floors
- Solar hot-water collectors
- Natural ventilation

Materials and Resources:
- Recycled cellulose acoustical ceiling
- Exposed structural materials
- Unsealed concrete floors

Indoor Environment Quality:
- Skylights/clerestory windows
- Low-VOC materials and finishes

PROJECT TEAM

California College of the Arts (formerly California College of Arts and Crafts)

Leddy Maytum Stacy Architects

Ove Arup & Partners

KCA Engineers Inc.

Architectural Lighting Design

Charles M. Salter Associates Inc.

Oliver & Company

Vancouver Island Technology Park

Victoria, British Columbia CAN

Current Owner: University of Victoria

Building Type: Commercial Office

Original Building Construction: 1976

Restoration/Renovation Completion: 2001

Square Footage: 171,750 ft^2

Percentage Renovated: 100%

Occupancy: 1,000–1,300 people (40–50 hours/week)

Recognition: LEED NC v2.0—Gold; VIATeC Environmental Award Finalist 2006; NRC Innovation Award for Sustainable Development 2003; BOMA Earth Award (sponsored by BC Hydro Powersmart) 2002; Minister's Environmental Award 2002; UDI Award for Excellence in Urban Development 2002; Greenways Developer's Award 2002

PROJECT DESCRIPTION

This project involved adaptive reuse of a 165,000-square-foot long-term-care hospital completed in 1976. While the building had an exceptional natural setting, a robust concrete structure, and an early but serviceable rainscreen wall system, it was deficient in current safety codes and had a tired-looking and dated institutional appearance.

The brief was to bring the building back to life in a cost-effective manner as a serviced shell building for high-technology tenants. Objectives included creation of larger floorplates, upgrading life-safety systems, renewing the building's appearance, and creating new "public contact" components—signage and wayfinding devices, as well as new entrances intended to convey clearly the image of a modern, high-tech working environment.

Figure 10.21 Part of an extensive stormwater-management plan, a grass- and gravel-paved parking area allows stormwater to filter directly into the ground, recharging the water table, but also oxidizing and biologically treating oil and gasoline drippings from cars. (Refer to Chapter 4.) Cars park on the grass-pave system and travel on the gravel cover. A water-management plan includes onsite ecological treatment of flows, quality, and temperature before discharge into Viaduct Creek, a habitat for salmon; incorporation of flood-plain management—1-in-10-year and 1-in-200-year stormwater runoff into treatment facilities; and incorporation of aquatic habitat to achieve drainage, aesthetic, recreational, and environmental benefits with no negative effects on aquatic life and no increase in stormwater discharge. © Christopher Rowe 2008

Figure 10.22 Computer modeling confirmed that the renovated building performs about 27.5 percent better than the requirements of ASHRAE/IESNA standard 90.1-1999. Thermal storage has been integrated into the water-loop heat-pump system at no premium cost. One benefit is that excess heat generated by the space or in computer rooms can be stored in the loop during winter. The heat is then available for early-morning warmup, as an alternative to heat supplied from the gas-fired boilers. In 2009, the facility began real-time monitoring to further improve operating efficiency. © *Christopher Rowe 2008*

Unreinforced concrete-block partitions and old hospital services were removed. Asbestos-containing materials found during the strip-out were abated. Seismic performance was brought up to current code requirements by the insertion of new, reinforced-concrete shear walls and steel braces. Useful mechanical and electrical services were identified and retained.

New Character

Existing covered exterior decks were converted to new floor space by the addition of high-performance windows, which increased perimeter glazing and daylighting. A dowdy, brown-and-beige exterior of stucco and brick was repainted in a new palette of soft greens, allowing the large complex to better blend into the natural viewscape. A new system of brightly painted steel pylons and signs creates landmarks at principal entrances, improves wayfinding on a large site, and provides a more modern "technical" image to the building.

Figure 10.23 The reuse of the building structure and shell generated a significant saving over building new. 99.9 percent of the building structure was reused; for shell elements, the reuse rate was about 91 percent. The 9 percent of shell not utilized was replaced with additional floor area by enclosing balconies, thereby increasing floor area without increasing the footprint of the building. © *Christopher Rowe 2008*

Figure 10.24 Conserving natural resources while minimizing the generation of waste and pollution was a key goal for VITP. With this in mind, existing ductwork was reused but is larger than necessary, given the needs of the new structure. Lower air speeds in ducts reduce energy consumption, as less energy is required for fans. The majority of concrete walls, columns, and ceilings have been left bare; concrete's durability means that these elements will require little maintenance— and they impart a desired high-tech/industrial design feel to the project. © *Christopher Rowe 2008*

GREEN DESIGN ELEMENTS

Vancouver Island Technology Park

Sustainable Sites:
- Bicycle accommodation
- Permeable paving material (green parking spaces)
- Retention ponds
- Xeriscaping
- Bioswales

Water Efficiency:
- Low-flow plumbing fixtures
- Dual-flush toilets
- Waterless urinals
- Aerator faucets (infrared sensor)

Energy and Atmosphere:
- Centrally located multiple-boiler plant
- Thermal storage in water-loop system
- High-efficiency T-5 fluorescent lighting
- High-performance windows
- Direct digital control system
- Building commissioning

Materials and Resources:
- Over 95 percent construction waste recycled or sold
- Recycled content materials
- Flyash concrete substitute

Indoor Environment Quality:
- Asbestos remediation
- IAQ construction management
- Low-VOC materials and finishes

Other Features:
- Occupant recycling program

User Amenities

New washrooms and common areas were inserted, employing inexpensive materials (drywall, vinyl composition tile) in vibrant colors. Primary amenities include a 5,600 SF business center with conference facilities, a fitness studio with changing rooms and showers, and a café. Extensive bicycle parking, secure and covered, is provided.

Achievable Sustainability

The natural conditions of the 35-acre site, reuse of a sturdy existing concrete structure, demolition- and construction-waste–reduction strategies, specification of appropriate materials, and a range of environmentally sensitive mechanical and electrical design strategies combine to make this project a showcase for achievable environmental sustainability. The development was awarded the first Gold Certification in Canada under the US Green Building Council LEED 2.0 in early 2002; at the time, it was one of only three projects worldwide that had achieved this ranking.

PROJECT TEAM

Vancouver Island Technology Park

BC Building Corporation

Idealink Architecture Ltd. (now part of Cannon Design)

Keen Engineering Co Ltd.

Blohm Peterson Vollan Galloway & Associates

Robert Freundlich & Associates

Bunting Coady Architects

1st Team Engineering

Aqua-Tex Scientific Consulting Ltd.

ENDNOTES

1. Jeanne Lambin and Adrian Scott Fine, "Rallying Support for Resources from the Recent Past," *Forum Journal*, vol. 18 (4) (Summer 2004).

2. U.S. Department of Energy Commercial Building Survey, 2003.

3. Lambin and Fine.

4. Theodore H. M. Prudon, *Preservation of Modern Architecture* (Hoboken, NJ: John Wiley & Sons, Inc., 2008), p. ix.

5. Mitchell Giurgola Architects, *Boomer Buildings: Mid-Centtury Architecture Reborn*, edited by Michael J. Crosbie. (Mulgrave, Vic., Australia: The Images Publishing Group, 2005), p. 6.

6. Maristella Casciato, "Modern Architecture Is Durable: Using Change to Preserve," 10th International DOCOMOMO Conference Programme, (2008), p. 3.

7. Richard Moe, "President's Report," *Forum Journal*, vol. 22 (2) (Winter 2008).

8. Ada Louse Huxtable, "The Beauty in Brutalism, Restored and Updated," *Wall Street Journal*, February 25, 2009, p. D7.

9. Lambin and Fine.

10. Prudon, p. viii.

11. Richard Klein, "Restoring the Twentieth Century," In *The Challenge of Change: Dealing with the Legacy of the Modern Movement. Proceedings of the 10th International DOCOMOMO Conference.* Dirk van den Heuvel, Maarten Mesman, Wido Quist, and Bert Lemmens (eds.) (Amsterdam: IOS Press BV, 2008), p. 263.

12. Huxtable, D7.

13. Bruce D. Snider, "At the Center of the Storm," *Preservation* (March/April 2009). Available at: www.preservationnation.org/magazine/2009/march-april/boston-city-hall.html.

14. Huxtable, D7.

15. Mitchell Giurgola Architects, p. 5, Foreword by Michael J. Crosbie.

16. Sadegh Hazrati and Stuart Harrad, "Causes of Variability in Concentrations of Polychlorinated Biphenyls and Polybrominated Diphenyl Ethers in Indoor Air," *Environmental Science & Technology*, vol. 40 (24) (2006): 7584–7589.

17. Nina Rappaport, "Sustainability, A Modern Movement." In *The Challenge of Change: Dealing with the Legacy of the Modern Movement. Proceedings of the 10th International DOCOMOMO Conference.* Dirk van den Heuvel, Maarten Mesman, Wido Quist, and Bert Lemmens (eds.) (Amsterdam: IOS Press BV, 2008), p. 337.

18. Michael J. Crosbie and Mitchell/Giurgola Architects, "Rejuvenating Boomers," *Architecture Week*, November 8, 2006, p. 81.1. Available at www.architectureweek.com/2006/1108/building_1-1.html.

19. Description of work available at http://www.som.com/content.cfm/lever_house_curtain_wall_replacement.

20. DPA Culture, "UN to Refurbish Historic Geneva Office, Go Green" (February 6, 2009); http://en.trend.az/news/world/wnews/1419581.html (accessed June 2010).

21. John Gendall "Michael Alderstein: U.N. Renovation Will 'Establish a Model' for Other Buildings," *Architect* (February 1, 2008). Available at http://www.architectmagazine.com/architecture/michael-alderstein-un-renovation-will-establish-a.aspx

22. The information on pp. 369–370 is derived from Susan Ross, "How Green Was Canadian Modernism; How Sustainable Will It Be?" *Docomomo*, no. 38 (March 2008), p. 72.

23. Nadav Malin, "National Geographic Society Upgrades Facilities with LEED-EB," *Environmental Building News* (December 2003), www.buildinggreen.com. Available at www.buildinggreen.com/auth/article.cfm/2003/12/1/National-Geographic-Society-Upgrades-Facilities-with-LEED-EB/?.

24. Prudon, p. xi.

25. Ibid.

26. Paul Goldberger, "Modernism," *Preservation* (May/June 2008). Available at www.preservation.org/magazine/2008/may-june/modernist-manifesto.html.

INDEX

WILEY BOOKS ON Sustainable Design

For these and other Wiley books on sustainable design, visit www.wiley.com/go/sustainabledesign

Alternative Construction: Contemporary Natural Building Methods
by Lynne Elizabeth and Cassandra Adams

Biophilic Design: The Theory, Science, and Practice of Bringing Buildings to Life
by Stephen Kellert, Judith Heerwagen, and Martin Mador

Contractor's Guide to Green Building Construction: Management, Project Delivery, Documentation, and Risk Reduction
by Thomas E. Glavinich and Associated General Contractors

Design with Nature
by Ian L. McHarg

Ecodesign: A Manual for Ecological Design
by Ken Yeang

Environmentally Responsible Design: Green and Sustainable Design for Interior Designers
by Louise Jones

Green BIM: Successful Sustainable Design with Building Information Modeling
by Eddy Krygiel and Brad Nies

Green Building Materials: A Guide to Product Selection and Specification, Second Edition
by Ross Spiegel and Dru Meadows

Green Development: Integrating Ecology and Real Estate
by Rocky Mountain Institute

Green Roof Systems: A Guide to the Planning, Design and Construction of Landscapes Over Structure
by Susan Weiler and Katrin Scholz-Barth

Guide to the LEED Green Associate Exam
by Michelle Cottrell

The HOK Guidebook to Sustainable Design, Second Edition
by Sandra Mendler, William O'Dell, and Mary Ann Lazarus

The Integrative Design Guide to Green Building: Redefining the practice of Sustainability
by 7group and Bill Reed

Land and Natural Development (Land) Code
by Diana Balmori and Gaboury Benoit

A Legal Guide to Urban and Sustainable Development for Planners, Developers and Architects
by Daniel Slone, Doris S. Goldstein, and W. Andrew Gowder

Materials for Sustainable Sites: A Complete Guide to the Evaluation, Selection, and Use of Sustainable Construction Materials
by Meg Calkins

Modern Sustainable Residential Design: A Guide for Design Professionals
by William J. Carpenter

Packaging Sustainability: Tools, Systems, and Strategies for Innovative Package Design
by Wendy Jedlicka

Sustainable Commercial Interiors
by Penny Bonda and Katie Sosnowchik

Sustainable Construction: Green Building Design and Delivery
by Charles J. Kibert

Sustainable Design: Ecology, Architecture, and Planning
by Daniel Williams

Sustainable Design of Research Laboratories
by KlingStubbins

Sustainable Healthcare Architecture
by Robin Guenther and Gail Vittori

Sustainable Residential Interiors
by Associates III

Sustainable School Architecture: Design for Elementary and Secondary Schools
by Lisa Gelfand with Eric Corey Freed

Sustainable Site Design : Criteria, Process, and Case Studies for Integrating Site and Region in Landscape Design
by Claudia Dinep, Kristin Schwab

Sustainable Urbanism
by Douglas Farr

 Environmental Benefits Statement

This book is printed with soy-based inks on presses with VOC levels that are lower than the standard for the printing industry. The paper, Rolland Enviro 100, is manufactured by Cascades Fine Papers Group and is made from 100 percent post-consumer, de-inked fiber, without chlorine. According to the manufacturer, the use of every ton of Rolland Enviro100 Book paper, switched from virgin paper, helps the environment in the following ways:

Mature trees	Waterborne waste not created	Water flow saved	Atmospheric emissions eliminated	Soiled Wastes reduced	Natural gas saved by using biogas
17	6.9 lbs.	10,196 gals.	2,098 lbs.	1,081 lbs.	2,478 cubic feet